# Autosegmental Studies in Bantu Tone

# Publications in African Languages and Linguistics

The aim of this series is to offer, at regular intervals, carefully worked out studies or collections of papers in African linguistics. In this way, it is hoped that important work can be brought to the attention of a wider linguistic audience including scholars who are not primarily concerned with African linguistics but who wish to keep abreast of recent advances in the fields of historical linguistics, theoretical phonology and linguistic typology, all of which, incidentally, tend to rely rather heavily on African language data.
At the same time, the editors intend to include occasional volumes which offer general accounts of major language groups, hoping that such surveys will be of assistance not only to linguists working on African languages but also to those who specialize in other areas.
Throughout the series an attempt will be made to strike a healthy balance between theory oriented and data oriented research.

G.N. Clements and J. Goldsmith (eds.)

# Autosegmental Studies in Bantu Tone

1984
FORIS PUBLICATIONS
Dordrecht - Holland/Cinnaminson - U.S.A.

*Published by:*
Foris Publications Holland
P.O. Box 509
3300 AM Dordrecht, The Netherlands

*Sole distributor for the U.S.A. and Canada:*
Foris Publications U.S.A.
P.O. Box C-50
Cinnaminson N.J. 08077
U.S.A.

ISBN 90 70176 98 X (Bound)
ISBN 90 70176 97 1 (Paper)



Printed in the Netherlands by ICG Printing, Dordrecht.

# Preface

One of the most striking features of the Bantu languages is the mobility of their tones, as shown in the freedom with which tones are mapped across the word or phrase. The present collection represents the result of an intensive comparative study of several typologically diverse Bantu languages aimed at exploring the nature of their tone and accent systems. One conclusion of this work is that while some Bantu languages can be shown to have retained the tonal system of the ancestral languages largely intact, others have innovated accentual systems which continue to reflect, to a greater or lesser degree, the tonal contrasts found in the proto-language.

The work represented here is the result of a collaborative effort on the part of all contributors. During a two-year period the various authors exchanged manuscript versions of their chapters and were able to incorporate many of the suggestions of their co-contributors into the final versions. The resulting volume reflects this close interaction. As will be evident from a reading of each chapter, no attempt was made by the editors to impose a uniformity of views on the individual contributors, and we hope that some of the vitality of current phonological research has managed to find expression in the variety of approaches reflected herein.

This volume does not claim to offer a definitive account of tone and accent in Bantu. We will consider ourselves fortunate if we have been able to suggest something of the analytical challenge to be found in the study of Bantu prosodic systems. We hope that this work will stimulate further investigation into the nature of Bantu tone and accent and its place in a general theory of phonology.

We take this opportunity to thank all the contributors for their cooperation in this joint venture, and offer our particular thanks to the President's Council on the Humanities of Indiana University and to the Harvard Graduate Society for Advanced Study and Research for the financial support which helped to make the publication of this book possible.

The editors

# Contents

*Chapter 1*

# Autosegmental Studies in Bantu Tone: Introduction

G.N. Clements and John Goldsmith

## 1. INTRODUCTION

1. This book introduces a new approach to the description of tone and accent in Bantu languages, based upon the theory of autosegmental phonology. The seven languages presented here vary in their degree of familiarity to linguists. Zulu and Kikuyu (and to a lesser extent, Tonga and Shona) have been the subject of an extensive descriptive literature, while Digo, Haya, and Ci-Ruri are relatively unfamiliar. It seems fair to say, however, that while a few Bantu languages have been described in considerable detail, none of them is well understood. Existing descriptions, while exemplary in many respects, present a confused and at times contradictory picture of the nature of Bantu tone systems as a whole, due largely to the absence, until now, of a unified, theoretically consistent framework for describing tone and accent. This book takes a first step toward remedying this situation. Each chapter presents a detailed analysis of the tone system of a particular Bantu language from a single point of view, that of autosegmental phonology. Taken together, these studies present a panoramic picture suggestive of the variety of tone and accent systems found in this linguistic area.

2. As anyone who has worked on this problem is well aware, the challenge raised for linguistic analysis by Bantu tone and accent systems is far from trivial. This is due not only to the richness and complexity of the rule systems of individual languages, but also, and more significantly, to the typological variety found throughout this area. The handful of detailed, reliable descriptions so far available suggest that a given Bantu language may fall anywhere along a scale from fully tonal systems (as in Kikuyu) to systems with no trace of linguistically distinctive tone (as in Swahili). In between fall a bewildering variety of intermediate types, most of which exhibit properties of both tone and accent languages in varying degrees.

Two major approaches have been offered in the earlier descriptive literature for describing Bantu tone and accent. The first, or tonal model, is exemplified in, for example, the work of Armstrong on Kikuyu (1940), Rycroft and Cope on Zulu (Rycroft 1963, 1979, Cope 1970), or Cole on Luganda (1967). In this approach, noun and verb stems are assigned to one of a small number of tone classes defined in terms of a pattern of tonal allomorphy found in a certain range of contexts, chosen to exemplify the full range of contexts in which any item may occur. Within each tone class subclasses may be recognized, varying according to the length or canonic structure of the stem, or certain other idiosyncratic properties.

The second model, an accentual one, derives essentially from the influential work of Meeussen (1954, 1963), and is further exemplified in the work of Carter (1971, 1972), Van Spaandonck (1967), Stevick (1969a), and others. This model, which is examined more closely in Goldsmith's chapter on Tonga, consists of a system which predicts surface tones on the basis of diacritic markings which designate certain vowels as "determinant" as opposed to others which are unmarked or "neutral". "Representation" or "realization" rules provide principles for assigning tones to words on the basis of the location of determinant and neutral syllables, as well as tonal information as it is introduced. Typically (although not as a matter of principle), such descriptions have the effect of "filling in" rather than changing tones. In this view, the diacritic marks used to identify determinant vowels function similarly to the traditional notion of accent, except that they are purely abstract features, permitting the prediction of observed tone patterns but having no intrinsic phonetic properties themselves.

These two descriptive models suggest a rigid dichotomy between tonal and accentual systems which does not exist in the languages themselves. The ambiguous status of some languages with respect to this principle of classification – Luganda is the best-known example – is reflected in the fact that they seem to be equally well (or poorly) treated in both models. It would seem, then, that a fully adequate model for describing Bantu prosodic systems should provide a natural way of describing the intermediate status of some languages between "fully tonal" and "fully accentual" systems.

A step in this direction has been taken by McCawley (1970, 1978). McCawley suggests that while the distinction between tone and accent languages may be well-defined in underlying representations (where accent is either present or not), it need not be well-defined in the phonological component itself, where rules of tonal assimilation and dissimilation, sometimes thought to characterize tone languages exclusively, may characterize languages with underlying pitch-accent as well. "Mixed" systems having both accent and tone rules may be distinguished according to how early in derivations tone rules are introduced. This model is proposed for languages as superficially diverse as Japanese and Luganda. We return below to the question of how McCawley's conception might be integrated into an autosegmental theory of Bantu tone.

It is quite pertinent to ask whether these conflicting analytical approaches reflect a genuine indeterminacy in the linguistic data, or whether they are simply a consequence of the theoretical experimentation which necessarily (and quite appropriately) arises in a field which has not yet developed a widely-agreed upon model. It is possible that both of these explanations are partly correct. Many Bantu languages can properly be regarded as transitional between "pure" tone languages – those requiring only tonal information in their lexical entries – and "pure" accent languages, in which surface tonal contours are determined at least partly by accentual information present in lexical representations. We do not believe that the conceptually well-defined opposition between tonal and accentual systems, each of which is independently well-attested, is weakened by the existence of such "transitional" systems. Much of the diversity in modern Bantu prosodic systems is due to the historical effect of such analytical indeterminacy, and can be plausibly explained in terms of it, as we shall argue below. On the other hand, it is also true that earlier phonological theory has not provided fully satisfactory models for tonal description, and that this field has been characterized by a wide variety of approaches (see, for example, the comprehensive overviews of the earlier literature given in Fromkin (1978) and Weidert (1981)). It is not unreasonable to think that at least some of the indeterminacy suggested by a reading of earlier descriptions results from inadequacies in the phonological models chosen. The only way of factoring out the respective contributions of data and theory to the problem of indeterminacy is to extend the data base, while at the same time reexamining already-available data from a theoretical perspective that offers some potential of consistency and unification.

It has been convincingly demonstrated that Proto-Bantu was a tone language with two distinctive tone levels, high (H) and low (L); see Greenberg (1948), Kähler-Meyer (1967/8), Guthrie (1967/71), Meeussen (1967, 1980) (and, for a dissenting view, Stevick (1969b) ). Certain details of the system are well established. Noun stems were generally bisyllabic and were characterized by one of the four tone melodies HH, HL, LH, or LL. Verb stems consisted of a monosyllabic radical characterized by H or L tone, and zero or more toneless (or, in an alternative analysis, L-toned) extensions, terminating in a final vowel with variable tone. On the basis of evidence from the verb alone, one could not conclusively identify Proto-Bantu as a tone language, since the verb could be described in terms of a system which assigns an underlying feature of accent to certain formatives but not to others. The evidence that Proto-Bantu was tonal rather than accentual resides largely in the nominals (nouns and adjectives); in the existence of a reconstructed tone assimilation rule which causes all extension syllables to acquire H tone preceding an inflectional suffix bearing H tone; and in the extensive comparative evidence showing that the closest relatives of Proto-Bantu were themselves tone languages (compare, for example, the tonal reconstructions given for Bantu by Guthrie (1967/71) with those proposed for the cognate forms in Western Nigritic (a term loosely co-extensive with Niger-Congo) by Mukarovsky (1976/7) ). Thus it must be assumed that the direction of change in the evolution of modern Bantu has been from tone languages to systems approaching accent languages, in varying degrees.

The details of this development are still unknown, due in large part to the lack of adequate descriptions (for a short bibliography of works on Bantu tone and accent see Hyman (1976)). It seems unlikely, however, that the drift from tone to accent is a regional or diffusional phenomenon. Even though the complex and, at least in part, irrecoverable patterns of historical migration within the Bantu-speaking area (Phillipson 1977a, 1977b, Bouquiaux et. al. 1980) make firm conclusions difficult, there is no evidence to suggest that the drift from tone to accent can be traced to an origin in one language or one language group from whence it would have spread to other areas. The effect of the loss of tonal distinctiveness is greatest in the western and eastern Bantu-speaking areas as opposed to the north, south, and center (see Guthrie, volume 1, topogram 4), and the mechanics of this loss present no coherent picture. Again, it is unclear to what extent this is an inherent feature of the data or the result of different and conflicting models of analysis. Nevertheless, one is forced to conclude on the basis of the available data that the loss of tonal distinctiveness is due at least in part to separate innovations and independent parallel development, with perhaps the added but localized contribution of certain common innovations. If this view is correct, then we are presented with the following challenging puzzle: what are the structural features of the Proto-Bantu linguistic system or of its immediate descendants that made it prey to an increasing tendency toward reanalysis as an accent system?

The fullest discussion of this problem to date is that of Carter (1973), who isolates a number of the recurrent types of tone change that define various degrees of deviation from the proto-model. Carter, drawing upon a tradition established in Van Spaandonck (1967) and earlier works, proposes the following rule-based typology of Bantu tone systems:

i. "etymological" or "clear tone" systems, which show a point-for-point correspondence with Proto-Bantu.
ii. "reversive" systems in which H replaces etymological L and L replaces etymological H.
iii. "tone doubling" systems in which a H tone is copied onto a following syllable.

iv. "tone anticipation" systems in which a H tone is copied onto a preceding syllable.

v. "displacement" or delayed realization systems in which basic H tone is realized on a tone-bearing element later than that with which it is lexically associated.

Several of these systems are found in combination; furthermore, some languages have, as noted earlier, lost all tonal distinctiveness. Carter's typology differs from Guthrie's functional classification mainly in that it is based upon an examination of tone rules of a fairly specific nature. Nevertheless, this system has not so far permitted the discovery of any general patterns of evolution. Carter drew the following conclusion, which is still valid at the present time:

> It may eventually be possible to construct a hypothesis of developments within particular languages, and of typical development of tonal to intonational system, or at least to isolate some feature or features which render a tonal system vulnerable to breakdown. At the moment there seems to be little association between e.g. the relative simplicity of a system, in terms of the number of rules operating, and the tendency to intonational development. The area where complete loss occurs shows *variety* of systems in surrounding languages, rather than a particular type of system. (Carter 1973, 47)

It is quite possible, of course, that the principles identified by Carter are not yet specific enough, and available descriptions not yet detailed enough, to permit a determination of linguistic groupings or of diffusional features based upon shared tone rules. It is also possible that the conditions leading to "tonal breakdown" are not only formal, but also functional in nature, having to do with the nature of the difficulties posed for acquisition (see for example Kiparsky (1973a, 1982)). But we must also consider the possibility that it is not the nature of the phonological rule system *per se* that is involved, but rather characteristics of the morphological structure shared by all Bantu languages, regardless of their specific tone rules.

It is tempting in this regard to speculate that a major source of the peculiarly Bantu penchant for accentual reanalysis lies in the morphological make-up of the verb. In most of the better-known tone languages, especially those of Asia and West Africa, morphological structure tends to be isolating, and there are fewer morphologically complex words. Bantu verbs, on the other hand, normally consist of a subject prefix, one or two tense prefixes, one or more object prefixes, a radical, one or more extensions, and a final vowel; further formatives may be present as well. All but the extensions typically have an independent, underlying tonal characterization.

The two most striking characteristics of the Bantu tone systems discussed in this book may be derived in some measure from this complex lexical structure. The first of these is the remarkable *mobility* of the tones. Considering Bantu languages of a wide variety of prosodic types, we see strong reason to believe that the domain of tone mapping in these languages is not the morpheme – as is the case with most other better-known tone languages – but rather the word as a whole. Thus typically, the statements that determine where a specific tone is to be placed or where an accent is to be realized are not local to the morpheme – in which case tone mapping would be trivial – but rather span domains consisting of two or several morphemes. Indeed, in one language considered in this collection, Digo, the domain of tone mapping is, in part, larger than the word, comprising verb-object sequences. The fact that the domain of tone mapping is typically the word, together with the rich morphological structure of the verb, opens up possibilities for tonal mobility that are not available in languages with a simpler morphological structure.

The second characteristic that is widely shared among Bantu languages, regardless of whether they are tonal or accentual, is the frequent occurrence of processes of tone spreading onto morphemes that bear no intrinsic tonal or accentual characteristics. A major source of this property lies once again in the structure of the verb, in this case in the presence of what may be potentially very long sequences of toneless (or accentless) extensions following the radical. These extensions acquire their tone from the tonal or accentual specifications of neighboring formatives, both in the most conservative Bantu tone systems as well as in the most innovative accentual systems. The property of free spreading, as we shall see below, is determined by the Well-formedness Condition of autosegmental phonology, and is a characteristic formal feature of accentual systems. Thus the presence of free spreading in a Bantu tone system is consistent with an analysis as an accent system, and could plausibly be taken as diagnostic of such a system. We note that here, once again, the formation of morphologically complex words is an important precondition for evidence that could point to an accentual analysis.

In our later discussion, we turn to the question of why a *potential* for accentual reanalysis should lead to *actual* reanalysis. For the present we merely point out that the two properties noted above, the tonal mobility resulting from taking long, morphologically complex words as the mapping domain together with the free spreading associated with toneless morphemes, are widely typical of Bantu languages but are much more limited in their appearance in the languages of West Africa, which in general show no propensity to accentual reanalysis. An interesting exception in this respect is Igbo, a language atypical of this area in having verbal extensions of the Bantu type. These extensions are of two types: a toneless class (Class 1 suffixes, in the terminology of Goldsmith 1976), and a low-toned class created from other verb stems (Class 2 suffixes). As Clark (1982) has pointed out, the addition of this new class of verbal elements creates a number of effects that are reminiscent of accentual systems such as that of Tonga. Clark suggests, in fact, that Igbo has already arrived at such an accentual analysis in the verbal system, consistently with our view that accentual reanalysis will arise first in the morphologically complex verb before extending to the noun.

It seems likely that the characteristics that we have attributed to the Bantu verb can be traced back to the ancestral system itself – or at least, to the latest common ancester of what Heine (1973) terms the Eastern Highland Group, including all the languages discussed in this collection. If this is true, then the only substantial obstacle to the historical drift toward a wholesale reanalysis of Bantu as an accentual system is the nominal, which, as we have seen, offers a convincingly reconstructed four-way opposition among HH, HL, LH, and LL tone classes in bisyllabic stems. But it will be noted that even this obstacle is a fragile one. It suffices for a Bantu language having the four-way opposition just described to acquire a rule reducing this opposition to a three-way one for the nominal system to become open to a reanalysis as an accentual one, in which the three remaining classes of bisyllabic stems will be treated as initial-accented, final-accented and unaccented. In fact, we know that Bantu languages have quite widely acquired such a rule (see the studies to follow), often consisting of one form or another of what we have termed Meeussen's Rule, which turns a HH sequence into a HL one, thereby eliminating the opposition between the Proto-Bantu *HH and *HL classes. Present information suggests that the addition of Meeussen's Rule or its equivalent to a grammar may be a necessary precondition for accentual reanalysis. It is not, however, a sufficient condition. In Zulu, as Laughren shows in her contribution to this volume, a very early rule of tonal metathesis survives as evidence that this language, while having undergone the historical neutralization of the contrast between *HH and *HL and showing several other traits of an accentual system, remains tonal all the way back to its underlying representations.

3. In the years following the publication of Chomsky and Halle's *The Sound Pattern of English* (1968), generative phonology could count a large number of successes in its program. Notions such as the phonological cycle, rule ordering and disjunctive application, and synchronically-moti-

vated abstract analyses gave the enterprise a vitality and an excitement that is still very much alive today.

The SPE framework enjoyed great successes in certain areas, but other traditional problems in phonology proved more intractable. The treatment of tone in African and Asian languages, for example, had long been viewed as an important area for phonology – indeed, a central issue, for the later London school – but remarkably little insight was produced by the SPE framework into the behavior of tone. The central tools in the generative framework at this point were rules that modified feature specifications and rules that deleted or inserted segments. Despite impressive attempts (Wang 1967, Smith 1968, Schachter and Fromkin 1968, Woo 1969), generative treatments of tonal problems remained generally unconvincing. SPE itself, notably, eschewed all discussion of the problem, as if in silent respect for Wittgenstein's dictum, "Wovon man nicht sprechen kann, darüber muss man schweigen."

The modification that was necessary in the SPE conception of phonology is one which, in retrospect, seems so compatible with the generative-transformational program that its late arrival is surprising. The fundamental insight that lay at the origin of autosegmental phonology was the proposal that phonological processes might not simply add or delete segments, or change the feature specification of those present in the representation; but that also, and perhaps primarily, phonological processes could modify the structure or *organization* of the representation. Within the SPE framework, phonological representations were extremely simple, as simple as earlier structuralist representations in fact (see e.g. Jakobson 1971). This was in striking contrast to the situation in generative syntax, where new notions of structure were being developed and refined.

The autosegmental proposal was to enrich the geometry of phonological representations, and in particular, to relax the assumption that these representations consist of single linear sequences of segments. Representations are instead multilinear sequences composed of several rows, or tiers, of segments:

(1)

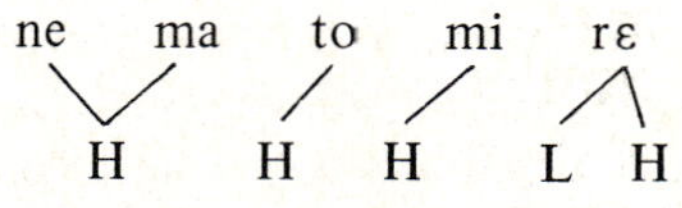


The separate, autonomous tiers contain sequences of segments specified for certain subsets of phonological features, and segments on one tier are related to segments on the adjacent tier by association lines. A single tone can be associated with more than one vowel, and similarly a vowel can be associated with more than one tone; furthermore, rules can modify associations, and not just affect the segments themselves. Thus in (1), which represents a verb in Kikuyu, the first tone is associated with two vowels, the second and third tone with one vowel each, and the final two tones with a single vowel, defining a tone pattern represented conventionally as [némátómírɛ̌].

The development of a formal system that permits co-equal and autonomous sequences of segments, as in (1), is a natural consequence of a number of earlier studies emphasizing what Gilbert Ansre has termed "tonal liberation". In particular, Williams (1971), in a study of tone mapping processes in Margi and Igbo, and Leben (1971, 1973), in studies of tonal processes in Hausa and Mende, brought out clearly several of the problems and paradoxes inherent in the treatment of tone systems within the generative framework available in the early 1970's. These studies showed that distributional constraints on underlying tone melodies and the regular principles of tone mapping could be most elegantly stated if tones were thought of as "suprasegmental" elements, rather than features of vowels. In Leben's more specific formulation of this model, it was claimed that tones were features of the morpheme with an equal status to that of consonants or vowels, but formally independent of them. Consequently, phonological rules could make reference to tones without referring to vowels and consonants, just as they could refer to consonants and vowels without mentioning tones. At a given point in a derivation, which must be idiosyncratically specified for each language, tones were "mapped" into individual tone-bearing segments, such as vowels; from that point onward in derivations they behaved just like other features of vowels with regard to phonological rules. Note that in this approach, rules referring both to tones and to non-tonal features were "intrinsically" ordered after rules that referred to tone "melodies" alone, due to the independent assumption that prior to mapping, tone rules could make only restricted reference (Williams) or no reference at all (Leben) to other phonological features of the morpheme.

This approach achieved striking solutions to problems that had remained intractable in earlier phonological theories. However, a number of problems remained. For example, the theory was unable to characterize the distinction between floating tones and associated tones in those (numerous) languages where floating tones do not constitute morphemes by themselves; see, for examples, the studies of Tonga, Zulu and Kikuyu in the present volume. It offered no formally coherent and empirically adequate way of characterizing contour tones as features of single short vowels. It was furthermore unable to account properly for the phenomenon of "tone stability" according to which phonological rules, applying after "tone mapping", delete vowels while leaving their tones behind. And it offered no way of characterizing systems in which "mapped" tones become "remapped" by later rules having the effect of altering the initially-assigned allocation of tones to tone-bearing units (see Kisseberth's treatment of Digo, below). All of the problems resulted from the single assumption that tonal representations and segmental representations are merged into single feature columns by the process of tone mapping. It is somehow necessary to express the fact that tones retain their autonomous status after the rules that assign tones to particular vowels have applied. As Leben has elsewhere pointed out (1978), the "suprasegmental" model had no way of expressing this generalization.

This problem finds a solution in the recognition that tone mapping rules do not merge tonal and segmental representations, but rather *associate* their elements by means of formal entities termed "association lines". The autosegmental framework, as first formulated in Goldsmith (1974a-d), posits phonological representations consisting of parallel tiers of phonological segments (both tonal and nontonal), as noted above. Separate autosegmental tiers remain independent of each other throughout derivations; thus, for example, (1) is a well-formed surface representation. Phonological rules may carry out operations on single tiers alone, or they may carry out operations affecting the set of associations between tiers; furthermore, phonological rules operating on single tiers may make reference, when necessary, to information available on other tiers.

A further innovation of autosegmental phonology is the notion of "Well-formedness Condition" governing autosegmental representations, originally formulated as below:

(2) Well-formedness Condition (WFC):
- i. All vowels are associated with at least one tone.
- ii. All tones are associated with at least one vowel.
- iii. Association lines do not cross.

This condition is not interpreted as a principle ruling out representations that do not conform to it, but rather as defining a neutral state from which any deviation is automatically corrected by convention. In subsequent formulations of the theory (see in particular Goldsmith 1976, 1979, 1981; Clements 1976, 1981a; Haraguchi 1977, 1979; Leben 1976, 1978; Clements and Ford 1979; Yip 1980; Halle and Kiparsky 1981; and McCarthy 1981, 1982, among others), it has been proposed that the mechanisms used to satisfy the Well-formedness Condition are universal (that is, invariant from language to language), and persist throughout the derivation, in the sense that they can and must apply immediately after each rule application. These mechanisms, termed Association Conventions by Haraguchi and later writers, add or delete association lines in order to bring any representation that deviates from the neutral state defined by the WFC into agreement with it. For example, in the hypothetical example

(3a) there are three unassociated or toneless vowels, thus creating a violation of condition (2i):

(3)

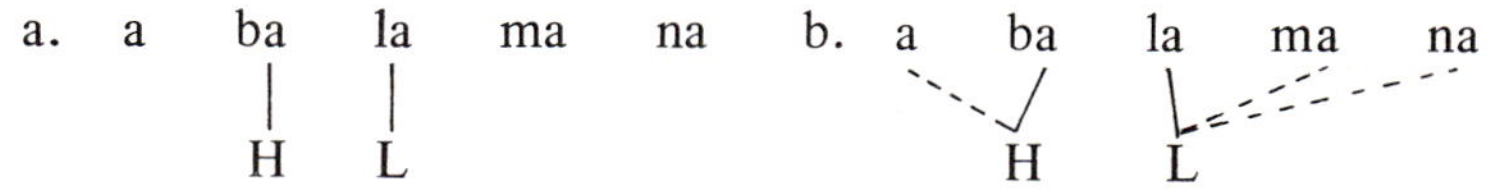


As shown by the dashed lines in (3b), the addition of three association lines is sufficient to bring the representation into conformity with the WFC. In cases where there is more than one way to satisfy the WFC, several specific principles have been proposed (for discussion see in particular Goldsmith 1976, Clements and Ford 1979):

(4) i. Associate free tones to free tone-bearing units from left to right;
ii. Associate free (unassociated) segments in preference to bound (associated) segments, (a) giving precedence to segments linked to unaccented elements, otherwise (b) giving precedence to segments on the left;
iii. Add the minimal number of association lines necessary to eliminate the violation.

These principles, applied in the order given, are sufficient to eliminate all cases of indeterminacy in the implementation of the WFC. The empirical motivation underlying the WFC should be clear. Its aim is to isolate the effects of rule application that are determined by general, language-independent conditions on phonological representation in such a way that the formulation of language-particular rules can be maximally free of superfluous (universally-determined) information.

Recent research has led to suggested modifications of some of the proposals mentioned above, all well within the spirit of the theory. Several of the chapters in this volume include discussion along these lines. As regards the Well-formedness Condition (2), the universality of one of its provisions, (2ii), has been called into question by Clements and Ford (1979), who argue that in Kikuyu, at least, floating tones must be allowed to remain afloat throughout the course of derivations. A more far-reaching proposal is that of Halle and Vergnaud (1982), who suggest that (2i) be replaced by a tone mapping rule which maps the first member of a sequence of free tones onto the first vowel of the domain, the second member onto the second vowel, and so on, finally associating the last tone in the sequence with any remaining toneless vowels to the right. Under this proposal, (2ii) remains in force but may be supplemented by language-particular well-formedness conditions of the type "no vowel may be associated with more than *n* tones," for some value *n*. One consequence of this proposal is that some vowels may remain toneless, in which case they surface with a "default" tone which is specified in their segmental matrix. Other alternative proposals have been made concerning not the statement of the WFC itself, but rather mechanisms of association such as those given in (4).

Many of these questions seem to be resolved by an observation made by Odden, in his contribution to this volume. Much work in the autosegmental framework has assumed that the mechanisms for removing violations of the WFC are in effect at all points in the derivation. In some languages, however, it is necessary to assume the existence of initial tone association rules which assign specific tones to specific tone-bearing units prior to the implementation of the WFC. This component may indeed be of major importance in the tonal phonology of some languages, as shown in the contributions by Kisseberth and by Hyman and Byarushengo. Odden points out that if violations of the WFC were everywhere resolved as soon as they arise, there would under most circumstances be no free vowels for such rules to assign tones to. It is thus within the logic of the theory that rules making reference to free tone-bearing units must take precedence over the implementation of the WFC, which thus serves to implement the "default" case. In fact, we may further observe that if Kiparsky's Elsewhere Condition (1973b) is understood as a regulative principle governing the operation of rule systems, then initial tone association rules and the WFC will always stand in the appropriate "elsewhere" relationship, and the rules, being more specific, will take precedence over the general mechanisms resolving the violations of the WFC. Odden concludes, therefore, that grammars need not specifically state the point in derivations at which the WFC comes into effect; it will always be applicable after the operation of the last rule which makes specific reference to a "free" tone-bearing unit.

One of the central claims of autosegmental phonology, then, is the proposal that there is a neutral or "well-formed" state, defined by the theory, from which representations may deviate. Language-particular rules may create violations of this well-formed state, but universal principles will automatically modify the geometry of the representation so as to restore it. This division of labor between language-specific rules and the universal WFC plays an important role in the studies which follow.

4. We have so far discussed the treatment of true "tone languages", that is, languages in which tonal information is part of the lexical representation of words and morphemes and in which accent plays no lexical role. In languages of this kind, we find a "Basic Mapping Principle" applying in case after case whose effect can be schematized as follows:

(5)
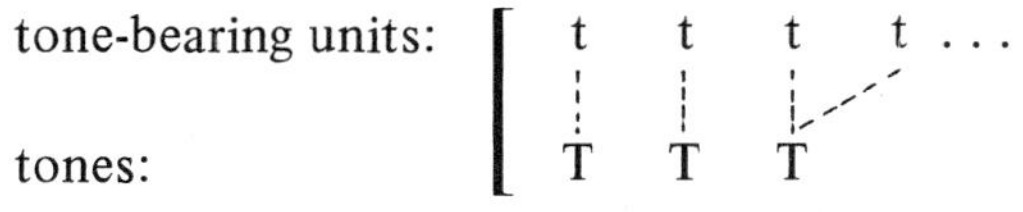


This principle is of course formally derived from the WFC (2) as implemented by the principles stated in (4). Regardless of the extent of language-specific variation in the details of this initial association procedure, it has long been clear that languages using such a procedure include all those whose underlying tone melodies are "unrestricted" (in the sense of Voorhoeve 1973), that is, the true tone languages.

On the other hand, other languages, often called "accent" languages, typically have a fixed, predictable tone melody which need not be specified in lexical representations but which is assigned to tone-bearing units in phonologically unpredictable ways. This "Basic Tone Melody" consists of a fixed sequence of two or three tones which are spread over a domain which is typically the word but which, in some languages, may be larger or smaller than the word. Tones associate with tone-bearing units not in the left-to-right fashion sketched in (5) but rather in the manner indicated in (6). As this figure shows, one of the tones in the melody is designated as accented, and is associated with the accented vowel as shown in (7). (Here and elsewhere we indicate the presence of an accent by the asterisk.)

(6)
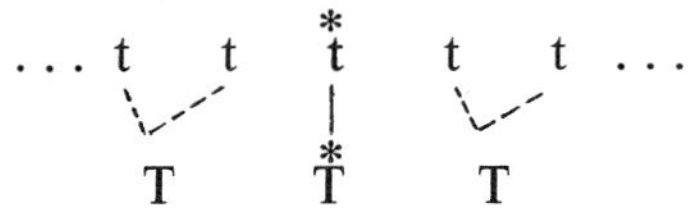


(7)
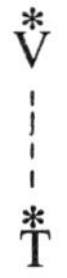


Principle (7) applies only to as-yet unassociated tones and tone-bearing units and thus takes precedence over the WFC. Tones and tone-bearing units unaffected by (7) are submitted to the mechanisms that implement the WFC. It should be borne in mind that this concept of accent bears no relation to particular phonetic properties such as stress or amplitude; it involves no more and no less than the association of basic tone melodies to the tone-bearing units of a word.

In this view, then, an accent language is identified as one in which a fixed Basic Tone Melody (or more rarely, two: see Haraguchi 1977) can be specified for all words, and in which the melody is assigned by rule (7) and the WFC. If the Basic Tone Melody of a language is, for example, HL (with either tone accented), then the underlying tonal tier of this language will consist of *n* copies of this melody: $(HL)^n$, where the number of copies (that is, the value of *n*) equals the number of accents in the representation at the point when (7) applies.

This view of accent systems, further elaborated upon in Goldsmith

(1982), can be summarized as in (8), which characterizes the accentual component of the system as feeding into the tonal component (see McCawley 1978 for an earlier statement of this view):

(8) Morphology ⟶ Underlying Representation

↓

| 1. Accent Rules<br>2. Basic Tone Melody Association |
|---|

↓

Underlying Tone Level

↓

| Tone Rules |
|---|

↓

Surface Phonetic Representation

In this model the accent rule component consists of rules which insert, delete, or shift accents. The underlying tone level is created by associating one copy of the Basic Tone Melody with each of the vowels that continue to bear accent after the operation of the accent rules, by the rule of Basic Tone Melody Association (7). The remainder of the tone rules then apply. The validity of this point of view, which conceives of an independent "accentual" part of the derivation preceding the tone rule component, clearly rests on the extent to which the concept of accent can simplify our account of tone systems and tone rules. We suggest, that is, that there are certain processes in languages that may ultimately have their surface manifestation in the tonal pattern of a word or phrase but which should best be viewed as involving a nontonal element – accent – which "sets the stage" for the tonal derivation to follow.

On this view, accent is not an element on a separate autosegmental tier; if it were, it would be no different formally from a tonal segment, and there would be little point in setting up an entity distinct from tone in underlying representations. Moreover, accent is not a binary feature: the notion of "[-accent]" (that is, "non-accent") plays no role in this account. We suggest that an accent is an element of the same type as a segment, but which can only exist as a feature or mark on another segment. Thus accent can be assigned, deleted, copied, or shifted, but it cannot "float", nor can it "associate", in the technical sense, since it is not assigned to an independent autosegmental tier.

It remains an open question at this point what constraints can be placed upon rule sensitivity to accents. Among several hypotheses that have at some time been envisaged are the following:

(9) i. Accents are erased after tone assignment.

ii. Accents are not erased, but cannot be introduced, shifted, or deleted after tone assignment.

Under the first of these hypotheses, tone rules would be unable to refer to accent. This hypothesis is difficult to reconcile with the recent studies of Luganda by Hyman (1982) and of Kimatuumbi by Odden (1982), where in both cases, the operation of tone rules appears to be crucially dependent upon the presence or absence of accents. The second, weaker hypothesis views accents as present after tones are introduced but as "immune" to the operation of further rules; that is, accents can be "looked at" but not affected. This view seems consistent with what is currently known about the operation of accentual systems and, if correct, imposes an intrinsic ordering between the accent rules and the tone rules. In sum, these remain interesting questions for further exploration, but will not be pursued further here.

5. As we have seen, an accentual system is more complex than a purely tonal one in one sense: an accentual system contains, in addition to the tonal derivation, an earlier accentual stage. Would considerations of simplicity, then, tend to weigh against accentual analyses of what superficially seem to be tone languages?

As noted above, the historical evidence shows that there has in fact been a distinct drift toward accentual reanalysis in Bantu languages. This evidence suggests that rather than being more complex linguistically, accentual systems may be simpler. In fact, one might conclude that it is just to the extent that an accentual analysis proves simpler than the best available tonal analysis that an accentual analysis will prevail.

A simple hypothetical illustration may help to make this point clear. Let us say that a tonal representation is *factorizable* if it can be analyzed as derived, by well-motivated rules, from a deeper level at which the tonal tier can be uniquely factored into a sequence of copies of a fixed tone melody. If we assume that such a basic tone melody must have at least two tones, then only a small set of tone languages will have the factorization property; well-studied languages like Igbo, Ewe or Yoruba can easily be seen not to have this property. In general, any language with few or no restrictions on underlying tone melodies will not be factorizable.

Suppose, however, that we encounter a case in which a factorization is possible into, say, a sequence of basic tone melodies of the form HL, and that moreover, we find one or more tone rules operating on certain instances of this melody as a unit, for example, deleting the second of two HL melodies occurring on successive syllables within the word. Two analyses are then possible, as summarized below:

| (10) | | tonal analysis: | | accentual analysis: |
|---|---|---|---|---|
| | a. | basic: HL | a. | basic: * |
| | b. | HL → Ø / HL__ | b. | * → Ø / *__ |
| | | | c. | Insert HL and associate by (7) |

In underlying representations (10a), the tonal analysis postulates sequences of the tone melody HL while the accentual analysis postulates accents. As (10b) shows, the tonal analysis has a rule deleting HL after HL while the accentual analysis has a rule deleting accent after accent. Finally (10c), under the accentual analysis the Basic Tone Melody HL is introduced, once for each remaining accented vowel, and associated by rule (7); this latter step, as it is determined by universal convention rather than being a language-specific rule, is cost-free in the grammar. It thus follows that the accentual analysis is simpler than the tonal analysis, on two counts: it has a simpler lexicon (requiring only one element, the accent, for every two tones required in the tonal analysis) and a simpler rule system (specifying only two units of information rather than four, for each such rule).

We may now express our view as follows: the language learner seeks to impose a factorization upon the tonal system wherever possible. What is meant by "seeks to impose?" The question is best answered by indirection. The construction, or acquisition of a grammar consists in developing analyses that maximize certain kinds of regularities. In particular, following a suggestion in Goldsmith (1976), chapter 4, we may propose that a system is more highly valued to the extent that its underlying representations consist of uniformly linear sequences in which all segments are fully specified for all features. Any departure from this type of regularity comes at a cost, in the sense that the learner must discover each instance of nonlinearity and enter it as a special condition on word structure in the developing grammar. Tone languages are typically systems in which this condition of linearity is not satisfied. Hence, at the point where the learner discovers any failure of one-to-one linkage between tones and tone-bearing units, in the form of floating tones, toneless vowels and the like, the learner will adopt the hypothesis that the system is underlyingly an accentual one and attempt to impose a factorization as described above. Lexical representations in accentual systems are of course fully linear as far as accent is concerned, since each segment either bears accent, or does not, and accents do not have the property of being able to "float", as noted in section 4.

In this view, "transitional" systems are precisely those which are susceptible to both tonal and accentual analysis, and in such cases we propose that the learner is biased toward the accentual account. Note in particular that the presence of toneless verbal suffixes, reconstructed at the level of Proto-Bantu, make linearization strictly impossible under a tonal analysis. Accentual reanalysis will be all the more compelling to the extent that no "counterevidence" exists in the form of tonal sequences that resist factorization, and even here, it seems reasonable to allow that learners may be inattentive to such counterevidence to the extent that it remains at the margins of the system.

6. This, then is our response to the question with which we began: how can we explain the widespread analytical indeterminacy which we encounter so frequently in Bantu tone and accent systems, and their apparent historical drift toward fully accentual systems? If we are correct, the problem of indeterminacy is not an artifact of inadequate linguistic models but on the contrary an inherent feature of the Bantu proto-system itself, which lent itself to dual analysis and gave rise to differing interpretations in the course of its later development. We have attributed this duality to the dynamics involved in the interplay of two opposed factors: the pressure toward factorization and linearization characterizing the language acquisition process itself, and the built-in nonlinearity of the proto-system, in which tones and tone-bearing units did not stand in a one-to-one relationship and where the domain of tone mapping, involving the morphologically complex, agglutinative structure of the verb, provided fertile ground for the increasing autonomy of the tonal and segmental tiers.

*Chapter 2*

# Tone and Accent in Tonga

John Goldsmith

## 1. INTRODUCTION

The tonal system of Tonga, a major language of Zambia, has been discussed in a series of papers of especial interest to Bantu scholars and phonologists more generally.[1] I hope to continue the discussion in this chapter, and illustrate how an accentual autosegmental theory can illuminate the intricacies of the Tonga verbal system. I have drawn heavily on material published by Hazel Carter (1962, 1971, 1972), and found inspiration in A.E. Meeussen's analysis of the morphotonology of Tonga (1963). I have also profited from discussions with Jerome Hachipola, a linguist and speaker of Tonga at Indiana University.

I shall generally assume an autosegmental theory of the form described in Chapter 1, and try to indicate ways in which the straightforward tonology of Tonga can best be treated autosegmentally, and, more importantly, show how the more complex accentual system can best be understood as the result of a small number of accentual, non-tonal rules which precede the Underlying Tone Level. At the Underlying Tone Level, a High-Low ($H\overset{*}{L}$) melody is assigned, with one copy per derived accent (i.e., one for each accent present at the Underlying Tone Level). These melodies are linked to the vowels of the word by a rule that associates the Low tone of the melody – the accented tone, as we shall call it – to the accented vowel in question.

In Section 2 below, we shall consider the nominal system, in which the basic $H\overset{*}{L}$ melody is most directly manifested. Section 3, the longest and central part of this paper, addresses the verbal system and its accentual rules. Finally, in Section 4 we shall consider the diachronic antecedents to the present-day accentual system found in Tonga.

## 2. THE NOMINAL SYSTEM

### *2.1 Introduction*

We shall first consider the tonal patterns on Tonga nominals in isolation, generally with the class prefix, which will be seen to be itself accentless, and thus tonally inert.

Guthrie notes that Tonga has three tonal classes in bisyllabic nominal stems, and not the four that might be expected of a two-tone language, and which were found in Proto-Bantu (see Section 4 below on the historical development). Carter (1962:13) notes that there are similarly three tonal classes of monosyllabic stems. Typical examples cited by Carter of the first class, Class A, include those in (1) and (2), where the stem is italicized for ease of identification.

(1) Class A monosyllabic stems

| | | |
|---|---|---|
| í + bú + *sì* | 'smoke' | (noun class 14) |
| í + kú + *pà* | 'to give' | (noun class 15) |

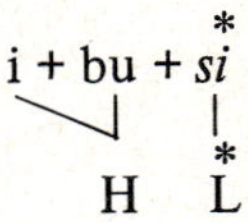


(2) Class A bisyllabic stems

| | | |
|---|---|---|
| í + má + *kànì* | 'news, affairs' | (cl. 6) |
| í + mó + *òmbè* | 'edge' | (cl. 3) |

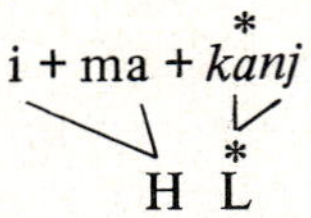


All nouns in class A fall into the autosegmental patterns of (1) or (2), with the L of a HL melody associated with the final syllable of the stem.

Class B2 is distinct from Class A in that all forms in Class B2 may be represented as in (3). The same HL melody is present, but the L toneme is not associated with the stem-initial vowel.

(3) Class B2

| | | |
|---|---|---|
| í + mú + *súnè* | 'ox' | (cl. 1) |
| í + mó + *ómbè* | 'calf' | (cl. 1) |

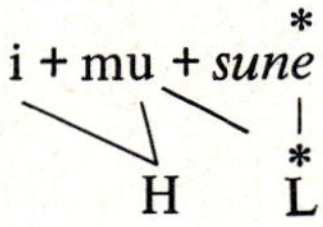


Carter identifies the crucial property here as the presence of H-tone on the stem-initial syllable, and includes as case B1 certain monosyllabic stems, as in (4), which may display either of two tone patterns. We shall assume that these are essentially Class A stems; their basic tone is thus that given first in (4). They must, however, be irregularly marked to undergo a final L-deletion rule.

(4) Class B1

| | | | | |
|---|---|---|---|---|
| í + má + *lì* | *or* | í + má + *lí* | 'money' | (cl. 6) |
| í + kú + *lè* | *or* | í + kú + *lé* | 'far away' | (cl. 17) |

The third class is composed of nouns with all syllables Low in tone, as in (5). These we shall analyze as being unaccented.

(5) Class C

| | | |
|---|---|---|
| ì + bù + *sù* | 'meal, flour' | (cl. 14) |
| ì + kù + *tì* + à | 'to pour' | (cl. 15) |
| ì + mà + *tòngò* | 'ruins' | (cl. 6) |
| ì + cò + *òlwè* | 'good fortune' | (cl. 7) |

```
i + bu + su
 \   |   /
     L
```

We shall return to these below.

In addition, there are polysyllabic stems of the sort illustrated in (6), with two Low-toned syllables interrupted by a High. We shall call these Class D.

(6) Class D

```
àcísyà      'uncle'   (cl. 1a)
| |  |
L H  L

tòmbélà     'lizard'  (cl. 1a)
|    | |
L    H L
```

When a prefix is attached, we find the tone pattern in (7).

```
(7)  a.  bá + !á  cí  syà          b.  bá + !tóm  bé  là
         |     \  /    |                |      \    /   |
         H (L)  H      L                H (L)    H      L
```

That is, the addition of the (otherwise inert) prefix rather strikingly alters the surface tone pattern in this case, putting the first and second syllables on the same tone (*!á cí*), while in the singular they had been on different tones (*à cí*). Clearly, however, the "slip-tone" or downstep observed in (7) and indicated by "!" is the effect of the L tone originally on *a*, but now unassociated. Tonga, we observe, is a language with downdrift; two High tones separated by a Low tone will be realized with the second High a bit lower in pitch then the first. The Low tone, we now see, need not be associated to effect this lowering.[2]

Thus we may hypothesize a rule as in (8). In fact, we shall see below that the two effects of (8) – the spreading leftward of the H tone following HL, and the disassociation of the L in a Rising pattern – should be separated, as in (9), (10).

(8) 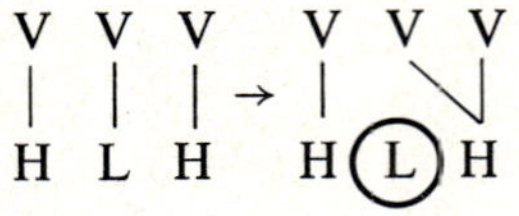

(9) 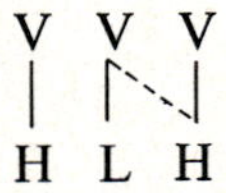

(10) 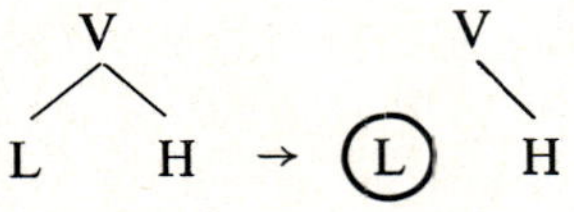

The question naturally arises as to the source of the four tonemes in (7a) and (7b). We shall see immediately below, when we consider accentless stems, that such prefixes as the *ba* in (7) have themselves no inherent tone, but rather accept the closest tone provided by the stem (see (5) above). The natural conclusion to draw, then, is that the entire sequence *HLHL* comes from the stems *acisya*/*tombela*.

Summarizing up to this point, we have found stems (Classes A and B) with a HL melody, and those (Class D) with a HLHL melody. In general, before the application of rules of tone-simplification, all words in Tonga display tone melodies of the form $(HL)_0^n$. Tonga thus has what we called in Chapter 1 the *factorization property*, and tone-assignment may be viewed as an accentual process. We need only specify the association of a fixed tone in the tone melody to a lexically determined vowel in a given word.

But which tone of the tone melody is accented? That is, which tone of the HL sequence is associated with the accented vowel? The hypothesis that the H is accented might work for Class B words, where we might say that a word like *ímá+súnè* was accented on the first vowel of the stem, as in (11).

(11) a.

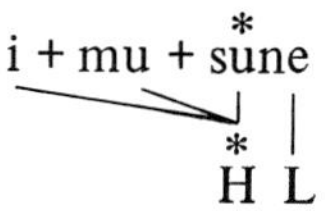


But this hypothesis gives way to the hypothesis that the basic melody is H$\overset{*}{\text{L}}$ (that is, that the Low tone is primarily associated with the accented vowel) when we consider Class A words, which can be naturally treated as initial-accent forms, as in (12). Class B forms are then analyzed not as in (11) but as in (13), with accent on a non-initial vowel.

(12) a.

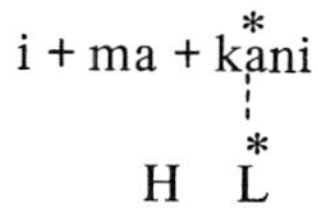


b.

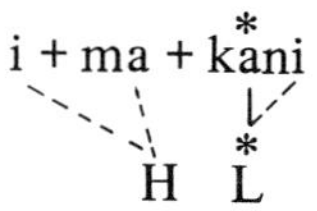


(13) a.

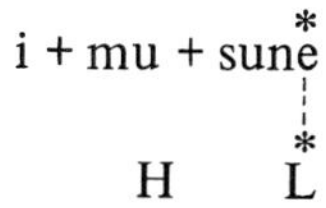


b.

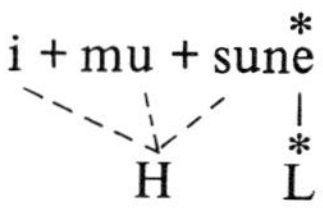


On this H$\overset{*}{\text{L}}$ analysis, then, we find that the accent can fall on any vowel, and there can be two accents in a single morpheme, a perhaps surprising result. It should also be observed that the accent has no other local phonetic effects. In a recent phonetic study, Luce (1981) showed that there was no influence on length caused by the accent in Tonga. There is also no perceptible loudness effect of the tonal accent.

In Class D, we find the possibility of the accent falling not only stem-initially, but also word-initially, as in (14).

(14)

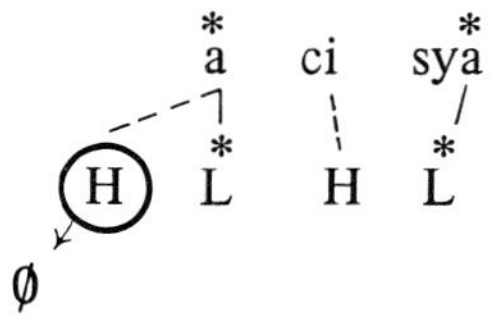


By the Well-formedness Condition, the initial H will be associated with the first vowel of the word, even in a case like (14), thus producing in effect a Falling tone. The surface L tone is the effect of the tone-simplification rule (15), which simplifies HL to L in absolute word-initial position.

(15)

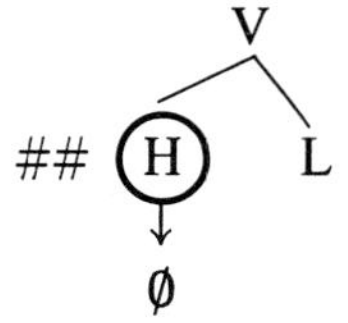

Finally, we must note that unaccented words must be assigned a Low melody, by what we might call a recessive tone rule. It is possible that this is achieved accentually, as Bill Poser has pointed out to me. If Tonga contains a rule that places an accent on the first syllable of any word that otherwise contains no accent, then this will provide the Low melody, through the effects of rule (15).

## 2.2 *Weak/Strong Forms*

An important role is played in Carter's grammar by the distinction between the *strong* and *weak* tonal patterns on nominals and verbs. Consider the contrast in (16), involving the Prehodiernal Past tense with an accented verb stem (see section 3.4).

(16) a. ndà-ká-tòlà nyàmà. 'I *took* meat.'
b. ndà-ká-!tólá nyàmà. 'I took *meat*.'

As Carter says, (16a) "implies, e.g., 'I didn't *bring* it'," (16b) "'I took nothing else'". Carter notes, "the strong series require no support and may stand at the end of an utternace; the weak series require the support of a following item, usually nominal or particle."

As the verb in (16) suggests, the shift from the (more basic) strong form to the weak form includes a raising of the entire sequence of final Low tones, though this sequence of now-High-toned vowels is separated from a preceding High by a downstep (the raised exclamation point of (16b)). Given rules (9) and (10), we may well conclude that (16b) is the surface realization of a structure as in (17) in which the verb and its object have formed a single phonological word with an accent peculiar to this construction placed on the first syllable of the object.

(17)
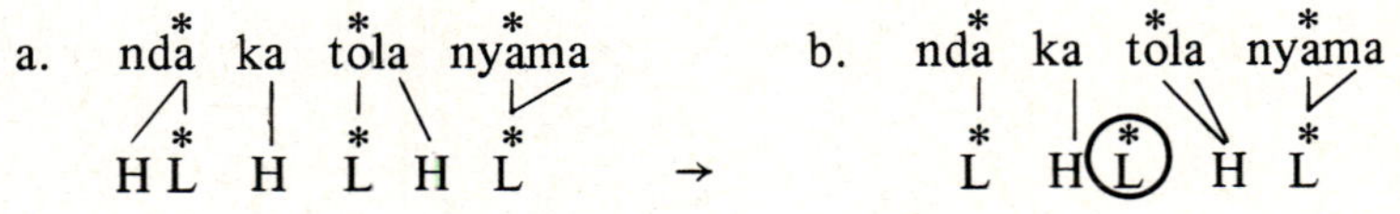


On this account, which we shall adopt, the weak series is formed by the application of a rule such as (18).[3]

(18) $[\ ]_V \#\# [CV \ldots] \rightarrow [\ ]_V + [C\overset{*}{V} \ldots]$

This analysis predicts that if the second word in a weak construction has itself an accent on a syllable other than the first syllable, then, when placed in this construction, it will appear to have two accents. This is correct, as we see in (19).

(19) a. músénè 'ox'
b. ndà ká ! tó lá ! mú sé nè 'I took an *ox*'
c.–d.

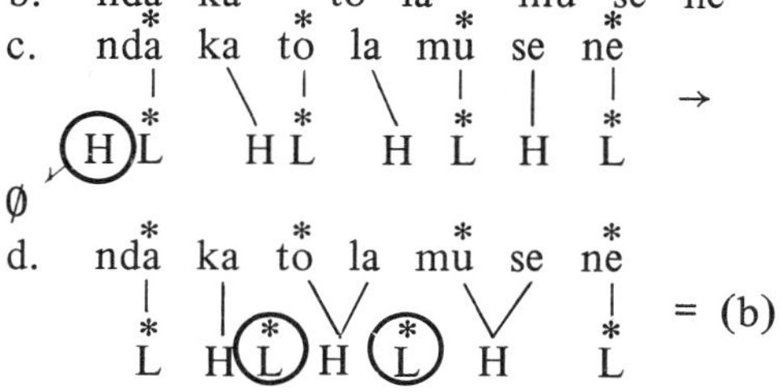

The connection between an induced initial-accent on the element immediately following a weak form is thus easily established tonally. That the two form a single phonological word is supported by such observations as the following, from Carter (1962:15): "Certain particles such as *!bíyó* or (!)*biyo* 'only' and the IN [independent nominal] *nzi?* 'what?', usually written as an enclitic, are always preceded by a weak pattern."

If the following word already has initial accent, the weak and the strong forms may be indistinguishable, as in Carter's example (1962:10) *twalyá zimbwali* 'we ate sweet potatoes'.

### *2.3 Accented Nominal Prefixes*

Unlike the usual class prefixes, which are unaccented, there are two kinds of accented nominal prefixes. Carter presents the following contrasts with the prefixes *a-* 'and,by,with' and *si-* 'one who Vs'.

(20)

| *Stem type* | *Word* | *'and a –'* | *V-er* | |
|---|---|---|---|---|
| accentless | (ì) lwèèndò | àlwèèndò | sìlwèèndò | 'traveller' |
| initial accent | (í) nkòndò | ànkóndò | sínkòndò | 'enemy' |
| non-initial accent | (í) kúkòlwà | àkúkòlwà | sìkúkòlwà | 'drunkard' |

We observe that the prefixes *a-* and *si-* are consistently Low in tone when they precede an accentless word, unsurprisingly, or when they precede a stem with accent at least one syllable away, as in the final row of (20). This is illustrated in (21).

(21) a. b.

However, when the prefix accent and the stem accent abut, the two prefixes respond in different ways. *a-* throws back the High tone from the stem, and since that H is not word-initial, it does not delete, but is simplified by a rule discussed below. Both cases in (22) illustrate the unusual situation in which two consecutive accents appear at the Underlying Tone Level.

(22)

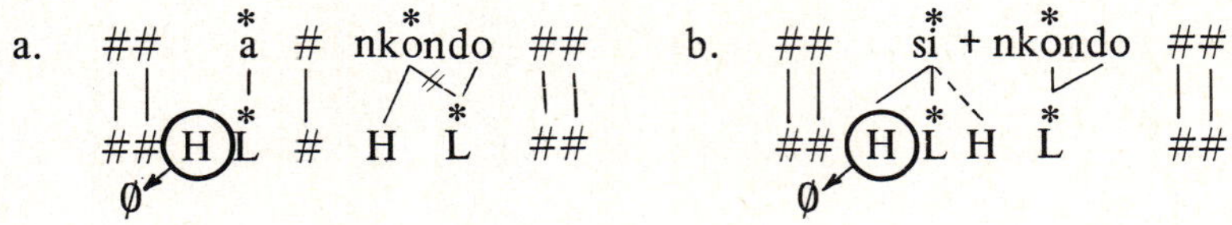


## 2.4 *Post-accenting Prefixes*

The view that Tonga morphemes may have accentual properties, but not tonal properties *per se*, is confirmed by the presence of nominal prefixes that fall neither into the unaccented nor the accented class. The Restricted Stabilizing Element (RSE) (Carter 1962:21) is, rather, a post-accenting element, symbolized here as $\vec{v}$. This post-accent is present as part of the underlying morphological representation. The phonological make-up of the RSE depends on the class of the nominal, but it begins with a nasal and is typically one syllable in length. The post-accent immediately shifts to the following syllable, due to its inherent properties, and the tonal pattern derived is provided at the Underlying Tone Level by the regular processes of the language. Thus words with accent on the second syllable (Class B) undergo a derivation as in (23a), and unaccented words as in (23b). Clear examples of Class A words are not available.

(23)

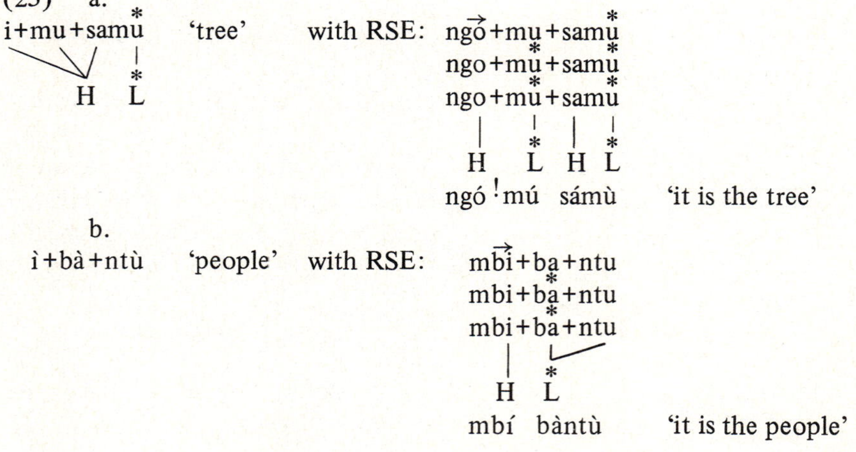

## 3. THE VERBAL SYSTEM

### *3.1 Introduction*

A.E. Meeussen's analysis of the tonal system of Tonga begins with a discussion of the tone found in the present perfect indicative, as in (24), and the present indicative, as in (25).

(24) Present Perfect

a. Verb stems of type *-lang-* 'look at'

| Subject | No Object | Type 1 Obj Prefix (sg.) | Type 2 Obj Prefix (pl.) |
|---|---|---|---|
| 1 sg. | ndí-lí-láng-ide | ndí-lí-mú-láng-ide | ndi-li-ba-láng-ide |
| 3pl. | ba-lí-láng-ide | ba-lí-mú-láng-ide | ba-lí-!bá-láng-ide |

b. Verb stems of type *-bon-* 'see'

| Subject | No Object | Type 1 Obj Prefix (sg.) | Type 2 Obj Prefix (pl.) |
|---|---|---|---|
| 1 sg. | ndi-li-bon-ide | ndi-li-mu-bon-ide | ndi-li-ba-bon-ide |
| 3 pl. | ba-lí-bon-ide | ba-lí-mú-bon-ide | ba-lí-ba-bon-ide |

(25) Present Indicative

a. *-lang-*

| Subject | No Object | Type 1 Obj Prefix (sg.) | Type 2 Obj Prefix (pl.) |
|---|---|---|---|
| 1 sg. | ndi-la-lang-a | ndi-la-mu-lang-a | ndi-la-ba-lang-a |
| 3 pl. | ba-la-lang-a | ba-la-mu-lang-a | ba-lá-ba-lang-a |

b. *-bon-*

| | | | |
|---|---|---|---|
| 1 sg. | ndi-la-bon-a | ndi-la-mu-bon-a | ndi-la-ba-bon-a |
| 3 pl. | ba-lá-bon-a | ba-lá-mú-bon-a | ba-lá-ba-bon-a |

Meeussen observes that each of the three major classes of morphemes - subject prefixes, object prefixes, and verb stems - can be subdivided into two classes, those which are always Low in tone (*ba*, *bon*, etc.) and those which may be either High or Low (*lang*, *mu*, *la*, *ndi*, etc.). In a singularly clever move, he suggests that we *underline* those morphemes that fall into the class that is everywhere Low. (25) can then be rewritten as (26). (Underlined morphemes are here italicized.)

| | | | |
|---|---|---|---|
| (26) | ndi la lang a | ndi la mu lang a | ndi la *ba* lang a |
| | *ba* la lang a | *ba* la mu lang a | *ba* lá *ba* lang a |
| | ndi la *bon* a | ndi la mu *bon* a | ndi la *ba* *bon* a |
| | *ba* lá *bon* a | *ba* lá mú *bon* a | *ba* lá *ba* *bon* a |

As Meeussen notes, "the rule is: elements of the first group [those not underlined] are high if and only if they occur between elements of the second group [those underlined]." While this procedure works, the algorithm is difficult to reinterpret from a generative point of view, as

McCawley (1973) points out. Taking the italicized elements to be either basically High or Low toned, the rule in question is curiously and peculiarly anti-assimilatory.

Meeussen himself felt no misgivings. He appended his algorithm with the caveat, "It is necessary to realize that this rule, no more than the grouping of sub-types into the categories "unmarked" and "marked", is neither true nor false; it can be more or less applicable, and this will have to be tested by examining other tenses."

Our own view is somewhat different. The theoretical framework being used here does force certain moves in the analysis, and forbids others; degrees of variation of the application of rules are not without limit. Meeussen's principle must surely be an artifact of something rather different.

Meeussen's division of prefixes and stems into two tonal classes is clearly both correct and necessary. In fact, it corresponds precisely to the notion of accented and unaccented vowel as developed in Section 2 above for nominals. That is, all of the morphemes that appear in such verbal forms as (24) and (25) also appear in nominal forms such as infinitives and free subject relatives. We find, perhaps not surprisingly, that the morphemes that Meeussen called "determinant" or "underlined" are, in our terms, precisely the accented morphemes. The rest are unaccented, and receive their tone by the Well-formedness Condition. This correspondence can be seen in such examples as (27).

| | | | | |
|---|---|---|---|---|
| (27) | a. | i ku b$\overset{*}{o}$n a | 'to see' | [í kú bon a] |
| | b. | i ku mu b$\overset{*}{o}$n a | 'to see him' | [í kú mú bon a] |
| | c. | i ku b$\overset{*}{a}$ b$\overset{*}{o}$n a | 'to see them' | [í kú ba bon a] |
| | d. | i ku lang a | 'to look at' | [i ku lang a] |

The principles developed in Section 2 lead to the correct nominal tone patterns in (27); the question arises, however, as to how to derive the verbal patterns of (25), for example, for which Meeussen's principle works.

The answer is clear. The verbal patterns in (24) and (25) differ from the corresponding nominal patterns in that a sequence of expected initial High syllables is Low (except in the first two forms in (24a), forms to which we return below). Forms with only a single accent do not present surface High tones. From an autosegmental perspective, we conclude that there is a rule as in (28) that deletes an initial H tone on the autosegmental tier, thus leaving the remaining L tone to associate leftward by the Well-formedness Condition, as in (29).

(28) $H \rightarrow \emptyset \ / \ [_{verb}\# \text{---}$

(29)

This analysis so far accounts for the nonoccurrence of High tones in verbs with only one accented syllable (holding aside the one exceptional case already noted); it also predicts that if a verb has two accents, as in (30), H tones will occur in between the accents, as Meeussen's algorithm notes, and that if the left-most of the two accents is not on the first syllable, the syllables to the left will be Low, as in (31). We shall see below that this is true.

(30)

(31)

It is worth emphasizing that on this autosegmental account, there is no special realization rule for verbal forms, as has been suggested in earlier analyses. We have the same basic melody, H$\overset{*}{\text{L}}$, in all cases, though there is a strictly tonological rule that operates on verbal forms. Those forms based on a verb root, but which are syntactically nominal, do not undergo H-deletion (28).

To pursue this point a moment, we might well imagine a system similar to Tonga's in which verbs and nouns were assigned accent in similar, or identical, ways, but in which the basic tone melody for nouns was H$\overset{*}{\text{L}}$ and that for verbs was $\overset{*}{\text{H}}$L. In such a system, we would find a rather striking difference between nouns and verbs, as in Tonga, but no convergence of the underlying tone melodies. Tonga's use of a *single* basic tone melody across categories, along with its tolerance of a tonal rule sensitive to lexical category, suggests (32).

(32) Conjecture: If an accentual language has only one basic tone melody for each lexical category, the respective melodies must be identical.

There is a second rule operative in the verbal data that we have considered so far. This rule is central to Tonga accentuation, and we shall refer to it as "Meeussen's Rule", for as Meeussen noted, "in a sequence of determinants [our acçents], only the first is treated as a determinant". We shall formalize this as in (33). Thus in a form like $\overset{*}{ba}$ *la* $\overset{*}{ba}$ $\overset{*}{bon}$ *a*, the accent on -$\overset{*}{bon}$- is deleted by an accentual rule before the Underlying Tone Level, and the $H\overset{*}{L}$ melodies are assigned as in (34a), not (34b).

(33) $\overset{*}{V} \rightarrow \overset{o}{V} \ / \ \overset{*}{V}\ C_o$ ——

(34)

## 3.2 *Present Indicative*

Consider the following data from Carter, consisting of forms in the Present Indicative. These verbs are all of the form:

| Subject markers | Tense marker | (object markers) | Verb stem | Final vowel |
|---|---|---|---|---|
| ndi 1 sg. | la | ndi 1 sg. | bon 'see' | a |
| u 2,3 sg. | | ku 2 sg. | lang 'look at' | |
| | | mu 3 sg. | etc. | |
| tu 1 pl. | | tu 1 pl. | | |
| mu 2 pl. | | mu 2 pl. | | |
| ba 3 pl. | | ba 3 pl. | | |

(35) Present Indicative

a. Accented stems

| *No Object Marker* | *Unaccented Object Marker* | *Accented Object Marker* |
|---|---|---|
| tu la bon a | tu la ku bon a | tu la ba bon a |
| tu la silik a | tu la ku silik a | tu la ba silik a |
| tu la swiilil a | tu la ku swiilil a | tu la ba swiilil a |
| | | |
| ba lá bon a | ba lá ndí bon a | ba lá ba bon a |
| ba lá silik a | ba lá ndí silik a | ba lá ba silik a |
| ba lá swiilil a | ba lá ndí swiilil a | ba lá ba swiilil a |

b. Unaccented stems

| | | |
|---|---|---|
| tu la lang a | tu la ku lang a | tu la ba lang a |
| tu la tobel a | tu la ku tobel a | tu la ba tobel a |
| tu la yandaul a | tu la ku yandaul a | tu la ba yandaul a |
| | | |
| ba la lang a | ba la ku lang a | ba lá ba lang a |
| ba la tobel a | ba la ku tobel a | ba lá ba tobel a |
| ba la yandaul a | ba la ku yandaul a | ba lá ba yandaul a |

By assigning underlying accent to 3rd person subjects and to plural object markers, as well as to stems such as *bon*, we find accent patterns as in (36). The circled accents represent accents deleted by Meeussen's Rule (33).

```
(36)  Present Indicative
       *                       *                    *  ⊛
tu la bon a          tu la ku bon a          tu la ba bon a
       *                       *                    *  ⊛
tu la silik a        tu la ku silik a        tu la ba silik a
         *                       *                  *    ⊛
tu la swiilil a      tu la ku swiilil a      tu la ba swiilil a

 *     *              *         *             *     *  ⊛
ba la bon a          ba la ndi bon a         ba la ba bon a
 *     *              *         *             *     *  ⊛
ba la silik a        ba la ndi silik a       ba la ba silik a
 *       *            *           *           *     *    ⊛
ba la swiilil a      ba la ndi swiilil a     ba la ba swiilil a

                                                    *
tu la lang a         tu la ku lang a         tu la ba lang a
                                                    *
tu la tobel a        tu la ku tobel a        tu la ba tobel a
                                                    *
tu la yandaul a      tu la ku yandaul a      tu la ba yandaul a

 *                    *                       *     *
ba la lang a         ba la ku lang a         ba la ba lang a
 *                    *                       *     *
ba la tobel a        ba la ku tobel a        ba la ba tobel a
 *                    *                       *     *
ba la yandaul a      ba la ku yandaul a      ba la ba yandaul a
```

These patterns extend the data given in (25) above.

If we look at Hachipola's Central dialect, we find a slightly different, and more interesting pattern, as in (37).

(37) a. Subject *u* (3rd singular)

| | | | |
|---|---|---|---|
| u lá ndí bon a | 'he sees me' | u lá tú bon a | 'he sees us' |
| u lá kú bon a | 'he sees you' | u lá mu bon a | 'he sees you' |
| u lá mú bon a | 'he sees him' | u lá bá bon a | 'he sees them' |

| | | |
|---|---|---|
| u la ndi lang a | 'he looks at me' | u lá tú lang a |
| u la ku lang a | etc. | u lá mu lang a |
| u la mu lang a | | u lá bá lang a |

b. Subject ndi (1st singular)

| | | | |
|---|---|---|---|
| ndi la ku bon a | 'I see you' | ndi la mu bon a | 'I see you-pl.' |
| ndi la mu bon a | 'I see him' | ndi la ba bon a | 'I see them' |

| | | |
|---|---|---|
| ndi la ku lang a | 'I look at you' | ndi la mu lang a |
| ndi la mu lang a | etc. | |

The tones in (37a) correspond to the accents indicated in (38).

(38) *u la ndi *bon a — *u la tu *bon a
*u la ku *bon a — *u la *mu *bon a
*u la mu *bon a — *u la ba *bon a

*u la ndi lang a — *u la tu *lang a
*u la ku lang a — *u la *mu lang a
*u la mu lang a — *u la ba *lang a

(the last three forms on the right are boxed; * marks the accented syllable)

We observe in the boxed data that an underlyingly accentless stem receives an accent when preceded by the object markers *-tu-* and *-ba-*. That is, in this dialect they are post-accenting; we summarize these forms in (39a). In (39b), we have indicated the forms from Carter's description of a closely related dialect.

(39) a. ndi $\overrightarrow{\text{tu}}$ — b. ndi *tu
ku *mu — ku *mu
mu $\overrightarrow{\text{ba}}$ — mu *ba

Let us postulate that the theory of accent contain within it post- and pre-accenting elements, indicated by $\vec{v}$ and $\overleftarrow{v}$, respectively. These elements, formally parallel to simple accents, will be everywhere subject to the convention that if $\vec{v}$ is followed by a syllable, it automatically and immediately shifts to the right one syllable and becomes a *. Similarly, $\overleftarrow{v}$ preceded by a syllable immediately shifts leftward and becomes a *.

Tonga is, we may note, undergoing a shift in the lexical marking of the plural object markers from accented (which is etymologically expected) to post-accenting, an interesting historical change. The resistance of the 2nd plural *mu* to this change is perhaps related to its near homophony to the 3rd singular object marker; the resistance to the change maximizes their surface distinctness.

A form like *u lá tú lang a* is derived as in (40).

(40) *u la $\overrightarrow{\text{tu}}$ lang a — UR
*u la tu *lang a — by convention
*u la tu *lang a — Tone Melody assignment

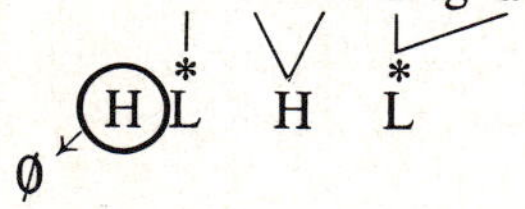


*3.3 Recent Past*

Let us turn now to the tone of the Recent Past tense (Carter's Tense 15 and 16). This tense is characterized by the tense marker *-a-* (accented), appearing immediately after the subject marker, parallel to the *-la-* in the Present Indicative. First we shall consider the tone pattern of this tense in the *weak* construction, that is, with a cliticized element following (a question word, for example). Rule (18) applies here, cliticizing the complement and assigning a * to the first syllable of the following object.

(41) Recent Past (Weak)

| | *No object* | **-less object* | **-ed object* |
|---|---|---|---|
| 'I' | ndabóná! | ndakú!bóná! | ndabábóná! |
| | ndasíilíká! | ndakú!síilíká! | ndabásíilíká! |
| | ndaswíílílá! | ndakú!swíílílá! | ndabáswíílílá! |
| 'they' | bábóná! | bákú!bóná! | bábábóná! |
| | básíilíká! | bákú!síilíká! | bábásíilíká! |
| | báswíílílá! | bákú!swíílílá! | bábáswíílílá! |
| 'I' | ndalángá! | ndakúlángá! | ndabálángá! |
| | ndatóbélá! | ndakútóbélá! | ndabátóbélá! |
| | ndayándáúlá! | ndakúyándáúlá! | ndabáyándáúlá! |
| 'they' | bálángá! | bákúlángá! | bábálángá! |
| | bátóbélá! | bákútóbélá! | bábátóbélá! |
| | báyándáúlá! | bákúyándáúlá! | bábáyándáúlá! |

The forms in (41) reflect an accentual pattern as in (42); as noted above, there is an accent (*) on the first syllable of the following object in each case due to rule (18). It is this following accent which gives rise to the downstep noted at the end of each word in (41).

(42) Recent Past (Weak)

```
     *  ⊛                  *     *                 *  ⊛  ⊛
ndi  a  bon  a       ndi  a  ku  bon  a      ndi  a  ba  bon  a
     *  ⊛                  *     *                 *  ⊛  ⊛
ndi  a  silik  a     ndi  a  ku  silik  a    ndi  a  ba  silik  a
     *  ⊛                  *     *                 *  ⊛  ⊛
ndi  a  swiilil  a   ndi  a  ku  swiilil  a  ndi  a  ba  swiilil  a

*  ⊛  ⊛              *  ⊛     *              *  ⊛  ⊛  ⊛
ba a  bon  a         ba a  ku bon  a         ba a  ba bon  a
*  ⊛  ⊛              *  ⊛     *              *  ⊛  ⊛  ⊛
ba a  silik  a       ba a  ku silik  a       ba a  ba silik  a
*  ⊛  ⊛              *  ⊛     *              *  ⊛  ⊛  ⊛
ba a  swiilil  a     ba a  ku swiilil  a     ba a  ba swiilil  a

     *                     *                       *  ⊛
ndi  a  lang  a      ndi  a  ku  lang  a     ndi  a  ba  lang  a
     *                     *                       *  ⊛
ndi  a  tobel  a     ndi  a  ku  tobel  a    ndi  a  ba  tobel  a
     *                     *                       *  ⊛
ndi  a  yandaul  a   ndi  a  ku  yandaul  a  ndi  a  ba  yandaul  a

*  ⊛                 *  ⊛                    *  ⊛  ⊛
ba a  lang  a        ba a  ku lang  a        ba a  ba lang  a
*  ⊛                 *  ⊛                    *  ⊛  ⊛
ba a  tobel  a       ba a  ku tobel  a       ba a  ba tobel  a
*  ⊛                 *  ⊛                    *  ⊛  ⊛
ba a  yandaul  a     ba a  ku yandaul  a     ba a  ba yandaul  a
```

Accents deleted by rule are indicated, again, by a circled star. As we see in (42), all sequences of consecutive *s reduce to the leftmost accent. Meeussen's rule (33) gives the right result in each case, whether applying simultaneously, or iterating from right to left.

The relation between the derived accentual patterns in (42) and the surface patterns in (41) is straightforward, given the principles discussed up to now, except in the case of the merger of syllables containing the subject markers *ndi-*, *b*$\overset{*}{a}$-, and the tense marker -$\overset{*}{a}$-. Note that the final H in the following examples comes from the accent on the initial vowel of the following object by (18).

(43)

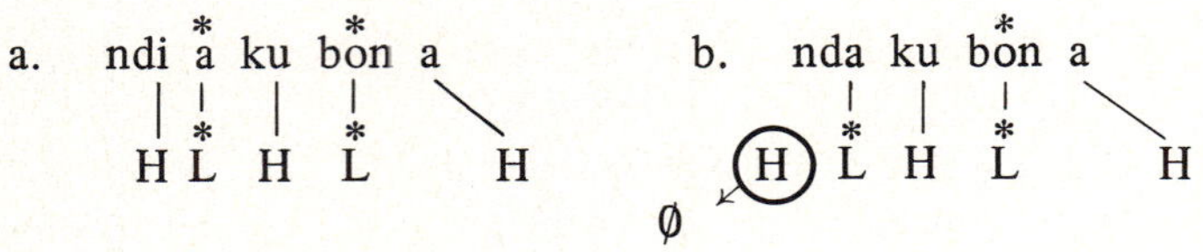

The underlying accent pattern is thus simple: the tense marker -$\overset{*}{a}$- is always accented; third person subjects are accented, first and second person are not; plural (personal) objects are accented, singular are not; and accents are deleted in accordance with Meeussen's Rule before the tone melodies are assigned.

The situation is considerably more complex, however, when we turn to the strong form of the Recent Past, the form in which the verb is not cliticized to the following object. The tone patterns are given in (44).

(44) Recent Past (Strong)

a. Accented Stems

| *No object* | **-less object* | **-ed object* |
|---|---|---|
| ndabóna | ndakúbona | ndabábona |
| ndasílika | ndakúsilika | ndabásilika |
| ndaswíilila | ndakúswiilila | ndabáswiilila |
| | | |
| wábona | wándíbona | wábabona |
| wásilika | wándísilika | wábasilika |
| wáswiilila | wándíswiilila | wábaswiilila |

b. Unaccented Stems

| | | |
|---|---|---|
| ndalanga | ndakulanga | ndabálanga |
| ndatobela | ndakutobela | ndabátobela |
| ndayandaula | ndakuyandaula | ndabáyandaula |
| | | |
| walanga | wandilanga | wábalanga |
| watobela | wanditobela | wábatobela |
| wayandaula | wandiyandaula | wábayandaula |

Given the principles discussed so far, these surface forms apparently reflect an accentual pattern as in (45).

(45) Recent Past (Strong)

```
        *  ⊛  *            *      *                      *  ⊛   *
A  ndi  a bon a       ndi  a ku bon  a        B  ndi  a  ba bon  a
        *  ⊛*              *      *                      *  ⊛  *
   ndi  a silik a     ndi  a ku silik a          ndi  a  ba silik a
        *    ⊛*            *       *                     *  ⊛    *
   ndi  a swi i lil a ndi  a ku swiilil a        ndi  a  ba swiilil a

   * ⊛  *             * ⊛       *                * ⊛  *   ⊛
C  u a bon a          u a ndi bon a           D  u a  ba bon a
   * ⊛ *              * ⊛      *                 * ⊛  *   ⊛
   u a silik a        u a ndi silik a            u a  ba silik a
   * ⊛   *            * ⊛        *               * ⊛  *    ⊛
   u a swiilil a      u a ndi swiilil a          u a  ba swiilil a

        *                  *                         *  ⊛  *
   ndi  a lang a      ndi  a ku lang a        E  ndi a  ba lang a
        *                  *                         *  ⊛   *
   ndi  a tobel a     ndi  a ku tobel a          ndi a  ba tobel a
        *                  *                         *  ⊛    *
   ndi  a yandaul a   ndi  a ku yandaul a        ndi a  ba yandaul a

   * ⊛                * ⊛                        * ⊛  *
   u a lang a         u a ndi lang a          F  u a  ba lang a
   * ⊛                * ⊛                        * ⊛  *
   u a tobel a        u a ndi tobel a            u a  ba tobel a
   * ⊛                * ⊛                        * ⊛  *
   u a yandaul a      u a ndi yandaul a          u a  ba yandaul a
```

Of the twelve triplets of forms in (45), the six boxed sets represent anomalies when compared to the apparently well-behaved forms of (41)-(42). We shall see that each anomaly allows of a simple resolution. Let us review what is puzzling in these cases.

In (A), the accent on the stem is absent, as expected, but an accent appears on the *following* syllable. This, in fact, is the key to all of the anomalous forms. Let us posit a rule (46) which shifts the accent one syllable to the right following -a- (with accent on -a-).

(46) Accent Shift

```
        *  *           *     *
   a.  -a- V  V  →   -a- V   V;     or,
        *  *           *     →
   b.  -a- V     →   -a-     V
```

Case (E) represents essentially the same problem, and is solved by the same rule (46) of Accent Shift. While *ba* has correctly lost its accent, the accentless stem that follows has picked up an accent somehow, and it is precisely through rule (46) that this arises.

All six boxed triplets pose a single problem as well: in each case, a sequence of three or more accents occurs, but the surface form is *not* formed by deleting all but the leftmost accent in the strong. *u a ba bon a* (with accents on u, a, ba, bon), which becomes *u a ba bon a* (with accents on u and ba), illustrates this strikingly.

Again, (46) Accent Shift is crucial to understanding this. And yet, the precise nature of the interaction of (46) Accent Shift and Meeussen's Rule is not statable within our current conception of rule interactions. Let us see why this is so.

It is clear, in the first place, that (33) Meeussen's Rule precedes, and bleeds, (46) Accent Shift. If *a*'s accent is lost by Meeussen's Rule, then it no longer triggers Accent Shift (46). This is seen in boxes (C), (D), and (F). Thus the deletion of *a*'s accent by Meeussen's Rule must precede (46).

However, while *a* can *undergo* Meeussen's Rule, in the sense that it can *lose* its accent, it cannot *trigger* the rule; that is, it cannot act as the left-hand vowel in Meeussen's Rule. *a* is thus a half-exception to Meeussen's Rule: it undergoes the rule, but it does not trigger it.

And yet, *a*'s half-hearted participation in Meeussen's Rule is due precisely to its involvement in rule (46). That is, (46) and (33) are two rules with similar inputs, and incompatible outputs. They both take a sequence of adjacent accents as their input, and while (46) turns the second of these two accents into a post-accent (see (46b)), (33) turns the same accent into a pre-accent (i.e., deletes it, since the pre-accent will immediately hop leftward onto an already present accent).

We arrive at the correct result if we modify Kiparsky's (1973) Elsewhere Condition in a minor way. We note, first, that the Elsewhere Condition is not (and was not proposed as) a principle predicting relative rule ordering. In particular, the Elsewhere Condition does *not* predict that the more specific of two rules in the appropriate relationship will apply first. Given the familiar "bleeding/counter-bleeding" relationship of the majority of cases discussed in the literature, it is not surprising that the more specific rule typically is ordered first, since otherwise it would never have a chance to apply; but that is not a *necessary* result, and the case at hand shows the contrary ordering.

The modification necessary in the Elsewhere Condition is that the more general rule should fail to apply not when the more specific rule *has* applied, but where the condition for the more specific rule is met.

We must say that all applications of (33) Meeussen's Rule apply before (46) Accent Shift, to ensure that (46) is properly bled; however, we must observe the potential case where (33) could apply to a sequence to which (46) would itself more specifically apply, as in (47). Precisely there, (33) does *not* apply.

```
        *  *  *   *                    *   *
(47) a. u  a  ba  bon  a     b.  ndi   a   ba  lang  a
        (33)                           (33) does not
           (33) does not apply              apply
              (33)
```

```
                  *    *                                   *   *
Output of (33):   u a ba bon a                     ndi a ba lang a
                  *    *                                   *     *
Output of (46):   u a ba bon a (no change)         ndi a ba lang a
```

Since (46) applies only when the verb is in the strong form, we see that the "exceptional" character of the non-application of (33) is the *direct* result of (46) being present to apply a moment later. In the case of the weak form, as in (48), rule (46) is not applicable, by stipulation. There Meeussen's Rule (33) applies across the board quite exceptionlessly, as we have already seen.[4]

```
                  * *  *   *                           *  *
(48)     a.       u a ba bon a            b.    ndi a ba lang a
                  *                                  *
Output of (33):   u a ba bon a                  ndi a ba bon a
```

*3.4 Prehodiernal Tense*

Tonga has a second past tense (Carter's Tense 18). This form is quite similar to that of the Recent Past, differing only in that its tense marker is *-a-ka-* (with * over *a*). Meeussen's Rule and our other tone rules work exceptionlessly here. Some sample forms are given in (49).

| | | | |
|---|---|---|---|
| (49) | nda ká bon a | nda ká kú bon a | nda ká ba bon a |
| | bá ká bon a | bá ká kú bon a | bá ká ba bon a |
| | nda ka lang a | nda ka ku lang a | nda ká ba lang a |
| | ba ka lang a | ba ka ku lang a | bá ká ba lang a |

These forms correspond to accentual patterns as in (50).

```
            *     *             *        *                *     *  ⊛
(50)   ndi a ka bon a     ndi a ka ku bon a        ndi a ka ba bon a
        *  ⊛      *        *  ⊛         *            *  ⊛    *   ⊛
       ba  a ka bon a     ba  a ka ku bon a        ba  a ka ba bon a

            *                   *                         *     *
       ndi a ka lang a    ndi a ka ku lang a       ndi a ka ba lang a
        *  ⊛               *  ⊛                     *  ⊛    *
       ba  a ka lang a    ba  a ka ku lang a       ba  a ka ba lang a
```

*3.5 Present Continuous*

The data and part of the analysis of this section come from Hachipola (1982). The tense morpheme *-ci-* of the Present Continuous displays certain puzzling aspects. Compare the following tonal patterns to those found either with an unaccented tense marker (*-la-* in (25), the Simple Present), or an accented tense marker (*-a-* (with * over *a*) in (41), the Recent Past).

(51) a. Accented Stem *-b$\overset{*}{o}$n-*

| *Subject* | *No Object Marker* | *Unaccented Object Marker* | *Accented Object Marker* |
|---|---|---|---|
| Unaccented | u ci bon a | u ci mu bon a | u ci ba bon a |
| Accented | (see text) | ba cí mú bon a | ba ci ba bon a |

b. Unaccented Stem *-lang-*

| | | | |
|---|---|---|---|
| Unaccented | u ci lang a | u ci mu lang a | u ci ba lang a |
| Accented | ba ci lang a | ba ci mu lang a | ba ci ba lang a |

The nearly complete lack of High tones in this pattern suggests that *-ci-* is accented, parallel to *-$\overset{*}{a}$-*. If we were to analyze *-ci-* in this way, all of the forms in (51b) would be correctly derived. However, *ba cí mú bon a* suggests that *-ci-* is unaccented, like *-la-*. More generally, *-ci-* appears to be underlyingly unaccented, but it becomes accented when a following morpheme is accented. Curiously, with the paucity of data available to us and the arrangement of the accentual system, we could equally well posit a rule that assigns accent to *-ci-* when an accented morpheme *precedes* it. Under either analysis, the assignment of accent to *-ci-* must precede Meeussen's Rule.

There remains, however, an unexplained point with respect to forms with accented subject and verb, but no object marker. On the account presented so far, we would expect a derivation as in (52a). As we see in (52b), however, this is correct only in certain cases.

(52) a.

| | | | |
|---|---|---|---|
| b$\overset{*}{a}$ ci b$\overset{*}{o}$n a | b$\overset{*}{a}$ ci s$\overset{*}{i}$lik a | b$\overset{*}{a}$ ci sw$\overset{*}{i}$ilil a | UR |
| b$\overset{*}{a}$ c$\overset{*}{i}$ b$\overset{*}{o}$n a | b$\overset{*}{a}$ c$\overset{*}{i}$ s$\overset{*}{i}$lik a | b$\overset{*}{a}$ c$\overset{*}{i}$ sw$\overset{*}{i}$ilil a | *-ci-* Rule |
| b$\overset{*}{a}$ ci bon a | b$\overset{*}{a}$ ci silik a | b$\overset{*}{a}$ ci swiilil a | M's Rule |
| *[bà cì bòn à] | [bà cì sìlìk à] | [bà cì swììlìl à] | Surface |

b. correct:

| | | |
|---|---|---|
| [bá cí bòn à] | [bà cì sìlìk à] | [bà cì swììlìl à] |

It appears that the only way to derive the correct form for *bá cí bon a* is to assume that the tense marker is *-aci-* in this form, and that neither syllable is accented. (This may weigh in favour of a formulation of the *-ci-* accent marking rule which copies accent from the left, for if that rule copies accent onto the irregular *-aci-*, making it *-$\overset{*}{a}$ci-*, Meeussen's Rule will undo its effects correctly in this case.) The rules we have postulated so far will then correctly derive the surface tonal pattern (*b$\overset{*}{a}$-aci-b$\overset{*}{o}$n-a* > *ba-ácí-bon-a* > *bácíbona*). We must leave this question for further investigation.

### *3.6 Final Vowel accent*

A major aspect of the treatment of Bantu verbal tone involves the behavior of the tone of the Final Vowel (FV). This morphological position is filled by a single vowel whose quality (*-e*, *-a*) is determined by the particular tense.

From the point of view of accent, the FVs of the various tenses may be accented or not, and the accented FVs furthermore fall into two categories, the stable FV accent, and the unstable FV accent. In all but one case, each tense whose FV is accented specifies whether the FV's accent is stable or unstable; in one case, however, the "stability" of the FV accent is predictable from context, and varies within the tense. This happens when there is no overt Tense Marker, as in the Dependent Affirmative tense, discussed in section 3.6.4.[5]

The stable FV accent is stable in a double sense. It is, first, immune to the effects of Meeussen's Rule. It thus does not become unaccented even when an accented verb stem immediately precedes.

The stable FV accent is also impervious to another process that could potentially remove it, a rule that shifts FV accent leftward onto an otherwise accentless verb stem. Before considering in detail the behavior of this leftward shift of the unstable accent, let us turn to one of the stable-accented tenses, the Hortative Affirmative.

#### *3.6.1 Hortative Affirmative*

In this tense, the final vowel *-a* is accented, and is immune to the effects of Meeussen's Rule; furthermore, it never deletes. The relevant data is displayed in (53), and the corresponding accentual patterns are seen in (54). The initial *ka* is a tense-mood marker.

(53) Hortative Affirmative

| *No Object Marker* | *Unaccented Obj Marker* | *Accented Obj Marker* |
|---|---|---|
| ka mu bón a | ka mu ndí !bón á | ka mu bá bón a |
| ka mu sílík a | ka mu ndí !sílík a | ka mu bá sílík a |
| ka mu swíílíl a | ka mu ndí !swíílíl a | ka mu bá swíílíl a |
| | | |
| ka mu láng a | ka mu ndí láng a | ka mu bá láng a |
| ka mu tóbél a | ka mu ndí tóbél a | ka mu bá tóbél a |
| ka mu yándáúl a | ka mu ndí yándáúl a | ka mu bá yándáúl a |

(54)

```
    *  ⊛  *               *      *  *           *  ⊛  ⊛  *
ka mu bon a           ka mu ndi bon a       ka mu ba bon a
    *  ⊛    *             *      *    *         *  ⊛  ⊛    *
ka mu silik a         ka mu ndi silik a     ka mu ba silik a
    *   ⊛     *           *       *     *       *  ⊛   ⊛     *
ka mu swiilil a       ka mu ndi swiilil a   ka mu ba swiilil a
```

| | | |
|---|---|---|
| ka mu* lang a* | ka mu* ndi lang a* | ka mu* ba⊛ lang a* |
| ka mu* tobel a* | ka mu* ndi tobel a* | ka mu* ba⊛ tobel a* |
| ka mu* yandaul a* | ka mu* ndi yandaul a* | ka mu* ba⊛ yandaul a* |

If we accept that the suffix *-a** is immune from deletion by Meeussen's Rule, then all of the data in (54) is as predicted: in a string of contiguous accents, only the leftmost remains. For this reason, and for another that will emerge below, we shall identify the stable FV as one preceded by word-boundary, while the unstable FV shall be represented as being preceded only by morpheme-boundary.

The tonal realizations of the accent patterns here are not totally transparent, however. The realization of *ka mu* ndi bo*n a** as *ka mu ndí! bón á* is curious. Why is the final syllable High in tone?

Notice that postulating a deletion of the FV accent in this case would predict the incorrect surface tonal pattern *ka mu ndí bon a*, as we see in (55).

(55) 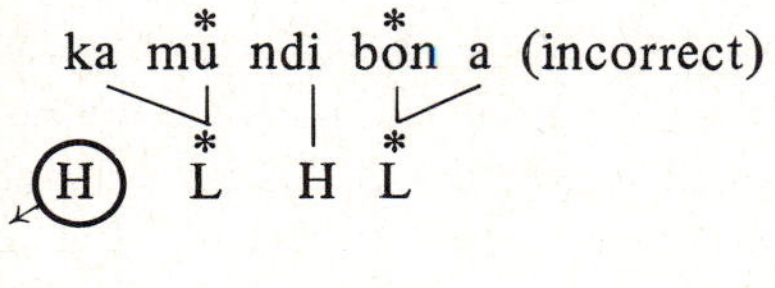


The raising of the tone on *bon* to downstepped High is in itself a direct indication that an accented syllable follows somewhere in the same word. However, we expect the form in (56) (compare (25b)).

(56) 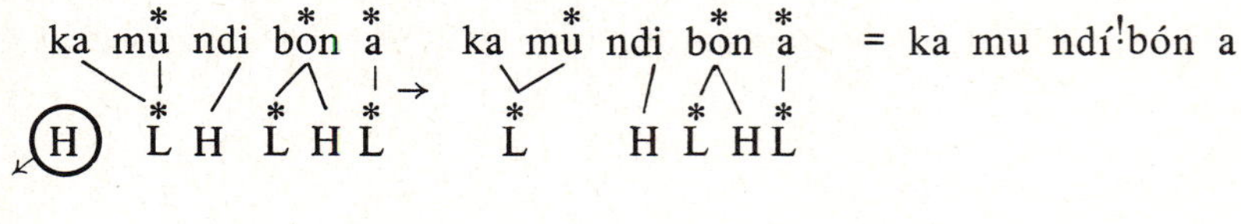


It is clear that the problem we face here is tonal, not accentual, in character. We have the correct tone pattern here, if we limit our sight to the tonal tier; the problem in (56) is the association to the syllabic tier. We might resolve the problem by positing a rule (57), Double-Accent Flop.

(57) Double-Accent Flop 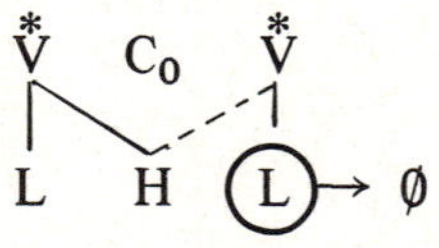


(57) is actually over-specified. Either (58a) or (58b) is sufficient.

(58) 

There are certain other forms in this tense that potentially interact with rule (57), forms that are complex and interesting in their own right. These involve verb stems that form a single syllable with the suffix *-a*. The suffix -$\overset{*}{a}$ never loses its accent in this tense, as we have seen, and so this syllable is potentially adjacent to a preceding accented syllable.

The stems in question may be either accented or unaccented, as we would expect. They consist either of stems of the form CV, such as *pe*, 'give', *ti* 'pour', or stems consisting of only a consonant. The phonological situation is complex, and I have had reference to unpublished work on the subject by Hachipola, but these matters do not figure centrally in the discussion that follows. The accent on the stem can be seen, as expected, in the infinitival form. Thus *íkúpà* contrasts tonally with *ìkùtyà.*

Consider these stems in the Hortative Affirmative in (59).

(59) Hortative Affirmative

| *Stem* | *No Object* | *Accentless Obj Marker* | *Accented Obj Marker* |
|---|---|---|---|
| Unaccented | ka mu tyá | (none given) | ka mwaá tyá |
| Accented | ka mu pá | ka mu ndí pa | ka mu tú pá |

The key to understanding these forms is to recognize that the mapping of tones to vowels occurs before syllable merger. (60) gives the accentual patterns of the forms in (59); the circled accents, as before, indicate accents that have been deleted.

(60) 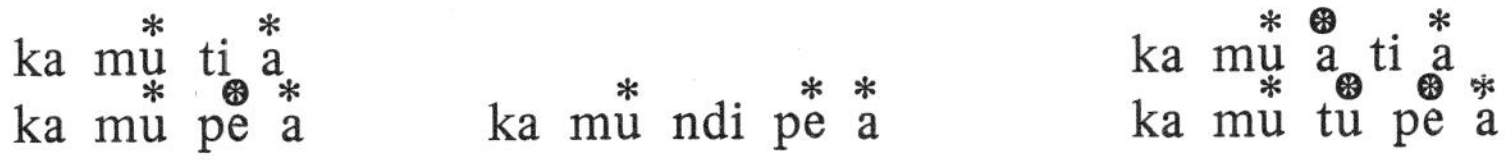

As in (54), the suffix -$\overset{*}{a}$ does not lose its accent. The forms in (59) are derived tonally as in (61).

(61) 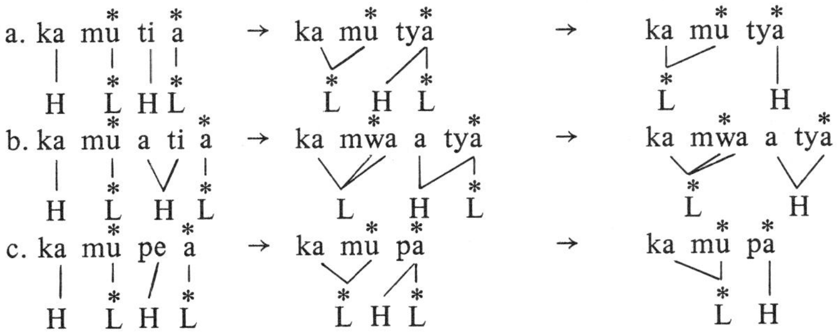

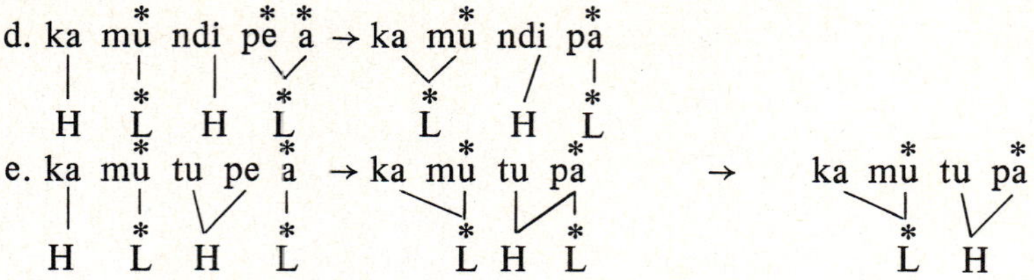


The first change in (61) involves initial High deletion and syllable merger, while the second involves a tonal simplification of non-initial Falling to High, as in (62), also seen in (58).

(62)

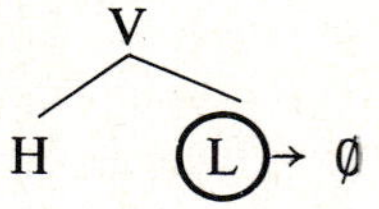


The derivation in (61d) has three accents in its first stage but only two tone melodies are inserted; furthermore, the accented L of the second melody specifically associates with the verb-stem vowel, not (only) the suffix vowel. This does not follow from the theory developed so far. We may conjecture that two (literally) adjacent accents merge to form a single accent, but the details remain much too underdetermined by the available data, unfortunately.

It is instructive to compare the analysis presented here with Meeussen's, and the elaboration of Meeussen's system developed by Carter (see especially Carter (1972)). It is particularly striking that Carter's system, which embodies both a notion of accent and of tonal realization of accent, is still unable to account for the various forms of the Hortative Affirmative in a uniform way, as Carter is at pains to point out (Carter (1972,58-62)). I would suggest that these results show that while an accentual treatment of Tonga is necessary, it is not sufficient; the tonal component of the Tonga analysis must also be autosegmental.

Carter suggests comparing the Hortative Affirmative with Independent Subject Relatives ("they who Verb . . ."). Carter observes that, under her analysis, no uniform treatment of the accentual property of the suffix is possible: "the results are very similar to those obtained for Tense 2 [Hortative Affirmative] in that no one solution stands out as most acceptable. Moreover, none is capable of a wider application, e.g., to Tense 2, which would tip the balance in its favour." (1972,61).

Consider the Independent Subject Relatives in (63).

(63) Independent Subject Relative

| *Stem* | *No Object Marker* | *Unaccented Object Marker* | *Accented Object Marker* |
|---|---|---|---|
| Unaccented | í bá tyá | | í bá ! á tyá |
| Accented | í bá pà | í bá ndí pà | í bá ! tú pá |

```
                              *                                                  *     *
Unaccented        i  ba  ti  a                                        i  ba  a  ti  a
                            *   *                            *   *                   *    ⊛   *
Accented          i  ba  pe  a          i  ba  ndi  pe  a       i  ba  tu  pe  a
```

Notice that the (bisyllabic) subject prefixes in this tense are not accented, unlike the Hortative Affirmative. This accounts for all of the differences in tonal realization between the two tenses. Note also that since these are not verbs (they are nominals), initial H-Deletion (28) does not apply. The reader may verify that the derivations that produce the tonal patterns from the accent patterns in (63) proceed precisely as in (61). (It should be noted that in Carter (1972), the High tone was accidentally left off the prefix in two of these forms.)

*3.6.2 Unstable Final Vowel Accent: Remote Dependent Affirmative*
Other tenses in Tonga have a FV which is underlyingly accented but which displays a rather different behavior from that studied in the preceding section. While the FV accent in the preceding example was unusual in that it did *not* delete where we would expect Meeussen's Rule to apply, in the Unstable FV tenses we find the accent on the FV missing or moved in more cases than Meeussen's Rule alone could account for.

Consider the following data, from the Remote Dependent Affirmative. *ka* is here the Tense Marker.

(64) Remote Dependent Affirmative

| *Stem* | *No Obj Marker* | *Unaccented Obj Marker* | *Accented Obj Marker* |
|---|---|---|---|
| Unaccented | tu ká láng e | tu ká mú láng e | tu ká!bá láng e |
| | tu ká tóbel e | tu ká mú tóbel e | tu ká!bá tóbel e |
| | tu ká yándaul e | tu ká mú yándaul e | tu ká!bá yándaul e |
| Accented | tu ká bon e | tu ká mú bon e | tu ká ba bon e |
| | tu ká silik e | tu ká mú silik e | tu ká ba silik e |
| | tu ká swiilil e | tu ká mú swiilil e | tu ká ba swiilil e |

(65)

| *Stem* | *No Obj Marker* | *Unaccented Obj Marker* | *Accented Obj Marker* |
|---|---|---|---|

```
              *          *                *                 *          *       *         *
Unaccented    tu ka lang e ⊛        tu ka mu lang e ⊛         tu ka ba lang e ⊛
              *        *                *            *            *       *       *
              tu ka tobel e ⊛       tu ka mu tobel e ⊛        tu ka ba tobel e ⊛
              *            *            *                *        *       *          *
              tu ka yandaul e ⊛     tu ka mu yandaul e ⊛      tu ka ba yandaul e ⊛
```

| | | | |
|---|---|---|---|
| Accented | t$\overset{*}{\text{ų}}$ ka b$\overset{*}{\text{ǫ}}$n $\overset{\circledast}{\text{ę}}$ | t$\overset{*}{\text{ų}}$ ka mu b$\overset{*}{\text{ǫ}}$n $\overset{\circledast}{\text{ę}}$ | t$\overset{*}{\text{ų}}$ ka b$\overset{*}{\text{ą}}$ b$\overset{\circledast}{\text{o}}$n $\overset{\circledast}{\text{ę}}$ |
| | t$\overset{*}{\text{ų}}$ ka s$\overset{*}{\text{į}}$lik $\overset{\circledast}{\text{e}}$ | t$\overset{*}{\text{ų}}$ ka mu s$\overset{*}{\text{į}}$lik $\overset{\circledast}{\text{e}}$ | t$\overset{*}{\text{ų}}$ ka b$\overset{*}{\text{ą}}$ s$\overset{\circledast}{\text{i}}$lįk $\overset{\circledast}{\text{e}}$ |
| | t$\overset{*}{\text{u}}$ ka sw$\overset{*}{\text{i}}$ilil $\overset{\circledast}{\text{e}}$ | t$\overset{*}{\text{u}}$ ka mu sw$\overset{*}{\text{i}}$ilil $\overset{\circledast}{\text{e}}$ | t$\overset{*}{\text{u}}$ ka b$\overset{*}{\text{a}}$ sw$\overset{\circledast}{\text{i}}$ilil $\overset{\circledast}{\text{e}}$ |

While the FV shows no sign of being accented in the case of the accented stems, there is an accent present in the case of the unaccented stems, clearly a contribution of the FV. However, only in the case of the monosyllabic stems is the FV accent actually located on the FV itself. In the other cases, it shifts leftward, with the result that the FV accent appears on the first vowel following the first vowel of the verb stem.

Thus we have two generalizations to deal with. In the case of an unstable FV accent, the FV accent *deletes* when it follows an accented stem, even when the two accents are not in contiguous syllables. Furthermore, when the verb stem that precedes the FV is itself unaccented, the FV accent shifts to the $V_2$ position, that is, the first vowel following the first vowel of the verb stem.

The second generalization is clearly the result of a leftward shift of the FV accent. The simplest statement of the shift makes use of the notion of post-accent discussed above. The FV accent shifts leftward and becomes a post-accent on the initial vowel of the verb stem, as in (66).

(66) $[_{\text{stem}} \overset{\ominus}{\text{V}} \ldots [_{\text{FV}} \overset{\circledast}{\text{V}}]\ ]$ (the $\circledast$ accent on the FV shifts leftward, as shown by an arrow, to become the post-accent on the stem vowel)

The post-accent immediately shifts rightward one vowel, giving the correct forms in (65), by the mechanism proposed above for post-accenting.

It is interesting to observe the effect of (66) on accented stems. As stated, it puts no condition on the accentual character of the first vowel of the stem. A similar process discussed in their paper on Haya by Hyman and Byarushengo in this volume is limited to cases where the stem is unaccented. In Tonga, however, no such condition need be placed on the rule. It is not *a priori* clear what will happen if both a post-accent and an accent arise on a single vowel. If they merge to become simply an accent, we arrive at the correct result; if, on the other hand, the post-accent hops, it will subsequently be deleted by Meeussen's Rule. Under either assumption, then, the FV accent will appear to vanish.

### *3.6.3 Unstable FV: Perfect Tense and the Restrictions on Initial High Deletion*

The data in (24), repeated here as (67), was used by Meeussen to motivate the Determinant/Neutral distinction in the verbal morphology. The first two forms are surprising, though; if the data in (67a) motivates placing an accent on $\overset{*}{\text{i}}$*de*, it remains surprising that any High tones appear in the first two forms, where only one accent is present. In all other verbal forms that we have seen, the single H$\overset{*}{L}$ associated with a word bearing only a single accent is simplified to $\overset{*}{L}$ by the initial High deletion rule (28).

(67) a. Unaccented Stem

| *Subject* | *No Obj Marker* | *Unaccented Obj Marker* | *Accented Obj Marker* |
|---|---|---|---|
| Unaccented | ndí lí láng ide | ndí lí mú láng ide | ndi li ba láng ide |
| Accented | ba lí láng ide | ba lí mú láng ide | ba lí!bá láng ide |
| b. Accented Stem | | | |
| Unaccented | ndi li bon ide | ndi li mu bon ide | ndi li ba bon ide |
| Accented | ba lí bon ide | ba lí mú bon ide | ba lí ba bon ide |

```
                          *                      *                  *     *
(68)  a.   ndi li lang ide      ndi li mu lang ide     ndi la ba lang ide
           *         *          *            *         *     *       *
           ba li lang ide       ba li mu lang ide      ba li ba lang ide
                  *   ⊛                  *   ⊛               *   ⊛   ⊛
      b.   ndi li bon ide       ndi li mu bon ide      ndi li ba bon ide
           *      *   ⊛         *        *   ⊛         *     *   ⊛   ⊛
           ba li bon ide        ba li mu bon ide       ba li ba bon ide
```

Meeussen concludes that the verbal formula is applicable "except if everything before the final is neutral, when all these neutrals are high, as if preceded by a determinant in preinitial position . . . . Since it would be awkward to introduce this into the formula, . . . the complication will better be stated as an auxiliary rule: when all elements, including a formative, are neutral before determinant extension or final, then all these elements are high." Carter (1971) states the exceptionality in a different way; she notes that all perfect tenses are realized under the "verbal" rule - Highs between Determinants - Except for the Present Perfect "with Neutral subject prefix and Neutral verbal radical, which is under the 'nominal' rule," i.e., has all Highs to the left of a Determinant.

In fact, the non-deletion of the H in these special Perfect verbs is part of a much more general phenomenon in Tonga which involves the tonology at the phrase level. The larger generalization that governs these forms is this: the only High tones that delete verb-initially by rule (28) are those whose tonal domain does not extend as far to the right as the verb stem. Thus an accent one or more syllables to the right of the verb stem will have its High tone associated with at least one vowel in the verb stem; and these High tones *never* delete by rule (28).

The precise manner in which (28) should be modified to express this generalization is not without theoretical interest. If we assume, perhaps gratuitously, that no structural morphological information is available on the tonal tier, the conditioning factors will be addressed on the syllabic tier as in (69), and a notation like the one suggested by Kahn (1976) will be necessary, according to which a trailing association line knotted at the end with an "x" indicates that part of the structural description of the rule in question is that there be *no* association lines in the indicated position. The association line indicated on the H in (69), then, will be taken to be the rightmost association of the H.

(69)

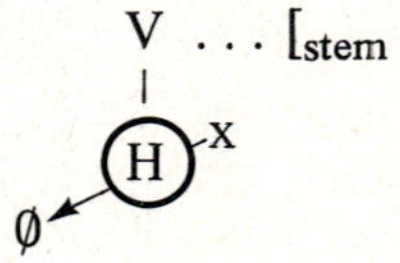


The more natural formulation of the rule in (70) is possibly only under certain assumptions regarding the way in which the tonal formula is morphologically organized. The crucial example here is *ndi-li-bon-ide*, where the initial H does in fact delete. The H from the single HL melody must be structurally outside of the verb stem for (70) to suffice; see (71).

(70)

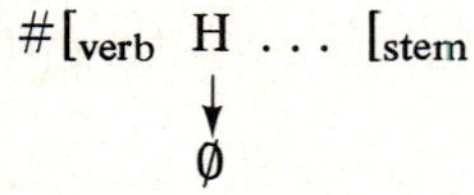


(71)

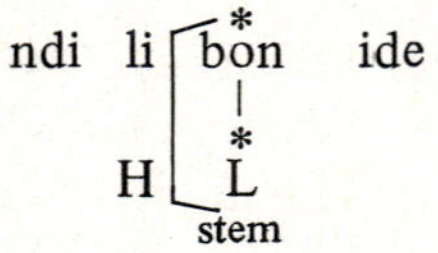


But whether the rule is formulated as in (69), (70), or otherwise, the apparent irregularity in the Perfect tonal pattern is in fact part of a more general phenomenon, as I indicated above, and must be interpreted as the result of a tonal rule, not an accentual rule.

Carter (1972) identifies certain problematic cases under her approach, cases where verbal elements appear to be tonally realized in a manner parallel to nominals, that is (according to our analysis), where initial H deletion does not apply. In the Near Future, tonally identical to the *-la-* Present Tense, there is, as Carter notes, "the possibility that the whole form may contain nothing but Neutral elements; and when this is so, and the tense is in D-link complex [i.e., the Weak construction discussed in Section 2.2 above], the realization is under the nominal rule". She gives the example in (72), slightly modified here.

(72)

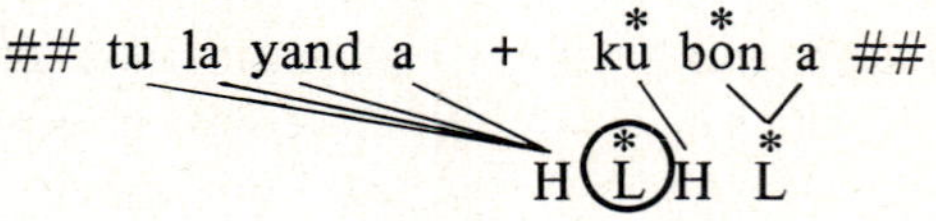


"we shall want to *sing*"

A simpler example of the same phenomenon is discussed later (Carter

1972,76) in connection with what Carter calls syntactic "composition", a fusion of the verb and its following object into a single phonological unit with the placement of an intrusive accent on the first vowel of the second element. There we find that the High tone that associates leftward into an accentless verb from an accented object (but not from an unaccented object) will not be deleted; see (73).

| | | | |
|---|---|---|---|
| (73) | tulaa mulimo | "we have work" | (unaccented object) |
| | túláá nhánda | "we have a house" | (*nhanda*, with * over the final a) |

All of these phenomena, and a number of other irregularities in Carter's and Meeussen's "verbal realization rule", follow directly from the revised formulation of the initial H-deletion rule given above.

### *3.6.4 Dependent Affirmative*

The final tense that we shall consider is the Dependent Affirmative, as in (74).

(74) a. Accented Stem

| *No Obj Marker* | *Unaccented Obj Marker* | *Accented Obj Marker* |
|---|---|---|
| tu bón e | tu kú bon e | tu ba bon e |
| tu sílík e | tu kú silik e | tu ba silik e |
| tu swíílíl e | tu kú swiilil e | tu ba swiilil e |

b. Unaccented Stem

| | | |
|---|---|---|
| tu láng e | tu kú láng e | tu bá láng e |
| tu tóbél e | tu kú tóbel e | tu bá tóbel e |
| tu yándáúl e | tu kú yándaul e | tu bá yándaul e |

```
(75)  a.  Accented Stem
*  ⊛  *              *     *  ⊛               *  *   *  ⊛
tu bon e             tu ku bon e              tu ba bon e
*  ⊛   *             *      *  ⊛              *  *  *   ⊛
tu silik e           tu ku silik e            tu ba silik e
*    ⊛    *          *       *    ⊛           *  *    *    ⊛
tu swiilil e         tu ku swiilil e          tu ba swiilil e
      b.  Unaccented Stem
*      *             *          *             *  *        *
tu lang e            tu ku lang e             tu ba lang e
                              *<-⊛                      *<-⊛
*        *           *                        *  *
tu tobel e           tu ku tobel e            tu ba tobel e
                                *<-⊛                      *<-⊛
*          *         *                        *  *
tu yandaul e         tu ku yandaul e          tu ba yandaul e
```

The first column clearly behaves like a tense with a stable FV accent, while the second and third columns behave like a tense with an unstable FV accent. This oddity appears to be limited to those tenses which have no overt tense marker following the subject marker; in these cases, the FV becomes a stable one when the stem is adjacent to the subject marker. If we indicate the stable FV by a preceding word-boundary, and an unstable FV by a preceding + boundary, then we can summarize this observation in (76).

(76) $[_{\text{subj}}]\ [_{\text{stem}}]\quad + \rightarrow \#$

## 4. THE DIACHRONIC PICTURE

In this final section, I would like to describe briefly how Tonga arrived where it is today from an earlier tone system, and how certain characteristics of Tonga today appear to be vestiges of the tonal innovations that made the shift from a tonal system to an accentual system possible.

It is our good fortune that Bantu historical studies are among the most developed of those available among all the language families of the world. We know that Proto-Bantu had the hallmark characteristics of a tonal system, with four tonal classes among the bisyllabic noun stems (HH, HL, LH, and LL), and a good deal about the correspondences between modern Tonga and Proto-Bantu has been established, especially by Guthrie (1967-1971) and Carter (1973).

The tonal correspondences are odd, at first sight, as we see in (73).

(77)

| *Proto-Bantu* | *Tonga/tone* | *Tonga/accent* |
|---|---|---|
| *(Stem)* | *(Prefix + Stem)* | *(Stem)* |
| H H | H + L L | $C\overset{*}{V}$ CV |
| H L | H + L L | $C\overset{*}{V}$ CV |
| L H | H + H L | CV $C\overset{*}{V}$ |
| L L | L + L L | CV CV |

The tonal evolution viewed in isolation is puzzling, though quite regular. The changes from HH to LL and from LH to HL suggest that H and L were exchanged, but HL merged with HH to form LL, and the *LL also stayed LL, though with the difference that its prefix is Low.

The puzzle vanishes when we compare the Proto-Bantu forms with the underlying accents in Tonga. Accent today appears, as Carter notes, where the first High tone in the proto-form did. As Guthrie observes, this collapsing of *HL and *HH occurs widely through his Zones F, G, and M.

Evidently, Proto-Bantu had a grammar in which the tone pattern of each noun was given explicitly. The prefixes were consistently Low in tone (with three exceptions which have been lost in Tonga). With a judicious choice of a Basic Tone Melody, this tonal system could be mimicked by an accentual system with minimal change or loss of information, as we have sketched in (78). Here we assume the original melody of accented stems was L$\overset{*}{\text{H}}$L. The forms represent a stage shared by a large class of Eastern Bantu languages, but I shall simply use the term Pre-Tonga to describe it.

(78)
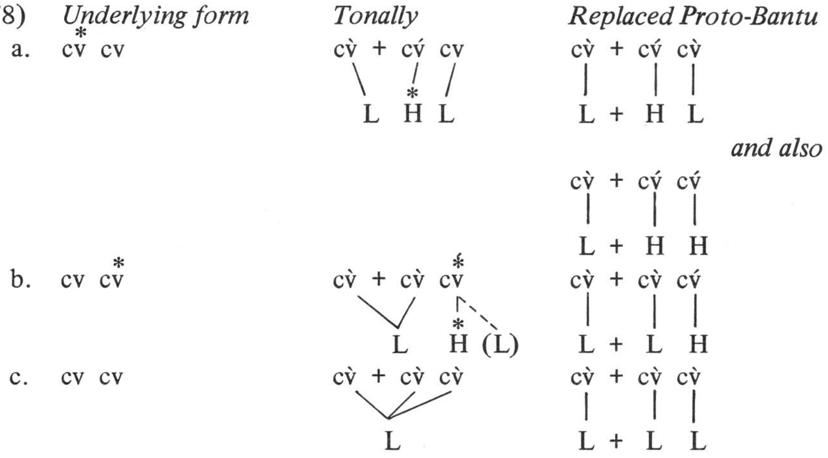


This pattern of development of accent from Proto-Bantu appears to be the typical one. Other evidence suggests that at a point subsequent to the change described in (78), the Basic Tone Melody was L$\overset{*}{\text{H}}$. Today, as we have seen, the Basic Tone Melody is H$\overset{*}{\text{L}}$.

As Carter (1973,45) notes, there is a regular class of exceptions to the schema in (78). A form for which we would expect a modern stem with initial accent (corresponding to PB *HH or *HL) will have accent on the second syllable if it has lost its initial consonant. Apparently what happened with the loss of the initial consonant was the creation of a contour tone as the class-prefix and the stem-initial vowel merged to form a single syllable, as in (75).

(79)
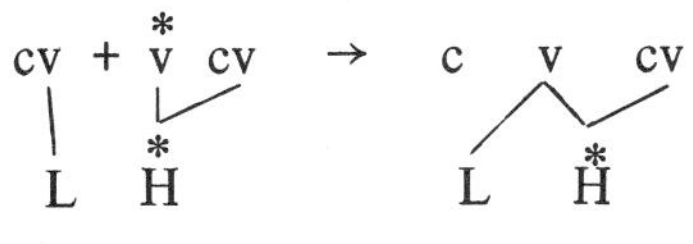

Tone is typically absorbed in such cases by the syllable with the like tone, as has been observed for many years; since these forms were reanalyzed as having final accent, the Rising tone in (75) must have simplified to Low suggesting that the following syllable was High. Hence, the melody was L$\overset{*}{\text{H}}$ at that point.

We are still faced with the more fundamental question as to why Proto-Bantu became accentual when it did, rather than earlier or later.

If Proto-Bantu had the tonal grammar T, what rule could it have been that was added to T to produce an output unequivocally reanalyzed as an accentual system by the next generation?

How could we possibly determine what rule R looked like? I would like to suggest that R must have been a tonal rule of which Meeussen's Accentual rule is a direct descendant. This rule would have been (80).

(80) H → L / H ——

If (80) were added to the tonal grammar, then the two cases that case (a) in (78) conflates would *already* have been collapsed on the surface by the addition of (80). Hence the reanalysis of tone as accent would have provided *no* less surface information than the earlier generation's grammar provided.

Secondly, whatever rule R actually was, we would expect some descendant rule in the accentual systems that grew out of the reanalysis. What rule do all, or most, of the accentual Bantu languages share? The answer is Meeussen's Rule (or its mirror-image, as in Rimi and Sukuma). It should be clear that if Proto-Bantu's grammar added rule (80), then in the verbal system we would find that any time High-toned morphemes were concatenated, only the first would surface as a High tone. Naturally, when the next generation noted this, they would interpret this as a loss of accent by the morphemes on the right. This is not circular; we know independently that High tone *was* reinterpreted as accent.

Much work remains to be done, clearly, to clarify this picture. Comparative work should lead us to a clearer picture of how a tonal system can evolve into the accentual system that we see today.

NOTES

1. I have had the good fortune to discuss the material presented in this paper with a number of linguists, and have profited from their comments in many ways. Among those I must thank are Nick Clements, Jerome Hachipola, Morris Halle, Larry Hyman, Chuck Kisseberth, and David Massamba. The initial stages of this work was done while I was an Andrew Mellon Faculty Fellow in the Linguistics Department at Harvard University, and I am grateful for the opportunity that this support provided me.

2. It is clearly necessary to permit specified segments on one tier to avoid the effects of the Well-formedness Condition, and thus to not associate. Consonants, for example, need not associate, though they may (see the discussion of depressor consonants by Laughren in this volume). A natural proposal to accommodate this observation is to suggest that two segments on opposite tiers may associate only if they share a feature specification. Normal (non-floating) tones would then be specified + syllabic, while floating tones would have no specification for the feature

syllabic at all. Depressor consonant tones would be marked -syllabic. On such an analysis, the change indicated in rule (10) would be in the value of the feature *syllabic* in the Low tone.

3. We will discuss below the notion of a *post-accent*, that is, an element which immediately shifts its position one syllable to the right when not in phrase-final position. Such an element will be represented on its vowel as $\vec{V}$. (18) would best be viewed, then, as reduction of the boundary between the verb and its object, and the placing of a post-accent on the Final Vowel.

4. The unusual behavior that we observe with the Tense Marker (TM) -$\overset{*}{a}$- clearly demands an explanation of a historical sort as well. The tonal data in (44) suggest that in Boxes A, B, and E (that is, those boxes where the Accent Shift rule (46) gets a chance to apply), the TM -$\overset{*}{a}$- functions to put a High tone on a following syllable. Such a notion is foreign to the prosodic system of present-day Tonga, where accent, realized as Low Tone, dominates the system. However, the peculiar character of the TM -a-'s accentual effects suggests that rule (46) arose out of an accentual reanalysis of surface forms from an earlier stage in which the TM *-a-* did precisely place a High tone on the following syllable. If we observe the Far Past in Luganda (Stevick (1969), we find that the TM -a- is indeed post-accenting, which has the effect in Luganda of placing a High Tone on the following syllable (*kù-gùl-à* in the infinitive, for example, becomes *yagúla* in the Far Past (3 sg.)). The *-a-* past tense discussed by Kisseberth in this volume also appears to be analyzable as possessing a post-accenting TM and an accented FV, while Ruri's Distant Past also has a post-accenting TM -a-. In fact, both Ruri and Rimi possess post-accenting TMs *-a-*; Ruri's undergoes a secondary accent shift to the right, displacing the High tone two syllables from the TM, while Rimi's undergoes only one displacement. See Massamba (1982) and Schadeberg (1979).

5. Tonga appears to have only one FV accent shifting rule, and it may be written to apply independently of the accent on the verb stem. As Hyman and Byarushengo show in their analysis of Haya in this volume, the shift of the FV accent may be dependent on the *lack* of accent in the verb stem, in other languages of this family. Luganda displays both patterns, with a rule like Tonga's in the Far Past, and a rule like Haya's in the Near Past.

The shift from the FV position to the second vowel of the stem represents a natural pattern of tone association, if the tone that is logically associated with the FV is associated with the vowels of the verb in the familiar one-to-one fashion (see Clements' chapter in this volume for a discussion of the pervasive one-to-one tone-to-vowel association pattern). Thus we may conclude that any stage at which such a shift is introduced is a tonal, pre-accentual stage of the language, a useful criterion in historical reconstruction.

*Chapter 3*

# A Model of Haya Tonology

Larry M. Hyman and Ernest Rugwa Byarushengo

## 0. INTRODUCTION

Over the past twenty years or so a tremendous advance has been made in the understanding of different kinds of prosodic systems. This advance, which has been made possible by our increased familiarity with the prosodic systems of the world's languages, as well as by theoretical innovations, is of two types. First, typologies of prosodic systems have become more adequate and sophisticated. Second, formal treatments of tonal and accentual systems have allowed more precise accounts of the phenomena in question.

Within this context the Bantu languages of Africa have played an important role. Their considerable complexity and theoretical interest have become known through the many descriptive studies available in the literature. Among the several hundred languages of this genetic group one finds prosodic systems which are clearly tonal, others which are clearly non-tonal, and still others which fall somewhere in between. Nearly every Bantu scholar agrees that the proto-language was characterized by two tones, H(igh) and L(ow), which occurred relatively freely within the Bantu word (see Greenberg 1948, Meeussen 1967, Kähler-Meyer 1967-68, Guthrie 1971; but cf. Stevick 1969, who argues for one tone in Proto-Bantu). As pointed out by Carter (1973), some Bantu languages show fairly complete and regular tonal correspondences with the reconstructions of H and L, while others have reduced the proto tonal oppositions in varying degrees. As these oppositions are lost, we arrive at what Voorhoeve (1973) termed a "restricted tone language", and finally to the non-tonal languages such as Swahili and some of the Tanzanian languages studied by Kähler-Meyer (1963).

In much of the typologizing, as well as in many descriptive studies, an essential characteristic of many Bantu tone systems is missed – namely, that the two reconstructed tones (H,L), which are still held to be underlying in synchronic (morphotonological) analyses (e.g., van Spaandonck 1971), do not behave like tones, but rather like *accents*. As originally pointed out by McCawley (1964, 1970), tones are expected (1) to combine relatively freely in the various morphological environments and (2) to partake in the same kinds of assimilation and simplification processes that segmental features undergo. In many Bantu languages, however, H tones are severely restricted in distribution. In addition, the tone rule universals proposed by Hyman (1973) and Hyman and Schuh (1974) based on West African languages are sometimes violated by Eastern Bantu tone systems. Finally, the kind of interaction found between tone and scope of focus in many Bantu languages is more typical of stress-accent systems than of the kind of tone system found in West Africa.

It thus behooves the Bantuist to address the accent vs. tone dichotomy and help establish a general theory of prosodic systems incorporating the exact parameters observed by the world's languages. In the present study we propose, within this context, to examine in some detail the prosodic system of Haya, a Bantu language of Meeussen's zone J spoken in Tanzania.[1] In an earlier version of this study, we argued that Haya is a "tonal accent" language and proposed to represent underlying tonal oppositions as one between * ("accented") vs. ° ("unaccented"). Recently, however, we have come to view Goldsmith's (1976a,b) asterisk notation as inadequate for the description of Bantu tone systems and therefore have opted for a more general framework that reveals in a more straightforward way the essential tonal character of these systems. Specifically, we shall argue that Haya (and many other closely related languages) is a version of Voorhoeve's restricted tone system in two senses. First, we shall argue that underlying forms are incompletely specified for tone (i.e., there will be many vowels which have no underlying tone). Second, the underlying tone which is indicated is restricted to H only. There thus is a stage where only H and "blanks" appear on the tonal tier, at which certain rules apply. This is the so-called "accentual level" of our earlier analysis. At a later stage the "blanks" are filled in by rule (receiving L tone in Haya) and another set of rules apply. This is the "tonal level" of the earlier model. Thus, the most general way of formalizing the difference between a pitch- or tonal accent system vs. a tone system is by allowing for underlying incomplete tonification in the former. Since "incomplete tonification" is not an all-or-nothing quality (e.g., some tone languages have a few affixes with no underlying tone), this approach makes the prediction that there will be a tone to tonal accent continuum. We believe this is correct and, if so, it is an important argument for the approach exemplified in this paper (see also the discussion in Hyman 1982a, b regarding the closely related Luganda system).

## 1. TONAL PRELIMINARIES: NOUN TONOLOGY

We begin by considering the distribution of surface tones in Haya nouns.

An initial study of the tone system of Haya was presented in Byarushengo, Hyman and Tenenbaum (1976). In that paper (henceforward, BHT) the major tone processes were discussed as was the notion of "assertion" and its effect on tone. The present statement is intended as a sequel to this earlier study. In essence, all of the observations of the 1976 paper remain intact except for the few statements which were made about verb tones (see section 2 below). The possible tone patterns found on bi-, tri- and quadri-syllabic nouns were illustrated in (1).

| (1) | surface | | | underlying |
|---|---|---|---|---|
| a. | L-L | ente | 'cow' | /e#N + te/<br>H |
| | H-L | émbwa | 'dog' | /e#N + bua/<br>H H |
| b. | L-L-L | enfulu | 'fish' | /e#N + fulu/<br>H |
| | | omuzi | 'root' | /o#mu + zi/<br>H |
| | L-H-L | empúnu | 'pig' | /e#N + punu/<br>H H |
| | | omúti | 'tree' | /o#mu + ti/<br>H H |
| | L-HL-L | enjôka | 'snake' | /e#N + joka/<br>H H |
| c. | L-L-L-L | okugulu | 'leg' | /o#ku + gulu/<br>H |
| | L-L-H-L | obugólo | 'snuff' | /o#bu + golo/<br>H H |
| | L-L-HL-L | omukôno | 'arm' | /o#mu + kono/<br>H H |
| | L-H-L-L | emótoka | 'car' | /e#motoka/<br>H H |

The tone marking used in the surface representations is that standardly used for Bantu languages: the acute accent (V́) indicates H tone, the circumflex accent (V̂) indicates falling tone (from H to L), and any unmarked vowel carries L tone.[2] In the case of vowel sequences, each vowel either carries an acute accent or is unmarked (e.g. V́V = a HL falling tone and [underlying] VV́ = a LH rising tone).

The following generalizations characterize the *surface* tone patterns in (1): (i) There are primarily two tones, H and L. (ii) There is no rising tone, and the observed falling tone can occur only in penultimate position (i.e. as -V̂CV or -V́VCV). (iii) H tone never appears immediately before pause. (iv) Only certain bisyllabic nouns such as *émbwa* 'dog' may begin with a H tone vowel after pause.

Given these observations concerning nouns pronounced in isolation (i.e. bounded by pauses), one might prematurely conclude that there is at most one mark of prominence per noun (i.e. either H or HL). This tempting conclusion is easily falsified, however, as soon as nouns are considered in context. Thus, in (2) it is observed that the trisyllabic noun 'tree' can appear in all eight logical combinations of H and L:

| | | | | |
|---|---|---|---|---|
| (2) | a. | L-L-L | omuti gwaa káto | 'a/the tree of Kato' |
| | | L-L-H | omutí gwange | 'my tree' |
| | | L-H-L | omúti | 'a/the tree' |
| | | L-H-H | omútí káto | 'a/the tree, Kato' [vocative] |
| | b. | H-L-L | okubón'[3] ómuti gwaa káto | 'to see a/the tree of Kato' |
| | | H-L-H | okubón' ómutí gwange | 'to see my tree' |
| | | H-H-L | okubón' ómúti | 'to see a/the tree' |
| | | H-H-H | okubón' ómútí káto | 'to see a/the tree, Kato' |

Since a lexical noun such as 'tree' can appear with all of the possible tonal configurations of H and L on three syllables, it would be difficult to deny the tonal nature of the Haya prosodic system. The following points were argued by BHT to account for the above observations: (i) There is indeed an underlying opposition between H and L. (ii) Any rising tone or falling tone not in penultimate position must be simplified to H (i.e. VV́ and [non-penultimate] V́V become V́V́). (iii) An initial H vowel which immediately follows pause becomes L, e.g. /$\underset{\text{H}}{\text{e}}$#N + te/ → [ente] 'cow'. (iv) In addition, it will be shown in this study that noun stems receive no more than one mark of prominence because of a constraint on underlying representations whereby there is *at most* one H tone per morpheme.

The two facts which were accounted for by BHT are the restriction of HL to penultimate position and the restrictions on a H tone vowel either immediately preceding or following a pause. Consider first the falling tones of 'snake' and 'arm' in (1). As seen in (3),

| | | | | | |
|---|---|---|---|---|---|
| (3) | a. | enjôka | 'snake' | enjóka yange | 'my snake' |
| | b. | omukôno | 'arm' | omukóno gwange | 'my arm' |

the syllable having this HL tone is realized H in most cases when the word is followed by something, i.e. when it is not prepausal. Given this alternation we propose that an underlying penultimate H tone becomes HL when a H-° sequence occurs before pause. (The symbol ° stands for a vowel slot which does not have a H associated with it.) However, in order to maintain this position, it is necessary to address those nouns which in fact have H-L before pause on the surface, e.g. 'tree' and 'snuff' in (1). As seen in (4),

| | | | | |
|---|---|---|---|---|
| (4) | a. omúti | 'tree' | omutí gwange | 'my tree' |
| | b. obugólo | 'snuff' | obugoló bwange | 'my snuff' |

these nouns also undergo an alternation when they are followed by something. In this case we have an alternation between H-L (before pause) vs. L-H (not before pause). If we compare (3) and (4) we see that the two sets of nouns in question run no risk of merging, since the nouns in (3) are pronounced H-L when not before pause, while the nouns in (4) are pronounced H-L when they *are* before pause.

Before concluding that there is a single rule operative before pause, consider the forms in (5).

| | | |
|---|---|---|
| (5) | a. enjôka káto | 'a/the snake, Kato' [vocative] |
| | omukôno káto | 'a/the arm, Kato' |
| | b. omútí káto | 'a/the tree, Kato' |
| | obugóló káto | '(the) snuff, Kato' |

In (5) the nouns appear in a context preceding the proper noun *káto*, which is used vocatively. Thus, these forms provide the answer to Kato's question, "what did you see?" (e.g. "a *snake* [is what I saw], Kato"). This is one of the contexts where a noun undergoes changes but is not prepausal. Further contexts were discussed in BHT, where it was argued that there is a phrase boundary (%) in such cases to which the following tone rules are sensitive:[4]

(6) a. H-L → HL-L / —— %
b. L-H → H-H / —— %

Thus, the HL tone rule is sensitive not to pause, but to the phrase boundary (which, as BHT demonstrated, marks the end of an assertion). Similarly, underlying L-H is affected by the same %, but crucially, as seen in the examples in (5b), it does not directly become H-L, as implied in the alternations in (4), but rather has an intermediate stage with final H-H. It is at this point that a later rule lowers any H tone vowel which precedes a pause. A similar process lowers the underlying H of the initial vowel (IV) when it *follows* a pause, as seen in (7).

| | | | | |
|---|---|---|---|---|
| (7) | enfulu | 'fish' | okubón' énfulu | 'to see fish' |

This initial vowel (or "preprefix") will have a surface H tone whenever the noun is preceded by anything: verb, adverb, preposition, etc. Thus, it is clear that the so-called preprefix has an underlying H tone.

The different realizations of word-final °-°, H-° and °-H are summarized in the table in (8).

| (8) Underlying: | °-° | H-° | °-H |
|---|---|---|---|
| Before % | L-L | HL-L | H-H |
| Before pause | L-L | HL-L | H-L |
| Before most modifiers | L-L | H-L | L-H |

As can be seen, °-° does not alternate in the different environments. Also note (cf. (1)) that there is no underlying final H-H in monomorphemic noun stems. In verbs, however, it is possible to distinguish a fourth H-H category.

## 2. VERB TONOLOGY

As is always the case in Bantu, verbs differ from nouns in Haya in their greater morphological complexity. They differ also in being capable of analysis into a (normally) monosyllabic verb radical (= root) preceded by prefixes (as in the case of nouns) and followed by suffixes. As seen in the infinitive forms in (9), there are two tone patterns for verbs in any given construction:

(9) a. okukôma 'to tie up' /o#ku + kom + a/
H H

b. okujuna 'to help' /o#ku + jun + a/
H

As indicated in the underlying representations to the right of the surface forms, verb radicals subdivide into H and ° tone classes (e.g. -k$\underset{H}{o}$m- and -jun-). The above forms are actually nominal in form, since as in the table in (1) above, they consist of a preprefix /$\underset{H}{o}$-/, followed by a noun class prefix /ku-/ (class 15). Unlike the nouns in (1), however, the final vowel (FV) is not part of the lexical stem, but rather is part of the morphology of the infinitival construction. Note, finally, that in (9) the H initial vowel becomes L after pause and the final HL-L of 'to tie up' is due to rule (6a).

Fully conjugated verb forms are considerably more complex than the nominal infinitive forms in (9). The formula in (10) summarizes the basic agglutinative structure of the Haya verbal unit (VU), i.e. the verb radical (R) with all of its prefixes and suffixes:

| | | | | | | | | | |
|---|---|---|---|---|---|---|---|---|---|
| (10) | (PI) # | SM + | N + | T/A + | OM + | <u>R</u> + | X + | FV # | (PF) |
| | V | V | CV | V | N | | V | V | CV |
| | CV | N | | VV | CV | | VC | | |
| | | CV | | CV | CVV | | | | |
| | | | | CVV | | | | | |

As seen in (10), the VU consists of a subject marker (SM), negation (N), tense/aspect (T/A), object marker(s) (OM), the verb radical (R), extension(s) (X), and a final vowel (FV). As also indicated, the VU can be preceded by a preinitial (PI) and followed by a post-final (PF) marker. Each of these is separated from the VU by an internal word boundary (#), as opposed to the ordinary morpheme boundary (+) separating the elements within the VU.[5] Except for the T/A, OM and X positions, each slot can have at most one morpheme. The possible syllable structures for each position are indicated except for the radical itself, which exhibits the possibilities in (11).

| | | | | | |
|---|---|---|---|---|---|
| (11) | -CVC- | /-kom-/ | 'tie up' | /-jun-/ | 'help' |
| | | H | | | |
| | -CVVC- | /-leet-/ | 'bring' | /-ziik-/ | 'bury' |
| | | H | | | |
| | -CVNC- | /-heɴd-/ | 'break' | /-biɴg-/ | 'chase' |
| | | H | | | |
| | -CV- | /-li-/ | 'eat' | /-si-/ | 'grind' |
| | | H | | | |

Verb radicals which often appear on the surface with an initial vowel are analyzed as having an underlying initial /y/, e.g. /-yij-/ 'come', /-y$\underset{\text{H}}{\text{i}}$t-/ 'kill' (cf. section 4).

In principle, the verb radical is monosyllabic as shown. Any seemingly longer form such as -t$\underset{\text{H}}{\text{o}}$bol- 'pierce' or -kulul- 'pull, drag' is to be analyzed as a monosyllabic radical (here -CVC-) followed by a -VC- extension (even though one or both may be unattested independently). The functions of the different slots in (10) are clear, with the following addenda: (i) The pre-initial slot can be filled with the initial vowel of the subject-relative construction, the progressive marker ni-, or the main clause negative marker ti-. (ii) The extensions can mark grammatical relations (e.g. -es-i- 'causative'), lexical relations (e.g. -oolol- 'reversive', as in -k$\underset{\text{H}}{\text{o}}$m-oolol- 'untie'), tense/aspect (e.g. -il- past tense occurring with the FV -e), or in the case of -aɴgan- 'reciprocal', participants. (iii) The FV is determined by tense/aspect, polarity and construction type. (iv) The post-final position is normally filled by a locative marker. An example of a rather complicated verbal unit is given in (12).

(12)

| | | | | | | | | | |
|---|---|---|---|---|---|---|---|---|---|
| a # | ba + | tá + | ka + | mu + | kóm + | e + | il + | é # | mu |
| Rel | they | Neg | Pf | him | tie | App | Pf | Pf | Loc |
| PI | SM | N | T/A | OM | R | X | X | FV | PF |

'they who have not tied him up in there'

Ideally in a Bantu language the tonal configuration of the complete VU will be a function of the tones of the parts. While this is usually the case, the process of establishing the principles of tonal realization is often not straightforward. Determining the underlying tones of the different morphemes usually requires considerable effort in substituting different markers (and $\phi$) in the different positions in the VU. Thus, one may find one tone pattern where there is no OM, but quite another pattern when the OM is present (especially in the imperative). It is normally the case that any of the slots in (10) can exhibit a tonal contrast between H and L (H and ° in Haya) except the extensions. These are generally "toneless", often assimilating to the tone of the FV (Meeussen 1967). These extensions are toneless also in Haya, which in our analysis means only that they contrast with H (and not that they constitute a third value in addition to H and L).

The first important observation about Haya verb forms is that no matter what the tense, polarity or construction type, there can be a maximum of only *one* surface H occurring in the span from the radical to the FV slot. In addition, there are exactly four possibilities for the placement of this H tone (including the one case where there is no H), as seen in (13).[6]

(13) a. $V_1$ : /ba + aa + kom + il + e/ → báákómile 'they have tied up' (Pf)
 H H

b. $\phi$ : /ba + aa + jun + il + e/ → báájunile 'they have helped' (Pf)
 H

c. FV : /ba + kom + il + e/ → bakomíle 'they tied up' ($P_2$)
 H H

d. $V_2$ : /ba + jun + il + e/ → bajunîle 'they helped' ($P_2$)
 H

The examples in (13a, b) are in the perfect (Pf) tense, which is characterized by a non-tonic (°) FV, while those in (13c, d) are in the $P_2$ (yesterday past) tense, which assigns an underlying H tone to the FV. (13a, c) involve the H tone radical -$\underset{\text{H}}{\text{kom}}$- 'tie up', while (13b, d) involve the non-tonic radical -jun- 'help'. The four possibilities, then, of H tone placement in nonprepausal forms (see note 6) are: (a) on the first vowel ($V_1$) of the radical; (b) no H; (c) on the FV; and (d) on the second vowel ($V_2$) counting from the initial radical boundary. Each of these patterns is relatively straightforward, with perhaps a brief comment in order on the $V_2$ H tone placement in (13d). The reason why this placement is stated as $V_2$, rather than being stated as the first vowel after the radical, is that radicals with a long (= underlyingly double) vowel require that the H be placed on the second vowel of the radical itself. Of interest from a Bantu point of view, the V preceding a NC sequence is considered short (= single). The relevant forms to compare with (13d) are given in (14).

| | | | |
|---|---|---|---|
| (14) a. ba-ziík-il-e | (→ bazííkile) | 'they buried' | /-ziik-/ |
| b. ba-biNg-íl-e | (→ babingîle) | 'they chased' | /-biNg-/ |

(14a) involves the radical /-ziik-/ 'bury', which receives its H tone $V_2$ from the FV (see (20)). By a tonal simplification rule, the resulting would-be LH rising tone becomes HH, as indicated. (14b), on the other hand, agrees with (13d), although vowels are often lengthened/doubled before NC sequences in other Bantu languages (cf. Byarushengo 1977).

The question that arises now is how best to account for the fact that the R-X-FV sequence allows only four tone patterns (no matter how many extensions are present). We have already said that extensions are toneless. This leaves the radical and final vowel to carry potential underlying H tones. We have seen that some radicals have a lexical underlyingly H, while others are non-tonic (i.e. underlyingly toneless). If we assume the same for the final vowel (a position which is well motivated from what is known about Bantu tonology in general), this would provide the four patterns of R + X + FV we need: $H+^\circ+^\circ$, $^\circ+^\circ+^\circ$, $H+^\circ+H$, and $^\circ+^\circ+H$, as indicated in the underlying forms of (13). Thus, a H is contributed by the radical in (13a, c) and by the FV in (13c, d). In addition to the non-tonic past extension -il- in all forms, the Pf tense assigns the marker $\underset{\text{H}}{\text{-aa-}}$ in the T/A slot. The rules which are needed to reduce the H of the radical in (13c) and shift the H of the FV to the $V_2$ in (13d) are given below.

The exact spelling out of the FV (and also the T/A markers) is determined by the tense/aspect, polarity and construction type in which the VU occurs. A table representing the major combinations of these grammatical factors is provided in Appendix II. In this table the major tense/aspects of Haya are listed vertically, while the columns represent main vs. (subject vs. object) relative clauses and affirmative vs. negative. Sample paradigms are seen in Appendix I.

In these appendices it is seen that not only do the tones vary according to tense/aspect, polarity and construction type, but so do the T/A markers themselves. Thus, for example, the $P_3$ (before yesterday past) tense marker is -ka- in main clause affirmative constructions, but -a- plus the ending -il-e in all other cases (with some tonal variation). Ideally, the tone differences observed between one construction type and another (e.g.

main vs. subject-relative clause or main affirmative vs. main negative etc.) should be in part or totally predictable from modifications on the underlying tones of the respective construction markers – especially the FV. It is a rare instance in Bantu, however, when one can change a main clause to a subject-relative clause simply by changing the tone of the FV in all tense-aspects. Instead, one finds enormous synchronic arbitrariness in present-day Haya, which masks the historical changes which have produced the language. This arbitrariness is captured by a number of morphological tone assignment rules, to be given in section 4 and Appendix II. The irregularities in the VU are thus to be captured in the morphology, not in the tonology per se. After the morphological assignment rules introduce the appropriate T/A and FV markers with their corresponding tones (H or °), this information, coupled with the underlying tone of the radical and other morphemes, can predict the rest automatically.

The three parameters of tense/aspect/mood, polarity and construction type define three FV morphological tone assignments: (a) non-tonic FV, as in the Pf in (13a, b); (b) H tone FV, as in the $P_2$ in (13c, d); and (c) "polar" (P) tone FV as, for example, in the $F_1$ (general future) tense, as seen in (15).

(15)a. /ba + laV + kom + aNgan + a/ → balaakómangana
H (under kom) — 'they will tie up each other'

b. /ba + laV + jun + aNgan + a/ → balaajunángana
H (under a) — 'they will help each other'

The examples in (15) involve the $F_1$ tense marker -laa- (underlyingly -laV-) and the reciprocal extension -aNgan-. The H tone is realized on the surface on the $V_1$ in (15a). Since we know that the radical has a H tone of its own, and that the derived $V_1$ pattern results from a H tone radical + a non-tonic FV, the FV of this tense must be underlyingly non-tonic, as indicated. However, in (15b), the H tone is associated with the $V_2$, i.e. on the first vowel of the extension. In order for this pattern to obtain, the FV must have an underlying H tone, as indicated. Thus, in the $F_1$ tense, the FV is non-tonic after a H tone radical but acquires a H tone after a non-tonic radical, hence the notion of "polar" tone.

Another fact that can be observed in Appendices I and II is that the tones of the T/A position also vary. They not only have different tones of their own, but can also affect the realization of the four patterns illustrated in (13). As an illustration, consider the data in (16), which differ from the corresponding sentences in (13) by the addition of the reflexive marker /-yee-/[7] in the OM slot:

(16)a. /ba + aa + yee + kom + il + e/ → bááyéékomile
H H H 'they have tied themselves up'

b. /ba + aa + yee + jun + il + e/ → bááyééjunile
H H 'they have helped themselves'

c. /ba + yee + kom + il + e/ → beekomíle
H H H 'they tied themselves up'

d. /ba + yee + jun + il + e/ → beejunîle
H H 'they helped themselves'

When compared with (13) two basic surprises are noted. First, in (16a) the H tone of -$\underset{\text{H}}{\text{kom}}$- is not realized. Second, the H of the reflexive /-$\underset{\text{H}}{\text{yee}}$-/ is not realized in (16c, d). Only (16b) follows our expectations: namely, that the H of the reflexive marker should be realized *and* it should not affect the realization of subsequent tones.

The alternations observed between the data in (13) and in (16) can be accounted for by the following two generalizations: (i) if, as in (16c, d) the FV has a H tone, *all* preceding H tones in the VU are reduced; and (ii) if the FV is non-tonic, there can be multiple H tones in a VU, but an underlying H which is immediately preceded by a H is reduced. We see this second generalization in effect also in the following examples having the H tone inceptive (In) marker -$\underset{\text{H}}{\text{la}}$- in the T/A slot:

(17)a. /ba + la + kom + il + e/ → balákomile
H H 'they have tied up before'

b. /ba + la + jun + il + e/ → balájunile
H 'they have helped before'

c. /ba + la + mu + kom + il + e/ → balámukómile
H H 'they have tied him up before'

In (17a), where -$\underset{\text{H}}{\text{la}}$- immediately precedes the H radical -$\underset{\text{H}}{\text{kom}}$-, only the former H is realized. The resulting form thus merges tonally with that in (17b), where the radical -jun- is non-tonic. In (17c), however, where the non-tonic OM -mu- 'him/her' appears between -$\underset{\text{H}}{\text{la}}$- and -$\underset{\text{H}}{\text{kom}}$-, the H tone of the radical is realized since it is not immediately preceded by H.

This process whereby one H causes an immediately following H to reduce is found in numerous Bantu languages (e.g. Tonga (Meeussen 1963), Luganda (Meeussen 1965), Makua (Cheng and Kisseberth 1979), etc.). In autosegmental terms it is formulated as in (18). (In this study association lines will usually be omitted in the case of one-to-one associations between tones and vowels.)

(18) V $C_0$ V
H H
⇓
L

This rule may reapply so as to reduce a H-H-H. . . sequence to H-L-L. . ., so its application must be specified either as simultaneous or as a right-to-left iterative rule. We specify the change in (18) as one from H to L, rather than H to °, although the latter would work for Haya. (It will not work for other languages, e.g. Luganda, since the "reduced tone" remains distinct from non-tonic specifications (see Hyman 1982a, b).) After rule (18) has applied, we then have a three-way tonal opposition: tonic H, tonic L, and non-tonic.

Another rule which is required reduces *all* H's to L within a VU which has a H tone FV:

(19) H → L / # X ___ Y V # (simultaneous multiple application)
H

Finally, rule (20) is needed to shift the H of the FV to $V_2$ position when the radical is non-tonic:

(20) $[_R$ C V $C_0$ V X V #
° H
⇓ ⇓
H L

In (20), the radical vowel must be specified as non-tonic (°) in order for the H tone to shift appropriately.[8] If rules (18) and (19) precede (20), then they must be formulated as H becoming L (rather than °) or else rule (20) will not be able to distinguish between underlyingly non-tonic radicals and derived non-tonic radicals, as in examples (13c, d) and (16c, d). Rule (18) may follow (20), in which case it can be formulated as a H tone deletion process. However, if rule (20) precedes rule (19), the latter is complicated considerably, requiring a double environment slash as in (21).

(21) H → L / # X ___ Y $_R[$ C ___ Z V W #
H

This formulation would have the H tone reductions occasioned by either a H FV or a H $V_2$, whence the need for such a complicated statement. In any case, rule (19) must *precede* rule (18) so that a form like /a + bon + a/ (H under *o* of bon, H under final *a*) 'he sees' becomes a + bon + $\underset{H}{a}$ [abóna] and *not* *a + b$\underset{H}{o}$n − $\underset{L}{a}$ [abôna]. We thus assume the ordering (19)-(18)-(20).

Although we have established rule (20) on the basis of verb forms, it also may apply in nouns as seen in the deverbal noun forms in (22).

(22)a. /e#li + kom + el + o/ → eikómelo 'place to tie up'
H H
b. /e#li + jun + el + o/ → eijunilo 'place to help'
H
c. /e#mi + kom + el + e/ → emikómele 'way to tie up'
H H
d. /e#mi + jun + el + e/ → emijunîle 'way to help'
H H

(22a-d) involve the extension /-el-/ (which becomes [il] after a radical with one of the vowels /i,u,a/). The FV is non-tonic -o in (22a, b) and polar -e in (22c, d). In (22d) we see the H of the FV shift to the $V_2$ position (and then become a HL tone by rule (6a)). The initial vowel /$\underset{H}{e}$-/ is realized with surface L tone in (22) because it occurs immediately after pause. It is otherwise protected from rule (19) by the # which separates it from the rest of the VU.

## 3. TONE VS. ACCENT

In the preceding sections we have assumed an autosegmental tonal framework without discussion. Two further aspects of the verb tonology suggest we are on the right track: (a) tone in reduplicated verb forms; and (b) tone in imperative forms whose only OM is a first person singular.

In Haya, most verbs can be reduplicated with a distributive meaning 'here and there', as seen in the infinitive forms in (23).

(23)a. okukôma 'to tie up' okukómaakoma 'to tie up here and there'
b. okujuna 'to help' okujunaajuna 'to help here and there'

The reduplicated part of the forms to the right is -aa- plus a copy of the radical. What is important is the assignment of tone to the reduplicated part. As is common in Bantu languages (cf. Lovins 1971 for Lomóngo, for example), the reduplicated parts are treated tonally as extensions, i.e. as toneless. That this is the case in Haya is seen from the forms in (24), which should be compared with those in (13).

(24) a. /ba + aa + kom + aa + kom + il + e/ → báákómaakomile
          H     H          'they have tied up here and there'
b. /ba + aa + jun + aa + jun + il + e/ → báájunaajunile
          H          'they have helped here and there'
c. /ba + kom + aa + kom + il + e/ → bakomaakomíle
          H          H          (← bakomaakomilé)
          'they tied up here and there'
d. /ba + jun + aa + jun + il + e/ → bajunáájunile
          H          (← bajunáajunile)
          'they helped here and there'

As in the case of unreduplicated verb forms, rules (19) and (20) realize a H tone on the FV in (24c), on the $V_2$ in (27d) and on each respective vowel in (24a, b), since there are no successive H tones to undergo rule (18). The question which arises is why in (24a, c) the H tone of the first occurrence of the radical -k$\underset{H}{\text{o}}$m- is not copied onto the corresponding reduplicated occurrence. That is, why don't we find the underlying representations in (25)?

(25) a. */ba + aa + kom + aa + kom + il + e/ (cf. 24a)
          H     H          H
b. */ba + kom + aa + kom + il + e/ (cf. 24c)
          H          H          H

First an observation: There is a pervasive constraint in the language against the occurrence of an underlying H tone anywhere between the $V_1$ and the FV. This constraint not only accounts for the lack of a tonal opposition on extensions, but also accounts for the non-occurrence of tonal contrasts on the second vowel of -CVVC- radicals. (That is, the only possible tonal contrast in long radicals is -C$\underset{H}{\text{V}}$VC- vs. -CVVC-, and not -C$\underset{H}{\text{V}}\underset{H}{\text{V}}$C- vs. -C$\underset{H}{\text{V}}$VC- or -CV$\underset{H}{\text{V}}$C- vs. -CVVC-.) The explanation for the non-reduplication of the H tone of the radical in (24a, c) naturally falls out from the autosegmental approach: reduplication involves only the segmental tier and not the tonal tier. The reduplicative process is thus a segmental one only, and the reduplicated syllables are treated as non-tonic, exactly as are the extensions.

The facts from reduplication argue strongly for a two-tiered approach to Haya tonology. So do the following imperative forms involving a first person singular OM (three dots indicate non-final tonal pronunciations):

(26) a. ń + kom + á . . . 'tie me up!' cf. tu + kóm + e . . . 'tie us up!'
ń + jun + á . . . 'help me!' tu + jun + é . . . 'help us!'
b. ń + kóm + el + á káto 'tie Kato up for me!'

| | | |
|---|---|---|
| | ń + jún + il + á káto | 'help Kato for me!' |
| c. | ń + kóm + óólol + á . . . | 'untie me!' (/-kom-/) <br> H |
| | ń + shúm + úúlul + á . . . | 'untie me!' (/-šum-/) |
| d. | ń + deet + á múno | 'bring me a lot!' |
| | ń + di + il + á múno | 'eat for me a lot!' |
| e. | m + pá káto | 'bring me Kato!' |

Looking at the forms in (26), the following irregularities can be noted: (i) The imperative normally takes the FV -e (with P tone) whenever an OM is present – the only exception to this being the first person singular OM, which takes the same -$\underset{H}{a}$ FV as in the corresponding zero forms *kóma* 'tie up!' and *júna* 'help!'; (ii) Whenever there is a H tone FV, the general rule is that all preceding H tones in the VU will reduce to L- the only exception being the first person singular OM, which in the imperative has a H tone which is realized; and (iii) there is no tonal contrast between H and non-tonic radicals, as seen in (26c). As can be seen most clearly in (26b, c), a H-L-H tonal pattern is distributed over the whole VU, preempting the normal tonal properties of the imperative. We may assume that N- '1st sg.' irregularly has an underlying H tone only in the -$\underset{H}{a}$ imperative. The result should theoretically be an initial H on the OM (subject to reduction via rule (19)) and a final H on the FV or $V_2$, depending on the tonicity of the radical. However, in order to obtain the correct tonal forms, there is instead a right-to-left association of the H-L-H pattern.[9]

In (26) the surface tonal forms are obtained by automatic application of this right-to-left association procedure. The form 'bring me Kato!' in (26e) only receives a L-H pattern, since there are fewer tone-bearing units than tones. This is achieved by stipulating that there can be one tone assigned per tone-bearing unit, and any left-over tone (here, the initial H of the H-L-H melody) simply fails to associate. Although anomalous when compared to the rest of the system, the existence of such a H-L-H "tonal melody" argues forcefully that tone should be represented on a separate autosegmental tier in Haya.

We accept then that the various morphemes in the VU may either have one underlying H tone specification or are non-tonic. By treating underlying forms as autosegmental representations of H and °, we have adhered to our assumption that Haya is at all stages of representation a "tone language". However, the properties of the underlying H tones are quite different from those found, for example, in the West African languages surveyed by Hyman and Schuh (1974). Whereas in the latter languages a H tone is expected to cause surrounding L tones to assimilate to it (especially through tone-spreading to the right), H tone in Haya seems at least in part "accentual" in nature. There is no evidence of H tone spreading in

Haya (other than the H-L-H melody we have just seen), and an underlying H "bumps off" an immediately following H. Thus, rules (18) and (19) represent *reduction* processes of the kind found in languages (with stress-) accent.

Because of the striking disparity between the underlying and surface prosodic units, Meeussen proposed that in certain Bantu languages tone be analyzed underlyingly with "determinant" vs. "neutral" elements (cf. Stevick's 1969 "tonic" vs. "non-tonic" distinction and the * vs. ° representations for languages such as Tonga and Luganda proposed by Goldsmith (this volume) and Hyman (1982a) respectively. A syllabic unit characterized as determinant is considered *marked*, while the neutral units lack this mark. Later in a derivation, the determinant/neutral opposition is reinterpreted by rules as an opposition between H and L tones.

In our study, rather than accepting representations of D vs. N or * vs. °, we claim that the marked nature of H tone in Haya and many other Bantu languages is captured by assuming an underlying opposition of H vs. °. In West African languages where two tonal values are more symmetric in nature, the underlying representation will be H vs. L. (Alternatively, a H vs. ° opposition will be spelled as one between H and L "earlier" than in Bantu languages.) Thus, a "tonal accent language" is not one characterized by the presence of an additional accentual subcomponent (represented by *'s).[10] In our framework, the tone vs. tonal accent dichotomy is a misconception. A tone language will be tonal-accent-like to the extent that there are stages in the derivation where there is incomplete tonification. To the extent that tonal processes take place at such stages the language will be accent-like, and the more such processes (or the more irrelevant the eventual tone of the non-tonic tone-bearing units), the more accent-like the language will appear.

In an earlier version of this study, we presented the following *functional* arguments for treating Haya as an accentual language:

(i) In Haya, no morpheme has more than *one* H tone per morpheme. This is exactly what we would expect if this H tone were an accent: a morpheme, no matter what its length, will have either one H or be non-tonic. Thus, H tone has a "culminative" function within morphemes: count the number of H tones in a word and you have at least as many morphemes.

(ii) There are rules assigning H tones at a distance in Haya. Thus we have seen that the H tone of a FV will be displaced onto the $V_2$ if the radical is non-tonic. Analyzed with complete tonification, this process is anomalous; analyzed as accentual via incomplete tonification, we are in the familiar realm of accent shifting, retraction etc.

(iii) There are numerous rules in Haya which "reduce" H tones to L in certain environments (cf. (18) and (19)). Taken as a tonal rule, (18) represents a dissimilation process. Taken as an accentual rule, it falls in with languages where adjacent (stress-) accents are reduced.

(iv) Although we have not seen the relevant examples yet, there is an important interaction between tone and scope of focus in Haya. Thus, consider the sentences in (27).

(27)a. ni kyo eki → ni ky' êki 'it's *this* one'
H HH
b. ni kyo eki → ní ky' êki 'it *is* this one'
H HH

The word in the gloss which is italicized would receive stress in the corresponding English sentences. The underlying H of the focus marker (FM) ni (H) 'it is' is reduced if the focus is on the demonstrative complement of the FM, as in (27a). If the focus is the FM itself, no reduction takes place, as in (27b). This type of interaction between prosody and focus is expected in an accent language, though not in a "pure tone" language.[11]

An adequate theory of prosodic systems must account for the occurrence and possible cooccurrence of the above properties in Bantu-like tone languages, where tone is "accent-like", but not, say, in Yoruba-like tone languages as found in West Africa. Our proposal to represent the underlying tonal opposition as one between H and ° in Haya accounts for this difference: (i) Since H in opposition to zero is a mark of prominence, it is natural for Haya to limit its occurrence to at most one per morpheme. (ii) Since H's are not separated from each other by L tones, but rather occur adjacent to each other on the tonal tier (prior to complete tonification), they may be subject to displacement over considerable distance, e.g. rule (20), which shifts a H from the FV to the $V_2$ position of the VU.[12] (iii) Because H is a mark of prominence (and not simply the plus value of a tonal feature [HIGH]), it is natural for there to be rules reducing the number of H's occurring within words or phrases. (iv) Finally, because H represents a prosodic prominence in Haya and similar languages, it is natural that its realization be tied up with considerations of focus, the marking of prominence par excellence.[13]

In the remainder of this section we shall consider the relevance of focus on tonal realizations in Haya. We begin with the O (present habitual) tense forms in (28).

(28)a. /ba + mu + jun + a/ → bamujúna 'they help him'
H
b. /ba + jun + a kato/ → bajuna káto 'they help Kato'
H H

In (28a) we observe that the SM, OM and radical are non-tonic while the FV carries an underlying H tone. By rule (6b) we derive *ba-mu-jún-á* before the % boundary, which then becomes *ba-mu-jún-a* by reduction of H before pause. In (28b) we have substituted the noun object 'Kato' for the OM -mu- 'him/her' which was found in (28a). The same underlyingly representation is in effect: the VU has a H only on its FV. However, as seen in the surface pronunciation, this H is reduced by rule. In this and other tenses in Haya (see (31)), wherever there is a post-verbal complement of any kind (noun, adverb, prepositional phrase etc.), *all* H tones in the VU are reduced. Since accent languages are known to undergo similar reduction processes dependent on the syntax, we have another case where our marked H tones behave in an accent-like fashion.

Looking at these facts a little more closely, it is not difficult to find a motivation for this H tone reduction. As demonstrated by Byarushengo and Tenenbaum (1976), Tenenbaum (1977) and Bennett (1977), the focus (or assertion) of a Haya utterance is placed *last* in a clause. Thus, in (28a) the VU contains the assertion ('they *helped* him'), while in (28b), the VU is not assertion-final: the two interpretations of (28b) are that either the VP ('helped Kato') or simply the noun object 'Kato' is the focus. Thus, this utterance answers either the question 'what do they do?' or the question 'Whom do they help?'. In order for Kato not to be part of the assertion, it can either be left-dislocated as in (29a), or right-dislocated, as in (29b).

| | | | |
|---|---|---|---|
| (29) | a. | kató ba-mu-jún-a<br>Kato they-him-help | 'Kato, they help him' |
| | b. | ba-mu-jún-á % káto<br>they-him-help Kato | 'they help him, Kato' |

As seen in (29), whenever an object is left- or right-dislocated, there must be a corresponding OM in the VU. In addition, a right-dislocated argument requires a % boundary before it (cf. BHT), while a left-dislocated argument is not marked by %. The explanation for this asymmetry is that % is inserted to mark the end of an assertion, and in a right-dislocation, what precedes the dislocated argument is always a full assertion. In fact, as demonstrated by BHT, when there is more than one right-dislocation, each one is preceded by %. Thus, in (29b), final H becomes H-H before %, as predicted by rule (6b).

To summarize thus far, the H tones which "survive" rules (18), (19) and (20) are still subject to the condition that their VU be *clause-final* (whether in a main or relative clause).

A second set of conditions makes it possible for H tones to survive even when the VU is not clause-final. We see a first example of this in

(30), which should be compared with (28).

(30)a. ni#ba + mu + jun + a → nibamujúna 'they are helping him'
                                   H
       Pr-they-him-help
    b. ni#ba + jun + a kato → nibajuná káto 'they are helping Kato'
                        H    H
       Pr-they-help Kato

These examples are in the Pr(ogressive) aspect. What is important is that this construction is built directly on the O tense seen in (28), with the same $\phi$ T/A marker and the same H tone FV – but with the addition of the PI *ni*-preceding the SM. The observed surface tones in (30a) are identical to those in (28a), but crucially, the H of the FV in (30b) is realized as H on the surface, while its counterpart in (28b) had to be reduced. The question is why.

The answer is to be found in studies of so-called "auxiliary focus" (Hyman 1979, Hyman and Watters 1980). The Pr aspect is an *intrinsically* focused verb form. The VU containing the Pr morpheme is treated as focused (i.e. as if it were clause-final) because the feature 'progressive' is itself semantically prominent. Such prominently marked VU's are exempt from H tone reduction of the type under discussion, even when the VU is not clause-final. As a first argument for this position, recall from (27) that /ni/ (H) is the general focus marker itself. Thus, 'they are helping Kato' can roughly be viewed as 'it's (that) they help Kato'.[14] Let us refer to a VU which is intrinsically focused as [+F].[15] In the last column of Appendix II we have indicated which verb forms are [+F] and which are [–F]: the latter forms undergo H tone reduction when not clause final, while the former do not. The two classes of verb forms are distributed as follows:

(31) [+F]
(a) all negative verb forms
(b) affirmatives of following:
- Pr (progressive)
- Pf (perfect)
- $P_3$ (before yesterday past; main clauses only)
- In (inceptive; experiential 'ever, before')
- Ps (perstitive 'still')
- Sj (subjunctive)
- Im (imperative)

[–F]
(a) affirmative verb forms of the following:
- O (present habitual)
- $P_1$ (today past)
- $P_2$ (yesterday past; stative)
- $P_3$ (before yesterday past; relative clauses only)
- PH (past habitual)
- $F_1$ (general future)
- $F_2$ (after tomorrow future)

As can be seen, all negative verb forms are [+F]. Affirmative verb forms fall into two categories: (a) Pr, Pf, $P_3$ [main clause only], In, Ps, Sj and Im (=[+F]); and (b) O, $P_1$, $P_2$, $P_3$ [except main clause], PH, $F_1$ and $F_2$ (=[−F]). Thus the controlling parameters of polarity, tense, aspect and mood require further comment.

Concerning negation, Givón (1978) has argued that speakers tend to use negative utterances when the content of the proposition has already been entered into the discourse. What this means is that negation, in the "unmarked case", constitutes at least part of the assertion of an utterance.[16] What Haya (and many other languages – see Hyman and Watters 1980) has done by requiring that all negative VU's be treated as intrinsically focused is extend this general tendency to *all* cases in terms of the obligatory [+F] designation. Thus, instead of the VU being marked semantically [+focus] whenever the negation is in focus (a choice of a speaker in a given context [ = pragmatic control of focus]), it is now the *language* that tells the speaker that negation is intrinsically [+F] [= grammatical control of focus]. We can therefore refer to negation as "marked polarity".

Similar factors which make a VU [+F] are "marked" tense, aspect and mood. That the subjunctive and imperative represent a departure from the unmarked indicative mood (and are therefore "marked") can be accepted on intuitive grounds. The perfect tenses (Pf and In) are here considered to be marked tenses, while the progressive tenses (Pr and Ps) are considered to be marked aspects. All remaining tense/aspect features are unmarked, i.e. non-progressive, non-perfect: O, $P_1$, $P_2$, $P_3$ [relative clauses only], PH, $F_1$ and $F_2$. In a formal analysis of the tense/aspect system, a feature matrix would be proposed to account for the different oppositions recognized in Haya. The perfect ('to have already X'ed') and inceptive ('to have X'ed before') would be two kinds of [+perf], while the progressive ('to be X'ing') and perstitive ('to be still X'ing') would be two kinds of [+prog]. The O and PH forms would be characterized as [−perf, −prog], which can be maintained as the unmarked aspectual category. Any category marked + for perfect tense, aspect, mood (presumably [+hortative], covering the subjunctive and imperative) or polarity will further be specified as [+F]. Alternatively, since past, future and habitual are the only categories further differentiated for tense in Haya, we might propose a feature [+tense], which redundantly takes a [−F] specification.

As for the main clause affirmative $P_3$ marker -ka-, it alone appears arbitrary in present day Haya in assigning [+F] to its VU. The corresponding relative construction for the $P_3$ does not involve -ka- and therefore does not receive a [+F] specification. The ultimate explanation for this anomaly is a historical one. The morpheme -ka- has three distinct non-overlapping functions in the auxiliary system: (a) in main clause affirmatives it is a $P_3$ marker; (b) in non-main affirmative clauses it is a past consecutive marker; and (c) in main and non-main negative clauses, it is a perfect marker, as can be seen from the negative forms of the Pf and In constructions in the Appendices. Mould (1979) has shown that -ka- has exactly these three meanings (past, perfect and consecutive) in different Bantu languages. Haya is unusual in having all three meanings realized by -ka-, though in complementary environments. Mould's reconstruction of *-ka- as a perfect marker in Proto-Bantu would explain its [+F] nature. In present day Haya we are forced to say that it is the morpheme itself which is [+F], rather than the feature(s) of which it is an exponent.

The rule which accounts for [−F] tone reduction will be given in section 4. It is important to note that a corresponding reduction process characterizes some noun phrases. In particular, the head nouns of an NP will undergo tone reduction if it is followed by any of the following modifiers: (a) a possessive pronoun [other than 1st and 2nd person singular]; (b) a possessive noun ("associative construction"); or (c) an adjective, providing that the modifier does not begin with a preprefix. Thus, consider the realization of the noun /$\underset{\text{H}}{\text{e}}$#ki + k$\underset{\text{H}}{\text{o}}$mbe/ 'cup' in (32), which is pronounced *ekikômbe* in isolation:

| | | |
|---|---|---|
| (32)a. | ekikombe kyáitu | 'our cup' (cf. ekikómb' ékáitu) |
| b. | ekikombe kyaa káto | 'Kato's cup' (cf. ekikómb' ékyaa káto) |
| c. | ekikombe kilúŋgi[17] | 'a beautiful cup' (cf. ekikómb' ékilúŋgi) |

As indicated in parentheses, when the modifier begins with a preprefix (giving it a relative clause-like interpretation, e.g. 'the cup which is mine'), tone reduction does not occur on 'cup'. As seen in (33), first and second person singular possessives, demonstratives and numerals do not condition tone reduction even when they lack the preprefix:

| | | |
|---|---|---|
| (33)a. | ekikómbe kyaŋge | 'my cup' |
| b. | ekikómbe kyaawe | 'your (sg.) cup' |
| c. | ekikómbe kîli | 'that cup (over there). |
| d. | ekikómbe kîmo | 'one cup' |

Since demonstratives and numerals generally occur later in the noun phrase than do possessives and adjectives, we can propose that they occur outside the $\bar{\text{N}}$ as expansions of the SPEC node. Possessives and adjectives, on the other hand, are expansions of the COMP node within $\bar{\text{N}}$. Thus, there is a relationship between the tightness of the bond between head noun and modifier and the occurrence of tone reduction. Since *any* post-verbal complement will cause tone reduction on a [−F] VU, the parallel between NP and VP tone reduction is an imperfect one.

The above suggestion does not immediately resolve the question of why first and second person singular possessors fail to condition tone reduction on the preceding head noun. It may be that in this case a head noun may acquire a [+F] specification as another kind of intrinsic focus. The alternative of deriving these possessives from the SPEC node is less attractive, especially since we may propose that preprefixed modifers originate in SPEC as do the semantically related relative clauses. As seen in the possessive pronoun constructions in (34), we shall need to set up a floating H tone preceding 'my', 'your sg.' and 'his/her':

| | | | | |
|---|---|---|---|---|
| (34) | ekitabó kyaŋge | 'my book' | ekitabo kyáitu | 'our book' |
| | ekitabó kyaawe | 'your sg. book' | ekitabo kyáanyu | 'your pl. book' |
| | ekitabó kye | 'his book' | ekitabo kyáabo | 'their book' |

The noun 'book' has the underlying form /$\underset{H}{e}$#ki + tabo), receiving the floating H on its final vowel when modified by a singular possessive pronoun. The form *ekikombê kye* 'his cup' indicates that the third person singular possessive also has a floating H before it, but in addition causes reduction of the penultimate H of /$\underset{H}{e}$#ki + k$\underset{H}{o}$mbe/.

A full table of possessive pronominal forms is given in Appendix III. The three rows of each form refer, respectively, to: (a) noun + possessive pronoun; (b) noun + $\phi$ copula + possessive pronoun; and (c) noun + relative copula + possessive pronoun. Representative examples with their glosses are repeated in (35).

(35) a. enkoní yange — 'my stick'
b. enkoni yange — 'the stick is mine'
c. ekony' éyánge — 'the stick which is mine'

The noun *enkoni* is, except for its preprefix, toneless underlyingly and therefore usually pronounced after pause with all L tones. In (35a), however, its final vowel receives the H floating tone referred to above. This floating H is absent in (35b), where there is a copular meaning, and hence the noun and possessive do not belong to the same NP. Finally, in (35c), there is a relative copular meaning expressed through the preprefix on the possessive pronoun. Note also in (35c) that the final -e must have an underlying H tone of its own (as opposed to the FV in (35a, b)), which undergoes rule (6b) when followed by %. The underlying forms for these examples are given in (36).

```
(36)a. /e#N + koni ##     i + a + Ng + e/
        H             H
    b. /e#N + koni ## i + a + Ng + e/
        H
    c. /e#N + koni ## e#i + a + Ng + e/
        H              H           H
```

To summarize the non-copular, non-relative forms: (a) 'my, you sg., his' involve the floating H; and (b) 'his, our, your pl., their' involve H tone reduction on the head noun. These two features thus define three situations: only (a) ['my, your sg.']; only (b) ['our, your pl., their']; both (a) and (b) ['his/her'].

## 4. TOWARDS A FORMAL MODEL

In the preceding sections we have argued for an approach to Haya tone which starts with incomplete tonification in underlying forms. The accentual nature of H tones was said to be captured by this formal property not obtaining in "pure tone" languages with completely tonified underlying forms. In this section we shall develop the model we have assumed in preceding discussions and present it in terms of the following rule types: (a) morphological H tone assignment rules; (b) morphophonemic H modification rules; (c) syllable structure rules; (d) tonification rules; (e) "tone" rules; and (f) "fast speech" rules. These sets of rules are crucially ordered with respect to one another, as indicated.

### *4.1 Morphological H Tone Assignment Rules*

As mentioned in our earlier discussion, H tones are either present lexically or are assigned by morphological rules. Especially in the case of the agglutinative VU, it will be necessary to specify, along with their segments, the tonal properties of each morpheme: subject markers, tense/aspect, relative and negative markers, final vowel, etc. In this section we shall be concerned only with the rules that are necessary to specify the tonicity of the FV (cf. Appendix II for additional tone assignment processes). Since a FV consists of one morpheme only, this means that the rules will assign either one or no H to it, depending on the tense/aspect/mood, polarity and construction type.

The features we shall use to specify the various parameters that determine the accentual value of the FV will be in part informal. The features Neg and Rel will refer, respectively, to negative and relative constructions, with the latter further subscripted S or O according to whether we refer to a subject-relative (Meeussen's "autonomous" construction) or an object-relative construction. [-neg, -rel] refers to main clause affirmatives, the unmarked construction. The various tense/aspect/moods will be referred to directly, rather than attempting a complete feature matrix for the different categories recognized by the language. Our data are from Appendix I, and we shall assume that our rules are ordered. In Appendix II it is seen that of the 72 FV's, 42 are tonic, 13 are non-tonic and 17 are tonic only if the radical is not tonic (i.e they have "polar" tone). In other words, 70% of the actual verb forms will have a non-tonic FV. It seems justified, then, for Haya at least, to propose rules that assign H, which therefore leave the majority of forms with a ° FV.[18] Among the several possibilities considered, the rules in (37) appear to be the optimal statement available:

(37)a. rules assigning H to the FV, independent of tone of radical

(i) $^{\circ} \rightarrow \mathrm{H} / + \bar{\mathrm{V}}]_{[\text{+neg: } P_2]}$

(ii) $^{\circ} \rightarrow \mathrm{H} / + \bar{\mathrm{V}}]_{[\text{+O rel: } F_2,\ O,\ P_1,\ P_2]}$

(iii) $^{\circ} \rightarrow \mathrm{H} / + \bar{\mathrm{V}}]_{[\text{-rel, -neg,: } F_2,\ O,\ Pr,\ P_2]}$

(iv) $^{\circ} \rightarrow \mathrm{H} / + \bar{\mathrm{V}}]_{[\text{Im (-Sm, -OM)}]}$ [19]

b. rules assigning H to the FV only if the radical is °

(i) $^{\circ} \rightarrow \mathrm{H} / + \bar{\mathrm{V}}]_{[F_1]}$

(ii) $^{\circ} \rightarrow \mathrm{H} / + \bar{\mathrm{V}}]_{[\text{+neg: O}]}$

(iii) $^{\circ} \rightarrow \mathrm{H} / + \bar{\mathrm{V}}]_{[\text{-neg, <+rel>: } <P_3>,\ \text{PH}]}$

(iv) $^{\circ} \rightarrow \mathrm{H} / + \bar{\mathrm{V}}]_{[\text{Sj}]}$

(v) $^{\circ} \rightarrow \mathrm{H} / + \bar{\mathrm{V}}]_{[\text{Im (+Sm or +OM)}]}$ [19]

c. miscellaneous

$^{\circ} \rightarrow \mathrm{H} / [\mathrm{C}\bar{\mathrm{V}} \ldots]_{[\text{+neg: } P_2]}$

In (37a) the rules which assign H to the FV independent of the radical tone are given. In (37b) the rules assigning H to the FV only if the radical is toneless are given. Finally, (37c) represents an anomalous rule assigning H to the radical in negative $P_2$ constructions.[20] It should be borne in mind that the ultimate morphological rules will have to refer not only to the tonal properties of the FV, but also to those of the pre-radical slots, where H's are introduced according to the same tense/aspect/mood, negative and relative feature specifications (see Appendix II). Finally, these morphological assignment rules will also specify the segmental content of the T/A and FV markers.

### *4.2 Morphophonemic H Modification Rules*

After the morphological H assignment rules have determined the location of the underlying H's, the morphophonemic rules determine which of these H's survive – and where. At this same point in the grammar there are morphophonemic segmental rules, just as there were segmental correlates to the morphological assignment rules of the preceding paragraph. Some of these morphophonemic rules involve consonant alternations and certain cases where the -il- extension undergoes fusion (see Byarushengo 1975, 1977 and rule (54) below).

The first rules which modify the underlying H tones are those given earlier as (19), (18) and (20), applying in that order. Rule (18) converts any contiguous sequence of H's to a H followed by a sequence of L's. Rule (19) reduces all H's to L's whenever the FV of the VU itself is H, and rule (20) shifts a FV H tone to $V_2$ position whenever the radical is non-tonic.

At this point two additional rules apply which assign a H to an object marker or T/A marker. The first rule *shifts* the H of a -C$\underset{H}{V}$- radical onto the preceding V when the -C$\underset{H}{V}$- radical is (a) preceded by a $\overset{\circ}{V}$ belonging to certain morphemes only, and (b) is followed by a non-tonic FV (i.e. when there are no extensions):

$$(38)\quad \begin{array}{ccccccc} \underset{\circ}{V} & ]_X & {}_R[ & C & \underset{H}{V} & + & V\,]_{VU} \\ \Downarrow & & & & \Downarrow & & \\ H & & & & L & & \end{array}$$

(where X = OM, $P_1$ -$\underset{H}{aa}$-, Ps -ki-$\underset{H}{aa}$-, or SM; i.e. X ≠ $P_3$ -ka-, $\overset{H}{F_1}$ -V-, or $\overset{H}{a}$ CV noun prefix, including the -ku- of Inf/Pr)

This rule accounts for the derivation of 'they ate it' ($P_3$) in (39a).

(39)a. ba+ka+ki+li+a → ba+ka+ki+li+a → ba+ka+ki+li+a [bákakîlya]
       H       H       H      H          H  L  H  L
       they-$P_3$-it-ate      (by 38)

b. ba+ka+li+a → ba+ka+li+a [bákálya] 'they ate' ($P_3$)
   H    H        H  L  H

Rule (38) does not apply in (39b), since the -ka- $P_3$ marker does not satisfy the condition on X. The phonetic forms are derived by assigning tones to toneless vowels and then applying (6a, b) and rule (69) below.

The second rule affects only OM's, the last of which receives a H if there is no subsequent H in the VU:

$$(40)\quad {}^\circ \rightarrow H \;/\; \_\_\_\_ \,]_{OM}\; X \,]_{VU} \qquad \text{(where X does not contain any H)}$$

Examples involving occurrences of an OM with the four combinations of H/° radical and H/° FV are provided in (41).

(41)a. ba+aa+mu+kom+il+e → báámukómile 'they have tied him up' (Pf)
       H       H
  b. ba+aa+mu+jun+il+e → báámújunile 'they have helped him' (Pf)
       H
  c. ba+mu+kom+il+e → bamukomíle 'they tied him up' ($P_2$)
       H   H
  d. ba+mu+jun+il+e → bamujunîle 'they helped him' ($P_2$)
       H

In these examples the OM has a H tone only in (41b), where both the radical and the FV are non-tonic. In the other examples, where either or both the radical and the FV have a H, the OM remains non-tonic.

In the following example involving the H tone inceptive marker -$\underset{H}{\text{la}}$-, we observe that (40) can create two H tones in immediate succession:

(42) ba+la+mu+jun+il+e → ba+la+mu+jun+il+e [balámújunile]
       H               H H
  they-In-him-help-In 'they have helped him before'

That the inceptive marker does not, by virtue of its underlying H, cause the reduction of the following OM H by rule (18) demonstrates that (40) must apply *after* (18). However, because the H of the OM is subject to reduction when the VU is [–F] and not clause final, (40) must precede the focus reduction rule, which we consider next.

We have already seen the relevance of focus to the realization of the H tones in Haya. As indicated in section 3 there are two different kinds of focus considerations, which Hyman and Watters (1980) refer to as constituent focus and auxiliary focus.

*Constituent focus* refers to whether or not a major constituent (argument or verb) receives focus marking. In Haya the only relevant environments will involve either the VU vis-à-vis its complements or a noun vis-à-vis its modifiers, i.e. X-COMP.

*Auxiliary focus* refers to cases of marked polarity, tense, aspect and mood which shield the accents of the VU from reduction.

We shall assume that a non-final VU or N which is exempt from H tone reduction will receive a [+F] specification on the basis either of the auxiliary features or noun phrase properties. This having been determined, the focus reduction rule can be formalized as in (43).

(43) $$H \rightarrow L \;/\; [\, X \bar{V} Y \,]_{\underset{[-F]}{N/VU}} \; Z \,]_{NP/VP} \qquad (\text{where } Z \neq \phi)$$

Any and all H tones become L on a head constituent (N or VU) which is

[–F] and followed by any complement within its phrase (NP or VP – or perhaps $\bar{N}$ and $\bar{V}$). We prefer this use of [–F] instead of listing all of the environments in (43) where focus reduction takes place since (i) the notion of focus incorporates the explanation for this reduction, and (ii) we would not be surprised to see these environments varying slightly from dialect to dialect or language to language in the area. [–F] could thus be defined differently in these cases.

Another reduction rule which is needed is given in (44).

(44) H → L / ___ OM [

A H is reduced before an object marker. This rule accounts for the following alternations:

| | | | |
|---|---|---|---|
| (45)a. | a#ba+jun+a<br>H H | → abájuna | 'they who help' |
| b. | a#ba+mu+jun+a<br>H H H | → abamújuna | 'they who help him' |
| c. | a#ba+ta+kom+a<br>H H H | → abatákoma | 'they who don't tie up' |
| d. | a#ba+ta+mu+kom+a<br>H H H | → abatamukôma | 'they who don't tie him up' |

(The H of the PI subject relative marker $\underset{\text{H}}{\text{a}}$- is reduced after pause by rule (50) and is disregarded here.) In (45a) there is a one-to-one relationship between the underlying H of the SM (see Appendix II) and its surface realization. In (45b), however, the H of the SM must reduce by rule (44), since it is followed by an OM. (The H of the OM -$\underset{\text{H}}{\text{mu}}$- is assigned by (40) and is irrelevant for the formulation of (44), as we see in (45d).) In (45c) the relative negative marker -$\underset{\text{H}}{\text{ta}}$- bears H tone, causing the H of the radical -$\underset{\text{H}}{\text{kom}}$- to reduce by rule (18). Finally, in (45d) this H on the negative marker is reduced by rule (44), leaving only the H of the verb radical. Other examples (e.g. the negative and relative $P_1$ forms in Appendix I) show that the H affected by (44) can not only belong to the SM or negative marker, but also to a T/A marker. The one morpheme which is exempt from (44) is the inceptive marker -$\underset{\text{H}}{\text{la}}$-; thus, cf. a+$\underset{\text{H}}{\text{la}}$+mu+$\underset{\text{H}}{\text{kom}}$+il+e → *alámukómile* 'he has tied him up before'.[21]

The next H modification rule is needed to account for the final H in the VU in (46a, b).

(46)a. ba+aa+jun+a byarushengo → baajuná byarushengo
H — 'they helped Byarushengo' ($P_1$)

b. ba+jun+il+e byarushengo → bajunilé byarushengo ($P_2$)
H

c. ba+ka+jun+a byarushengo → bákajuna byarushengo ($P_3$)
H

Whenever a toneless VU is followed by a toneless complement of any kind (object, adverb, etc.) a H tone is optionally found on its FV. In (46a, b) the underlying H tone is reduced by (43). Thus, the surface forms in (46a, b) are optional variants of the forms *baajuna byarushengo* and *bajunile byarushengo*. In (46c), where the VU is exempt from (43) because the $P_3$ -ka- form is [+F], the H on the SM is preserved and a H is not assigned to the FV by rule (47).

(47) $[\ X\ \underset{o}{V}\ ]_{VU}\ [\ Y\ ]$ (where X and Y do not contain H)

⇓

H

The above optional rule is only approximate since it must capture variations such as those seen in (48).

(48)
a. batweekeile byarushengo kasheijage 'they sent Kasheijage to
b. batweekeilé byarushengo kasheijage Byarushengo' ($P_2$)
c. batweekeile byarushengó kasheijage
d. *batweekeilé byarushengó kasheijage

(48a) represents the all-L tone realization we expect from a [–F] VU which has undergone (43) and which is followed by two toneless NP's. (48b) has the H tone FV we expect from the operation of rule (47). However, as seen in (48c), an alternative is to place the H on the last vowel of the first accentless NP complement. (48d) shows that it is unacceptable to place a final H on both the VU and the first NP. We have not investigated all of the logical contexts where (47), or some extension of it, may or may not apply. We have, however, determined that the application of this rule is fairly general. Thus, as a final illustration, consider the application of (47) before the adverb /ge/ 'well' in (49).

(49) /ba+mu+kom+a ge/ → bamukoma ge ~ bamukomâ ge
H H 'they tie him up well'

First rule (19) removes the H from the radical -kom-; then (43) removes the H of the FV. This is followed by the optional application of (47) which puts a H back on the FV of the VU. Rule (6a) converts this H to HL.

The last H modification rule to be discussed in this section is given in (50).

(50) $(\underset{H}{V})^{n}_{1}$ / // ____
⇓
o

All consecutive post-pause H toned vowels are deleted (cf. derivation in (70) below). This most frequently applies to the preprefix in nouns and the subject relative PI in verbs; e.g. /$\underset{H}{o}$#mu + ntu/ 'person' is realized [omuntu] after pause. The derivation in (51) shows the one instance we have found where more than one $\underset{H}{V}$ is affected by (50):

(51) a#a + li + a → a#a + li + a → a#a + li + a [alya] 'he who eats'
      H    H          H  H

The underlying form has a H on the PI and on the radical $\underset{H}{\text{-li-}}$ 'eat'. This latter H is first shifted on the preceded SM a- 'he' by rule (38). This creates a sequence of two $\underset{H}{V}$'s, both of which then reduce to $\mathring{V}$ by rule (50).

### *4.3 Syllable Structure Rules*

At this point rules which affect syllable structure apply. We shall consider two rules which affect the *number* of syllables. After these rules have applied, syllable structure is introduced. While it is possible to assume syllables from the beginning of the derivation, we have found no reason to do so.

The first rule fuses the -il-e tense/aspect extension with a preceding l or n which is either preceded by a VV sequence or is part of an extension (e.g. the applied extension -el-). Examples are seen in (52) from the $P_2$ tense.

| | | | |
|---|---|---|---|
| (52)a. | a+zaal+il+e<br>   H    H | → azáíle | 'she gave birth' |
| b. | a+zaan+il+e<br>        H | → azáine | 'he played' |
| c. | a+kom+el+il+e<br>   H      H | → akoméíle | 'he tied up for (s.o.)' |
| d. | ba+kom+angan+il+e<br>    H         H | → bakomangáíne | 'they tied each other up' |

When the vowel preceding the l or n is single, fusion does not take place:

(53)a. a + kol + il + e ⟶ akozíle 'he worked'
H H

b. a + gon + il + e ⟶ agonîle 'he snored'
H

c. a + bon + il + e ⟶ abóíne 'he saw'
H H

An exception is the radical -bon- (H) 'see', as seen in (53c), which undergoes fusion even though the radical consonant is preceded by a single vowel. Probably the best way to account for these facts is as formulated in (54).

(54) $_{R}[\ \mathrm{C\ X\ V\ l, n\ +\ il\ +\ e}\ ]_{VU}$ (where $X \neq \phi$)
$\ \ 1\ 2\ 3\ \ 4\ \ \ \ 5 6\ \ 7 \rightarrow$ $1\ 2\ 3\ 5\ 4\ \phi\ 7$

The second rule affecting the number of syllables is the process of y-deletion shown in (55).

(55) $y \rightarrow \phi\ /\ +\ C\ V\ +\ \_\_\_$

The segment y deletes whenever preceded by a CV morpheme (i.e. there can be no + between the C and the V, contrary to the usual situation).[22] Thus we observe the following:

(56)a. /a + yee + jun + a/ → ayeejúna 'he helps himself'
H H

b. /ba + yee + jun + a/ → beejúna 'they help themselves'
H H

Deletion does not take place in (56a) because the preceding morpheme a- does not consist of a CV. It does take place in (56b), where the preceding CV-morpheme ba- then coalesces with the reflexive marker (next paragraph).

Both rule (54) and (55) potentially create sequences of more than two V's, e.g. (52a) has an intermediate form azaaile (H), and (56b) has an intermediate form baeejuna (H). The following table, modified from Byarushengo (1977) illustrates the V (H) + V coalescence properties of Haya:

(57) $V_1 + V_2$ ⟶ (rows: $V_1$ ↓)

| | i | e | a | o | u |
|---|---|---|---|---|---|
| i | ii | ye(e) | ya(a) | yo(o) | — |
| e | ei | ee | aa | oo | — |
| a | ai | ee | aa | oo | — |
| o | oi | ee | aa | oo | — |
| u | ui | we(e) | wa(a) | wo(o) | — |

/u/ is not found second in a VV sequence. The parentheses in the first and last rows indicate a difference which depends on the presence vs. absence of a C preceding the vowel sequence: if a C is present, the vowel length is preserved (e.g. Ci-a → Cyaa);[23] if a C is not present, the vowel is lost (e.g. i + a → ya).[24] The only sequences of unlike vowels allowed are ei, ai, oi and ui, i.e. sequences where /i/ is the second vowel. Following Clements' (1981) treatment of Luganda, we present the necessary rules in a non-linear or three-dimensional framework (McCarthy 1979; Halle and Vergnaud 1980):

(58)a.

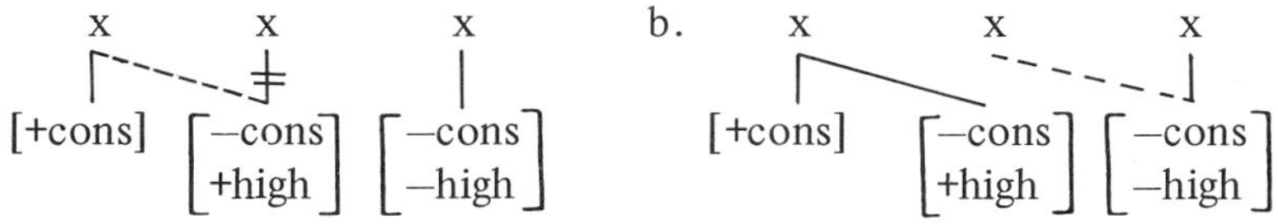


(59)a.

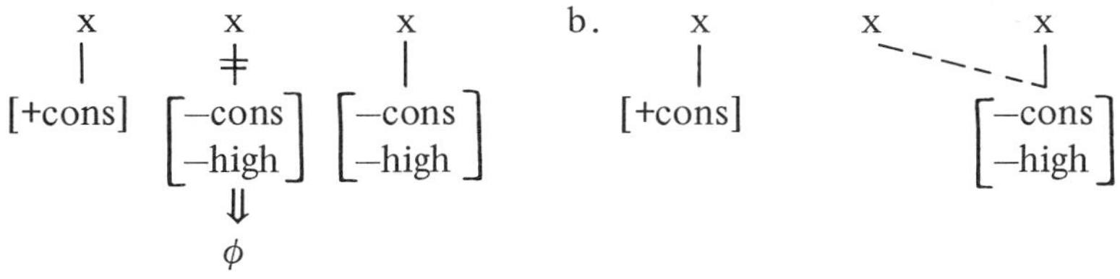


Departing from the above mentioned works, we replace the CV tier with a bare [+seg] specification or "x" to which segmental features are associated (and on the basis of which syllabification rules apply). In (58a) the [−cons, +high] features refer to /i/ and /u/, which reassociate with the initial [+cons] x. In (59a) the [−cons, −high] features refer to /e, o, a/, which delete when followed by another vowel. In (58b) and (59b) the features of the second vowel extend their association to the x left stranded by (58a) and (59a). It is this creation of like vowel sequences that must be blocked if the [−cons, +high] segment is not in turn preceded by a [+cons] segment. In this case we obtain i + a → [ya] and u + a → [wa], i.e. with a single vowel. We accept Steriade's (1982) proposal that a CV sequence will universally syllabify into an onset and nucleus. To this we add a Haya-specific rule that assigns /i/ and /u/ to the *onset* of a syllable when (a) preceded by #(#) and (b) followed by a [−cons, −high] segment. When preceded by a consonant, /i/ and /u/ are universally assigned to the rime of their syllable and are only later reassigned to the onset by rule (58a).[25] It will be noted that the gliding and deletion processes in (58) and (59) do not interfere with tone, since the tone bearing units, the x's, remain intact.[26]

It appears that syllable construction takes place in two stages: (a) within ## boundaries, and (b) across ## (and even %) boundaries. This assumption will simplify the tone rules to follow. In this context, a syllable is formed of an onset and as many V's as follow in sequence.[27]

*4.4 Tone Assignment Rules*

After such $(C)V_1^n$ syllables are constructed *within* words, the following two tone assignment rules apply:

(60)a. extend the association of a H tone to all V's within the same syllable;
b. assign a L to each *sequence* of remaining untoned (C)V's.

(60a) simplifies potential contour tones by effecting a one-to-many association of a H tone to all tautosyllabic contiguous vowels, as in (61).

(61)a.
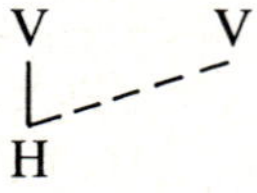

b.
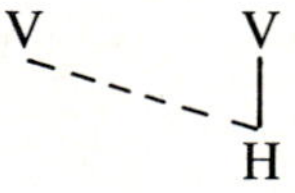


In cases of more than two V's in sequence, the H will undergo multiple associations. (60b) proposes to assign a *single* L to any stretch of untoned material. Thus, (62a) becomes (62b), not (62c).

(62)a. ba + ka + jun + a     'they helped' ($P_3$)
H
b. ba + ka + jun + a
H
L
c.*ba + ka + jun + a
H L L L

The arguments are mostly theoretical, since (62b) and (62c) would be pronounced identically. (62b) does represent, however, a more economical "default tone" assignment process than (62c), even for Haya.

*4.5 Tone Rules*

The remaining rules to be considered include (a) an optional tonal metathesis rule (not exemplified up to now); (b) tonal modifications before %; (c) lowering of H before pause; and (d) V-trimming.

Consider the following derivations:

```
(63)a. ni#ba+kom+angan+a mu            → nibakomangána mú. . .
                 (H)        H   H       'they are tying each other up in it'
    b. ba+ka+mu+jun+il+a e#N +bua    → bákamújuníl' embwá. . .
       H     H         H     H          'they helped dogs for him' (P3)
    c. ti#ba+mu+kom+e+il+e N +bua    → tibamukoméíle mbwá. . .
                (H)        H     H     'they didn't tie up dogs for him'
                                                                   (P2)
```

In each of the tonal outputs in (63) the italicized H tone is unaccounted for by the rules seen up to this point. (All forms are as pronounced when not occurring before %.) In (63a) a VU with a H tone FV is followed by a H tone enclitic $/m\underset{H}{u}/$ 'in it'; in (63b) a non-tonic FV is followed by a bisyllabic noun with a H tone preprefix and a final H tone vowel; and in (63c) a H tone FV is followed by a bisyllabic noun with a final H tone vowel. The generalization covering these three situations and others like them can be summed up as follows: whenever two syllables preceding a ## word boundary are both H toned (by (60a)), the H tone of the penultimate syllable becomes L and is anticipated on the preceding antepenultimate L tone syllable. In order for the rule to apply, there must, however, be a ## boundary also in the *penultimate* syllable:

(64)

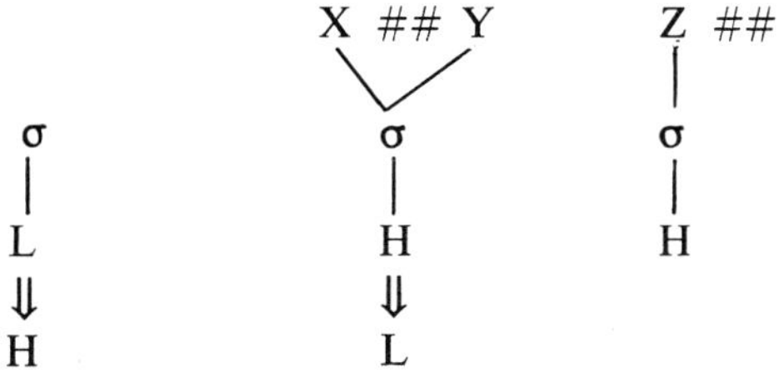


(where X can be $\phi$, or Y can be $\phi$, but not both)

This rule must apply after all of the tone reduction rules (e.g. (43)), since these may bleed (64). As written, (64) will guarantee that only mono- or bisyllabic words will ever satisfy the structural description of the rule. Because this rule must refer to syllables, we receive an important indication that syllable structure must be introduced by this stage. Also noteworthy about (64) is that it may remove the H from a preprefix internal to an utterance, as seen in (63). Finally, it can be seen in (65) that (64) also applies to appropriate noun phrases:

```
(65)a. bu + golo ki               →  bugólo kí . . . 'which snuff?'
                 H  H
    b. e #N + koni i + a e #N + bua →  enkoní y'embwá. . .
       H             H       H                  'the stick of the dog'
```

Rule (64) is either an optional rule or is characteristic of certain speech styles or dialects. Thus, while we were not able to determine what conditions the variants, the utterances in (63) and (65) can also be heard with the italicized H tone one syllable to the right.

The next tone rules required are the formal correlates to (6a) and (6b), which have been referred to numerous times in the discussion. These may be reformulated as in (66).

(66)

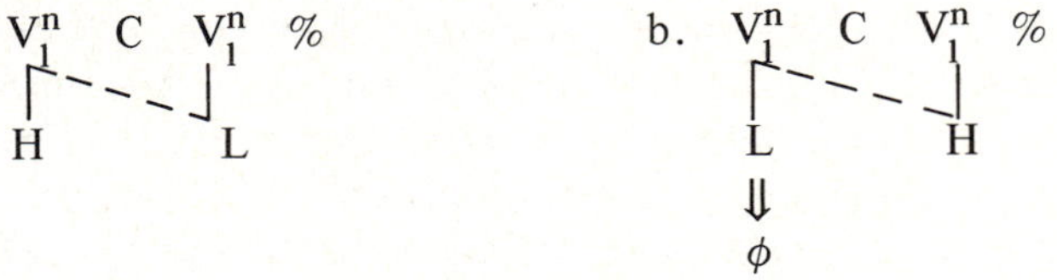


Another possibility would be to conflate the two rules as in (67).

(67)

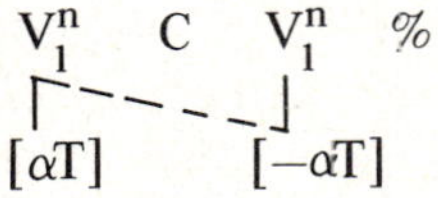


This formulation would require a subsequent LH rising tone simplification rule, duplicating part of the intent of (66b). Since contour simplification will have to apply in any case to the result of resyllabification across ## and % boundaries, (67) seems a viable alternative to (66a, b). We shall not further address this issue here, nor the surface adjustments necessary in the last stage of the derivation in (68).

(68)

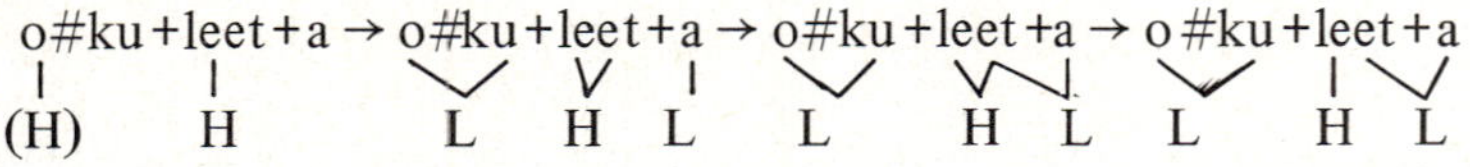


'to bring'

That is, rather than deriving *okuléêta*, where a H *and* L are associated to the second /e/, we obtain *okuléeta,* with H on the first and L on the second /e/, by the contour simplification rule just mentioned.

The final tone rule to be considered here is given in (69).

(69)

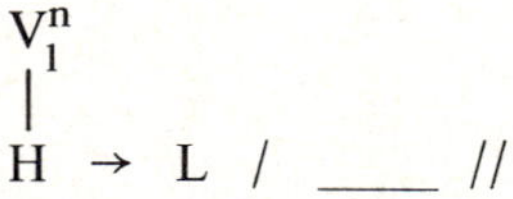


A H tone syllable becomes L before a pause. We now can give a complete derivation for the noun $/\underset{H}{e}\#N + bu\underset{H}{a}/$ 'dog':

(70)
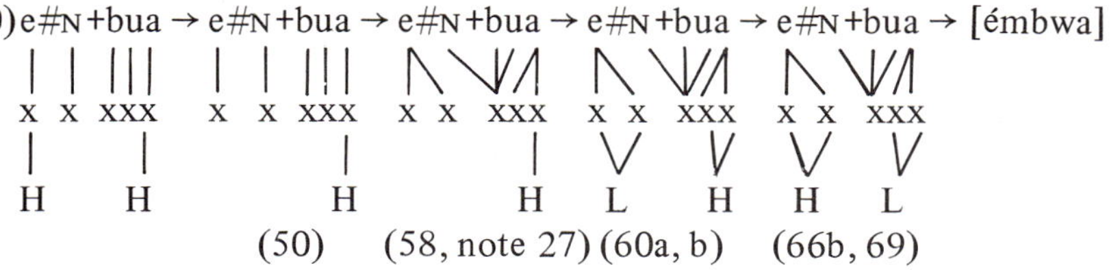


The underlying form is as given in the left-most column. The first rule which applies is (50), deleting the H of the preprefix vowel after pause. Then the segmental features reassociate according to rule (58) and the rule described in footnote 27. Tone assignment (60a, b) places a L on the first two x's and extends the H to both [−cons] x's of the second syllable. Then, rule (66b) derives H-H, which becomes H-L by rule (69).[28] Finally, a rule of V-trimming (Clements 1981) of the form in (71) applies:

(71)
$$V \rightarrow \phi \; / \; \underline{\quad\quad} \; V \quad \left\{ \begin{matrix} NC \\ V \\ // \end{matrix} \right\}$$

A VV sequence is shortened to V before either (i) an x which has a NC feature sequence associated to it; (ii) another V; or (iii) a pause. We have written this rule as a left-to-right rule which can apply more than once to a sequence (e.g. VVVV will become VV). In the last output of (70) we observe that *eembwaa* undergoes two parts of (71): trimming before a NC sequence and trimming before pause.

The rules characterizing syllable structure now reapply across word and phrase boundaries. In our earlier paper an attempt was made to do syllabification in one (late) stage, but this led to complications. The complications arising from our decision to isolate two syllabification processes are not dealt with in this paper.[29]

### *4.6 Fast Speech Rules*

There are certain rules that operate in fast speech which modify the segmental output of the preceding sections. These do not, however, affect the syllabic or tonal structure, and so are considered to be late, low-level rules. We shall consider two of these here.

The first concerns the optional rule in (72).

(72) $h \rightarrow \phi$ (optional and dialectal)

Any h may be deleted. That this rule must operate subsequent to all of the above tonal rules is seen in (73).

(73) a + hiNg + a → ahínga ~ aínga 'he exchanges'
H

The first variant, *ahínga*, is derived by applying rules (66b) and (69). The second variant differs only in the deletion of h by rule (72). This however creates a LH rising tone which is *not* subject to contour simplification. Thus it must be a very late rule.

The second rule concerns optional simplifications of grammatical morphemes of the shape -mu- and -ni-, which may be realized, respectively, as syllabic [m] and [N] (i.e. the latter, but not the former, assimilates in place of articulation to the following consonant):

(74)a. mu → m̩ b. ni → N̩

Thus, consider the optional variants in (75).

(75) ba-ka-mu-biNg-a → bákamúbinga ~ bákaḿbinga 'they chased him'
H H (P3)

The second pronounciation, resulting from (74a), creates a LH rising tone which, as in (73), is not subject to contour simplification. Thus, the changes represented in (74) must also have a low-level application.

## 5. CONCLUSION

In the above sections it has been argued that Haya (i) shares important properties with accentual languages not having tone, and (ii) fails to share other properties with tonal languages not having accent. First, H tones in Haya have a restricted distribution (at most one per morpheme) and are subject to reduction processes and shifting at a distance. They also interact with the focus system. Second, Haya fails to have tone spreading rules of the type dicussed by Hyman and Schuh (1974). Instead, it has anticipation conditioned by the % boundary in (66), a property characteristic of accent (cf. Becker 1978; Hyman 1978). We leave open the possibility that the final two syllables before a % boundary constitute a *foot*.

In an earlier version of this study we proposed to represent underlying tonal contrasts as contrasts between * and °. Asterisks were originally used by Goldsmith (1976a, b), Leben (1976) and Haraguchi (1977) to line up tones with tone bearing units – in "pitch accent" languages such as Japanese, as well as in stress-accent languages such as English. However, asterisks on tone-bearing units have been abandoned by some writers in favor of other devices for the mapping of intonational melodies in stress-accent languages (see, for example, Pierrehumbert 1980). Thus, the assumption that the asterisk notation provides a unified formal identity among all stress- and pitch-accent languages is open to question.

We claim that Bantu tone languages such as Haya, Luganda, Kinande, Digo, Makua etc. start out only with H tones. That is, the underlying opposition is H vs. °. Certain rules may apply to change some H tones to L, thereby creating a three-way opposition of H vs. L vs. °. The advantages of this system over the */° approach are not enormous in Haya, but appear as soon as other languages are taken into consideration. First, it can be noted that in Sukuma (Batibo 1976), a L which comes from an underlying H is *lower* in pitch than a L which, in this analysis, would come from underlying °. Thus, the default tone spelling rule will assign a kind of mid or neutral pitch level to °'s. Assigning L or M in a default tone spelling rule is not the only possibility. If in Tonga we started with underlying L vs. °, a rule would insert a H tone between L's. In Sukuma, where a H often appears two syllables to the right of its underlying position, it is possible to start with L vs. ° and have H inserted on the basis of the location of underlying L.

While the full range of variation and the potentials of this model are yet to be explored, it seems the most promising way of establishing parameters in tone and pitch-accent languages. The Eastern Bantu languages all start out with one underlying tone (usually H). The more tone-like languages such as Kikuyu assign the L to untoned vowels early; the more accent-like languages such as Haya assign the L to untoned vowels late. The two logical extremes would be, on the one hand, a language with all vowels specified for tone in the underlying forms and, on the other hand, a language with no tones specified underlyingly. As close approximations we can cite Yoruba and Somali. In the latter language there is only one H tone per word, which, according to placement rules, occurs either on a penultimate or final vowel (see Hyman 1981 and references therein). (Untoned vowels receive their non-high pitch, which scholars transcribe as L or M, but which should probably just be viewed as "neutral", by low-level detail rules.)

Note, finally, that this approach allows for the coexistence of tone and accent. The asterisk is available, for example, for stem accent, which may cooccur with tone (e.g. Kikuya, as described by Paulian 1975). If there are tone languages which, as Pulleyblank (1982) has recently proposed for Kimatuumbi, require accentual feet, the H designation can serve the same function as the * in other analyses. We believe that this approach will ultimately prove superior and more general in characterizing different tone and pitch-accent systems than the asterisk notation we originally adopted along with Goldsmith (1982).

NOTES

1. The present study represents the culmination of several years of thinking and rethinking of the Haya tone system. During this period we have had the opportunity to share our ideas with others and to receive invaluable feedback from the many people to whom we have subjected the Haya tone system. Most recently we have benefitted from discussions with Nick Clements, John Goldsmith and Will Leben, who provided comments on an earlier version of this study. All phases of research were conducted at the University of Southern California, and all data are based on the Kihanja dialect of Haya, as spoken by the second author. The first author has been supported by a National Science Foundation grant no. SOC75-16487 and a Guggenheim Fellowship; the second author has been supported by a scholarship from the University of Dar es Salaam. We gratefully acknowledge this support, without which the present study would not have been possible.

2. An unmarked nasal consonant in a NC sequence carries the same tone as the endpoint of the preceding tone, e.g. a H tone in *ekigúnju* 'animal' and a L tone in *olumbûmba* 'clay'. The one exception is when the nasal occurs initially in an utterance, In this case it is syllabic and carries a L if unmarked or a H if marked, e.g. *ḿbwá ki* 'which dog?', *mpúnú ki* 'which pig?'.

3. The apostrophe (') indicates that a vowel has been elided (here, the final vowel -a of the infinitive /$\underset{\text{H}}{\text{o}}$ #ku + $\underset{\text{H}}{\text{bon}}$ + a/ 'to see') and that the remaining vowel is lengthened.

4. As indicated, these rules apply after complete tonification (e.g. after assignment of L tones by (60b) ). See (66) and (67) for formal restatements of (6a, b).

5. In these and other examples, # indicates an internal word boundary, + a morpheme boundary, and – a grammatical boundary of either category. Note that the PI is separated from the VU by a # boundary because its H tone is exempt from the tone reduction process formulated below in (43). Rule (18) also does not apply if a # boundary intervenes between the two H tones. Finally, the PF is separated from the VU by *at least* a # boundary because it functions as part of the post-VU Z causing focus reduction in (43).

6. The forms given to the right of the arrow in (13) are as pronounced before pause. The non-prepausal pronounciations of (13c) and (13d) are *bakomilé*. . .and *bajuníle* . . ., i.e. with FV and $V_2$ H tones, respectively.

7. The reflexive morpheme has the allomorph [ee] in certain environments (see rule (55) ). Note that the tones of $\underset{\text{H}}{\text{-aa-}}$ and $\underset{\text{H}}{\text{yee-}}$ are motivated directly by their interaction with rule (18): $\underset{\text{H}}{\text{-aa-}}$ does not cause lowering of a following H, while $\underset{\text{H}}{\text{-yee-}}$ does. Furthermore, $\underset{\text{H}}{\text{-yee-}}$ does not itself undergo lowering when preceded by a H.

8. The presence of at least three vowels in the structural description of rule (20) indicates that there will be no change if there are only two vowels from the initial radical boundary to the end of the VU. When there is only a non-tonic -CVC- radical and a H tone FV, the FV is already the $V_2$. Since it carries its underlying H, there is no change and (20) does not apply.

9. Because of the forms in (26d), this H-L-H must be distributed by *syllable*: the final H is assigned to the final syllable, the L to the penultimate syllable and the remaining H to all preceding syllables. If we were to map tones to vowels, the forms in (26d) would come out **ń-déet-á múno* and **ń-dí-il-á múno*. These forms could not be claimed to undergo a simplification process to derive the correct output, since the general rules of Haya can only convert unacceptable HL contours to H. Thus we assume the correctness of syllable mapping.

10. It is too early to evaluate the proposal of Pulleyblank (1982) that Kimatuumbi – and perhaps other Bantu tone languages – have underlying accentual feet. It would be possible in Haya to construct a two-syllable foot before % which would then be subject to rules (6a, b). In this interpretation, the rules in (6) would be motivated not directly by the % boundary, but rather by the fact that the interacting syllables are *coupled* into a foot.
11. There may be a separate tonal morpheme marking in or out of focus in a "pure tone" language, thereby giving the impression of a possible counterexample to our claim. Such cases are not relevant, since what we are claiming for accent languages is an interaction between focus and *phrasing*, the surface manifestation of the latter being a tonal interaction between constituents.
12. A more dramatic example is Digo (Kisseberth, this volume), where the H may be distantly displaced onto a following word.
13. Other languages with an interaction between focus and tone include Luganda, Tonga, Bemba and Rundi. Tonal differences between "strong" vs. "weak" boundaries in these languages are a direct reflection of differences in focus.
14. The same development of a progressive form from prefixing the focus marker to a zero present tense is observed in Efik (Cook 1979).
15. This [+F] is a *morphological* feature and should be distinguished from any feature such as [+focus] which might mark a focused or asserted constituent. The latter feature in a transformational framework might correlate with syntactic movement rules and also serve as input to semantic interpretation. The feature specification [+F] is of morphological interest only, although it clearly derives from focus considerations. An alternative to the [+F] approach taken here might be establishing different boundaries between a [+F] VU and its complement(s) vs. a [–F] VU and its complement(s), e.g. a ## boundary reduces to # if the VU is [–F] (cf. Hyman 1982a, where a curious rule of this type is described for Luganda). The reduction rule would then apply to VU # COMP, but not to VU ## COMP (and corresponding structures in the noun phrase).
16. It is not hard to imagine contexts where the negation is not part of the assertion. Thus, if after someone has said 'John didn't eat an apple', we assert, 'no, John didn't eat a *pear*', the negation has been presupposed (i.e. the x such that John didn't eat x is a pear [ not an apple]). Cf. also the negative WH-question, 'what didn't John eat?', which presupposes that John didn't eat something. Negation is treated as intrinsically focused in Aghem (Hyman 1979) and many other African languages.
17. (32c) differs from the corresponding copular construction in tone only; cf. *ekikómbe kilúngi* 'the cup is beautiful'. Non-copular adjectives tend to occur with a preprefix.
18. In reality, we suspect that some of the T/A forms may have to receive their tonal properties together and as a whole, rather than by individual rules such as in (37). For example, the perstitive (Ps) always receives a ° SM, the T/A markers -ki-$\underset{\text{H}}{\text{a}}$a-, and a FV -a. In rules such as (37), where H is assigned to the FV and ° is the default specification, there is no one place where, for example, the FV of the Ps is specified as °.
19. The imperative FV and tones are somewhat complicated. The FV will be $\underset{\text{H}}{\text{-a}}$ if the imperative is singular (in which case there is no SM) and if there is no OM (except for the first person singular – see (26) ). It will be $\underset{\text{H}}{\text{-e}}$ if there is a SM (as in the second person plural imperative) but no OM, and it will be $\underset{\langle\text{H}\rangle}{\text{-e}}$ with polar tone (⟨H⟩) if there is an OM other than first person singular (whether or not there is a SM).
20. The reason why a H must be exceptionally assigned to a non-tonic radical is that

*all* verb forms show H on the FV in the $P_2$ negative (see forms in Appendix I). The same irregularity occurs in the Pf negative in Luganda, which is cognate with the Haya $P_2$ negative.

21. Alternatively, certain morphemes could be assigned a H when directly preceding the radical, but this would be considerably more complex to state (e.g. the SM would get such a H pre-radically only in relative clauses, etc.).

22. There are a few exceptional roots which must be marked so as not to undergo (55), e.g. $\underset{H}{a}$#ma + yaga 'dance (n.)', $\underset{H}{e}$#i + yengo 'wave', etc. It should be noted that there is also a rule which deletes y whenever it is followed by i. Thus, cf. *yógya* 'wash!', but *íta* 'kill!', from /$\underset{H}{\text{yit}}$ + $\underset{H}{a}$/. This underlying form is justified by the realization of /n + $\underset{H}{\text{yit}}$ + $\underset{H}{a}$/ 'I kill' as [ññíta]. Since the root -ntu of *omunto* 'person' has the realization [eñintu] 'tall slender people' in class 10, the underlying forms /$\underset{H}{o}$#mu + yintu/ and /$\underset{H}{e}$#N + yintu/ are motivated. An additional rule absorbs the i into the following NC complex.

23. The resulting double vowel may become shortened, however, before a NC sequences, another V or pause (see rule 71)).

24. In order for the rules to work out properly, it is necessary to assume that word-initial morphemes of the shape e- and o- are /i-/ and /u-/ underlyingly. This is required in the case of SM's. Thus, /u + $\underset{H}{\text{aa}}$ + $\underset{H}{\text{bon}}$ + a/ becomes *wáábôna* 'you saw' ($P_1$), but /u + $\underset{H}{\text{bon}}$ + $\underset{H}{a}$/ 'you see' becomes *obóna*. The rule that lowers /i/ and /u/ to [e] and [o] word-initially also affects forms such as $\underset{H}{o}$ + ku + gulu 'leg', which can be represented abstractly as /$\underset{H}{u}$ + ku + gulu/. We shall continue to indicate preprefixes as /e/ and /o/, the forms they take after this vowel lowering process.

25. A sequence such as [yaa] is however possible if the y is followed by an underlyingly double vowel, e.g. /i + $\underset{H}{\text{aa}}$ + $\underset{H}{\text{bon}}$ + a/ 'he saw' ($P_1$) is pronounced *yáábôna.*

26. The only possible problem with this statement would derive from a sequence of ## $\underset{H}{i}$ + a or ## $\underset{H}{u}$ + a, which would become $\underset{H}{\text{ya}}$ and $\underset{H}{\text{wa}}$ with something having to happen to the H now associated with a glide. Luckily such sequences do not occur in Haya since all [+high] +V+ morphemes having to undergo this rule are non-tonic.

27. The presence of NC complexes poses a potential problem. The facts are these: +N+ morphemes must be underlyingly syllabic, since they potentially carry a H (e.g. the OM -N- 'me', class 9/10 N-, etc.); otherwise, NC complexes are counted as single prenasalized consonants, i.e. internally to a morpheme as in -biNg- 'chase'. We represent the nasal morphemes as $\overset{N}{x}$ and the internal NC complexes as $\overset{NC}{x}$. As in Luganda (Clements 1981), there must be a rule which changes any V + N + C sequences to VV followed by a prenasalized consonant, e.g.

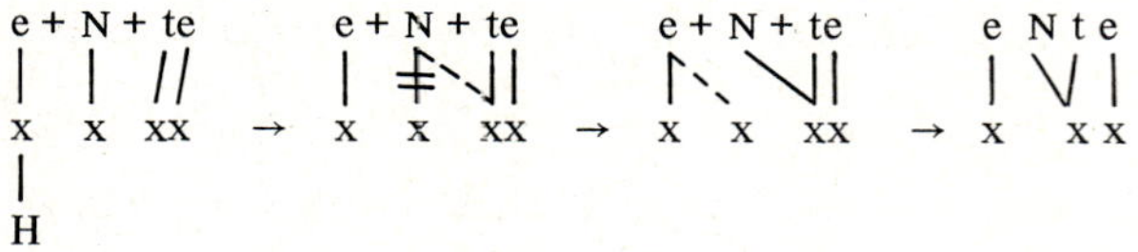


This procedure, which recognizes an intermediate *eente* which becomes *ente* by V-trimming (rule (71)), is restricted to the +N+ morphemes only (i.e. it does not apply to +CVNC+ morphemes because of derivations such as (14b)).

28. Note that the derivation in (70) demonstrates the rules (50) and (69), which lower post- and pre-pause H tone vowels cannot be collapsed as a mirror-image rule.

29. These complications include a few cases where rules (58) and (59) are not followed within a word, e.g. /ti#a + bon + a/ 'he doesn't see' is pronounced [tábona],
H H
not *tyáábona or even *táábona. Note also that [y] deletes following s and z within the same word (e.g. o-ku-si-a 'to grind' is pronounced *okusa*), but not across words
H
(e.g. o#bu + nyaasi ## o #bu is pronounced *obunyáasy'óbu* 'this grass').
H H H H

## APPENDIX I: HAYA VERB FORMS

In the following sections we provide representative Haya verb paradigms, which are organized as follows:

A. *By construction*
  1. Affirmative
    a. main clause
    b. subject relative clause
    c. object relative clause
  2. Negative
    a. main clause
    b. subject relative clause
    c. object relative clause

B. *By tense/aspect*
  1. O (present habitual)
  2. $P_1$ (today past)
  3. $P_2$ (yesterday past)
  4. $P_3$ (before yesterday past)
  5. PH (past habitual)
  6. $F_1$ (general and near future)
  7. $F_2$ (after tomorrow future)
  8. Pr (progressive)
  9. Pf (perfect)
  10. In (inceptive; 'to have (n)ever X'ed')
  11. Ps (perstitive; 'to be still X'ing')
  12. Sj (subjunctive)
  13. Im (imperative)

C. *By content*
  1. $\phi$ (bare verb form)
  2. OM (verb form + object marker -mu- 'him/her')
  3. Rfl (verb form + reflexive marker -yee- 'self')
H
  4. Rec (verb form + reciprocal extension -angan- 'each other')
  5. Comp (verb form + noun complement 'Kato' [a name])

With respect to the construction type (A), it will be noted that although main, subject relative and object relative clauses have different tonal properties in the affirmative, the three constructions follow a single tonal pattern in the negative. The subjunctive and imperative form (B.12-13) are given at the end of the paradigms, since they show fewer constructional distinctions than the other tense/aspects. The subject of all of the forms (except the imperative) is ba- 'they'. The H tone verb radical -$\underset{\text{H}}{\text{kom}}$- 'tie up' appears in the left column, while the non-tonic verb radical -jun- 'help' appears in the right column. Thus, the first five rows in the left column mean, respectively: (a) 'they tie up'; (b) 'they tie him/her up'; (c) 'they tie themselves up'; (d) 'they tie each other up'; and (e) 'they tie up Kato'. A tabular summary follows these forms.

*Important note:*
Forms are given with *surface* tones. Thus, it should be recalled that final phonetic H-L and HL-L derive, respectively, from underlying final vs. penultimate H tone. Morphological boundaries are indicated by hyphens, although they are imperfect in cases of coalescence and fusion, e.g. -angain-e derives from -angan-il-e.

1a. *Main Clause Affirmative* ('they tie/help')

| | | |
|---|---|---|
| O | ba-kóm-a | ba-jún-a |
| | ba-mu-kóm-a | ba-mu-jún-a |
| | b-ee-kóm-a | b-ee-jún-a |
| | ba-kom-angán-a | ba-jun-ángan-a |
| | ba-kom-a káto | ba-jun-a káto |
| $P_1$ | b-áá-kôm-a | b-áá-jun-a |
| | b-áá-mu-kôm-a | b-áá-mú-jun-a |
| | b-áá-yéé-kom-a | báá-yéé-jun-a |
| | b-áá-kóm-angan-a | b-áá-jun-angan-a |
| | b-aa-kom-a káto | b-aa-jun-a káto |
| $P_2$ | ba-kom-íl-e | ba-jun-îl-e |
| | ba-mu-kom-íl-e | ba-mu-jun-îl-e |
| | b-ee-kom-íl-e | b-ee-jun-îl-e |
| | ba-kom-angáín-e | ba-jun-ángain-e |
| | ba-kom-il-e káto | ba-jun-il-e káto |
| $P_3$ | bá-ka-kôm-a | bá-ka-jun-a |
| | bá-ka-mu-kôm-a | bá-ka-mú-jun-a |
| | bá-k-éé-kom-a | bá-k-éé-jun-a |
| | bá-ka-kóm-angan-a | bá-ka-jun-angan-a |
| | bá-ka-kóm-a káto | bá-ka-jun-a káto |
| PH | ba-a-kóm-ag-a | ba-a-jun-âg-a |
| | ba-a-mu-kóm-ag-a | ba-a-mu-jun-âg-a |
| | ba-a-yéé-kom-ag-a | ba-a-yéé-jun-ag-a |
| | ba-a-kóm-angan-ag-a | ba-a-jun-ángan-ag-a |
| | ba-a-kom-ag-a káto | ba-a-jun-ag-a káto |
| $F_1$ | ba-laa-kôm-a | ba-laa-jún-a |
| | ba-laa-mu-kôm-a | ba-laa-mu-jún-a |
| | ba-laa-yéé-kom-a | ba-laa-yee-jún-a |
| | ba-laa-kóm-angan-a | ba-laa-jun-ángan-a |
| | ba-laa-kom-a káto | ba-laa-jun-a káto |
| $F_2$ | ba-li-kóm-a | ba-li-jún-a |
| | ba-li-mu-kóm-a | ba-li-mu-jún-a |
| | ba-ly-ee-kóm-a | ba-ly-ee-jún-a |
| | ba-li-kom-angán-a | ba-li-jun-ángan-a |
| | ba-li-kom-a káto | ba-li-jun-a káto |

| | | |
|---|---|---|
| Pr | ni-ba-kóm-a | ni-ba-jún-a |
| | ni-ba-mu-kóm-a | ni-ba-mu-jún-a |
| | ni-b-ee-kóm-a | ni-b-ee-jún-a |
| | ni-ba-kom-angán-a | ni-ba-jun-ángan-a |
| | ni-ba-kom-á káto | ni-ba-jun-á káto |
| Pf | b-áá-kóm-il-e | b-áá-jun-il-e |
| | b-áá-mu-kóm-il-e | b-áá-mú-jun-il-e |
| | b-áá-yéé-kom-il-e | b-áá-yéé-jun-il-e |
| | b-áá-kóm-angain-e | b-áá-jun-angain-e |
| | b-áá-kóm-il-e káto | b-áá-jun-il-e káto |
| In | ba-lá-kom-il-e | ba-lá-jun-il-e |
| | ba-lá-mu-kóm-il-e | ba-lá-mú-jun-il-e |
| | ba-l-éé-kom-il-e | ba-l-éé-jun-il-e |
| | ba-lá-kóm-angain-e | ba-lá-jun-angain-e |
| | ba-lá-kom-il-e káto | ba-lá-jun-il-e káto |
| Ps | ba-ky-áá-kôm-a | ba-ky-áá-jun-a |
| | ba-ky-áá-mu-kôm-a | ba-ky-áá-mú-jun-a |
| | ba-ky-áá-yéé-kom-a | ba-ky-áá-yéé-jun-a |
| | ba-ky-áá-kom-angan-a | ba-ky-áá-jun-angan-a |
| | ba-ky-áá-kóm-a káto | ba-ky-áá-jun-a káto |

1b. *Subject relative clause affirmative* ('the ones/they who tie/help')

| | | |
|---|---|---|
| O | a-bá-kom-a | a-bá-jun-a |
| | a-ba-mu-kôm-a | a-ba-mú-jun-a |
| | a-b-éé-kom-a | a-b-éé-jun-a |
| | a-bá-kom-angan-a | a-bá-jun-angan-a |
| | a-ba-kom-a káto | a-ba-jun-a káto |
| $P_1$ | a-bá-á-kom-a | a-bá-á-jun-a |
| | a-ba-a-mu-kôm-a | a-ba-a-mú-jun-a |
| | a-ba-a-yéé-kom-a | a-ba-a-yéé-jun-a |
| | a-bá-á-kom-angan-a | a-bá-á-jun-angan-a |
| | a-ba-a-kom-a káto | a-ba-a-jun-a káto |
| $P_2$ | a-bá-kom-il-e | a-bá-jun-il-e |
| | a-ba-mu-kóm-il-e | a-ba-mú-jun-il-e |
| | a-b-éé-kom-il-e | a-b-éé-jun-il-e |
| | a-bá-kom-angain-e | a-bá-jun-angain-e |
| | a-ba-kom-il-e káto | a-ba-jun-il-e káto |
| $P_3$ | a-ba-a-kóm-il-e | a-ba-a-jun-îl-e |
| | a-ba-a-mu-kóm-il-e | a-ba-a-mu-jun-îl-e |
| | a-ba-a-yéé-kom-il-e | a-ba-a-yee-jun-îl-e |
| | a-ba-a-kóm-angain-e | a-ba-a-jun-ángain-e |
| | a-ba-a-kom-il-e káto | a-ba-a-jun-il-e káto |
| PH | a-ba-a-kóm-ag-a | a-ba-a-jun-âg-a |
| | a-ba-a-mu-kóm-ag-a | a-ba-a-mu-jun-âg-a |
| | a-ba-a-yéé-kom-ag-a | a-ba-a-yee-jun-âg-a |
| | a-ba-a-kóm-angan-ag-a | a-ba-a-jun-ángan-ag-a |
| | a-ba-a-kom-ag-a káto | a-ba-a-jun-ag-a káto |
| $F_1$ | a-ba-laa-kôm-a | a-ba-laa-jún-a |
| | a-ba-laa-mu-kôm-a | a-ba-laa-mu-jún-a |
| | a-ba-laa-yéé-kom-a | a-ba-laa-yee-jún-a |
| | a-ba-laa-kóm-angan-a | a-ba-laa-jun-ángan-a |

| | | |
|---|---|---|
| | a-ba-laa-kom-a káto | a-ba-laa-jun-a káto |
| $F_2$ | a-ba-lí-kom-a | a-ba-lí-jun-a |
| | a-ba-li-mu-kôm-a | a-ba-li-mú-jun-a |
| | a-ba-ly-éé-kom-a | a-ba-ly-éé-jun-a |
| | a-ba-lí-kom-angan-a | a-ba-lí-jun-angan-a |
| | a-ba-li-kom-a káto | a-ba-li-jun-a káto |
| Pr | a-ba-lí-ku-kôm-a | a-ba-lí-ku-jun-a |
| | a-ba-lí-ku-mu-kôm-a | a-ba-lí-ku-mú-jun-a |
| | a-ba-lí-kw-éé-kom-a | a-ba-lí-kw-éé-jun-a |
| | a-ba-lí-ku-kóm-angan-a | a-ba-lí-ku-jun-angan-a |
| | a-ba-lí-ku-kóm-a káto | a-ba-lí-ku-jun-a káto |
| Pf | a-b-áá-kóm-il-e | a-b-áá-jun-il-e |
| | a-b-áá-mu-kóm-il-e | a-b-áá-mú-jun-il-e |
| | a-b-áá-yéé-kom-il-e | a-b-áá-yéé-jun-il-e |
| | a-b-áá-kóm-angain-e | a-b-áá-jun-angain-e |
| | a-b-áá-kóm-il-e káto | a-b-áá-jun-il-e káto |
| In | a-ba-lá-kom-il-e | a-ba-lá-jun-il-e |
| | a-ba-lá-mu-kóm-il-e | a-ba-lá-mu-jun-il-e |
| | a-ba-l-éé-kom-il-e | a-ba-l-éé-jun-il-e |
| | a-ba-lá-kom-angain-e | a-ba-lá-jun-angain-e |
| | a-ba-lá-kom-il-e káto | a-ba-lá-jun-il-e káto |
| Ps | a-ba-ky-áá-kôm-a | a-ba-ky-áá-jun-a |
| | a-ba-ky-áá-mu-kôm-a | a-ba-ky-áá-mu-jun-a |
| | a-ba-ky-áá-yéé-kom-a | a-ba-ky-áá-yéé-jun-a |
| | a-ba-ky-áá-kóm-angan-a | a-ba-ky-áá-jun-angan-a |
| | a-ba-ky-áá-kóm-a káto | a-ba-ky-áá-jun-a káto |

1c. *Object relative clause affirmative* (owó . . . 'the one they tie/help for')

| | | |
|---|---|---|
| O | ba-kom-él-a | ba-jun-îl-a |
| | ba-mu-kom-él-a | ba-mu-jun-îl-a |
| | b-ee-kom-él-a | b-ee-jun-îl-a |
| | ba-kom-angan-íl-a | ba-jun-ángan-il-a |
| | ba-kom-el-a káto | ba-jun-il-a káto |
| $P_1$ | ba-a-kom-él-a | ba-a-jun-îl-a |
| | ba-a-mu-kom-él-a | ba-a-mu-jun-îl-a |
| | ba-a-yee-kom-él-a | ba-a-yee-jun-îl-a |
| | ba-a-kom-angan-íl-a | ba-a-jun-ángan-il-a |
| | ba-a-kom-el-a káto | ba-a-jun-il-a káto |
| $P_2$ | ba-kom-éíl-e | ba-jun-íil-e |
| | ba-mu-kom-éíl-e | ba-mu-jun-íil-e |
| | b-ee-kom-éíl-e | b-ee-jun-íil-e |
| | ba-kom-angan-ííl-e | ba-jun-ángan-iil-e |
| | ba-kom-eil-e káto | ba-jun-iil-e káto |
| $P_3$ | ba-a-kóm-eil-e | ba-a-jun-íil-e |
| | ba-a-mu-kóm-eil-e | ba-a-mu-jun-íil-e |
| | ba-a-yéé-kom-eil-e | ba-a-yee-jun-íil-e |
| | ba-a-kóm-angan-iil-e | ba-a-jun-ángan-iil-e |
| | ba-a-kom-eil-e káto | ba-a-jun-iil-e káto |
| PH | ba-a-kóm-el-ag-a | ba-a-jun-íl-ag-a |
| | ba-a-mu-kóm-el-ag-a | ba-a-mu-jun-íl-ag-a |
| | ba-a-yéé-kom-el-ag-a | ba-a-yee-jun-íl-ag-a |
| | ba-a-kóm-angan-il-ag-a | ba-a-jun-ángan-il-ag-a |

| | | |
|---|---|---|
| | ba-a-kom-el-ag-a káto | ba-a-jun-il-ag-a káto |
| $F_1$ | ba-laa-kóm-el-a | ba-laa-jun-îl-a |
| | ba-laa-mu-kóm-el-a | ba-laa-mu-jun-îl-a |
| | ba-laa-yéé-kom-el-a | ba-laa-yee-jun-îl-a |
| | ba-laa-kóm-angan-il-a | ba-laa-jun-ángan-il-a |
| | ba-laa-kom-el-a káto | ba-laa-jun-il-a káto |
| $F_2$ | ba-li-kom-él-a | ba-li-jun-îl-a |
| | ba-li-mu-kom-él-a | ba-li-mu-jun-îl-a |
| | ba-ly-éé-kom-él-a | ba-ly-ee-jun-îl-a |
| | ba-li-kom-angan-íl-a | ba-li-jun-ángan-il-a |
| | ba-li-kom-el-a káto | ba-li-jun-il-a káto |
| Pr | ba-lí-ku-kóm-el-a | ba-lí-ku-jun-il-a |
| | ba-lí-ku-mu-kôm-el-a | ba-lí-ku-mú-jun-il-a |
| | ba-lí-kw-éé-kom-el-a | ba-lí-kw-éé-jun-il-a |
| | ba-lí-ku-kóm-angan-il-a | ba-lí-ku-jun-angan-il-a |
| | ba-lí-ku-kóm-el-a káto | ba-lí-ku-jun-il-a káto |
| Pf | b-áá-kóm-eil-e | b-áá-jun-iil-e |
| | b-áá-mu-kóm-eil-e | b-áá-mú-jun-iil-e |
| | b-áá-yéé-kom-eil-e | b-áá-yéé-jun-iil-e |
| | b-áá-kóm-angan-iil-e | b-áá-jun-angan-iil-e |
| | b-áá-kóm-eil-e káto | b-áá-jun-iil-e káto |
| In | ba-lá-kom-eil-e | ba-lá-jun-iil-e |
| | ba-lá-mu-kóm-eil-e | ba-lá-mú-jun-iil-e |
| | ba-l-éé-kom-eil-e | ba-l-éé-jun-iil-e |
| | ba-lá-kom-angan-iil-e | ba-lá-jun-angan-iil-e |
| | ba-lá-kom-eil-e káto | ba-lá-jun-iil-e káto |
| Ps | ba-ky-áá-kóm-el-a | ba-ky-áá-jun-il-a |
| | ba-ky-áá-mu-kóm-el-a | ba-ky-áá-mú-jun-il-a |
| | ba-ky-áá-yéé-kom-el-a | ba-ky-áá-yéé-jun-il-a |
| | ba-ky-áá-kom-angan-il-a | ba-ky-áá-jun-angan-il-a |
| | ba-ky-áá-kóm-el-a káto | ba-ky-áá-jun-il-a káto |

2a. *Main clause negative* ('they do not tie/help')

| | | |
|---|---|---|
| O | ti-bá-kom-a | ti-ba-jún-a |
| | ti-ba-mu-kôm-a | ti-ba-mu-jún-a |
| | ti-b-éé-kom-a | ti-b-ee-jún-a |
| | ti-bá-kom-angan-a | ti-ba-jun-ángan-a |
| | ti-bá-kom-a káto | ti-ba-jun-á káto |
| $P_1$ | ti-bá-á-kom-a | ti-bá-á-jun-a |
| | ti-bá-á-mu-kôm-a | ti-bá-á-mú-jun-a |
| | ti-bá-á-yéé-kom-a | ti-bá-á-yéé-jun-a |
| | ti-bá-á-kom-angan-a | ti-bá-á-jun-angan-a |
| | ti-bá-á-kom-a káto | ti-bá-á-jun-a káto |
| $P_2$ | ti-ba-kom-íl-e | ti-ba-jun-íl-e |
| | ti-ba-mu-kom-íl-e | ti-ba-mu-jun-íl-e |
| | ti-b-ee-kom-íl-e | ti-b-ee-jun-íl-e |
| | ti-ba-kom-angáín-e | ti-ba-jun-angáín-e |
| | ti-ba-kom-il-é káto | ti-ba-jun-il-é káto |
| $P_3$ | ti-bá-á-kom-il-e | ti-bá-á-jun-il-e |
| | ti-bá-á-mu-kóm-il-e | ti-bá-á-mú-jun-il-e |

| | | |
|---|---|---|
| | ti-bá-á-yéé-kom-il-e | ti-bá-á-yéé-jun-il-e |
| | ti-bá-á-kom-angain-e | ti-bá-á-jun-angain-e |
| | ti-bá-á-kom-il-e káto | ti-bá-á-jun-il-e káto |
| PH | ti-bá-á-kom-ag-a | ti-bá-á-jun-ag-a |
| | ti-bá-á-mu-kóm-ag-a | ti-bá-á-muú-jun-ag-a |
| | ti-bá-á-yéé-kom-ag-a | ti-bá-á-yéé-jun-ag-a |
| | ti-bá-á-kom-angan-ag-a | ti-bá-á-jun-angan-ag-a |
| | ti-bá-á-kom-ag-a káto | ti-bá-á-jun-ag-a káto |
| $F_1$ | ti-ba-a-kôm-e | ti-ba-a-jún-e |
| | ti-ba-a-mu-kôm-e | ti-ba-a-mu-jún-e |
| | ti-ba-a-yéé-kom-e | ti-ba-a-yee-jún-e |
| | ti-ba-a-kóm-angan-e | ti-ba-a-jun-ángan-e |
| | ti-ba-a-kóm-e káto | ti-ba-a-jun-é káto |
| $F_2$ | ti-bá-li-kom-a | ti-bá-li-jun-a |
| | ti-bá-li-mu-kôm-a | ti-bá-li-mú-jun-a |
| | ti-bá-ly-éé-kom-a | ti-bá-ly-éé-jun-a |
| | ti-bá-li-kom-angan-a | ti-bá-li-jun-angan-a |
| | ti-bá-li-kom-a káto | ti-bá-li-jun-a káto |
| Pr | ti-bá-li-ku-kôm-a | ti-bá-li-ku-jun-a |
| | ti-bá-li-ku-mu-kôm-a | ti-bá-li-ku-mú-jun-a |
| | ti-bá-li-kw-éé-kom-a | ti-bá-li-kw-éé-jun-a |
| | ti-bá-li-ku-kóm-angan-a | ti-bá-li-ku-jun-angan-a |
| | ti-bá-li-ku-kóm-a káto | ti-bá-li-ku-jun-a káto |
| Pf | ti-bá-ka-kóm-il-e | ti-bá-ka-jun-il-e |
| | ti-bá-ka-mu-kóm-il-e | ti-bá-ka-mú-jun-il-e |
| | ti-bá-k-éé-kom-il-e | ti-bá-k-éé-jun-il-e |
| | ti-bá-ka-kóm-angain-e | ti-bá-ka-jun-angain-e |
| | ti-bá-ka-kóm-il-e káto | ti-bá-ka-jun-il-e káto |
| In | ti-bá-ka-kóm-ag-a | ti-bá-ka-jun-ag-a |
| | ti-bá-ka-mu-kóm-ag-a | ti-bá-ka-mú-jun-ag-a |
| | ti-bá-k-éé-kom-ag-a | ti-bá-k-éé-jun-ag-a |
| | ti-bá-ka-kóm-angan-ag-a | ti-bá-ka-jun-angan-ag-a |
| | ti-bá-ka-kóm-ag-a káto | ti-bá-ka-jun-ag-a káto |
| Ps | ti-bá-ky-áá-kôm-a | ti-bá-ky-áá-jun-a |
| | ti-bá-ky-áá-mu-kôm-a | ti-bá-ky-áá-mú-jun-a |
| | ti-bá-ky-áá-yéé-kom-a | ti-bá-ky-áá-yéé-jun-a |
| | ti-bá-ky-áá-kóm-angan-a | ti-bá-ky-áá-jun-angan-a |
| | ti-bá-ky-áá-kóm-a káto | ti-bá-ky-áá-jun-a káto |

2b. *Subject relative clause negative* ('the ones/they who do not tie/help')

| | | |
|---|---|---|
| O | a-ba-tá-kom-a | a-ba-ta-jún-a |
| | a-ba-ta-mu-kôm-a | a-ba-ta-mu-jún-a |
| | a-ba-t-éé-kom-a | a-ba-t-ee-jún-a |
| | a-ba-tá-kom-angan-a | a-ba-ta-jun-ángan-a |
| | a-ba-tá-kom-a káto | a-ba-ta-jun-á káto |
| $P_1$ | a-ba-tá-á-kom-a | a-ba-tá-á-jun-a |
| | a-ba-tá-á-mu-kôm-a | a-ba-tá-á-mú-jun-a |
| | a-ba-tá-á-yéé-kom-a | a-ba-tá-á-yéé-jun-a |
| | a-ba-tá-á-kom-angan-a | a-ba-tá-á-jun-angan-a |
| | a-ba-tá-á-kom-a káto | a-ba-tá-á-jun-a káto |

| | | |
|---|---|---|
| $P_2$ | a-ba-ta-kom-íl-e | a-ba-ta-jun-íl-e |
| | a-ba-ta-mu-kom-íl-e | a-ba-ta-mu-jun-íl-e |
| | a-ba-t-ee-kom-íl-e | a-ba-t-ee-jun-íl-e |
| | a-ba-ta-kom-angáín-e | a-ba-ta-jun-angáín-e |
| | a-ba-ta-kom-il-é káto | a-ba-ta-jun-il-é káto |
| $P_3$ | a-ba-tá-á-kom-il-e | a-ba-tá-á-jun-il-e |
| | a-ba-tá-á-mu-kóm-il-e | a-ba-tá-á-mú-jun-il-e |
| | a-ba-tá-á-yéé-kom-il-e | a-ba-tá-á-yéé-jun-il-e |
| | a-ba-tá-á-kom-angain-e | a-ba-tá-á-jun-angain-e |
| | a-ba-tá-á-kom-il-e káto | a-ba-tá-á-jun-il-e káto |
| PH | a-ba-tá-á-kom-ag-a | a-ba-tá-á-jun-ag-a |
| | a-ba-tá-á-mu-kóm-ag-a | a-ba-tá-á-mú-jun-ag-a |
| | a-ba-tá-á-yéé-kom-ag-a | a-ba-tá-á-yéé-jun-ag-a |
| | a-ba-tá-á-kom-angan-ag-a | a-ba-tá-á-jun-angan-ag-a |
| | a-ba-tá-á-kom-ag-a káto | a-ba-tá-á-jun-ag-a káto |
| $F_1$ | a-ba-ta-a-kôm-e | a-ba-ta-a-jún-e |
| | a-ba-ta-a-mu-kôm-e | a-ba-ta-a-mu-jún-e |
| | a-ba-ta-a-yéé-kom-e | a-ba-ta-a-yee-jún-e |
| | a-ba-ta-a-kóm-angan-e | a-ba-ta-a-jun-ángan-e |
| | a-ba-ta-a-kóm-e káto | a-ba-ta-jun-é káto |
| $F_2$ | a-ba-tá-li-kom-a | a-ba-tá-li-jun-a |
| | a-ba-tá-li-mu-kôm-a | a-ba-tá-li-mú-jun-a |
| | a-ba-tá-ly-ée-kom-a | a-ba-tá-ly-éé-jun-a |
| | a-ba-tá-li-kom-angan-a | a-ba-tá-li-jun-angan-a |
| | a-ba-tá-li-kom-a káto | a-ba-tá-li-jun-a káto |
| Pr | a-ba-tá-li-ku-kôm-a | a-ba-tá-li-ku-jun-a |
| | a-ba-tá-li-ku-mu-kôm-a | a-ba-tá-li-ku-mú-jun-a |
| | a-ba-tá-li-kw-éé-kom-a | a-ba-tá-li-kw-éé-jun-a |
| | a-ba-tá-li-ku-kóm-angan-a | a-ba-tá-li-ku-jun-angan-a |
| | a-ba-tá-li-ku-kóm-a káto | a-ba-tá-li-ku-jun-a káto |
| Pf | a-ba-tá-ka-kóm-il-e | a-ba-tá-ka-jun-il-e |
| | a-ba-tá-ka-mu-kóm-il-e | a-ba-tá-ka-mú-jun-il-e |
| | a-ba-tá-k-éé-kom-il-e | a-ba-tá-k-éé-jun-il-e |
| | a-ba-tá-ka-kóm-angain-e | a-ba-tá-ka-jun-angain-e |
| | a-ba-tá-ka-kóm-il-e káto | a-ba-tá-ka-jun-il-e káto |
| In | a-ba-tá-ka-kóm-ag-a | a-ba-tá-ka-jun-ag-a |
| | a-ba-tá-ka-mu-kóm-ag-a | a-ba-tá-ka-mú-jun-ag-a |
| | a-ba-tá-k-éé-kom-ag-a | a-ba-tá-k-éé-jun-ag-a |
| | a-ba-tá-ka-kóm-angan-ag-a | a-ba-tá-ka-jun-angan-ag-a |
| | a-ba-tá-ka-kóm-ag-a káto | a-ba-tá-ka-jun-ag-a káto |
| Ps | a-ba-tá-ky-áá-kôm-a | a-ba-tá-ky-áá-jun-a |
| | a-ba-tá-ky-áá-mu-kôm-a | a-ba-tá-ky-áá-mú-jun-a |
| | a-ba-tá-ky-áá-yéé-kom-a | a-ba-tá-ky-áá-yéé-jun-a |
| | a-ba-tá-ky-áá-kóm-angan-a | a-ba-tá-ky-áá-jun-angan-a |
| | a-ba-tá-ky-áá-kóm-a káto | a-ba-tá-ky-áá-jun-a káto |

2c. *Object relative clause negative* (owó . . . 'the one they do not tie/help for')

(Forms are identical to 2b. except the preprefix is absent, e.g. owó ba-ta-mu-kóm-el-a 'the one they do not tie him up for.')

3a. *Subjunctive clause affirmative* ('let him tie/help')

| | |
|---|---|
| ba-kóm-e | ba-jún-e |
| ba-mu-kôm-e | ba-mu-jún-e |
| b-éé-kom-e | b-ee-jún-e |
| ba-kom-angán-e | ba-jun-ángan-e |
| ba-kom-é káto | ba-jun-é káto |

3b. *Subjunctive clause negative* ('let them not tie/help')

| | |
|---|---|
| ba-tá-kom-a | ba-ta-jún-a |
| ba-ta-mu-kôm-a | ba-ta-mu-jún-a |
| ba-t-éé-kom-a | ba-t-éé-jún-a |
| ba-tá-kom-angan-a | ba-ta-jun-ángan-a |
| ba-tá-kom-a káto | ba-ta-jun-á káto |

4a. *Imperative singular affirmative* ('tie/help')

| | |
|---|---|
| kóm-a | jún-a |
| (+ OM = 3a.) | (+ OM = 3a.) |
| yéé-kom-e | yee-jún-e |
| kom-angán-a | jun-ángan-a |
| kom-á káto | jun-á káto |

4b. *Imperative negative, plural affirmative, singular affirmative with OM*
(Forms are identical with 3a. in affirmative or 3b. in negative.)

APPENDIX II: SEGMENTAL & TONAL MORPHOLOGY OF THE VERBAL UNIT

| | MAIN AFF. | MAIN NEG. | S REL AFF. | S REL NEG. | O REL AFF. | FOCUS |
|---|---|---|---|---|---|---|
| O | ba-R-a<br>H | ti-ba-R-a<br>H ⟨H⟩ | a-ba-R-a<br>H H | a-ba-ta-R-a<br>H H ⟨H⟩ | ba-R-a<br>H | –+–+–+ |
| $P_1$ | ba-aa-R-a<br>H | ti-ba-a-R-a<br>H H | a-ba-a-R-a<br>H H | a-ba-ta-a-R-a<br>H H H | ba-a-R-a<br>H | –+–+–+ |
| $P_2$ | ba-R-ile<br>H | ti-ba-R-ile<br>H H H | a-ba-R-ile<br>H H | a-ba-ta-R-ile<br>H H H H | ba-R-ile<br>,H | –+–+–+ |
| $P_3$ | ba-ka-R-a<br>H | ti-ba-a-R-ile<br>H H | a-ba-a-R-ile<br>H H ⟨H⟩ | a-ba-ta-a-R-ile<br>H H H | ba-a-R-ile<br>⟨H⟩ | ++–+–+ |
| PH | ba-a-R-aga<br>⟨H⟩ | ti-ba-a-R-aga<br>H H | a-ba-a-R-aga<br>H H ⟨H⟩ | a-ba-ta-a-R-aga<br>H H H | ba-a-R-aga<br>⟨H⟩ | –+–+–+ |
| $F_1$ | ba-laV-R-a<br>⟨H⟩ | ti-ba-V-R-e<br>⟨H⟩ | a-ba-laV-R-a<br>H <H> | a-ba-ta-V-R-e<br>H ⟨H⟩ | ba-laV-R-a<br>⟨H⟩ | –+–+–+ |
| $F_2$ | ba-li-R-a<br>H H | ti-ba-li-R-a<br>H | a-ba-li-R-a<br>H H | a-ba-ta-li-R-a<br>H H H | ba-li-R-a<br>H H | –+–+–+ |
| Pr | ni-ba-R-a<br>H | ti-ba-liku-R-a<br>H H | a-ba-liku-R-a<br>H H | a-ba-ta-liku-R-a<br>H H H | ba-liku-R-a<br>H | ++++++ |
| Pf | ba-aa-R-ile<br>H | ti-ba-ka-R-ile<br>H | a-ba-aa-R-ile<br>H H | a-ba-ta-ka-R-ile<br>H H | ba-aa-R-ile<br>H | ++++++ |
| In | ba-la-R-ile<br>H | ti-ba-ka-R-aga<br>H | a-ba-la-R-ile<br>H H | a-ba-ta-ka-R-aga<br>H H | ba-la-R-ile<br>H | ++++++ |
| Ps | ba-kiaa-R-a<br>H | ti-ba-kiaa-R-a<br>H | a-ba-kiaa-R-a<br>H H | a-ba-ta-kiaa-R-a<br>H H H | ba-kiaa-R-a<br>H | ++++++ |
| Sj | R–e / R–e<br>H ⟨H⟩ | | | ba-ta-R-a<br>H ⟨H⟩ | | + + |
| Im | R–a<br>H | | | (= Sj) | | + |

It should be noted that the object relative negative forms are the same as the subject relative negative forms, except that the PI vowel is absent. We shall use the following abbreviations for the five columns of forms: MCA, MCN, SRA, SRN, ORA and ORN (not shown). The +/– features in the last column refer to whether or not the respective column is [+F].

The assignment of H tones to the VU takes place as follows:

(i) PI: ni and ti are tonic, while the preprefix used in the SRA/SRN forms is tonic (lowered after pause, however, by rule (50)).

(ii) SM: Those consisting solely of a vowel (including the syllabic nasal) are always non-tonic. These include: n- '1st sg.', o- '2nd sg.', a- '3rd sg.', e- 'class 4, class 9'. The remaining SM's are CV in structure and are non-tonic except in the following cases: (a) immediately preceding the T/A marker -ka-; (b) all tenses in the MCN except $F_1$, $F_2$ and Ps; and (c) with the O and $P_2$ tenses in the SRA. The above table illustrates these tonal patterns with the SM ba- 'they' (class 2).

(iii) NEG: $\underset{\text{H}}{\text{-ta-}}$ is always tonic except in the $F_1$.

(iv) T/A: (a) $\underset{\text{H}}{\text{-aa-}}$ always occurs tonic on its first V (MCA $P_1$; Pf and Ps); (b) $\underset{\text{H}}{\text{-a-}}$ is tonic in MCN, SRA, SRN and ORN, but non-tonic in the ORA; (c) $F_1$ -là- and -V- are both non-tonic (the latter indicating the doubling of whatever vowel precedes it); (d) $F_2$ $\underset{\text{H}}{\text{-li-}}$ is tonic; (e) In $\underset{\text{H}}{\text{-la-}}$ is tonic; (f) Ps -ki- is non-tonic; (g) Pr -$\underset{\text{H}}{\text{li}}$-ku is tonic on its first vowel ($\underset{\text{H}}{\text{-li-}}$ is as in $F_2$, while -ku- is the infinitive prefix); and (h) -ka- is non-tonic.

(v) OM: The reflexive OM is tonic on its second vowel, i.e. -y$\underset{\text{H}}{\text{ee}}$-; all other OM's are non-tonic but may receive a H tone by rule (40). Recall also the irregular tonal behaviour of the 1st sg. OM in imperatives in (26).

(vi) R: A radical is either tonic or non-tonic on its first vowel; all subsequent vowels are non-tonic and are the equivalent of extensions in this regard.

(v) X: All extensions are non-tonic.

(vi) FV: The rules for assigning accents to FV's were given in (37). Those FV's marked ⟨H⟩ in the table receive a H only if the R does not have a H. In addition, the FV is either -a or -e. It is -e in the following cases: (a) in any verb form using the -il- past or perfect extension; (b) $F_1$ negative forms; and (c) subjunctives.

APPENDIX III: TONE PATTERNS OF NOUN + POSSESSIVE PRONOUN SEQUENCES

| *Noun* | *'my'* | *'your sg.'* | *'his/her'* | *'our'* | *'your pl.'* | *'their'* |
|---|---|---|---|---|---|---|
| ente | enté yange | enté yaawe | enté ye | ente yáitu | ente yáanyu | ente yáabo |
| *cow* | ente yange | ente yaawe | ente ye | ente yáitu | ente yáanyu | ente yáabo |
| | ent' éyánge | ent' éyááwe | ent' éye | ent' éyáitu | ent' éyáanyu | ent' éyáabo |
| émbwa | embwá yange | embwá yaawe | embwá ye | embwa yáitu | embwa yáanyu | embwa yáabo |
| *dog* | embwá yange | embwá yaawe | embwâ ye | embwá yáitu | embwá yáanyu | embwá yáabo |
| | embw' éyánge | embw' éyááwe | embw' éye | embw' éyáitu | embw' éyáanyu | embw' éyáabo |
| enkoni | enkoní yange | enkoní yaawe | enkoní ye | enkoni yáitu | enkoni yáanyu | enkoni yáabo |
| *stick* | enkoni yange | enkoni yaawe | enkoni ye | enkoni yáitu | enkoni yáanyu | enkoni yáabo |
| | enkony' éyánge | enkony' éyááwe | enkony' éye | enkony' éyáitu | enkony' éyáanyu | enkony' éyáabo |
| empúnu | empunú yange | empunú yaawe | empunú ye | empunu yáitu | empunu yáanyu | empunu yáabo |
| *pig* | empunú yange | empunú yaawe | empunû ye | empunú yáitu | empunú yáanyu | empunú yáabo |
| | empunw' éyánge | empunw' éyááwe | empunw' éye | empunw' éyáitu | empunw' éyáanyu | empunw' éyáabo |
| omwáana | omwáána wange | omwáána waawe | omwaaná we | omwaana wáitu | omwaana wáanyu | omwaana wáabo |
| *child* | omwáána wange | omwáána waawe | omwáána we | omwáána wáitu | omwáána wáanyu | omwáána wáabo |
| | omwáán' ówánge | omwáán' ówááwe | omwáán' ówe | omwáán' ówáitu | omwáán' ówáanyu | omwáán' ówáabo |
| omukâma | omukáma wange | omukáma waawe | omukamá we | omukama wáitu | omukama wáanyu | omukama wáabo |
| *chief* | omukáma wange | omukáma waawe | omukáma we | omukáma wáitu | omukáma wáanyu | omukáma wáabo |
| | omukám' ówánge | omukám' ówááwe | omukám' ówe | omukám' ówáitu | omukám' ówáanyu | omukám' ówáabo |
| omugóle | omugolé wange | omugolé waawe | omugolé we | omugole wáitu | omugole wáanyu | omugole wáabo |
| *bride* | omugolé wange | omugolé waawe | omugolê we | omugolé wáitu | omugolé wáanyu | omugolé wáabo |
| | omugol' ówánge | omugol' ówááwe | omugol' ówe | omugol' ówáitu | omugol' ówáanyu | omugol' ówáabo |
| omulimi | omulimí wange | omulimí waawe | omulimí we | omulimi wáitu | omulimi wáanyu | omulimi wáabo |
| *farmer* | omulimi wange | omulimi waawe | omulimi we | omulimi wáitu | omulimi wáanyu | omulimi wáabo |
| | omulimy' ówánge | omulimy' ówááwe | omulimy' ówe | omulimy' ówáitu | omulimy' ówáanyu | omulimy' ówáabo |
| enkúlungo | enkúlungó yange | enkúlungó yaawe | enkulungó ye | enkulungo yáitu | enkulungo yáanyu | enkulungo yáabo |
| *grinding* | enkúlungo yange | enkúlungo yaawe | enkúlungo ye | enkúlungo yáitu | enkúlungo yáanyu | enkúlungo yáabo |
| *stone* | enkúlung' éyánge | enkúlung' éyááwe | enkúlung' éye | enkúlung' éyáitu | enkúlung' éyáanyu | enkúlung' éyáabo |

*Notes:* 1. The three rows for each form refer, respectively, to (a) noun + possessive pronoun; (b) noun + $\phi$ copula + possessive pronoun; (c) noun + relative possessive pronoun, e.g. (a) 'my cow'; (b) 'the cow is mine'; (c) 'the cow which is mine'.

2. The third line of the 'his/her' forms can optionally have a H tone on the syllable immediately preceding the relative possessive pronoun, e.g. ént' éye, omulímy' ówe.

3. The first H tone in the first line of 'my' and 'your sg.' + 'grinding stone' can optionally be deleted.

*Chapter 4*

# Digo Tonology

Charles W. Kisseberth

## 1. INTRODUCTION

During 1979 I had the opportunity to collect a fairly substantial body of data on a restricted number of morphological forms and syntactic phrases in Digo (E. 73 in Guthrie's 1971 classification of the Bantu languages). The present study incorporates the results of my analysis of these data. This analysis must be regarded as preliminary and fragmentary for two reasons: first, there are no doubt other morphological forms and syntactic phrases as yet unexamined which would shed additional light on the phenomena dealt with here; second, the data are so complex as to make any detailed comparative examination of the various possible approaches to the data impossible in the space available here. As a consequence of this space limitation, I have opted for presenting one basic approach to the tonal pattern of Digo, without always giving due attention to competing approaches. This decision should not be misinterpreted as indicating that I do not consider the alternative approaches worthy of serious consideration. The tonal facts of Digo are, I believe,

* I would like to express my gratitude to the University of Illinois Research Board and to the African Studies Program of the University of Illinois for providing the funds that made possible this research on Digo tonology.
I would also like to thank the National Science Foundation, whose Grant No. BNS-7924523 greatly facilitated the writing of this paper. The data in this paper reflect the speech of Mr. Mfundo Jumaa Mfundo and were gathered while Mr. Mfundo was studying at the University of Illinois. I have not yet had the opportunity to compare his speech with that of other native speakers of Digo. I would like to express my deep gratitude to Mr. Mfundo for the enthusiasm and patience with which he assisted me in the study of his language.
I am also deeply indebted to Chin-Chuan Cheng, who has collaborated with me over the past few years on the study of Bantu tonology and who rechecked all of my transcriptions of the Digo material I collected. Finally, I would like to thank John Goldsmith and Nick Clements for their many comments and suggestions regarding the analysis of Digo; I have not always followed their suggestions, and in the end perhaps I will regret not having done so. But their encouragement has always been a stimulation to me.

extremely interesting and amply justify the existence of the present study, despite its preliminary and fragmentary nature.

I will attempt to establish that (a) the surface location of Digo pitch contrasts does not generally represent the underlying location of the contrasts - indeed, that while a pitch contrast may be realized phonetically in one word, its point of origin may be in a preceding word; (b) the difference between the surface and the underlying location of pitch contrasts is the result of the existence in Digo of several rules that *relocate* a high tone, moving it from its point of origin to some designated vowel later in the word or phrase; (c) there is evidence that at least two of the tonal principles of Digo must apply *cyclically;* and (d) the tone pattern of Digo is rendered highly opaque not just as a result of the rules that relocate high tones, but also because of various processes that simplify contour tones, spread a high tone from one vowel onto a preceding vowel, change a high tone into a low tone, etc.

## 2. POLYSYLLABIC VERB STEMS IN THE INFINITIVE

An examination of the infinitive form of the verb provides the best point of departure for any discussion of Digo tonology. The infinitive in Digo, as in many other Bantu languages, consists of a prefix *ku-* followed by the verb stem and the suffixal vowel *-a.* The verb stem is in a few cases entirely consonantal, but generally has one or more vowels in it. I shall restrict myself in this section to cases where there are at least two vowels in the stem. Between the *ku-* and the stem, an object prefix may occur. Initially, I shall ignore forms containing an object prefix, but later in the section I will examine the tonal properties of forms where an object prefix is present.

When polysyllabic verb stems in the infinitive are examined, one finds that three tonal patterns are possible, two of which can easily be seen to be superficial variants of a single fundamental type. There are thus just two basic tonal shapes for polysyllabic stems in the infinitive. In (1)–(3) I list a few examples of each of the three surface patterns.

| | | |
|---|---|---|
| (1) | ku-ambir-a | 'to tell' |
| | ku-changamuk-a | 'to be cheerful' |
| | ku-dekez-a | 'to spoil s.o.' |
| | ku-erek-a | 'to carry on the back' |
| | ku-gandamiz-a | 'to press, squeeze' |
| | ku-tsumbur-a | 'to unearth' |

| | | |
|---|---|---|
| (2) | ku-arŭk-â | 'to begin, start' |
| | ku-bomŏr-â | 'to demolish' |
| | ku-gongomě-â | 'to hammer' |
| | ku-furukŭt-â | 'to move restlessly' |
| | ku-sindĭk-â | 'to shut the door' |
| | ku-yakinĭsh-â | 'to confirm' |

| | | |
|---|---|---|
| (3) | ku-dunduríz-a | 'to place in reserve' |
| | ku-fukíz-a | 'to apply heat' |
| | ku-koróg-a | 'to stir' |
| | ku-kurúg-a | 'to smoothen by rubbing' |
| | ku-siríg-a | 'to rub' |
| | ku-tanyiríz-a | 'to drive off predators' |

Vowels that are unmarked for tone are pronounced with relatively low pitch, except that when such a vowel occurs in penultimate position (in the phrase) it will be pronounced with some falling quality. Penultimate vowels are also ordinarily lengthened to some degree, but I have not indicated this lengthening in my transcriptions. The symbol ´ indicates a high-toned vowel, the symbol ˇ indicates a vowel with a rising tone, and the symbol ˆ indicates a vowel with a falling tone. I use B to indicate a bilabial continuant that behaves like a sonorant.

The items in (1) are pronounced with relatively low pitch; the items in (2) have a rising tone on the penult vowel and a falling tone on the ultimate vowel; the items in (3) have a high tone on the penult vowel. The patterns exhibited in (2) and (3) are in complementary distribution; verb stems such as those in (3) always have a voiced obstruent following the penult vowel, whereas verb stems such as those in (2) either have no consonant following the penult vowel or a consonant that is not a voiced obstruent. The verbs in (1), on the other hand, show no restrictions as to what follows the penult vowel. I assume, therefore, that the examples in (1) represent one basic tonal type, and that the examples in (2) and (3) represent a second basic tonal type. I shall show below that there is a great deal more evidence for identifying the tone patterns in (2) and (3) as instances of a single basic type than just the fact that these two superficially different patterns are in complementary distribution.

There is no doubt but that these two basic tonal types in Digo are reflexes of the Proto-Bantu tonal system. In Proto-Bantu there was a tonal contrast in verb stems only on the first vowel of the stem, that vowel being either high- or low-toned. Let me refer to verb stems having a high-toned first vowel as "high-toned verbs" and verb stems having a low-toned first vowel as "low-toned verbs". Examination of Guthrie's comparative Bantu materials (Guthrie 1967-71) and the "starred forms" that he constructs (which for my present purposes I will regard as approximations of Proto-Bantu sounds, though Guthrie himself does not regard the symbols used in his starred forms as representing the pronunciation of the items in the protolanguage) reveals a systematic relationship between Proto-Bantu tones and the Digo tonal patterns. Polysyllabic Digo stems having the pitch pattern of (1) regularly correspond to low-toned verbs in Proto-Bantu, while polysyllabic stems having the pitch patterns of (2) and (3) regularly correspond to high-toned verbs in Proto-Bantu. The data in (4) and (5) exemplify this point. Note that in Guthrie's starred forms ` indicates a low tone.

| | | | | |
|---|---|---|---|---|
| (4) | *Guthrie's starred form* | | *Digo infinitive* | |
| | *-gàmb- | 'speak' | ku-ambir-a | 'to tell' |
| | *-gàduk- | 'turn *intr.*' | ku-garuk-a | 'to turn *intr.*' |
| | *-dàmuk- | 'wake up *intr.*' | ku-ramuk-a | 'to wake up *intr.*' |
| | *-dàgud- | 'practice medicine' | ku-ragur-a | 'to treat medically' |
| | *-còmud- | 'pull out' | ku-tsomor-a | 'to pull, draw out' |
| | *-cààgud- | 'choose' | ku-tsagur-a | 'to choose' |
| | *-cààkad- | 'become worn out' | ku-tsakar-a | 'to become worn out' |

| | | | | |
|---|---|---|---|---|
| (5) | *Guthrie's starred form* | | *Digo infinitive* | |
| | *-kódud- | 'cough' | ku-korǒr-â | 'to cough' |
| | *-kádaŋg- | 'fry; roast' | ku-karǎng-â | 'to fry' |
| | *-kúmbat- | 'hold in arm' | ku-kumbatǐy-â | 'to embrace' |
| | *-pápat-/ pápaṭi- | 'touch; grope' | ku-BaBǎs-â | 'to touch, grope' |
| | *-yánik- | 'spread to dry' | ku-anǐk-â | 'to put in sun to dry' |
| | *-kṹnik- | 'cover' | ku-fwinǐk-â | 'to cover' |
| | *-búdag- | 'kill' | ko-orág-a | 'to kill' |

We have seen that the present-day contrast in Digo between verb stems such as those in (1) and those in (2)–(3) is derivable from the historical contrast between low- and high-toned verb stems in Proto-Bantu (where the locus of this contrast was on the first vowel of the stem). The pitch contrasts in Digo infinitives are located phonetically (primarily) on the penultimate vowel of the word. Does this difference in location reflect a fundamental reorganization of the tone system from Proto-Bantu to Digo? I do not think so. I shall argue instead that the tone contrasts in Digo infinitives must be located underlyingly on a vowel earlier in the word than the penult – indeed, I shall ultimately suggest that there is some reason to believe that the contrast is located on the first stem vowel, just as in Proto-Bantu.

One piece of evidence favoring this view is that the verbal *root* determines the tone pattern of the infinitive, even when it is a non-root vowel that occurs in the penult and phonetically carries the tonal contrast. Consider the examples in (6) and (7).

| | | | | |
|---|---|---|---|---|
| (6) | ku-vugur-a | 'to untie' | ku-vugurir-a | 'to untie for/with' |
| | ku-rongoz-a | 'to lead' | ku-rongozer-a | 'to lead for/with' |
| | ku-tsukur-a | 'to carry' | ku-tsukurir-a | 'to carry for/with' |

| | | | | |
|---|---|---|---|---|
| (7) | ku-fwinǐk-â | 'to cover' | ku-fwinikǐr-â | 'to cover for/with' |
| | ku-bundúg-a | 'to pound' | ku-bundugǐr-â | 'to pound for/with' |
| | ku-ezěk-â | 'to thatch' | ku-ezekěr-â | 'to thatch for/with' |

These examples show that the addition of a derivational suffix (or "extension", to use the terminology of Bantuists) such as *-ir-/-er-* 'for/with' to a verb stem does not alter the over-all tonal pattern exhibited by that verb. If the unextended verb has the low pattern, the extended verb will be in the low pattern (cf. (6)); if the unextended verb has the high pattern, the extended verb will be in the high pattern (cf. (7)). The verb root determines the tone pattern of the infinitive, not the extension, even though it is the extension vowel that is the phonetic locus of the tonal contrast.

It might be noted at this point that the data in (7) represent further evidence that the two surface tonal shapes represented by *ku-fwinǐk-â* and *ku-bundúg-a* are in fact variants of the same fundamental pattern. Given that it is the verbal root that determines the tonal shape of the infinitive, notice that when *ku-bundúg-a* is extended by the suffix *-ir-,* the result is *ku-bundugǐr-â.* Although *ku-bundúg-a* has, on the surface, a level high tone on the penult vowel, and *ku-bundugǐr-â* has a rising-falling pattern over the final two vowels, this difference follows from the fact that the post-penult consonant in the former case is a voiced obstruent and in the latter case is not a voiced obstruent. The parallelism between *ku-fwinikǐr-â* and *ku-bundugǐr-â* provides support for the claim that /fwinik/ and /bundug/ are verbs of the same fundamental type.

In (6) and (7) we have examples where a single extension follows the verb root. In (8) I show that the same facts can be observed when two extensions follow the verb root.

| | | |
|---|---|---|
| (8) | ku-kwaruz-a | 'to scratch' |
| | ku-kwaruzir-a | 'to scratch for/with' |
| | ku-kwaruziran-a | 'to scratch for one another' |
| | ku-chekěch-â | 'to sift' |
| | ku-chekechěr-â | 'to sift for/with' |
| | ku-chekecherǎn-â | 'to sift for one another' |

The reciprocal extension *-an-* may be combined with the *-ir-/-er-* extension, as illustrated by *ku-kwaruziran-a* and *ku-chekecherăn-â*. The vowel of the reciprocal extension is the phonetic locus of the contrast in these two forms, but the source of the difference must reside in the fact that /kwaruz/ and /chekech/ are representatives of two distinct tonal types. In these examples the reciprocal extension is separated from the verb root by another extension, but this fact does not in any way alter the situation: the verbal root determines the phonetic realization of the penult vowel, even if that penult vowel is part of an extension that is separated from the root by another extension.

Additional evidence that tonal contrasts in Digo that are phonetically associated with the penult vowel are underlyingly located elsewhere is provided by infinitive forms that contain an object prefix. The examples in (9) illustrate this point.

| | | |
|---|---|---|
| (9) | ku-vugurir-a | 'to untie for' |
| | ku-ni-vugurir-a | 'to untie for me' |
| | ku-ku-vugurir-a | 'to untie for you sg.' |
| | ku-mu-vugurir-a | 'to untie for him/her' |
| | ku-u-vugurǐr-â | 'to untie for us' |
| | ku-a-vugurǐr-â | 'to untie for you pl./them' |

As I have shown earlier, the stem /vugur/ is one that triggers the low pattern. The addition of the singular human object prefixes *-ni-* 'me', *-ku-* 'you sg.', and *-mu-* 'him/her' does not alter the surface tonal shape of the word. But the addition of the plural human object prefixes *-u-* 'us' and *-a-* 'you pl./them' causes the low pattern to be replaced by the high pattern. The tonal difference between *ku-vugurir-a* and *ku-u-vugurǐr-â* clearly resides in the object prefix found in the latter example rather than in the penultimate vowel which is the superficial bearer of the contrast.

The paradigm in (10) is, I would claim, entirely parallel to that in (9).

| | | |
|---|---|---|
| (10) | ku-raBiz-a | 'to insult' |
| | ku-ni-raBiz-a | 'to insult me' |
| | ku-ku-raBiz-a | 'to insult you sg.' |
| | ku-mu-raBiz-a | 'to insult him/her' |
| | ku-u-raBíz-a | 'to insult us' |
| | ku-a-raBíz-a | 'to insult you pl./them' |

The difference between *ku-u-vugurǐr-â* and *ku-u-raBíz-a* is, once again, to be attributed to the fact that the post-penult consonant in the former case is not a voiced obstruent while in the latter case it is a voiced obstruent. These examples thus provide further evidence that the different tonal shapes illustrated in (2) and (3) above are variants of the same fundamental tonal type. For it is only this assumption that allows us to claim that the object prefixes *-u-* and *-a-* produce the *same* tonal change in (9) and (10).

We have seen so far that certain verbal roots (e.g. /fwinik/ and /chekech/) and certain object prefixes (e.g. *-u-* and *-a-*) are alike in that when they are present in an infinitival form, that form is characterized by either a rising-falling pattern over the last two vowels or else a level high tone on the penult (the choice between the two patterns being a function of the nature of the post-penult consonant). Furthermore, we have seen that the verb roots that trigger these patterns regularly correspond to high-toned verbs in Proto-Bantu. It should be noted that in a number of Bantu languages, the plural human object prefixes cognate with Digo *-u-* and *-a-* are high-toned whereas the singular human object prefixes cognate with Digo *-ni-*, *-ku-*, and *-mu-* are low-toned. Thus it seems reasonable to conclude that the Digo tone patterns in question are, from an historical point of view, the direct consequence of the presence of a high tone either on the verb root or on an object prefix. I will therefore refer to the pitch patterns of (2) and (3) as the "high" pattern, and I will refer to the roots and prefixes that trigger this pattern as "high" roots and "high" prefixes. I will refer to the pattern of (1) as the "low" pattern, and I will refer to the roots and prefixes that trigger this pattern as "low" roots and "low" prefixes.

Further support for associating the surface pitch contrasts found on the penultimate vowel with an underlying tonal contrast located elsewhere in the word is provided by an examination of the present tense paradigm in Digo. I will restrict my attention at the present time to the present tense paradigm of low-toned verb roots. (11) illustrates the paradigm.

| | | |
|---|---|---|
| (11) | ku-togor-a | 'to praise' |
| | ni-na-togor-a | 'I am praising' |
| | u-na-togor-a | 'you sg. are praising' |
| | a-na-togŏr-â | 'he/she is praising' |
| | tu-na-togor-a | 'we are praising' |
| | mu-na-togor-a | 'you pl. are praising' |
| | ma-na-togŏr-â | 'they are praising' |

Examination of (11) reveals that present tense forms of verbs such as /togor/ are pronounced with the low tone pattern when the subject is first or second person, but with the high tone pattern when the subject is third person. The shift from the low to the high pattern thus is clearly associated with the third person subject prefix rather than with the penultimate vowel – even though the penultimate vowel is the primary locus of the contrast between the two tonal patterns. This, then, is another instance where the underlying source of the superficial tonal contrast is shown to reside earlier in the word than the penult vowel. It should be noted that in a number of Bantu languages one can find cases where a third person subject prefix bears a high tone whereas first and second person subject prefixes are low-toned. Thus it seems reasonable to conclude that from an historical point of view the pitch pattern observed in *a-na-togŏr-â* is to be seen as the consequence of a high-toned vowel in the word.

The present tense paradigm provides additional evidence that the two pitch patterns exhibited in (2) and (3) are best regarded as superficial variants of a single basic tonal type. Consider the examples in (12).

| | | | |
|---|---|---|---|
| (12) | a. | ni-na-vugur-a | 'I am untying' |
| | | a-na-vugŭr-â | 'he is untying' |
| | | ni-na-Bukus-a | 'I am shelling corn' |
| | | a-na-Bukŭs-â | 'he is shelling corn' |
| | | ni-na-ramuk-a | 'I am waking up' |
| | | a-na-ramŭk-â | 'he is waking up' |
| | b. | ni-na-raBiz-a | 'I am insulting' |
| | | a-na-raBíz-a | 'he is insulting' |
| | | ni-na-gandamiz-a | 'I am pressing' |
| | | a-na-gandamíz-a | 'he is pressing' |
| | | ni-na-onjerez-a | 'I am adding to' |
| | | a-na-onjeréz-a | 'he is adding to' |

In (12a) the third person subject prefix triggers the pitch pattern of (2) while in (12b) the same prefix triggers the pitch pattern of (3). By analyzing (2) and (3) as variants of a single tonal type, we can claim that the third person subject prefix triggers the *same* tonal change in all forms. The third person forms in (12a) have the rising-falling pitch pattern because the post-penult consonant is not a voiced obstruent, while the third person forms in (12b) have the level high pattern on the penult vowel because the post-penult consonant is a voiced obstruent.

I have now given three arguments to the effect that a pitch feature associated with the penult vowel is properly to be attributed to a morphological element that does not in fact (necessarily) occur in the penult position. This morphological element may be the verb root, an object prefix, or a subject prefix. I have furthermore suggested that these elements were (at some earlier stage of the language) high-toned. Viewed from an historical perspective, then, what has happened is that a high tone earlier in the word has been *displaced* to later in the word. The issue that we must now turn to is the following: what is the best treatment of Digo tonology from a synchronic point of view?

Two analyses suggest themselves. The first analysis - call it the phonological analysis - claims that the elements in question (verb roots such as /fwinik/, object prefixes such as /u/ and /a/, third person subject prefixes /a/ and /ma/ in the present tense) have associated with them in underlying structure a high tone. A rule of High Tone Displacement must apply, then, to reassociate these high tones with a vowel later in the word (up to this point, it would appear to be the penult vowel - but I shall ultimately hypothesize it to be the ultimate vowel). This displaced high tone will eventually be realized either as a rising-falling pattern over the last two vowels of the word, or as a level high tone on the penult, depending on the nature of the post-penult consonant. The second analysis – call it the diacritic analysis - would associate a diacritic feature with the morphological elements in question and then assign a high tone to the last vowel (or penult, depending on one's analysis) of any word containing one of these diacritically-marked morphemes. In such an analysis we would have a diacritically-induced high tone assignment rule instead of a high tone displacement rule. Under both analyses, words which have no high tone or no diacritic (as the case may be) will have a low tone assigned to each vowel, except that the penult will be assigned a mid-falling tone when the word is phrase-final.

I prefer the phonological analysis to the diacritic analysis for the simple reason that I prefer to account for phonetic contrasts in terms of phonological rather than diacritical contrasts, especially when there is a direct relationship between the postulated phonological contrast and the phonetic facts. In the data so far presented, the high tone postulated by the phonological analysis is realized either as a level high tone (as in *ku-bundúg-a*) or as a sequence of rising and falling tones (as in *ku-fwinĭk-â*). As more and more data are examined, I will show that the level high tone manifestation of underlying high tones is in fact the usual case and that the rising-falling manifestation is a consequence of a very simple, natural rule. Thus there is a direct correlation between underlying high tone and surface high tone (although their *location* differs). I will not discuss the diacritic analysis here, but I believe that the data analyzed throughout this study present insurmountable problems for a diacritic solution.

Let us look more closely at the phonological analysis. I shall assume an essentially autosegmental approach to Digo tonology where the tones are represented on a tier parallel to but independent of the tier containing the segments which bear the tones; these two tiers are connected by means of association lines linking the tones and the tone-bearing segments. These association lines may or may not be present in the underlying structure, but they must be present in the surface representation. Furthermore, they must conform to a universal set of Well-formedness Conditions (e.g. association lines must not cross, every tone-bearing unit must be associated with at least one tone, every tone must be associated with at least one tone-bearing unit), though it is of course by no means settled what these well-formedness conditions are in detail (for some discussion see Chapter 1). Association lines may be supplied by language-particular rules or by universal principles of tone association. The precise nature of these universal principles of tone association, and the point or points in the derivation where they apply, are not discussed here. It should be noted that within the autosegmental approach, a single tone may be associated with more than one tone-bearing unit, and a single tone-bearing unit may be associated with more than one tone.[1]

When one attempts to apply this framework to Digo, certain points are rather clear while others are quite murky. It is clear that certain morphemes must have a high tone associated with them in underlying structure (though it is not clear whether that high tone is associated with a particular vowel of the morpheme or not). Furthermore, it is clear that this high tone must, in the course of the derivation, come to be associated with a vowel that is not (necessarily) part of the morpheme with which the high tone is underlyingly associated. We can assume, therefore, that Digo has a language-specific rule of tone association - call it High Tone Displacement - which adds an association line between a high tone and some designated vowel. Which vowel? At first glance, it would appear most likely to be the penultimate vowel of the word - cf. *ku-dunduríz-a,* where the penult vowel has a level high tone and all the remaining vowels of the word are low-toned. However, I am going to ultimately argue that High Tone Displacement in fact associates a high tone with the ultimate vowel of the word rather than the penultimate. The crucial evidence for this hypothesis comes from the phrasal tonology, which will not be examined until later in the paper; I will simply assume, for now, the reasonableness of having High Tone Displacement associate a high tone with the ultimate vowel. Given such a formulation of High Tone Displacement, we will need to explain (a) why this ultimate high tone gets realized phonetically as a rising-falling pattern in examples such as *ku-fwinǐk-â* and (b) why this ultimate high does not appear in *ku-dunduríz-a* but instead a high tone appears on the penult vowel.

Before I can begin to address the problem of accounting for the pitch patterns exhibited by *ku-fwinǐk-â* and *ku-dunduríz-a,* another problematic aspect of an autosegmental analysis of Digo must be confronted. Given that certain morphemes have a high tone associated with them underlyingly, what about the remaining morphemes? Do they have a low tone associated with them, or do they simply lack any tonal specification? The issue here is whether one needs to have low tones associated with roots such as /tsumbur/ and grammatical affixes such as the infinitive prefix /ku-/, the present tense prefix /-na-/, and the 1 sg. object prefix /-ni-/ in order to explain the appearance of low-toned syllables in words such as *ku-tsumbur-a, a-na-vugǔr-â, ku-dundurǐz-a,* etc. (the morphemes that I earlier referred to as "low-toned" morphemes), or whether the low-toned syllables in these words can be derived without having recourse to underlying low tones associated with the so-called low-toned morphemes.

I will attempt to show that an analysis which involves underlying low tones for /tsumbur/, /ku-/, etc., is by no means necessary and even represents a complication for the analysis. The evidence will, however, only gradually emerge. At the present point in the exposition, I will simply present an analysis where these morphemes are treated as toneless in underlying structure. This analysis is based on the idea that each utterance in Digo has associated with it an unassociated initial low tone and an unassociated final low tone - call these "boundary tones". Under this approach, the representations for *ku-tsumbur-a* and *ku-fwinǐk-â* will be:

```
L          L                L    H    L

$ku-tsumbur-a$              $ku-fwinik-a$
```

In the former example, the universal well-formedness conditions will guarantee that all of the vowels in the word be associated with some tone. Since the only tones in the word are low, it is clear that whatever the precise details of this association might be, all of the vowels of the word will be low-toned. And this, of course, is the desired result. (I am assuming that the fact that a low-toned vowel in phrase-penultimate position is pronounced with a mid-falling quality is to be attributed to a low-level phonetic rule.) In the latter example, the High Tone Displacement rule will associate the H with the ultimate vowel yielding:

```
L       H L
         \
$ku-fwinik-a$
```

If we can assume a universal principle whereby an unassociated tone will become associated with any vowel that is unassociated, then the initial boundary tone will become associated with the first three vowels of the word:

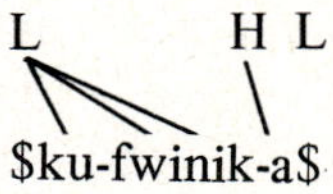


If we also assume that an unassociated tone must associate with a vowel, then the final boundary tone will become associated with the last vowel of the word:

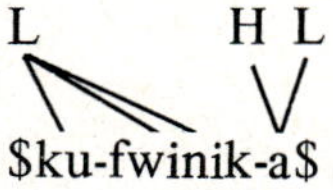


This representation is very close to being the correct surface representation of *ku-fwinǐk-â*. In order to produce the correct surface form, we will simply need a rule that will add an association line between a high tone (which is associated with the ultimate vowel in a phrase) and a preceding vowel. This rule - call it Leftwards High Spread - will yield the final representation:

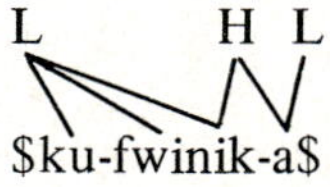


Notice that in the above account of *ku-fwinǐk-â*, the principle associating the initial boundary tone with all unassociated vowels must apply before Leftwards High Spread. If the reverse sequencing obtained, the syllable *ni* would be linked to a H by virtue of Leftwards High Spread and thus could not become linked with the initial boundary tone (since the unassociated boundary tone is associated only with unlinked vowels by the universal principle mentioned earlier). I have also assumed that High Tone Displacement is applied before this principle, since the association of the H with the ultimate vowel determines which vowels in a word are unlinked.

The above analysis of *ku-fwinǐk-â* seems to me quite well-motivated given that all of the assumptions that underlie it are highly plausible ones. The assumption that an unassociated tone will link by a universal principle with all unassociated vowels is supported by the fact that just such a principle has already been proposed for autosegmental phonology.[2] Similarly, the assumption that an unassociated tone must link with a vowel is another principle that has been independently proposed.[3] Finally, the postulation of a rule such as Leftwards High Spread is rendered plausible by the fact that just such a rule has been hypothesized for other Bantu languages in Tanzania.[4] I will assume, therefore, that the "boundary tone" analysis of the low tones in words such as *ku-tsumbur-a* and *ku-fwinǐk-â* is indeed an attractive one.

My analysis of Digo has, so far, accounted just for the tone patterns in (1) and (2). The pattern in (3) – cf. *ku-dunduríz-a* – has not yet been explained. The proper explanation of this pattern cannot, I believe, be discovered until the phrasal tonology is examined; therefore I will postpone further analysis of this pattern until section 8, where the phrasal phenomena are investigated.

## 3. MONOSYLLABIC VERB STEMS.

Up to this point I have restricted my attention to polysyllabic verb stems. Turning to verb stems of the shape $-C_O VC_O-$, we find that at first glance they do not appear to differ in any marked way from the polysyllabic stems. In terms of superficial phonetic shape, there are three pitch patterns observable for these monosyllabic stems, and these three patterns can again be reduced to two basic types. Examples are given in (13)-(15).

| | | | | |
|---|---|---|---|---|
| (13) | ku-rir-a | 'to laugh' | ku-chit-a | 'to pierce' |
| | ku-tsam-a | 'to move' | ku-rim-a | 'to cultivate' |
| | ku-riB-a | 'to pay' | ku-Bond-a | 'to pound (in mortar)' |
| | ku-miz-a | 'to swallow' | ku-bwag-a | 'to knock down' |
| (14) | ku-něn-â | 'to speak' | ku-rǒr-â | 'to marry' |
| | ku-dǔng-â | 'to string beads' | ku-měnz-â | 'to like, love' |
| | ku-fǔnd-â | 'to teach' | ku-kwěr-â | 'to climb' |
| | ku-rěh-â | 'to bring' | ku-vǔndz-â | 'to break s.t.' |
| (15) | ku-úz-a | 'to ask' | ku-ádz-a | 'to name, mention by name' |

The infinitive forms in (13) are parallel to the examples in (1); the forms in (14), with a rising-falling sequence over the final two vowels, are parallel to the examples in (2); and the forms in (15), with a level high tone on the penult, are parallel to the examples in (3). Again, the pitch patterns in (14) and (15) are in complementary distribution; the pattern in (15) occurs just in case the post-penult consonant is a voiced obstruent, while the pattern in (14) occurs when there is either no consonant or a consonant other than a voiced obstruent in post-penult position. The pattern in (13) occurs regardless of the nature of the post-penult consonant. Thus it would appear that monosyllabic verb stems are entirely parallel to polysyllabic stems. But this apparent parallelism is deceptive, and the actual situation is more complex.

There are numerous monosyllabic verb stems that on the surface appear to be similar to those in (13) in not having a high tone associated with them, but which upon further investigation behave quite differently – indeed, behave as though they are high-toned. Some verbs of this rather anomalous type are listed in (16).

| | | | | |
|---|---|---|---|---|
| (16) | ku-Bis-a | 'to avoid, give way' | ku-kur-a | 'to grow' |
| | ku-heg-a | 'to trap' | ku-rum-a | 'to bite |
| | ku-som-a | 'to read' | ku-ond-a | 'to get thin' |
| | ku-tsun-a | 'to skin' | ku-wad-a | 'to roast' |
| | ku-vwin-a | 'to sing' | ku-on-a | 'to see' |

The verbs in (16), when pronounced in isolation, sound exactly like the verbs in (13). The difference between the verb stems in (16) and those in (13) appears as soon as we consider the phenomenon of verbal derivation. Recall that the extension *-ir-/-er-* 'for/with' can be appended to a verb stem. This extension does not have a high tone associated with it (none of the extensions in Digo do), as can be seen from the examples in (6), where we see that the addition of this element to the stem /vugur/ yields *ku-vugurir-a.* This pronunciation, of course, is one that results when there is no high tone associated with the word. Let us now look at what happens when *-ir-/-er-* is appended to the verb stems in (13) and (16).

| | | | | |
|---|---|---|---|---|
| (17) | ku-rir-a | 'to cry' | ku-ririr-a | 'to cry for' |
| | ku-rim-a | 'to cultivate' | ku-rimir-a | 'to cultivate for/with' |
| | ku-guz-a | 'to sell' | ku-guzir-a | 'to sell to' |
| | ku-riB-a | 'to pay' | ku-riBir-a | 'to pay with' |
| | ku-chit-a | 'to pierce' | ku-chitir-a | 'to pierce with' |
| | ku-dzeng-a | 'to build' | ku-dzenger-a | 'to build for/with' |
| | ku-vut-a | 'to pull' | ku-vutir-a | 'to pull for/with' |

| | | | | |
|---|---|---|---|---|
| (18) | ku-tsun-a | 'to skin' | ku-tsunǐr-â | 'to skin for/with' |
| | ku-wad-a | 'to roast' | ku-wadǐr-â | 'to roast for/with' |
| | ku-vwin-a | 'to sing' | ku-vwinǐr-â | 'to sing to' |
| | ku-som-a | 'ro read' | ku-somĕr-â | 'to read to/for/with' |
| | ku-vug-a | 'to cook' | ku-vugǐr-â | 'to cook for/with' |
| | ku-fur-a | 'to wash (clothes)' | ku-furǐr-â | 'to wash for/with' |
| | ku-shon-a | 'to sew' | ku-shonĕr-â | 'to sew for/with' |

Assuming that the verbs in (13) are low-toned, then we would expect that the addition of the *-ir-/-er-* extension would in no way change their tonal structure. The examples in (17) show this to be true. The extended forms are pronounced according to the pattern of low-toned words. The verbs in (16), on the other hand, behave anomalously. When they are extended, as in (18), the extended form is pronounced with the pitch pattern characteristic of a word that contains a high tone. But where did this high tone come from? The verbs in (16) are, in isolation, pronounced as though they have no high tones associated with them. I take the data in (18) to be suggestive that the verbs in question really do have a high tone associated with them in underlying structure, but that this high tone is replaced by a low tone in the unextended form of the verb. Call this rule Neutralization. The rule of Neutralization will be discussed in more detail momentarily, but first an historical aside is in order.

Examination of Guthrie's comparative Bantu materials reveals that in fact the verbs that behave like those in (13) regularly derive from low-toned Proto-Bantu verb stems, whereas the verbs that behave like those in (16) regularly derive from high-toned Proto-Bantu verb stems. This point is illustrated in (19) and (20), respectively.

| | | | | |
|---|---|---|---|---|
| (19) | *Guthrie's starred form* | | *Digo* | |
| | *-gùd- | buy | ku-gur-a | 'to buy' |
| | *-dụ̀t- | pull | ku-vut-a | 'to pull' |
| | *-dìd- | cry, wail | ku-rir-a | 'to cry' |
| | *-dìp- | pay | ku-riB-a | 'to pay' |
| | *-jèŋg- | build | ku-dzeng-a | 'to build' |
| | *-dìm- | cultivate | ku-rim-a | 'to cultivate' |
| | *-pònd- | pound | ku-Bond-a | 'to pound' |
| | *-cààm- | move one's residence | ku-tsam-a | 'to move' |
| | *-mị̀d- | swallow | ku-miz-a | 'to swallow' |

| | | | | |
|---|---|---|---|---|
| (20) | *Guthrie's starred form* | | *Digo* | |
| | *-dụ́g- | cook, boil | ku-vug-a | 'to cook' |
| | *-tég- | set (trap) | ku-heg-a | 'to trap' |
| | *-bị́n- | dance; sing | ku-vwin-a | 'to sing' |
| | *-dúm- | bite | ku-rum-a | 'to bite' |
| | *-kúd- | grow up | ku-kur-a | 'to grow' |
| | *-bón- | see | ku-on-a | 'to see' |

On the basis of the data in (19) and (20), it would certainly appear to be the case that the contrast between high- and low-toned monosyllabic stems in Proto-Bantu has been neutralized when these roots appear unextended (in the infinitive – for other verbal forms, see below). Both types of verb are pronounced as low-toned stems. But if it is true that high-toned monosyllabic stems in Digo have been neutralized with low-toned stems, what about the examples in (14) and (15)? These are monosyllabic roots and they have not lost their underlying high tone. Why not? From a synchronic point of view, I do not believe that there is an explanation for why these verb stems do not undergo Neutralization – they simply must be regarded as exceptions. There does, however, appear to be an historical explanation. Consider the data in (21).

| | | | | |
|---|---|---|---|---|
| (21) | *Guthrie's starred forms* | | *Digo* | |
| | *-tóód- | marry | ku-rǒr-â | 'to marry' |
| | *-néén- | speak | ku-něn-â | 'to speak, say' |
| | *-kúér- | go up | ku-kwěr-â | 'to climb' |
| | *-déét- | bring | ku-rěh-â | 'to bring' |
| | *-dų́ík- | clothe | ku-vwǐk-â | 'to clothe' |
| | *-bį́ád- | bear (child) | ku-vyǎr-â | 'to give birth' |

We see from the examples in (21) that Proto-Bantu had verb roots of the shape -CV́V́C-. The descendants of these verb roots in Digo are pronounced with the high-tone pattern, but they do not have two vowels in their stems. They are identical in pronunciation to Proto-Bantu -CVC- roots as far as vowel length is concerned. That is to say, the vowel of /nen/ is pronounced short in all environments except penultimate in the phrase, where it is pronounced long; this is exactly the same behavior as the historically short vowel of /heg/, for instance. It appears, then, that while -CV́C- stems lost their high tone in the historical development of Digo, -CV́V́C- stems did not. However, -CVVC- stems eventually merged with -CVC- stems in terms of vowel length, but this merger did not affect the tonal behavior of the items in question.

There are some problems for this historical explanation of the data in (14) and (15). For instance, there are a number of examples like *ku-vǔndz-â, ku-měnz-â, ku-dǔng-â,* and *ku-fǔnd-â* where the high tone associated with a -CVNC- stem has not been neutralized. Since vowel-lengthening before an NC cluster is widespread in Bantu, it might be suggested that these stems in Proto-Bantu had two vowels (a long vowel equaling two short vowels) and that this fact prevented the loss of the high tone associated with these stems. But there are other -CVNC- stems that had a high tone in Proto-Bantu and did undergo high tone loss. Thus *ku-ond-a* 'to get thin' derives from **-yónd-*, having undergone the high tone loss. Why isn't *ku-ond-a* pronounced *ku-ǒnd-â* (like *ku-měnz-â*)? Despite this problem, there is some reason for thinking that the existence of monosyllabic stems in Digo that have failed to undergo Neutralization is due to the fact that Proto-Bantu stems of the shape -CV́V́C- preserved their underlying high tone even though they ultimately merged with -CV́C- stems from a segmental point of view.

Let me now turn to an examination of the formulation of Neutralization. I assume that this rule will change an H to L (at a later point, I will show why the H must be changed to L rather than simply deleting). The immediate issue is - which H's are subject to this rule? I have shown that an H underlyingly associated with a monosyllabic stem neutralizes. No other high tones are subject to Neutralization. For instance, consider the examples in (22) and (23).

| | | |
|---|---|---|
| (22) | ku-ni-chit-a | 'to pierce me' |
| | ku-ku-chit-a | 'to pierce you sg.' |
| | ku-mu-chit-a | 'to pierce him/her' |
| | ku-u-chǐt-â | 'to pierce us' |
| | ku-a-chǐt-â | 'to pierce you pl./them' |

| | | |
|---|---|---|
| (23) | ni-na-chit-a | 'I am piercing' |
| | u-na-chit-a | 'you sg. are piercing' |
| | a-na-chǐt-â | 'he/she is piercing' |
| | tu-na-chit-a | 'we are piercing/ |
| | mu-na-chit-a | 'you pl. are piercing' |
| | ma-na-chǐt-â | 'they are piercing' |

Notice that in (22) the high tone underlyingly associated with the object prefixes /u/ and /a/ does not neutralize, but rather displaces to the ultimate vowel and triggers Leftwards High Spread. Similarly, in (23) the high tone underlyingly associated with the third person prefixes /a/ and /ma/ does not neutralize, but instead displaces to the ultimate vowel and triggers Leftwards High Spread.

Given that Neutralization must (somehow) be restricted just to the tone of a monosyllabic stem, let me consider briefly the issue of where this rule might be ordered relative to High Tone Displacement. If High Tone Displacement is ordered first, and if the H of verbs such as those in (16) is allowed to undergo this displacement, then we would have difficulty formulating Neutralization since it would not be possible to distinguish an ultimate high tone that originated from a monosyllabic verb from an ultimate high tone that originated from an object prefix or a subject prefix or a polysyllabic stem. Thus it appears that we must either (a) prevent the H on a monosyllabic stem from undergoing High Tone Displacement or (b) order Neutralization before High Tone Displacement. While the latter course of action might appear promising, I will present data later in this study that argue against it. Consequently, I will propose an analysis where High Tone Displacement is restricted so that it may not apply to a high tone associated with a monosyllabic stem (the stems in (14) and (15) will have to be marked as exceptions to this restriction).

Thus a representation such as

```
L    H    L
     |
$ku-som-a$
```

will fail to undergo High Tone Displacement, and ultimately Neutralization will change the H to L. I have assumed here that the H of the verb stem is underlyingly associated with the vowel of the verb stem since in order to apply High Tone Displacement we must know whether an H is associated underlyingly with a monosyllabic stem or with some other morpheme. Given the above assumptions, the rule of Neutralization can be formulated so as to lower an H that is associated with the penultimate vowel in a word (later, I will show that actually it is not the word but the phrase), since subsequent to High Tone Displacement the only high tones associated with the penultimate vowel are, in fact, the high tones associated with monosyllabic verb stems that have failed to displace due to the restriction on High Tone Displacement.[5]

The derivation of *ku-som-a* as opposed to *ku-a-chĭt-â* is illustrated in (24).

```
(24)  L   H   L          L  H      L
          |                 |
      $ku-som-a$         $ku-a-chit-a$

                         L        HL
                                  |
      inapplicable       $ku-a-chit-a$       High Tone Displacement⁶

      L   L   L
          |
      $ku-som-a$         inapplicable        Neutralization

      L   L   L          L        HL
      \   |   /          \  \   \ /
      $ku-som-a$         $ku-a-chit-a$       association principles plus
                                             Leftwards High Spread
```

4. VERBS WITH TWO HIGH TONES

Up to this point I have restricted the data to instances where there is just one high tone in the underlying structure of a word. In this section I look at cases where there are two high tones. Consider first what happens when a high-toned object prefix appears in a word with a high-toned verb stem.

| | | |
|---|---|---|
| (25) | ku-pupŭt-â | 'to beat' |
| | ku-ni-pupŭt-â | 'to beat me' |
| | ku-ku-pupŭt-â | 'to beat you sg.' |
| | ku-mu-pupŭt-â | 'to beat him/her' |
| | ku-u-pupŭt-â | 'to beat us' |
| | ku-a-pupŭt-â | 'to beat you pl./them' |

| | |
|---|---|
| ku-on-a | 'to see' |
| ku-ni-on-a | 'to see me' |
| ku-ku-on-a | 'to see you sg.' |
| ku-mu-on-a | 'to see him/her' |
| ku-tu-ǒn-â | 'to see us' |
| ku-a-ǒn-â | 'to see you pl./them' |

The underlying representation of *ku-a-pupǔt-â* has two high tones - one associated with the object prefix /a/ and the other associated with the verb stem /puput/. The surface realization of this underlying form does not, however, differ in any way from *ku-ni-pupǔt-â* which has just one high tone in its underlying structure (the object prefix in this case being a low-toned one). We must therefore provide an analysis of these data whereby the two high tones in *ku-a-pupǔt-â* will yield the same phonetic result as a single underlying high tone. This might be accomplished in one of two ways. One solution would be to allow High Tone Displacement to associate both of the high tones with the ultimate vowel. A well-motivated universal convention could then come into play whereby two successive identical tones associated with the same vowel are reduced to a single tone. The other analysis would assume the existence of a rule that eliminates one of the two high tones. Both of these analyses will be evaluated as we proceed.

The facts with respect to the verb /on/ differ from those with respect to /puput/, although both verbs are underlyingly high-toned. The underlying representation of *ku-a-ǒn-â* is like *ku-a-pupǔt-â* in having two high tones, whereas the representation of *ku-ni-on-a* is like *ku-ni-pupǔt-â* in having one high tone. But whereas *ku-ni-pupǔt-â* and *ku-a-pupǔt-â* are identical in their tonal shapes, *ku-ni-on-a* and *ku-a-ǒn-â* differ. The reason for this difference is in part obvious - /on/ is subject to Neutralization whereas /puput/ is not. In order to specify precisely how Neutralization will account for the difference between *ku-ni-on-a* and *ku-a-ǒn-â,* we must apply the two approaches cited above to the problem of what happens when there are two high tones in underlying structure.

Suppose that we were to follow the analysis that allows High Tone Displacement to associate both high tones in *ku-a-pupǔt-â* with the ultimate vowel. Consider what would happen, then, in the case of a representation such as:

```
L  HH  L
   | |
$ku-a-on-a$
```

The H associated with the verb stem could not displace onto the ultimate vowel since high tones on monosyllabic verb stems will be exempted from High Tone Displacement. But if the stem H cannot become associated with the ultimate vowel, the prefixal H cannot either - at least not without violating one of the most fundamental parts of the Well-formedness Condition on autosegmental representations: namely, that association lines may not cross. In order for the prefixal H to associate with the ultimate vowel, the association line connecting them would have to cross the association line connecting the stem H with the stem vowel. (This discussion, of course, presupposes that there is indeed an association line connecting the stem H with the stem vowel prior to High Tone Displacement. As I proceed, more support for this assumption will be forthcoming.) If the prefixal H is thus unable to associate with the ultimate vowel, the wrong output will be generated : **ku-á-on-a.*

Let us now consider how *ku-a-ŏn-â* would be derived in an analysis where instead of associating both highs in a word with the ultimate vowel we have a rule that would delete one of these highs. Deletion of a high tone would occur when there is both a high tone on the prefix and a high tone on the stem. The question that immediately arises is: which high tone deletes? Given the account of Neutralization that I have proposed, the answer must be: the stem high. If the prefixal high were deleted, then the stem high would be the only high in the word and it would fail to displace to the ultimate vowel (since High Tone Displacement cannot affect highs on monosyllabic stems) and would subsequently undergo Neutralization. The result would be a word with no high tones: **ku-a-on-a.* If, on the other hand, it is the stem high that deletes, then there will still be a high on the prefix and this high will be able to displace to the ultimate vowel. Notice that it is critical to my analysis that the high associated with the stem be *deleted* rather than being replaced by a low tone. If the stem high were replaced by a low tone, then the prefix high would not be able to associate with the ultimate vowel because to do so would require crossing the association line linking the stem vowel to the low tone. I will refer to the rule that eliminates the stem high when a high-toned object precedes as High Tone Deletion. This rule is one that is the Digo counterpart to a widely occurring process in Bantu that disallows successive high tones.[7]

The derivations of *ku-a-pupŭt-â* and *ku-a-ŏn-â* are shown below:

```
(26)  L  H H    L     L  HH  L
         | |             ||
      $ku-a-puput-a$  $ku-a-on-a$

      L  H      L     L  H   L
         |               |
      $ku-a-puput-a$  $ku-a-on-a$        High Tone Deletion
```

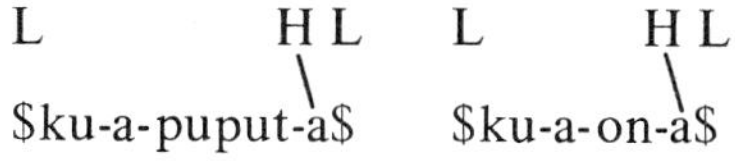


High Tone Displacement

inapplicable inapplicable Neutralization

association principles,
Leftwards High Spread

So far I have considered just one environment where two high tones can appear in the underlying structure of words - namely, forms with a high-toned object prefix and a high-toned verb stem. Another environment where two high tones can occur underlyingly is in the present tense paradigm of a high-toned verb stem.

(27) ni-na-pupǔt-â 'I am beating'
u-na-pupǔt-â 'you sg. are beating'
a-na-púpút-â 'he/she is beating'
tu-na-pupǔt-â 'we are beating'
mu-na-pupǔt-â 'you pl. are beating'
ma-na-púpút-â 'they are beating'

ni-na-tanyiríz-a 'I am driving off predators'
a-na-tányíríz-a 'he/she is driving off predators'

ni-na-furukǔt-â 'I am moving about restlessly'
a-na-fúrúkút-â 'he/she is moving about restlessly'

ni-na-chimbǐr-â 'I am running away'
a-na-chímbír-â 'he/she is running away'

ni-na-sindǐk-â 'I am shutting the door'
a-na-síndík-â 'he/she is shutting the door'

ni-na-BaBǎs-â 'I am groping in the dark'
a-na-BáBás-â 'he/she is groping in the dark'

Recall that in the present tense paradigm, the third person subject prefixes /a/ and /ma/ have a high tone associated with them. Thus when these prefixes occur in a verbal form with a high-toned stem, we have another instance where two high tones occur in underlying structure. But notice that in all such forms in (27), there is a different surface tone shape from cases where only one high tone occurs in the underlying form. Third person subject, present tense forms of high-toned verb stems are characterized by a sequence of high tones throughout the verb stem followed by a falling tone on the final vowel. (Actually, this surface pattern is not characteristic of *all* third person present tense forms, but more about this later.)

Given that *a-na-púpút-â* derives from a representation such as

```
LH     H     L
 |     |
$ a-na-puput-a$
```

we have further reason for dismissing the proposed analysis whereby all high tones in a word would displace to the ultimate vowel. For if both of the highs in the above representation were to displace to the ultimate vowel (and then simplify, by convention, into a single H), we would be unable to account for the presence of high tones on the stem vowels. On the other hand, if we assume the existence of a rule such as High Tone Deletion to account for the loss of the stem high in examples like *ku-a-pupŭtâ* and *ku-a-ŏnâ,* then it is clear that we must restrict High Tone Deletion so that it cannot apply to the third person present tense forms in (27). For if High Tone Deletion did apply, then the third person forms should be identical in pronunciation to the non-third person forms (which have just one high tone in their underlying form). I will assume that High Tone Deletion is a rule that is restricted to just the case where a high-toned stem is preceded by a high-toned object prefix, but additional data will need to be considered before it becomes clear why I have taken High Tone Deletion to be basically morphologically-governed.[8]

Before I attempt to develop an analysis of the tone pattern of forms such as *a-na-púpút-â,* some additional data need to be presented. First, consider third person present tense forms of high-toned verbs when an object prefix is included:

| | | |
|---|---|---|
| (28) | a-na-mú-púpút-â | 'he/she is beating him/her' |
| | a-na-á-púpút-â[9] | 'he/she is beating them' |

Underlyingly, the first example in (28) has two high tones - one on the subject prefix and the other on the stem. The second example in (28) has three underlying high tones - one on the subject prefix, one on the object prefix, and the other on the stem. But High Tone Deletion will eliminate the stem high tone in the second example. Consequently, after High Tone Deletion, the forms in (28) will have the following representations:

```
LH        H    L          LH   H      L
 |        |                |   |
$a-na-mu-puput-a$         $a-na-a-puput-a$
```

Notice that despite the difference in the location of the second high tone, both of these forms end up phonetically with the same tone pattern – namely, a high tone associated with all of the vowels from the object prefix up to the end of the word.

Next consider the case where a low-toned verb occurs in the present tense with object prefixes.

| | | |
|---|---|---|
| (29) | ni-na-tsukur-a | 'I am taking' |
| | ni-na-mu-tsukur-a | 'I am taking him/her' |
| | ni-na-a-tsukŭr-â | 'I am taking them' |
| | a-na-tsukŭr-â | 'he/she is taking' |
| | a-na-mu-tsukŭr-â | 'he/she is taking him/her' |
| | a-na-á-tsúkúr-â | 'he/she is taking them' |

In *ni-na-tsukur-a* none of the morphemes has a high tone associated with it. The addition of the low-toned object prefix /mu/ does not alter the picture, but the incorporation of the high-toned object prefix /a/ yields an underlying form with a high tone that will displace to the ultimate vowel and then trigger Leftwards High Spread. In the case of *a-na-tsukŭr-â*, there is a high tone associated with the subject prefix. The incorporation of the object prefix /mu/ does not change the situation, but the incorporation of /a/ adds a second high tone. The representation underlying *a-na-á-tsúkúr-â* is exactly like that underlying *a-na-á-púpút-â* once High Tone Deletion has applied to the latter example, and their surface tonal shapes are also identical.

Another environment in Digo where two high tones occur in the underlying representation is provided by the *-ka-* tense. In (30) I give the paradigm for a low-toned verb in the *-ka-* tense.

| | | |
|---|---|---|
| (30) | ni-ka-tsukŭr-â | 'I have carried' |
| | u-ka-tsukŭr-â | 'you sg. have carried' |
| | a-ka-tsukŭr-â | 'he/she has carried' |
| | tu-ka-tsukŭr-â | 'we have carried' |
| | mu-ka-tsukŭr-â | 'you pl. have carried' |
| | ma-ka-tsukŭr-â | 'they have carried' |

Each member of this paradigm is pronounced as one expects when there is one high tone associated with the word. But the stem /tsukur/ is a low-toned stem, so where does the high tone in this paradigm come from? The simplest assumption appears to be that the high tone is associated underlyingly with the *-ka-* tense/aspect prefix, since every verbal form containing this prefix does have at least one high tone. Of course, one could claim that it is the subject prefixes in (30) that provide the source for the high tone rather than *-ka-*, but this is a less straightforward analysis since these subject prefixes are by no means generally associated with high tones. (We have already seen that in the present tense, non-third person subject prefixes are low-toned while third person subject prefixes are high-toned.) I assume, therefore, that *-ka-* has a high tone associated with it in underlying structure, and that in the case of the examples in (30) High Tone Displacement will associate this high with the ultimate vowel (triggering Leftwards High Spread as a consequence). I assume that all subject prefixes are low-toned in the *-ka-* tense.

If we now consider the paradigm for a high-toned verb stem in the *-ka-* tense, we see that in this paradigm there will be two high tones - one associated with the *-ka-* and one associated with the stem.

| | | |
|---|---|---|
| (31) | ni-ka-kúmbúkír-â | 'I have remembered' (cf. ku-kumbukǐr-â) |
| | u-ka-kúmbúkír-â | 'you sg. have remembered' |
| | a-ka-kúmbúkír-â | 'he/she has remembered' |
| | tu-ka-kúmbúkír-â | 'we have remembered' |
| | mu-ka-kúmbúkír-â | 'you pl. have remembered' |
| | ma-ka-kúmbúkír-â | 'they have remembered' |

Notice that in these forms High Tone Deletion does not apply to the stem high, even though it is immediately preceded by a high toned tense/aspect prefix (whereas the stem high is deleted when it is preceded by an object that is high-toned). The surface tone shape of the items in (31) is entirely analogous to examples such as *a-na-púpút-â* (high on subject prefix and stem), *a-na-á-tsúkúr-â* (high on subject prefix and on object prefix), etc.

The incorporation of object prefixes into *-ka-* forms is illustrated in (32), where the stem is low-toned, and in (33), where the stem is high-toned.

| | | |
|---|---|---|
| (32) | a-ka-rimǐr-â | 'he/she has cultivated for' |
| | a-ka-ni-rimǐr-â | 'he/she has cultivated for me' |
| | a-ka-ú-rímír-â[10] | 'he/she has cultivated for us' |

| | | |
|---|---|---|
| (33) | a-ka-púpút-â | 'he/she has beaten' |
| | a-ka-ní-púpút-â | 'he/she has beaten me' |
| | a-ka-ú-púpút-â | 'he/she has beaten us' |

In (32), the first two items have just one high tone in their underlying structure (which displaces to the ultimate vowel and triggers Leftwards High Spread); the last item has two highs, one on the *-ka-* and one on the object prefix. These highs are unaffected by High Tone Deletion and trigger the same tonal pattern as we observed earlier for *a-na-á-tsúkúr-â* (where there were high tones on the subject prefix and on the object prefix). In (33), the first two examples have two underlying high tones - one on the *-ka-* and the other on the verb stem. Again, these two high tones trigger a surface tone pattern where there is a high associated with all of the vowels of the word beginning with the object prefix, if there is one, otherwise with the first stem vowel. In the last example there are three high tones underlyingly - on the *-ka-*, on the object prefix, and on the stem. But High Tone Deletion removes the high from the stem, resulting in a form with two high tones which trigger exactly the same tonal pattern as in the first two examples of (33).

I have now shown a fairly wide range of situations where two high tones occur in underlying structure in Digo, and I have demonstrated that only the conjunction of a high-toned object prefix and a high-toned stem triggers the application of High Tone Deletion. Since the high tones in this case occur in adjoining morphemes, it would be tempting to treat High Tone Deletion as a very general rule which eliminates the second of two high tones on adjoining morphemes. However, if the prefix *-ka-* is regarded as being the bearer of a high tone in the paradigms illustrated in (30) and (31), then such a generalized form of High Tone Deletion is not possible since the *-ka-* will appear adjacent to high toned stems (cf. (31)) and high-toned object prefixes (cf. (32)) without triggering High Tone Deletion. A more specific restriction on High Tone Deletion seems to be required - namely, it affects just a stem high after a high on an object prefix. This is not a particularly ad hoc condition if we take into consideration the fact that (a) there is otherwise at most one high tone associated with a verb stem in Digo, no matter how long that verb stem may be, and (b) in many Bantu languages there is evidence that the object prefix coheres with the verb stem in a particularly close way. For example, in Makua (a Bantu language spoken in Tanzania and Mozambique) certain verb tenses require that a high tone be assigned to the second vowel of the verb stem; when an object prefix is included in the construction, the object prefix is included in the determination of what constitutes the "second" vowel. Evidence that in Digo the object prefix is somehow included in the verb stem can be found in the fact that when a word has two high tones in its underlying structure (after High Tone Deletion), the word is pronounced with a series of high tones that begins on the first vowel of the verb stem proper if there is no object prefix present - cf. *a-na-púpút-â* - but on the object prefix if there is one - cf. *a-na-ú-púpút-â.* (I turn to the analysis of this this pattern immediately below.) If we assume, then, that the object prefix is included with the verb stem proper into a larger unit - call it the verbal complex - then High Tone Deletion can be formulated as in (34).

(34) $$\text{Verbal Complex}\begin{bmatrix} \text{H} & & \text{H} \\ 1 & & 2 \end{bmatrix} \rightarrow \quad 1 \quad \emptyset$$

At this point, let us look in more detail at the cases where there are two high tones in the underlying representation of a word and these high tones are not affected by High Tone Deletion. In the examples cited so far, these two high tones have resulted in a surface tone pattern where all the vowels of the word (starting from the first vowel in the verbal complex) have a high tone associated with them. This tonal shape is not, however, the only surface manifestation that two underlying high tones exhibit. Consider the data in (35).

| | | |
|---|---|---|
| (35) | ni-na-babadŭr-â | 'I am forcing s.t. apart' |
| | a-ná-babadŭr-â | 'he/she is forcing s.t. apart' |
| | ni-na-garagăr-â | 'I am tossing around' |
| | a-ná-garagăr-â | 'he/she is tossing around' |
| | ni-na-dundurĭk-â | 'I am walking stealthily' |
| | a-ná-dundurĭk-â | 'he/she is walking stealthily' |
| | ni-na-zungumúz-a | 'I am conversing' |
| | a-ná-zungumúz-a | 'he/she is conversing' |
| | ni-na-vurúg-a | 'I am stirring' |
| | a-ná-vurúg-a | 'he/she is stirring' |

These examples involve high-toned verb stems in the present tense. When the subject prefix is *ni-*, which is low-toned, there is just one high tone in the word. This high tone of course displaces to the ultimate vowel – resulting in the application of Leftwards High Spread in the case of stems whose penult-consonant is not a voiced obstruent. (Recall that I have not yet accounted for the forms with a voiced obstruent in post-penult position.) When the subject prefix is *a-*, which is high-toned, there are two high tones in the underlying structure of the word. The phonetic realization of these two high tones differs from what we have previously encountered. Here we find a level high tone on the present tense prefix *-na-* and another high tone that has displaced to the ultimate vowel. (I will not continue to repeat the point that a high tone that displaces to the ultimate vowel will subsequently trigger either Leftwards High Spread or whatever process(es) that may be involved in the surface pattern exhibited by stems whose post-penult consonant is a voiced obstruent.) The vowels that are in between the *-na-* prefix and the displaced high tone are low-toned.

What distinguishes the examples in (35) from the comparable data in (27)? The answer is clear. The verbs in (35) all have an initial voiced obstruent, whereas the verbs in (27) do not. Thus the tonal difference between *a-na-púpútâ* and *a-ná-dundurǐk-â* ultimately derives from the difference in the voicing of the initial obstruent of the stem. Further evidence for this difference is provided by the examples in (36).

| | | |
|---|---|---|
| (36) | ni-na-gurir-a | 'I am buying for' |
| | ni-na-a-gurǐr-â | 'I am buying for them' |
| | a-na-gurǐr-â | 'he/she is buying for' |
| | a-na-á-gurǐr-â | 'he/she is buying for them' |
| | | |
| | ni-na-demurir-a | 'I am scolding' |
| | ni-na-a-demurǐr-â | 'I am scolding them' |
| | a-na-demurǐr-â | 'he/she is scolding' |
| | a-na-á-demurǐr-â | 'he/she is scolding them' |

In (36) I give two examples of low-toned verb stems in the present tense. In an example like *ni-na-demurir-a,* there are no high tones. The incorporation of the object prefix /a/ in *ni-na-a-demurǐr-â* results in a word that has one high tone which displaces to the ultimate vowel. In *a-na-demurǐr-â* there is a high tone associated with the subject prefix which displaces to the ultimate vowel. The incorporation of the object /a/ in this form results in a word with two high tones. The first high tone is associated with the object prefix and the second high tone has displaced to the ultimate vowel - but the vowels in between are low-toned. This contrasts with a form such as *a-na-á-tsúkúr-â* in (29) where all of the vowels beginning with the initial vowel of the verbal complex are high-toned. Again, what distinguishes the verbs in (36) is that they begin with a voiced obstruent as compared to *a-na-á-tsúkúr-â* where the verb begins with a voiceless obstruent.

Yet more evidence of the relevance of the nature of the initial consonant of the verb stem is provided by the *-ka-* tense. Consider the examples in (37) of high-toned verbs in the *-ka-* tense and compare them with the previous example in (31).

| | | |
|---|---|---|
| (37) | ni-ká-bomǒr-â | 'I have demolished' |
| | ni-ká-vwinǐr-â | 'I have sung for' |
| | ni-ká-doněr-â | 'I have kissed' |
| | ni-ká-gongomě-â | 'I have hammered' |

The forms in (37) have two high tones in their underlying representation; one of these highs is associated with the *-ka-* prefix and the other with the verb stem. Although this same situation produces a sequence of high tones throughout the stem in *ni-ka-kúmbúkír-â* (31), we find a different surface pattern in *ni-ká-gongomě-â, ni-ká-doněr-â*, and the like. The examples in (37) all begin with a voiced obstruent in stem-initial position, in contrast to the verb /kumbukir/ and the additional examples given below in (38).

| | | |
|---|---|---|
| (38) | ni-ka-síchír-â | 'I have heard' |
| | ni-ka-chékéch-â | 'I have sifted' |
| | ni-ka-káráng-â | 'I have fried' |
| | ni-ka-páyúk-â | 'I have gotten thin' |
| | ni-ka-fwíník-â | 'I have covered' |
| | ni-ka-túrúk-â | 'I have gone out' |
| | ni-ka-nyámár-â | 'I have kept quiet' |
| | ni-ka-yáyús-â | 'I have melted s.t.' |

I have shown so far that when a verbal word has two high tones, a different surface tonal pattern results when the stem-initial consonant is a voiced obstruent from when the stem-initial consonant is not a voiced obstruent. Actually, the situation is much more complicated than this statement suggests, for the presence of a voiced obstruent at other places in the stem affects the surface tonal pattern as well. This is illustrated in (39).

| | | |
|---|---|---|
| (39) | *high-toned verbs in the -ka- tense* | |
| | a-ka-ézěk-â | 'he/she has thatched' |
| | a-ka-wézěsh-â | 'he/she has enabled' |
| | a-ka-tábǐk-â | 'he/she has become distressed' |
| | a-ka-tábǎng-â | 'he/she has spoiled by mixing with s.t.' |
| | a-ka-súrúbǐk-â | 'he/she is strong/firm' |
| | a-ka-ézekěr-â | 'he/she has thatched with/for' |
| | *low-toned verbs in the -ka- tense with a high-toned object prefix* | |
| | a-ka-ú-tógǒr-â | 'he/she has praised us' |
| | a-ka-ú-ságǐr-â | 'he/she has ground s.t. for us' |
| | a-ka-ú-rágǔr-â | 'he/she has treated us (medically)' |

The surface tonal pattern exhibited by these forms is quite consistent: starting from the beginning of the verbal complex, there is a sequence of high tones that stops at the point where a voiced obstruent is first encountered; in addition, there is a high tone that has associated with the ultimate vowel (and triggered the application of Leftwards High Spread in all of the examples cited). In the event the post-penult consonant is a voiced obstruent, the high tone associated with the ultimate vowel will be realized as a level high tone on the penult vowel (with a low-toned ultimate vowel); for example, *a-ka-ígíz-a* 'he/she has imitated'. Superficially, *a-ka-ígíz-a* appears as though it has a series of high tones that begins at the start of the verbal complex and continues up to the post-penult voiced obstruent – in other words, it looks just like *a-na-tányíríz-a.* But I claim that *a-ka-ígíz-a* is structurally like *a-ka-tábi̋k-â* – i.e. the series of high tones that begins with the first vowel of the verbal complex stops when the *g* of /igiz/ is encountered, and the high on the penult vowel is just the high that occurs as a consequence of displacement to the ultimate vowel. In *a-na-tányíríz-a,* on the other hand, the sequence of highs that originates at the beginning of the verbal complex continues up to the post-penult voiced obstruent. There is no prior voiced obstruent to impede its progression through the word. The high tone on the penult vowel, of course, has a dual source. It represents a part of the sequence of highs that originates at the beginning of the verbal complex – but it can also be viewed as the consequence of displacement to the ultimate vowel. In other words, there are two separate reasons for the penult vowel to be high toned.

At this point, let me summarize the facts about the surface realization of words with two high tones (subsequent to High Tone Deletion). If there are no voiced obstruents in the verbal complex, each vowel of the complex has a level high tone except the last vowel, which has a falling tone. In words where there are one or more voiced obstruents in the verbal complex, there is a series of level high tones in the complex up to, and including the vowel preceding the first voiced obstruent. There is also a high tone that has displaced to the ultimate vowel. Let us now consider what sort of analysis these data suggest.

The evidence provided by the items where there is a voiced obstruent in the verbal complex suggests clearly that one of the two highs in the word must displace to the ultimate vowel. I will assume that it is the rightmost high in the word that displaces. The motivation for this assumption will appear below. Given that the rightmost high in the word displaces to the ultimate vowel, what about the preceding high? Does it simply remain associated with the vowel to which it is underlyingly linked? The answer must be a negative one, otherwise we would expect pronunciations like **a-ká-tábi̋k-â* where the *-ka-* prefix would bear a high tone since it is underlyingly specified as high and is not subject to displacement (since the stem high tone is rightmost in the word and is thus subject to displacement). Similarly, instead of *a-na-á-guri̋r-â* we would expect **ǎ-ná-á-guri̋r-â* where the subject prefix *a-* would bear a high tone since it is underlyingly specified as high and is not subject to displacement (the high tone of the object prefix being rightmost in the word and thus subject to displacement).[11] Another rule must be posited, therefore, that will have the effect of displacing the first high in the word to the verbal complex. For instance, underlying forms such as

```
L  H H  L                    LH  H        L
   |  |                       |   |
$a-ka-tabik-a$               $a-na-a-gurir-a$
```

must undergo High Tone Displacement, yielding:

```
L  H      HL                 LH           HL
   |       |                  |            |
$a-ka-tabik-a$               $a-na-a-gurir-a$
```

and also this second displacement process, call it Displacement-To-Stem, which will result in:

```
L     H   HL                 L    H       HL
      |    |                      |        |
$a-ka-tabik-a$               $a-na-a-gurir-a$
```

If we assume that Displacement-To-Stem applies after High Tone Displacement, then the former rule will (given the data so far presented) simply displace any high that is not associated with the ultimate vowel to the first vowel of the verbal complex. There is one complication, however. If the verbal complex begins with a voiced obstruent, the first high in the word cannot associate with the verbal complex, but instead must associate with the vowel immediately preceding the verbal complex; cf. *a-ná-dundurĩk-â* shown earlier in (35) (from an underlying representation where the *a-* subject prefix is high-toned and the verb stem is high-toned). The rule of Displacement-To-Stem is provisionally formulated as in (40):

(40)
$$\begin{matrix} H & & \\ | & & \\ V_i & (Y) & V_j \end{matrix} \Rightarrow \begin{matrix} & & H \\ & & | \\ V_i & (Y) & V_j \end{matrix}$$

Condition: Y is the maximal string of sounds which contains neither a voiced obstruent nor a vowel belonging to the verbal complex. $V_i$ = a vowel that is not part of the verbal complex.

Rule (40) says that a high tone (associated with a vowel other than the ultimate vowel) will associate with a vowel as far to the right as possible subject to the constraint that (a) it may not associate to the right of a voiced obstruent and (b) it may not associate to the right of a vowel in the verbal complex.

Confirmation of the above formulation of Displacement-To-Stem is provided by an example such as *a-ká-ga-tanyiríz-a* 'he/she has driven them off'. This item includes the high-toned object prefix /ga/, which has an initial voiced obstruent. The high tone associated with the *-ka-* is not able to displace to the right since it cannot do so without crossing a voiced obstruent.

The attentive reader will perhaps have noted that the examples *a-ka-tábǐk-â* and *a-na-á-gurǐr-â* can be accounted for without recourse to a rule such as Displacement-To-Stem if one were to assume that High Tone Displacement affects the first H in a word, metathesizing it to the right of any subsequent H's in the word and associating it with the ultimate vowel. Under this analysis, representations such as

```
L   H H    L            LH    H      L
    | |                 |     |
$a-ka-tabik-a$          $a-na-a-gurir-a$
```

would be converted by High Tone Displacement into the following representations:

```
L      H   HL           L     H      HL
       |   |                  |      |
$a-ka-tabik-a$          $a-na-a-gurir-a$
```

This analysis so far fails to explain *a-ná-dundurǐk-â* and *a-ká-ga-tanyiríz-a.* These items have the following underlying representations:

```
LH     H       L          L  H H         L
|      |                     | |
$a-na-dundurik-a$         $a-ka-ga-tanyiriz-a$
```

(In the latter case, I have assumed the prior application of High Tone Deletion; /tanyiriz/ is underlyingly high-toned.) If High Tone Displacement were to affect the first high tone in the word, we would derive the following representations:

```
L      H       HL         L     H          HL
       |       |                |          |
$a-na-dundurik-a$         $a-ka-ga-tanyiriz-a$
```

These representations are not yet surface forms since they have a high tone associated with the first vowel of the verbal complex rather than with the vowel immediately preceding the verbal complex. To obtain the correct results, it would be necessary to postulate a rule of High Tone Retraction. High Tone Retraction would, presumably, affect a high associated with a vowel and reassociate it with the preceding vowel just in the event a voiced obstruent occurs between the two vowels in question.[12] The result of the application of High Tone Retraction to the above representations would be:

```
L  H           HL         L  H             HL
   |           |             |             |
$a-na-dundurik-a$         $a-ka-ga-tanyiriz-a$
```

We have now correctly associated a high tone with the vowel immediately preceding the verbal complex rather than with the first vowel of that complex.

I have sketched two analyses of *a-ná-dundurǐk-â* and *a-ká-ga-tanyiríz-a.* One analysis involves a rule of High Tone Displacement that affects the rightmost high in a word and a rule of Displacement-To-Stem; the other analysis involves a rule of High Tone Displacement that affects the leftmost high in a word and a rule of High Tone Retraction. Both of these analyses will also account for an example such as *a-na-ní-dungǐr-â* 'he/she is piercing for me'. This word has the underlying structure:

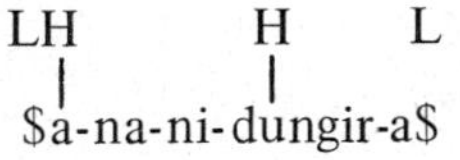


The first analysis predicts that the stem H will associate with the ultimate vowel and the high on the subject prefix will displace to the first vowel in the verbal complex (which is the vowel of the low-toned object prefix /ni/). The second analysis predicts that the prefix high will displace to the ultimate vowel and the high of the stem /dungir/ will retract back onto the preceding vowel (which is the vowel of the /ni/ object prefix). Thus both analyses will correctly associate one high with /ni/ and the other high with the ultimate vowel.

I will argue below that the analysis involving Displacement-To-Stem is superior to the analysis involving High Tone Retraction. But before I can examine the relevant evidence, certain other matters and certain additional data must be discussed and analyzed.

Both of the analyses under discussion have produced the following representations:

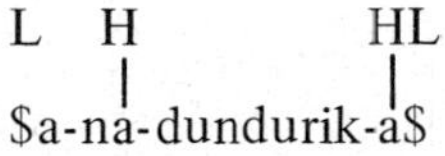


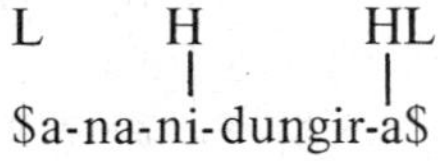


(I am ignoring the example *a-ká-ga-tanyiríz-a* since it involves the special case where a voiced obstruent precedes the ultimate vowel and I have not yet developed the analysis of this situation.) The principles governing the association of unlinked tones and unlinked vowels should produce the following (incorrect) results when applied to the above representations:[13]

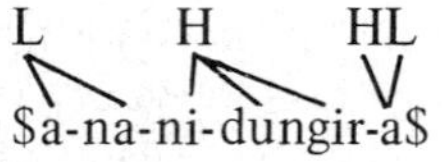


Even if the rule of Leftwards High Spread were to apply to such representations, it would have no visible effects, and the result would be that incorrect surface representations would be generated: **a-ná-dúndúrík-â* and **a-na-ní-dúngír-â.*

The problem that confronts us here clearly derives from the fact that prior to the application of the general principles governing the association of unlinked tones and vowels, we need representations where there is a *low* tone in front of the ultimate high. Where could this low tone come from? One possibility, of course, is that we assume that in the underlying representation of stems such as /dundurik/ and /dungir/, the first vowel has a high associated with it but the remaining vowels have low tones associated with them. Such an analysis runs counter to my proposal to regard vowels as being either linked to a H underlyingly or unspecified for tone. In addition, such an analysis would create complications for data to be discussed below. Another possibility - and the one that I will adopt here - is to assume that voiced obstruents are assigned (by rule) a low tone. Call this rule Low Insertion. Given the application of Low Insertion, we will derive (prior to the application of the universal principles governing unlinked tones and vowels) the following representations:[14]

If the general principles governing the association of unlinked tones and vowels are stated so that when an unlinked vowel is between two linked tones, it associates to the left rather than to the right (see note 13), then we will derive the following representations:

The application of Leftwards High Spread will then yield the correct surface shape:

The postulation of the rule of Low Insertion does not seem to me an implausible move (see Laughren, this volume, for a similar rule in Zulu). The correlation between voiced consonants and low tones is one that has been widely recognized in the literature.[15] Furthermore, the postulation of Low Insertion will account not just for the medial low-toned vowels in *a-ná-dundurǐk-â* and *a-na-ní-dungǐr-â,* but will also remove the need for one of the ad hoc restrictions I placed earlier on Displacement-To-Stem. Recall that in my formulation of that rule in (40), it was necessary to stipulate that a non-ultimate high cannot be displaced *past* a voiced obstruent. However, if Low Insertion is applied before Displacement-To-Stem, then the inability of a high tone to associate past a voiced obstruent would simply reduce to a case of not being able to cross an association line. Incidentally, since High Tone Displacement *does* associate a high tone with the ultimate vowel regardless of whether there are voiced obstruents in between the point of origin of the high tone and the ultimate vowel, Low Insertion will have to be ordered after High Tone Displacement.

Up until this point we have examined just cases where a voiced obstruent occurs at the beginning of the verb stem or at the beginning of the object prefix. If a voiced obstruent occurs medially in the verb stem, we get surface forms like *a-ka-súrúbiǩ-â*. The underlying representation of this item is:

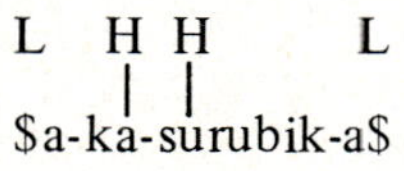


Both of the analyses I have considered (High Tone Displacement affecting the rightmost high plus Low Insertion plus Displacement-To-Stem, or High Tone Displacement affecting the leftmost high plus Low Insertion plus High Tone Retraction) will yield the same result when applied to the above representation:

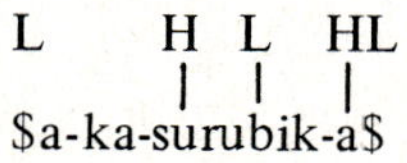


Notice that if we now apply the general principles governing the association of unlinked tones and vowels - and if we again assume that an unassociated vowel located between two linked tones associates to the left rather than to the right, we will derive the following structure:

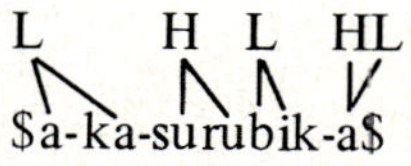


The application of Leftwards High Spread will then produce the correct surface representation:

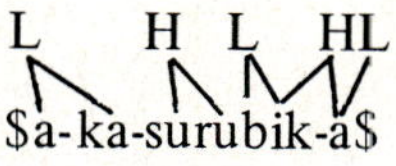

The discussion of the above example has shown that the principle that associates unlinked vowels to the left (when these vowels occur between two linked tones) will account for the fact that a *sequence* of high tones appears on the verbal complex in *a-ka-súrúbǐk-â.* The fact that this sequence is halted by the presence of a voiced obstruent is explained by the fact that the voiced obstruent is linked to a low tone and this association line will prevent any vowels to the right from being affected by a high tone to the left.

I have now accounted for all the data involving words with two high tones where there is a voiced obstruent in the verbal complex (excluding the case where there is a voiced obstruent immediately before the ultimate vowel, since this case involves a complexity that cannot be seen until the phrasal tonology is examined in section 8). Let me now consider examples like *a-na-púpút-â.* This item has the underlying structure:

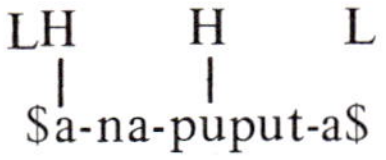


The analyses that I have considered will both convert this structure to:

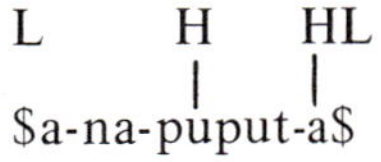


The general principles governing the association of unlinked tones and vowels will then yield the structure:

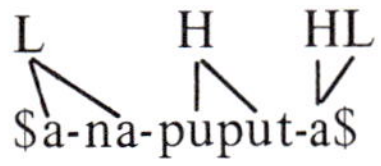


The application of Leftwards High Spread to this representation will produce no visible change. The above representation gives, of course, a correct account of the phonetics of *a-na-púpút-â*

Notice that if instead of a rule of Low Insertion we had claimed that the medial low tones in *a-ná-dundurǐk-â, a-na-ní-dungǐr-â,* and *a-ka-súrúbǐk-â* were to be attributed to the fact that the non-initial vowels in the verbs /dundurik/, /dungir/, and /surubik/ all are underlyingly associated with a low tone, then we would have difficulty explaining why the second vowel of the verbal complex in *a-na-púpút-â* does not have a low tone associated with it in phonetic representation. I take the ungrammaticality of **a-na-púpǔt-â* to be evidence that there is no low tone associated with the non-initial vowels of polysyllabic verb stems, and that therefore Low Insertion is a preferred analysis.

I can now adduce evidence in favor of the analysis involving Displacement-To-Stem over the analysis involving High Tone Retraction. If a low-toned object prefix is introduced into *a-na-púpútâ*, we get the following surface forms: *a-na-ní-púpút-â* 'he/she is beating me'. This item has the underlying structure:

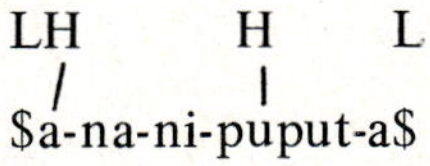


Consider the analysis involving displacement of the leftmost high. It would convert the above representation into:

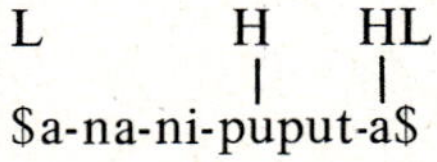


Now, the rule of High Tone Retraction cannot apply to this representation since it retracts a high tone onto a preceding vowel just in case a voiced obstruent intervenes. The general principles governing the association of unlinked tones and vowels will then produce the following incorrect representation:

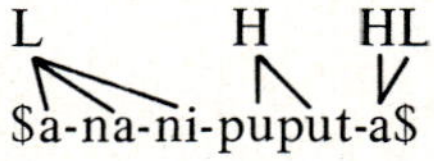


Thus it can be seen that the analysis involving High Tone Displacement affecting the leftmost high in a word plus High Tone Retraction cannot explain why in *a-na-ní-púpút-â* there is a high tone associated with the object prefix.

On the other hand, the analysis involving Displacement-To-Stem will yield the correct results. Given the underlying structure

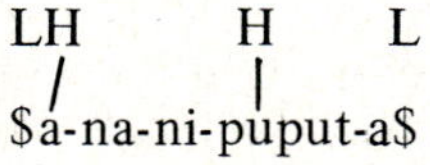


High Tone Displacement will yield

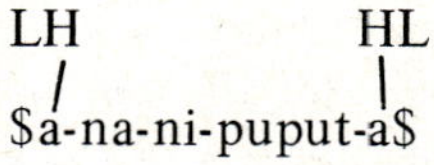


and then Displacement-To-Stem will give the following structure:

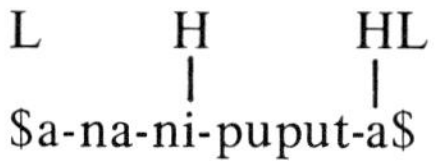


The general principles governing the association of unlinked tones and vowels will generate the correct phonetic representation:

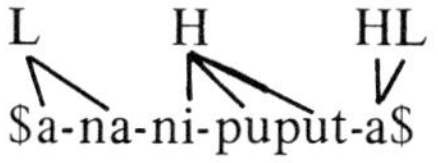


(The application of Leftwards High Spread will not alter the phonetic realization of this item.) On the basis of forms like *a-na-ní-púpút-â,* then, I conclude that High Tone Displacement must affect the rightmost high and that a rule of Displacement-To-Stem is motivated.

All of the data presented so far containing two high tones (subsequent to High Tone Deletion) have involved verb stems that are not subject to the rule of Neutralization. I would like now to examine data where there are two high tones in the word, the rightmost of which is associated with a stem that is subject to Neutralization. Consider the examples in (41).

| | | |
|---|---|---|
| (41) | a-na-hêg-a | 'he/she is trapping' |
| | a-na-sôm-a | 'he/she is reading' |
| | a-na-chêm-a | 'he/she is shouting' |
| | a-na-îm-a | 'he/she is standing' |
| | a-na-mêg-a | 'he/she is breaking off a piece' |
| | a-ná-ban-a | 'he/she is pressing' |
| | a-ná-vug-a | 'he/she is cooking' |
| | a-ná-zim-a | 'he/she is extinguishing' |
| | a-ná-dony-a | 'he/she is choking' |
| | a-ná-jibu | 'he/she is answering' |

All of the verbs in (41) are monosyllabic stems that are subject to Neutralization. They can be contrasted with monosyllabic high-toned stems that are exceptional in that they do not undergo Neutralization:

| | | |
|---|---|---|
| (42) | a-na-nén-â | 'he/she is speaking' |
| | a-na-nyór-â | 'he/she is shaving' |
| | a-na-tány-â | 'he/she is stopping a fight' |
| | a-na-Béh-â | 'he/she is sifting grain' |
| | a-ná-dŭng-â | 'he/she is piercing' |
| | a-ná-vyăr-â | 'she is giving birth' |
| | a-ná-bănd-â | 'he/she is hitting so as to break s.t. in two' |

The verbs in (41) can also be contrasted with monosyllabic low-toned verbs:

| | | |
|---|---|---|
| (43) | a-na-tsǒng-â | 'he/she is carving' |
| | a-na-rǐr-â | 'he/she is crying' |
| | a-na-Bǒnd-â | 'he/she is pounding' |
| | a-na-sǔk-â | 'he/she is plaiting' |
| | a-na-fǐk-â | 'he/she is arriving' |
| | a-na-vwǐk-â | 'he/she is dipping s.t. in' |
| | a-na-gǔr-â | 'he/she is buying' |
| | a-na-dzěng-â | 'he/she is building' |
| | a-na-zǎm-â | 'he/she is stooping/bending' |

The derivation of the items in (42) and (43) does not really require any discussion. The words in (43) have a single high tone (associated with the subject prefix) which will be displaced to the ultimate vowel and then trigger Leftwards High Spread. The words in (42) have two high tones: one of these high tones is associated with the subject prefix and the other is associated with the stem. The stem high is marked as exceptional in that it will undergo High Tone Displacement even though there is an otherwise general restriction on that rule which bars it from affecting a high associated with the penultimate vowel of the word. Consequently, given the underlying form

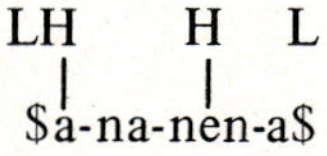


High Tone Displacement and Displacement-To-Stem will correctly derive the representation:

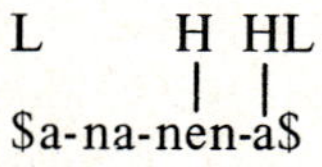


The general principles governing the association of unlinked tones and vowels will yield the surface representation:

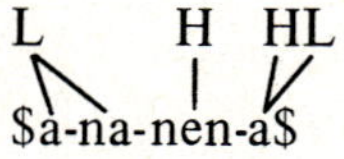


Items such as *a-ná-dǔng-â* present no problems, since they are entirely parallel to examples like *a-ná-dundurǐk-â.*

The data in (41), however, do require some discussion. The underlying forms of *a-na-sôm-a* and *a-ná-dony-a* are:

```
LH    H  L            LH     H   L
 |    |                |     |
$a-na-som-a$          $a-na-dony-a$
```

Recall that in my analysis, High Tone Displacement is blocked from applying to a high tone that is associated with the penultimate vowel of the word. Since High Tone Displacement affects just the rightmost high in a word, we have here a situation where High Tone Displacement simply cannot apply to these representations. Low Insertion will apply to the second representation to assign the stem-initial voiced obstruent a low tone:

```
LH    LH   L
 |    \\
$a-na-dony-a$
```

On the basis of the examples in (41), it appears that we can derive the correct phonetic forms by simply allowing Neutralization and Displacement-To-Stem to apply. Neutralization will change a H associated with the penultimate vowel into a L, yielding:

```
LH    L  L            LH    LL   L
 |    |                |    \\
$a-na-som-a$          $a-na-dony-a$
```

and Displacement-To-Stem will associate a non-ultimate high as far to the right as possible (provided it does not cross an association line or a stem vowel):

```
L    HL  L            L  HLL   L
     V                   | ||
$a-na-som-a$          $a-na-dony-a$
```

Finally, the principles governing the association of unlinked tones and vowels will produce the correct surface forms:

```
L    HL  L            L  HLL   L
 \   V  /             \  | ||  /
$a-na-som-a$          $a-na-dony-a$
```

As attractive as this analysis is, I will show that actually it is not Displacement-To-Stem that associates the non-ultimate high in these examples but rather a third displacement rule – a displacement rule that is in fact triggered by a neutralized high and attracts a preceding high to the neutralized high. The data motivating the postulation of a third displacement rule (which I will refer to as Low Attraction) will be examined later in the study (section 6) and I will not pursue a discussion of this matter at the present time.

I will conclude this section by noting the existence of one class of examples that provides a certain complication for the analysis of Digo that I have so far developed. There are a handful of verbs in Digo which have verb stems that contain no vowel (although historically these verb stems presumably did have a vowel). One such verb is *ku-ty-a* 'to obey'. The present tense paradigm of this verb is illustrated in (44).

| | | |
|---|---|---|
| (44) | ni-na-ty-a | 'I am obeying' |
| | u-na-ty-a | 'you sg. are obeying' |
| | a-nâ-ty-a | 'he/she is obeying' |
| | tu-na-ty-a | 'we are obeying' |
| | mu-na-ty-a | 'you pl. are obeying' |
| | ma-nâ-ty-a | 'they are obeying' |

Clearly, the verb /ty/ – even though it has no vowel – must have a high tone associated with it in underlying structure. Furthermore, this high tone must undergo Neutralization. In order to undergo Neutralization, it must *not* undergo High Tone Displacement (since Neutralization affects penultimate highs, not ultimate highs). In order to not undergo High Tone Displacement, it must be associated with the penultimate vowel in the word (recall that penultimate high tones are exempted from High Tone Displacement, at least in the regular case). Consequently, in order for the high tone associated with /ty/ to undergo Neutralization it must – prior to the application of High Tone Displacement – get shifted from /ty/ onto the preceding (penultimate) vowel. Call this rule High Shift. Presumably this rule shifts a high from a morpheme that has no tone-bearing element onto the preceding vowel. Given the postulation of this rule, the paradigm in (44) can be readily derived. (45) gives representative derivations:

```
(45)   L      H  L   LH     H  L
                      |
       $ni-na-ty-a$   $a-na-ty-a$

       L   H     L   LH H     L
           |          / |
       $ni-na-ty-a$   $a-na-ty-a$      High Shift

       inapplicable   inapplicable     High Tone Displacement
```

```
L   L   L      LH  L    L
    |           |  |
$ni-na-ty-a$   $a-na-ty-a$        Neutralization

               L HL     L
                  V
inapplicable   $a-na-ty-a$        Low Attraction

L   L   L      L   HL   L
 \  |  /        \  V   /
$ni-na-ty-a$   $a-na-ty-a$        association principles
```

At this point in the exposition, let me point out how the data I have considered in this section provide evidence in favor of certain assumptions that I made earlier about the formulation of High Tone Displacement and Neutralization.

First, recall that I claim that High Tone Displacement associates a high tone with the ultimate vowel of the word rather than with the penult vowel. Given the assumption that High Tone Displacement must precede Neutralization (an assumption that I will justify in the section on phrasal tonology later in section 8), and given the assumption that Neutralization affects penultimate high tones (an assumption that explains why *ku-som-a* undergoes Neutralization but *ku-somĕr-â* does not, as well as helping to explain some additional data examined in the treatment of the imperative verb in section 6), then it follows that High Tone Displacement cannot displace a high tone to the penultimate vowel of the word. If it did so, then this displaced high should undergo Neutralization, but it does not!

Second, recall that I assume that Neutralization changes a high to a low rather than simply deleting the high from the tonal tier. My motivation for making this assumption comes from the forms in (41) like *a-na-sôm-a.* In particular, the falling tone on the penultimate vowel of this word needs explanation. The high portion of the fall clearly has its origin in the high tone associated with the subject prefix /a/. But what about the low portion of the fall? It does not appear that this low can in any way be explained as deriving from the final boundary low, since there would be no need for this low to associate with the penult vowel given that this vowel has a high linked to it (as a consequence of the rule that I have referred to as Low Attraction, which attracts a preceding H to the neutralized vowel). If however, we accept the claim that Neutralization changes a high into a low, then the low portion of the falling tone receives an explanation.

## 5. THE -A- PAST TENSE

The morphological structure of the past tense in Digo is SP+a+(OP)+VS+a, where SP = subject prefix, OP = object prefix, and VS = Verb Stem. The choice of a given subject prefix does not alter the tonal shape of the past tense form in any way; consequently, all of the examples cited will be with the same SP - namely, the 1 sg. subject prefix, which is ordinarily *ni-* but assumes the form *n-* in front of the *-a-* past tense marker. Examples of this construction are given in (46).

(46) a. *low-toned stems*

| | |
|---|---|
| n-a-tsúkúr-â | 'I carried' |
| n-a-wóchér-â | 'I received' |
| n-a-róngóz-a | 'I led' |
| n-a-tsór-â | 'I picked up' |
| n-a-píg-a | 'I hit' |
| n-á-gǔr-â | 'I bought' |
| n-á-vugǔr-â | 'I untied' |
| n-á-vumikíz-a | 'I agreed' |
| n-a-tógǒr-â | 'I praised' |
| n-a-rágǔr-â | 'I treated (medically)' |
| n-á-dzěng-â | 'I built' |

b. *high-toned verb stems that undergo Neutralization*

| | |
|---|---|
| n-á-meg-a | 'I broke off a piece' |
| n-á-san-a | 'I forged' |
| n-á-rum-a | 'I bit' |
| n-á-Bah-a | 'I got' |
| n-á-hem-a | 'I cleared forest' |
| n-á-vwin-a | 'I sang' |

c. *high-toned verb stems that undergo High Tone Displacement*

| | |
|---|---|
| n-a-kúmbúkír-â | 'I remembered' |
| n-a-túrúk-â | 'I went out' |
| n-a-púpút-â | 'I beat' |
| n-a-nén-â | 'I spoke' |
| n-á-vwinǐr-â | 'I sang for' |
| n-á-dunduríz-a | 'I put something aside' |
| n-á-garagǎr-â | 'I rolled about in pain' |
| n-á-dǔng-â | 'I pierced' |
| n-a-ézěk-â | 'I thatched' |

Consider first the data in (46a). The verb stems in question are low-toned at the lexical level. Nevertheless, the tonal shapes that the items in (46a) exhibit are entirely analogous to verbal forms that contain two high tones. This can be seen by comparing (46a) with the high-toned verbs in the *-ka-* tense illustrated in (37), (38), and (39). It seems clear, then that any satisfactory account of the data in (46a) requires that there be two high tones in the underlying structure of these words. The only question is: where are these two high tones located (underlyingly)?

The data in (46a) show that the rightmost high has been able to displace to the ultimate vowel. Consequently, we know that this high tone must *not* be associated with the penultimate vowel (since penultimate highs cannot displace). This means that the stem cannot be the locus of the rightmost high tone - for if the stem were where this high tone originated, then we could not explain an example like *n-ágŭr-â.* The stem vowel in this example is the penultimate vowel of the word; therefore, if it had a high tone associated with it, that high tone would fail to undergo High Tone Displacement and would subsequently undergo Neutralization. But this would produce incorrect results. I conclude that the rightmost high tone in the words in (46a) is not associated with the stem. It could (conceivably) be associated with the ultimate vowel, or it could be associated with the past tense marker *-a-*.

The data in (46a) show that the first high tone in the underlying structure of these words displaces to(wards) the stem. Since in all other cases Displacement-To-Stem affects a prefixal high, it seems likely that the first high in these words must be associated with a prefix. Which prefix? If the rightmost high were assumed to be associated with the final vowel *-a* underlyingly, then the first high in the word could conceivably be associated either with the subject prefix or with the past tense marker *-a-*. However, if the rightmost high were assumed to be associated with the past tense marker *-a-*, then presumably the first high must be located on the subject prefix (assuming that it would be theoretically unviable to have *two* high tones associated with the *-a-* prefix).

We have learned all that we can from the data in (46a). Consider now the examples in (46b). The verb stems here all have a high tone associated with them at the lexical level. Furthermore, this high tone is associated with a vowel that is penultimate in the word. As a consequence, this high tone will be unable to undergo High Tone Displacement and will undergo Neutralization. Suppose that we were to assume in the past tense there is a high tone associated with one of the prefixes and with the ultimate vowel. Then we would have an underlying representation for *n-á-san-a* such as:

```
L    H H  HL
     | |  |
$n(i)-a-san-a$
```

While the rule of Neutralization could account for the fact that the medial H in this representation is changed to L, there would be no independently motivated rule to account for why the H associated with the ultimate vowel is changed to L. Not only would there be no independently motivated rule to account for this change, the change would not be a motivated one either - why should this H be lowered? There does not appear to be any natural phonetic process that would account for such a change.

On the other hand, suppose that both of the high tones associated with the past tense are located on the prefixes. Then the underlying representation for *n-á-san-a* would be:

```
L HHH  L
  | | |
$n(i)-a-san-a$
```

High Tone Displacement will fail to apply to this representation (since the rightmost H is on the penult and cannot undergo the rule); Neutralization will then yield:

```
L HH L  L
  | | |
$n(i)-a-san-a$
```

We have now successfully accounted for the fact that there is a low tone associated with the penult vowel and no high tone associated with the ultimate vowel. What remains to be explained is why in *n-á-san-a* there is a high tone associated with the *-a-* past tense marker but not with the verb stem's vowel. For we do have a rule that would be expected to associate a prefixal high with the neutralized vowel - cf. *a-na-sôm-a,* derived earlier. I have referred to this rule as Low Attraction. (Recall that I have not yet given the evidence that distinguishes Low Attraction from Displacement-To-Stem. In the examples under discussion, the neutralized vowel is the first vowel in the stem; consequently, the displacement of a high to the neutralized (low) vowel is indistinguishable from the displacement of a high to the first stem vowel.)

Below I will suggest an analysis of *n-á-san-a,* and the other data in (46b), though I readily admit that the data do not unambiguously support this analysis over other conceivable ones. Suppose that, after Neutralization has applied to produce the representation cited above, Low Attraction associates the high linked to the past tense marker with the neutralized vowel.[16] This would produce the representation:

```
L H   HL  L
  |   \/
$n(i)-a-san-a$
```

Assume furthermore that the first H in this word is unable to undergo any displacement process (it isn't subject to High Tone Displacement since it isn't the rightmost H in the word at the point where that rule applies; it isn't subject to Low Attraction because it isn't the H that immediately precedes the penult low; I will discuss below how to insure that it isn't subject to Displacement-To-Stem). If we now allow the universal association principles to apply, they will produce the following structure (given the elision of the vowel of the *ni-* prefix):[17]

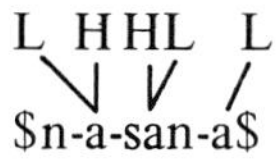


At this point we can invoke an extremely plausible rule (cf. Hyman and Schuh 1974) which would delete the H from a HL sequence linked to a penult vowel when the preceding vowel is associated with another high tone. Call this rule Fall Simplification.[18] It will yield the following:

This, of course, is not quite the correct phonetic output. It is still necessary to postulate a rule that would eliminate the initial L from a LH sequence on the first vowel of the word. (There are no rising tones on the first vowel of a word except those that originate from Leftwards High Spread - see examples like *kǎndê* 'food' in the section on nouns below.)

At first glance it might seem as though the need to eliminate the initial low in the above derivation provides evidence *against* the boundary tone analysis, since it is only the assumption of such tones that requires there to be an initial low tone in the underlying representation of *n-á-san-a.* However, if one did not assume the existence of boundary tones and claimed that in the past tense the first morpheme of the word has associated with it a high tone, one would account for why *n-á-san-a* begins with a high tone but one would leave unexplained why the examples in (46a) like *n-a-tsúkúr-â* begin with a low tone. If the first morpheme in the past tense construction (namely, the subject prefix) has a high tone associated with it, then an initial boundary tone is needed to explain why the *-a-* in *n-a-tsúkúr-â* is realized as a low-toned vowel.

Another tack that could be adopted in order to account for the loss of the initial L in *n-á-san-a* is to revise the general principles for associating unlinked tones and vowels. In particular, one might claim that an unlinked tone will associate (by universal rule) only in the event there is an unlinked vowel available for the tone to link up with. In the case of *n-á-san-a,* the first vowel of the word is linked to an H, therefore the initial boundary tone would be left stranded - there would be no available unlinked vowel for it to associate with. We could then assume a convention whereby unlinked tones are simply omitted from the phonetic representation. While this revision of the general principles for associating unlinked tones and vowels would explain the failure of the initial boundary tone to appear in *n-á-san-a,* it would not explain why the final boundary tone *does* appear in items such as *n-a-tsúkúr-â,* etc. We have seen that the final L does associate with the ultimate vowel even though the ultimate vowel has a H associated with it as a consequence of High Tone Displacement. It would be necessary, under the proposed revision of the general principles for associating unlinked tones and vowels, to postulate a language-specific rule of Digo that would have the effect of linking a final unassociated L with the final vowel of the word. Thus, whatever analysis we adopt, there will be a need for some rule specific to Digo - either a rule to eliminate the initial boundary tone from *n-á-san-a* or a rule to link the final boundary tone regardless of whether the ultimate vowel is already linked to a tone. The choice between these two analyses will, of course, depend on what turns out - on universal grounds - to be the appropriate conventions for associating unlinked tones and vowels.

While the above account of the derivation of *n-á-san-a* is doubtless problematic in various respects, I do feel that an appeal to a rule such as Fall Simplification to account for the absence of a falling tone on the neutralized vowel is extremely attractive. The difference between *a-na-sôm-a* and *a-ná-san-a* clearly seems to be that in the former case the neutralized vowel is not preceded by a high tone whereas in the latter case it is. And, furthermore, it seems reasonable to conclude that the reason there is a high tone on the *-a-* prefix in *n-á-san-a* is due to the fact that there is a high tone in this word which has been unable to displace to the neutralized vowel. And it seems reasonable to conclude that the reason this high tone cannot displace to the neutralized vowel is that there is another high in the word that has displaced to the neutralized vowel, but which does not actually appear on the surface (having been eliminated by Fall Simplification). For the remainder of this paper, then, I will assume that some such account of *a-ná-san-a* is appropriate. Later, when I turn to the phrasal tonology, additional relevant data will emerge.

Let me now turn to the data in (46c). The verb stems here are ones that have a high tone associated with them at the lexical level, and this high tone is one that is subject to High Tone Displacement (*contra* the stems in (46b)). Thus we will have underlying structures of the following sort:

```
L H H H         L
   |  |  |
$n(i)-a-kumbukir-a$
```

High Tone Displacement will associate the rightmost H with the ultimate vowel. Displacement-To-Stem will associate the medial H with the first vowel of the verbal complex. The result is:

```
L H    H        HL
   \    |        |
$n(i)-a-kumbukir-a$
```

The elision of the vowel of *ni-* would cause the H associated with this vowel to shift onto the *-a-* prefix. But notice that this result is not a desirable one, for we do not want to end up with a high tone associated with the *-a-*. In the correct surface representation *-a-* will have to be associated just with the initial boundary (low) tone.

There are obviously several approaches one might adopt in order to solve this problem. I will suggest one that involves a modification of a rule suggested earlier. Recall that earlier I suggested that instead of the expected **n-ǎ-san-a* we get *n-á-san-a* due to the application of a rule that simplifies rising tones on the first vowel of a word. Call this rule Rising Tone Simplification. It will convert a rising tone to a level high tone in the case of *n-á-san-a.* Now, I would like to suggest that instead of the expected **n-ǎ-kúmbúkír-â* we get *n-a-kúmbúkír-â* as a result of this same Rising Tone Simplification rule. Only in this case we get a level low tone instead of a level high tone. Whether the rising tone simplifies to a high tone or a low tone depends on the following vowel: if the following vowel is low-toned, the rise simplifies to high; if the following vowel is high-toned, the rise simplifies to low. Some additional support for this analysis will arise in the next section of the paper.[19]

In discussing the data in (46c) I have so far mentioned only an example such as *n-a-kúmbúkír-â* where there are no voiced obstruents to complicate matters. Let me now consider examples where there is a voiced obstruent in the stem. The underlying representation of *n-a-ézěk-â* is:

```
L HHH    L
  | | /
$n(i)-a-ezek-a$
```

High Tone Displacement will associate the rightmost H with the ultimate vowel; Low Insertion will assign a L to the *z* of /ezek/; and Displacement-To-Stem will then associate the H of the *-a-* prefix with the first stem vowel. The result will thus be:

```
L H   HL   HL
  \   ||    |
$n(i)-a-ezek-a$
```

The vowel of the *ni-* prefix will elide, and the general principles associating unlinked tones and vowels will associate the first L and H in the word with the prefix *-a-*; they will also associate the L linked to *z* with the penultimate vowel and the final boundary (low) tone with the ultimate vowel. The result is:

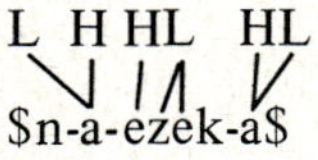


Rising Tone Simplification will simplify the rising tone on the first vowel of the word to a level low tone (since the next vowel in the word is high-toned) and Leftwards High Spread will add an association line between the penultimate vowel and the H associated with the ultimate vowel. These two changes produce the correct surface form.

Finally, consider the example *n-á-vwinǐr-â.* It has the underlying form:

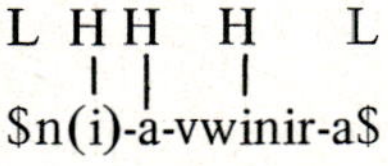


High Tone Displacement will associate the rightmost H with the ultimate vowel; Low Insertion will assign a L to the stem-initial consonant; and Displacement-To-Stem will be unable to move the H from the *-a-* onto the first stem vowel, since Displacement-To-Stem is barred from crossing an association line. The output of the above rules will thus be:

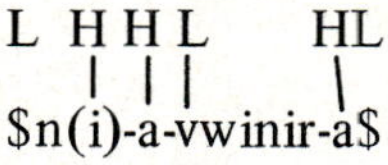


The vowel of *ni-* will elide. The general principles for associating unlinked tones and vowels will associate the first L and H in the word with the prefixal vowel *-a-*. This will, however, trigger the loss of one of the H's, since two successive identical tones on the same vowel must reduce to a single tone by general convention. The L associated with the *v* will associate with the antepenult and penult vowels. The final boundary (low) tone will associate with the ultimate vowel. We will thus derive the representation below:

Rising Tone Simplification will reduce the rising tone on the first vowel of the word to a level high tone. The reason that Rising Tone Simplification produces a level high in this example (rather than a level low) is that a low tone follows the rising tone. This low tone is associated with a consonant rather than a vowel, but that does not appear to matter. Thus the proper formulation of Rising Tone Simplification is: the rise becomes high when a low follows and low when a high follows. Leftwards High Spread will also apply, adding an association line between the penult vowel and the high associated with the ultimate vowel. The result is the correct surface form:

The past tense is clearly a complex construction which poses a number of difficulties for any satisfactory analysis. It is interesting, however, despite its problematic aspects, because it provides for the possibility of a representation where there are *three* high tones. I will show in section 8 that the phrasal tonology provides instances where there are three high tones, and that the facts encountered there parallel the data discussed in this section. Thus while there are details of the analysis of the past tense that are still unclear, there will be independent evidence that it is correct to assume that (46b) and (46c) represent instances where there are three underlying high tones.

## 6. THE IMPERATIVE

In this section I will examine some aspects of the tonal structure of the imperative in Digo. This form has neither a subject prefix nor a tense prefix. The final vowel is *-a* when there is no object prefix present or when the OP is the 1 sg. *-ni-*, otherwise the final vowel is *-e*. The suffix *-ni* is added to indicate a plural subject. Although I will give the plural imperative forms when I cite data, these forms are problematic in certain respects and I will not attempt to give a full account of them here. In (47) I illustrate the imperative of a low-toned verb, /tsukur/ 'carry'.

| | | | | |
|---|---|---|---|---|
| (47) | tsukur-a | 'carry!' | tsukur-ǎ-nî | 'pl. carry!' |
| | ni-tsukur-a | 'carry me!' | ni-tsukur-ǎ-nî | 'pl. carry me!' |
| | a-tsukûr-e | 'carry them!' | a-tsúkúr-é-nî | 'pl. carry them!' |

The key to understanding the imperative construction, tonally-speaking, is provided by the example *a-tsukûr-e*. The pitch pattern of this item is identical to forms such as *a-na-sôm-a,* thus it seems reasonable to conclude that their underlying structures must be parallel. This pitch pattern derives from there being (a) a high tone on the penultimate vowel which will fail to undergo High Tone Displacement and instead will undergo Neutralization, and (b) a high tone on a prefix which will displace to the neutralized vowel. In the case of *a-tsukûr-e,* we have independent evidence that the object prefix /a/ has a high tone associated with it. Thus, in order to make this item parallel to *a-na-sôm-a,* all that is necessary is to assume that in this construction there is a high tone associated with the last vowel of the verb stem (which is the penultimate vowel of the word). This high on the last stem vowel is presumably supplied by the morphology rather than being "lexical" in nature (since we know that /tsukur/ has no highs associated with it lexically).

The derivation of *a-tsukûr-e* is shown in (48) below.

(48)
```
LH     H  L
 |     |
$a-tsukur-e$

inapplicable          High Tone Displacement

LH     L  L
 |     |
$a-tsukur-e$          Neutralization

L      HL  L
       \/
$a-tsukur-e$          Low Attraction

L      HL  L
 \     \/  /
$a-tsukur-e$          association principles
```

If the derivation in (48) is accepted, then we have critical evidence in support of the proposition that we need a rule of Low Attraction distinct from Displacement-To-Stem. Notice that the prefixal H is associated underlyingly with an object prefix, and it ends up associated with the neutralized vowel. But Displacement-To-Stem predicts that the prefixal H should remain located on the first vowel of the verbal complex. That rule in no way predicts that the prefixal H will end up on the ultimate vowel of the verbal complex. Thus we need a rule which will associate a H with the neutralized vowel (the neutralized vowel, of course, is simply a penultimate vowel linked to a low). I have called this rule Low Attraction.

I assume that Low Attraction will be formulated so that a H is attracted to a *low* penult vowel. This means that Neutralization must precede Low Attraction, since Neutralization creates the L that triggers the application of Low Attraction. Furthermore, I assume that Low Attraction cannot associate a H with the neutralized vowel if to do so would cause a crossing of association lines. Thus the presence of a L linked to a voiced obstruent will prevent a high from associating with the neutralized vowel, as in examples like *a-ná-vug-a* (see section 4). The prefixal H *does* reassociate as close to the neutralized vowel as possible - thus in the example just cited the H associated with the subject prefix /a/ moves over the vowel of /na/, even though it cannot move all the way to the neutralized vowel.[20] From the above observation it can be seen that Low Insertion must apply before Low Attraction, since the former rule supplies the linked low tones that prevent Low Attraction from associating the prefixal H with the neutralized vowel in examples like *a-ná-vug-a.*

Let us pause briefly to consider the interaction of Low Attraction and Displacement-to-Stem. The ordering of these two rules is by no means obvious. Consider the derivation in (48), for instance. We could allow Displacement-to-Stem to apply before Low Attraction. If we did this, the prefixal H would get displaced to the first vowel of the verbal complex - but since the object prefix /a/ *is* the first vowel of the verbal complex, the application of Displacement-to-Stem would be vacuous. Low Attraction could then reassociate the H in question with the neutralized vowel. On the other hand, if we apply Low Attraction before Displacement-to-Stem, then the prefixal H will get associated with the neutralized vowel before Displacement-to-Stem ever has a chance to affect it. Either ordering of the rules will thus account for *a-tsukûr-e.*

Examples such as *a-na-sôm-a* and *a-ná-vug-a* also do not provide any relevant data since in these words Low Attraction and Displacement-to-Stem would in any case associate the prefixal H with the *same* vowel. Thus it is impossible to tell which rule has actually applied. The one sort of example that is interesting is *n-á-san-a,* derived earlier. In this word we have two high tones before the neutralized vowel, one associated with the subject prefix *n(i)-* and one associated with the past tense prefix *-a-*. I have suggested that the rightmost of these prefixal highs does displace to the neutralized vowel, although it then undergoes Fall Simplification. The leftmost high does not displace onto the neutralized vowel. This can be explained if we restrict Low Attraction so that it affects just the first H before the neutralized vowel. But this leftmost prefixal high also does not displace to the first vowel of the verbal complex (which is, of course, also the neutralized vowel). Thus it appears that it must be prevented from undergoing Displacement-to-Stem as well as Low Attraction. The leftmost high *does* associate with the *-a-* prefix, but there is no good evidence that this association is to be attributed to the application of Displacement-to-Stem. I have suggested earlier that when the subject prefix *ni-* elides its vowel, the H associated with that vowel will reassociate with the following vowel (the *-a-* prefix) as a consequence of the general principles governing autosegmental representations. Thus we have no reason at all to think that Displacement-to-Stem has operated in the derivation of *n-á-san-a.* Consequently, Displacement-to-Stem must be formulated so that it will not affect the leftmost high in the underlying structure of *n-á-san-a.*

If Displacement-to-Stem is ordered before Low Attraction, then we could restrict the former rule so that it applies just to the *first* H before a verbal complex (just as we necessarily restricted Low Attraction to the first H before a neutralized vowel). This formulation is possible since (in the case of *n-á-san-a*) there would still be two high tones before the verbal complex at the point where Displacement-to-Stem applies, Low Attraction not yet having associated the rightmost prefixal high with the neutralized vowel. If, on the other hand, Low Attraction is applied before Displacement-to-Stem, then after the former rule has applied the leftmost of the underlying prefixal highs will be the only high located before the verbal complex (Low Attraction having moved the rightmost prefixal high to the neutralized vowel). Thus, if we are to prevent this leftmost prefixal high from associating with the first vowel of the verbal complex, we must constrain Displacement-to-Stem so that it cannot apply when there is already a high associated with that vowel (due to the prior application of Low Attraction).[21] Instead of adding such a complication to the statement of Displacement-to-Stem, I prefer to order that rule before Low Attraction. Such an analysis means that a high tone that undergoes Low Attraction will necessarily have already undergone Displacement-to-Stem. For simplicity's sake, in the remainder of this paper I will simply speak of a high tone undergoing Low Attraction, ignoring the fact that it will actually undergo Displacement-to-Stem first under the rule ordering I am assuming.[22]

At this point, let us return to a consideration of the data in (47). I have explained the example *a-tsukûr-e.* The forms *tsukur-a* and *ni-tsukur-a* present no problems. They each have a single high tone, associated with the penultimate vowel, which will undergo Neutralization. Thus in the surface representation of these words there are no high tones. The example *tsukur-ǎ-nî* shows that the addition of the suffix *-ni* causes the high tone associated with the last vowel of /tsukur/ to no longer be located on the penultimate vowel of the word and thus to no longer be exempted from High Tone Displacement. That rule will associate the high on the last vowel of /tsukur/ with the ultimate vowel of the word, eventually triggering Leftwards High Spread. The example *ni-tsukur-ǎ-nî* is entirely parallel to *tsukur-ǎ-ní.* The example *a-tsúkúr-é-nî* can be accounted for in a straightforward fashion within the analysis I have developed, but some of the later data involving the plural imperative with a high-toned object prefix contain complexities that cannot be examined in detail in the present study. Consequently, I will not attempt to pursue an analysis of such forms here.

Consider now the data in (49).

| | | | | |
|---|---|---|---|---|
| (49) | vumikiz-a | 'say yes!' | vumikiz-ǎ-nî | 'pl. say yes' |
| | ni-vumikiz-a | 'say yes to me!' | ni-vumikiz-ǎ-nî | 'pl. say yes to me!' |
| | á-vumikiz-e | 'say yes to them!' | á-vumikiz-é-nî | 'pl. say yes to them!' |

The example *á-vumikiz-e* is, for my present purposes, the most interesting form in (49). It has a high tone associated with the /a/ object prefix and with the last vowel of the verb stem. Notice that the high associated with the object prefix is unable to associate with the neutralized vowel; this failure is presumably due to the voiced obstruent at the beginning of the stem /vumikiz/. Low Insertion will associate a low tone with this consonant, and the presence of this linked low tone will prevent Low Attraction from associating the prefixal high with the neutralized vowel; the high tone on the object prefix must therefore remain associated with that prefix. The penultimate high, of course, cannot displace to the ultimate vowel, but rather undergoes Neutralization. Consequently, there will be no high tone in the word except for the high associated with the prefix.

Consider next the case of a low-toned verb stem with a stem-medial voiced obstruent.

| | | | | |
|---|---|---|---|---|
| (50) | rejezer-a | 'soak for!' | rejezer-ǎ-nî | 'pl. soak for!' |
| | ni-rejezer-a | 'soak for me!' | ni-rejezer-ǎ-nî | 'pl. soak for me!' |
| | a-réjezer-e | 'soak for them!' | a-réjezer-é-nî | 'pl. soak for them!' |

The form that is of interest to us here is *a-réjezer-e.* Notice that the high tone associated with the object prefix has moved away from that prefix as far towards the neutralized vowel as possible. It is prevented from reaching the neutralized vowel by the presence of a low tone associated with the voiced obstruent *j* as a consequence of Low Insertion. (Notice that even if the *j* were not present, the prefixal high could still not reach to the neutralized vowel since there is another voiced obstruent (*z*) whose linked low tone would block the association of the prefix high with the neutralized vowel.) It is important to note, however, that the prefixal high does move as close to the neutralized vowel as it can get without crossing an association line, thus it does associate to the vowel preceding *j*.[23]

So far in my discussion of the imperative I have only illustrated the behavior of low-toned verbs. In (51) I illustrate a high-toned verb. (Recall that B indicates a bilabial continuant that does not behave as an obstruent.)

| | | | | |
|---|---|---|---|---|
| (51) | Birik-a | 'send it!' | Birik-ǎ-nî | 'pl. send it!' |
| | ni-Birik-a | 'send me!' | ni-Birik-ǎ-nî | 'pl. send me!' |
| | a-Birîk-e | 'send them!' | a-Bíríḱ-é-nî | 'pl. send them!' |

These examples parallel precisely the data in (47) – suggesting that perhaps in the imperative the lexical tone specification of a verb is deleted and a H is assigned to the last vowel of the verb stem for *all* verbs. Further support for this proposed merger of (lexical) low and high verbs is found in (52).

| | | | | |
|---|---|---|---|---|
| (52) | vwinir-a | 'sing to!' | vwinir-ǎ-nî | 'pl. sing to!' |
| | ni-vwinir-a | 'sing to me!' | ni-vwinir-ǎ-nî | 'pl. sing to me!' |
| | á-vwinir-e | 'sing to them!' | á-vwinir-é-nî | 'pl. sing to them!' |

These data parallel precisely the data in (49) involving the low-toned verb /vumikiz/. There is no trace of any difference between the imperative of /vwinir/, a high-toned verb, and the imperative of /vumikiz/, a low-toned verb.

Although the data available to me at the present time are unfortunately skimpy on this particular point, there is some evidence that the merger between low and high verb stems in the imperative is only partial. In particular, it appears that high-toned verbs lose the high tone associated with their first vowel just in the event the first stem vowel is in antepenult position in the word. Compare the data in (53) with the examples in (51) and (52).

| | | | | |
|---|---|---|---|---|
| (53) | chekecher-a | 'sift for!' | chekecher-ǎ-nî | 'pl. sift for!' |
| | ni-chekecher-a | 'sift for me!' | ni-chekecher-ǎ-nî | 'pl. sift for me!' |
| | a-chékécher-e | 'sift for them!' | a-chékéchér-é-nî | 'pl. sift for me!' |

I suggest that the underlying representation of *a-chékécher-e* has a high associated with the object prefix /a/, a high associated with the first stem vowel, and a high associated with the last vowel of the stem. The following derivation provides the correct surface representation, given this underlying structure.

```
(54) LH  H   H  L
      |  |    \
     $a-chekecher-eS
```

inapplicable — High Tone Displacement

```
     LH  H   L  L
      |  |    \
     $a-chekecher-e$
```

Neutralization

LH HL L
$a-chekecher-e$ — Low Attraction

LH HL L
$a-chekecher-e$ — association principles

LH L L
$a-chekecher-e$ — Fall Simplification

LH L L
$a-chekecher-e$ — Rising Tone Simplification

The only point about the derivation in (54) that needs clarification is the ordering of the general principles for associating unlinked tones and vowels *before* Fall Simplification. Recall that Fall Simplification says that a HL sequence on a single vowel reduces to L just in case the preceding vowel has a H associated with it. In the above example, the HL sequence is not preceded by a high-toned vowel until *after* the general principles governing autosegmental representations add the relevant association lines. Thus it is necessary that Fall Simplification apply to the output of these general principles.[24]

Notice that throughout this study I have assumed that the general principles apply at some *point* in the derivation (e.g. after such rules as High Tone Displacement, Low Insertion, Low Attraction, and Displacement-to-Stem, but before such rules as Fall Simplification, Rising Tone Simplification, and Leftwards High Spread). An alternative view would have the general principles apply at every stage in the derivation - i.e. to the underlying representation and to the output of each rule in the grammar. This alternative view, if adopted for Digo, would require certain modifications in my analysis, and these modifications might be viable ones. However, to examine this issue in detail would take us beyond the scope of this study.[25]

## 7. NOUN TONOLOGY

In the preceding sections of this study I have examined a few of the verbal tenses in Digo and provided an analysis of the complex tonal patterns that they exhibited. Since some of the most significant evidence concerning the nature of Digo tonology derives from an examination of phrases consisting of a verb plus a noun, it is necessary to examine and to analyze the tonal behavior exhibited by nouns outside the scope of such phrases so that we can properly appreciate the results of combining these nouns with verbs into verbal phrases. The study of noun tonology, however, is itself a matter that requires extended treatment and cannot be dealt with fully here. In any case, much research is still required for a complete understanding of the full range of noun tonal patterns; all that I can do here is to motivate the existence of three tonally distinct groups of nouns which represent the simplest cases (from a tonal perspective) and also the most frequent types in the language.

The best way to begin to get at the tonal structure of nouns in Digo is to compare the simple noun with its locative form. Locatives in Digo are derived by suffixing *-ni* to the simple noun. In (55) below I illustrate a very large class of nouns which both in their simple form and in their locative form are pronounced with the tonal pattern associated with all low words.[26]

| | | | |
|---|---|---|---|
| (55) | n-jira | 'path(s)' | n-jira-ni |
| | mu-hama | 'millet' | mu-hama-ni |
| | tsongo | 'bird(s)' | tsongo-ni |
| | mu-hambo | 'trap' | mu-hambo-ni |
| | ma-ruwa | 'flowers' | ma-ruwa-ni |
| | gari | 'car' | gari-ni |
| | tunda | 'fruit' | tunda-ni |
| | banda | 'shed' | banda-ni |
| | goma | 'drum' | goma-ni |
| | chi-ronda | 'sore' | chi-ronda-ni |

Nouns such as the above are, I claim, best regarded as being ones which do not have a high tone associated with any of their vowels. I will refer to these as low-toned nouns.

Another very large class of nouns in Digo is illustrated in (56). In their simple form, these nouns are pronounced with the tonal pattern characteristic of words that lack any high tone. However, in their locative form, these nouns are pronounced with the tonal pattern characteristic of a word that has one high tone (which has displaced to the ultimate vowel, etc.).

| | | | |
|---|---|---|---|
| (56) | biga | 'water pot' | bigǎ-nî |
| | renje | 'pumpkin' | renjě-nî |
| | fumo | 'spear' | fumǒ-nî |
| | tsui | 'leopard(s)' | tsuǐ-nî |
| | vi-yogwe | 'sweet potatoes' | vi-yogwě-nî |
| | mu-kono | 'hand, arm' | mu-konǒ-nî |
| | ny-umba | 'house(s)' | ny-umbǎ-nî |

| | | | |
|---|---|---|---|
| | ny-ungu | 'pot(s) | ny-ungŭ-nî |
| | gunguhi | 'bed leg' | gunguhĭ-nî |
| | m̩-fumbati | 'side-bar of bed' | m̩-fumbatĭ-nî |

Nouns such as those in (56) are, I claim, best regarded as being nouns which have a high tone associated with their penultimate vowel, this high tone being thus subject to Neutralization. When the noun appears in its simple form, the penult H will fail to undergo High Tone Displacement and instead undergo Neutralization. The result is an all low word. In the locative form, the high on the noun is no longer penultimate, thus it is subject to High Tone Displacement and ends up associated with the ultimate vowel (eventually triggering Leftwards High Spread).

Let us at this point turn our attention to a third type of noun, which is illustrated in (57).

| | | | |
|---|---|---|---|
| (57) | kŭndê | 'beans' | kundé-nî |
| | kăndê | 'food' | kandé-nî |
| | chi-kŏpwê | 'sweet potato leaves' | chi-kopwé-nî |
| | pwéza | 'octopus' | pwéză-nî |
| | zódo | 'cooked mangos' | zódŏ-nî |
| | bătâ | 'duck' | batá-nî |
| | bŭndâ | 'bunch' | bundá-nî |
| | sahănî | 'plates(s)' | sahaní-nî |
| | kofĭyâ | 'hat(s)' | kofiyá-nî |
| | báda | 'cassava meal' | bádă-nî |
| | dŏnâ | 'hard porridge' | doná-nî |
| | chi-tábu | 'book' | chi-tábŭ-nî |

The simple forms of the nouns in (57) indicate quite clearly that these nouns have a high associated with them in underlying structure – a high tone that does not fall within the scope of Neutralization. The high tone on these nouns displaces to the ultimate vowel, where it yields the two surface patterns that we have observed from the very beginning of this paper: a rising-falling sequence over the last two vowels of the word, or a level high on the penult (the latter occurring when the post-penult consonant is a voiced obstruent). Since the H associated with the nouns in (57) is not the neutralizing type, that means that it must either be associated with a vowel other than the penult, or if it is associated with the penult, it must be marked as an exception to the restriction barring High Tone Displacement from affecting penult highs (recall that *ku-nĕn-â,* for example, represents an instance of a verb that must be so marked). For my present purposes it is not necessary to determine the location of the H on (each of) the nouns in (57); all that is crucial is that these are nouns that have a high tone that displaces to the ultimate vowel. The locative forms in (57) are problematic and I will not attempt to develop an analysis of them here.[27]

Suffixation of the locative element *-ni* provides clear evidence for the existence of three types of nouns – low-toned nouns, as in (55); high-toned nouns subject to Neutralization, as in (56); and high-toned nouns that undergo High Tone Displacement, as in (57). Much additional support for this three-way distinction among nouns can be found from examining various noun phrases in Digo, but I believe that the validity of the preceding analysis will be amply justified in the course of my examination of the tonal pattern of phrases consisting of a verb plus noun. It is to these phrases that I turn in the next section.

## 8. PHRASES CONSISTING OF A VERB AND A NOUN

Although a complete study of the tonology of Digo sentences is absolutely essential to an adequate understanding of Digo tone, I have sufficient materials to explore in detail just one sort of phrase, namely, those consisting of a verb plus a single (unmodified) noun. Such phrases, however, shed considerable light on the workings of tone in Digo.

### *8.1. Phrases Involving Verbs with No High Tones*

I will consider first phrases involving verbs that lack any high tones. In (58) I illustrate the case when a low-toned noun follows such a verb.

| | | | |
|---|---|---|---|
| (58) | a. | ku-gur-a ŋombe | 'to buy a cow' |
| | | ku-henz-a mu-ganga | 'to look for a doctor' |
| | | ku-sag-a mu-hama | 'to grind millet' |
| | b. | ni-na-pig-a goma | 'I am beating a drum' |
| | | ni-na-guw-a tunda | 'I am peeling a fruit' |

In (59) I illustrate the case where a high-toned noun subject to Neutralization follows a low-toned verb.

| | | | |
|---|---|---|---|
| (59) | a. | ku-takas-a ny-ungu | 'to clean a pot' |
| | | ku-rand-a chi-tanda | 'to spread a bed' |
| | b. | ni-na-jit-a vi-yogwe | 'I am cooking sweet potatoes' |
| | | na-na-gur-a shoka | 'I am buying an axe' |

In (60) I illustrate the case where a high-toned noun subject to High Tone Displacement follows a low-toned verb.

| | | | |
|---|---|---|---|
| (60) | a. | ku-sag-a ma-pěmbâ | 'to grind maize' (cf. ma-pěmbâ 'maize') |
| | | ku-vugur-a fũndô | 'to untie a knot' (cf. fũndô 'knot') |
| | | ku-andik-a chi-tábu | 'to write a book' (cf. chi-tábu 'book') |
| | b. | ni-na-tsor-a chi-dǎfû | 'I am picking a young coconut' (cf. chi-dǎfû 'young coconut') |
| | | ni-na-vugur-a fũndô | 'I am untying a knot' |

Examination of the data in (58)-(60) establishes that after a verb which contains no high tone in its underlying structure, a noun is pronounced exactly as it is pronounced in its isolation form. The noun is in no way affected by being located after a low-toned verb.

### *8.2. Phrases Involving Verbs with One High Tone*

Next I turn to phrases where the verb contains a single H in its underlying structure. In (61) I give examples of low-toned nouns after such verbs.

| | | | |
|---|---|---|---|
| (61) | a. | ku-onyes-a n-jǐrâ | 'to show the way' (cf. ku-onyěs-â, n-jira) |
| | | ku-afun-a ny-ǎmâ | 'to chew meat' (cf. ku-afǔn-â, ny-ama) |
| | | ku-anik-a n-gǔwô | 'to dry clothes in sun' (cf. ku-anǐk-â, n-guwo) |
| | b. | ni-na-ezek-a bǎndâ | 'I'm thatching a shed' (cf. ni-na-ezěk-â, banda) |
| | | ni-na-reh-a chi-gwázo | 'I'm bringing a peg' (cf. ni-na-rěh-â, chi-gwazo) |
| | | ni-na-ádz-a mǔ-tû | 'I'm mentioning someone' (cf. ni-na-ádz-a, mutu) |
| | c. | a-na-henz-a mu-gǎng-â | 'he's looking for a doctor' (cf. a-na-hěnz-â, mu-ganga) |
| | | a-na-jit-a mǎngâ | 'he's cooking cassava' (cf. a-na-jǐt-â, manga) |
| | | a-na-píg-a gǒmâ | 'he's beating a drum (cf. a-na-píg-a, goma) |
| | | a-na-ragíz-a kalǎmû | 'he's ordering a pen' (cf. a-na-ragíz-a, kalamu) |
| | d. | a-ka-gur-a n-gǔwô | 'he has bought clothes' (cf. a-ka-gǔr-â, n-guwo) |

| | |
|---|---|
| a-ka-jit-a má-zu | 'he has cooked bananas' (cf. a-ka-jǐt-â, ma-zu) |
| a-ka-ragíz-a kalǎmû | 'he has ordered a pen' (cf. a-ka-ragíz-a, kalamu) |

There are two immediately striking facts about the data in (61). First, the low-toned nouns are pronounced just like words that have a high tone displaced onto their ultimate vowel. Second, the verbs are (for the most part – and herein lies a very interesting story) pronounced as though they have no H associated with them. In other words, it seems as though the verb (which contains a H underlyingly) gives up its high to the low-toned noun that follows!

The analysis of this phenomenon is fairly obvious. Namely, all that we need to do is assume that High Tone Displacement operates on phrases as well as words. Thus if the rightmost H in the phrase is located on the verb, it will still displace to the ultimate vowel in the phrase, even though that ultimate vowel is in fact part of a noun that follows the verb. For instance, given the underlying representation

```
LH                  L
 |
$a-na-henz-a mu-ganga$
```

High Tone Displacement will apply to reassociate the H on the prefix /a/ with the last vowel of /mu-ganga/. The general principles governing unlinked tones and vowels plus the rule Leftwards High Spread will then create the correct surface shape.

There is one significant question that must be raised with respect to this analysis of the data in (61). Does the rule High Tone Displacement operate *once* on the entire phrase, or does it operate *twice* – first on the verb word, and then again to the phrase consisting of the verb plus following noun? Given the example *a-na-henz-a mu-gǎngâ*, either approach would achieve the correct results. If High Tone Displacement applies just to the entire phrase, it will reassociate the H of the verbal prefix /a/ with the last vowel of the noun. If High Tone Displacement applies twice, it first will reassociate the H of the prefix /a/ with the last vowel of the verb word, and then it will apply at the phrasal level to reassociate the H on the last vowel of the verb word with the last vowel of the noun. In either case, the prefix H ends up on the last vowel of the noun.

Evidence in favor of saying that High Tone Displacement applies in some sort of cyclic fashion (first to the verb, and then again to the phrase) is provided by several examples in (61) like *a-na-píg-a gǒmâ, a-na-ragíz-a kalǎmû*, and *ni-na-ádz-a mǔ-tû*. Although in underlying structure these phrases contain just a single H - originating on the 3 sg. subject prefix in the first two examples and on the verb stem in the last example, the surface forms clearly reflect *two* high tones. Where does this second H come from? The answer to this question will lead to the conclusion that High Tone Displacement must be a cyclic rule.

The critical fact about examples like *a-na-píg-a gŏmâ* is that the verb words in question are ones that have a voiced obstruent in post-penult position. But recall that it is exactly such verb words that I have up to this point left unexplained. I have not yet accounted for why a high-toned verb such as *ku-koróg-a* has a high tone on its penult vowel and a low-toned ultimate vowel, when what my rules predict is that there should be a high tone associated with the ultimate vowel of this word. Phrases such as *a-na-píg-a gŏmâ* suggest that the ultimate vowel of such words *does* have a high associated with it (at some point in the derivation, at least) and that in phrases where the verb is followed by a low noun, this high will displace onto the ultimate vowel of the noun. In other words, *a-na-píg-a gŏmâ* has as an intermediate stage in its derivation the representation:

```
L        H H      L
         | |
$a-na-pig-a goma$
```

But the underlying representation of this phrase is:

```
LH                L
 |
$a-na-pig-a goma$
```

How could the necessary intermediate stage have arisen? Presumably High Tone Displacement would convert the underlying representation into:

```
L          H      L
           |
$a-na-pig-a goma$
```

(I am assuming the cyclic analysis here. See below for more discussion.) At this point it is necessary to postulate a new rule, call it High Doubling. This rule will say that if (a) the ultimate vowel has a high associated with it, and (b) if a voiced obstruent precedes that ultimate vowel, then insert a high tone into the tonal tier and associate it with the penultimate vowel. The result of applying High Doubling to the above representation will be just the intermediate representation that will be necessary in order to explain *a-na-píg-a gŏmâ.*

If we assume, then, that High Doubling is involved in the derivation of verb words which have a high tone associated with their ultimate vowel and a voiced obstruent in post-penult position, we are now able to explain why a word such as *ku-koróg-a* has a high tone on its penult vowel: this high tone is the result of the application of High Doubling. What then needs explanation is why there is no high tone on the ultimate vowel of such words when they occur at the end of the phrase (*a-na-píg-a gǒmâ* shows that the ultimate high *is* retained when the verb is not final in the phrase, at least in the examples so far considered).

I propose the following derivation for such words. Given the underlying representation:

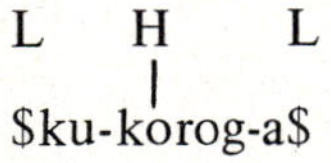


High Tone Displacement associates the H with the ultimate vowel and High Doubling will then associate a H with the penultimate vowel. I assume that Low Insertion will then associate a low tone with the voiced obstruent *g*. The resulting representation will be:

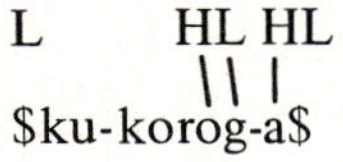


The general principles governing autosegmental representations will then add association lines between the initial low boundary tone and the first two vowels of the word and between the final low boundary tone and the ultimate vowel:

At this point I assume that a new rule, call it Final Fall Simplification, will eliminate the H from a HL sequence associated with a final vowel when that H is *not* associated with any other vowel. I am assuming here that the rule Leftwards High Spread is applied before Final Fall Simplification and that it is the application of the former rule that prevents the application of the latter rule to a representation such as that of *ku-pupǔt-â:*

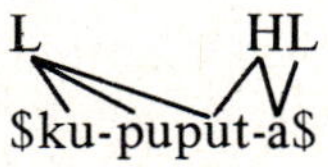

In the above representation, the H of the HL sequence associated with the last vowel is also associated with the penultimate vowel as a result of Leftwards High Spread. This association line will bar Final Fall Simplification from applying. Of course, in the derivation of *ku-koróg-a,* Leftwards High Spread will not be able to add an association line between the ultimate H and the penultimate vowel because to do so would require crossing an association line (and I have been assuming throughout that the rules in Digo that associate tones and vowels do not cross association lines).

Let us now turn back to the question of whether High Tone Displacement applies just once, to the entire phrase, or whether it applies in a cyclic fashion, first to the verb and then to the entire phrase. The example *a-na-píg-a gǒmâ* demonstrates conclusively that the answer must be that the rule is applied in cyclic fashion. For if High Tone Displacement applied just once to the whole phrase, it would take the H associated with the subject prefix /a/ in the verb word and reassociate it with the ultimate vowel of the noun. There would be no point in the derivation where a high tone is associated with the ultimate vowel of the verb. But if there is no high tone on the ultimate vowel of the verb, then High Doubling will not have an opportunity to apply and assign a high tone to the penultimate vowel of the verb. Thus we could not explain why there is a high tone on the penult vowel of the verb. I conclude that High Tone Displacement must be cyclic. Of course, High Doubling must be cyclic as well, since it must apply after the first application of High Tone Displacement and before the second application. This sequencing is necessary since if the application of High Tone Displacement at the phrasal level preceded High Doubling, the former rule would remove the high tone from the ultimate vowel of the verb and thus destroy the conditions for the latter rule.

In (61) I just gave examples where the H on the verb word is one that is subject to High Tone Displacement when the verb is pronounced in isolation. In (62) I give examples where the H on the verb word is one that would be subject to Neutralization if the verb were pronounced in isolation. The nouns that follow are, again, low-toned nouns.

| | | | |
|---|---|---|---|
| (62) | a. | ku-heg-a n-gurǔwê | 'to trap a pig' (cf. ku-heg-a, n-guruwe) |
| | | ku-heg-a n-jǐyâ | 'to trap a pigeon' (cf. n-jiya) |
| | | ku-ih-a mu-gǎngâ | 'to call a doctor' (cf. ku-ih-a, mu-ganga) |
| | b. | ni-na-Bah-a ma-tǔndâ | 'I'm getting fruit' (cf. ni-na-Bah-a, ma-tunda) |
| | | ni-na-vug-a w-ǎrî | 'I'm cooking rice' (cf. ni-na-vug-a, w-ari) |

ni-na-tsun-a ŋǒmbê 'I'm skinning a cow'
(cf. ni-na-tsun-a, ŋombe)

The most striking fact about these data is that the rule of Neutralization has not applied to change the H of the verb stem to L – the H remains and eventually gets displaced (via High Tone Displacement) to the ultimate vowel of the noun. In order to prevent Neutralization from applying to the phrases in (62), we must formulate Neutralization so that it applies to a penult high not in the *word,* but rather in certain *phrases.* In other words, Neutralization cannot affect the high tone associated with the penultimate vowel of the verb words in (62) because these highs are not located on the penultimate vowel in the phrase. Much work on Digo syntax will be required before I can state precisely the nature of the phrases that are the domain of the Neutralization process, but the data considered here show that a verb plus following noun object constitutes one such phrase.

Let me at this point return to one aspect of the analysis of Digo that I did not provide justification for earlier. Recall that I proposed to order High Tone Displacement before Neutralization. In order to maintain this sequencing, it was necessary for me to put a condition on the former rule to exempt penultimate highs from undergoing it. In effect I claimed that the failure of penultimate highs to displace to the ultimate vowel is independent of the fact that they neutralize to low. The motivation for dissociating these two rules comes from a consideration of phrases such as *ku-heg-a n-gurŭwê.* The underlying structure of this phrase is:

```
L     H               L
      |
$[[#ku-heg-a#] [#n-guruwe#]]$
```

Given my proposed analysis, High Tone Displacement will not be able to affect the H of the verbal word on the first cycle (i.e. the cycle that considers just the inner constituents) since that H is associated with the penult vowel in the representation. Since High Tone Displacement does not associate the high with the ultimate vowel of the verb, High Doubling will not be applicable either. On the second cycle, High Tone Displacement will associate the H of the verb with the ultimate vowel of the noun. The verbal H cannot escape High Tone Displacement since it is no longer on the penultimate vowel of the representation when the entire phrase is being considered.

Suppose that instead of the above analysis we claimed that Neutralization is ordered before High Tone Displacement, and that the reason a penult high does not displace is because it is changed to low by Neutralization before High Tone Displacement has an opportunity to apply. Since

Neutralization is inapplicable in the case of a phrase such as *ku-heg-a n-gurǔwê,* the analysis I just sketched would predict that on the first cycle High Tone Displacement will move the H of the verb onto the last vowel of the verb. High Doubling would then assign a H to the penult vowel of the verb. On the next cycle, the high on the ultimate vowel of the verb would displace to the ultimate vowel of the noun. But we would be left with a high tone incorrectly located on the verb: **ku-hég-a n-gurǔwê.* I conclude, therefore, that the analysis that makes failure to undergo High Tone Displacement independent of Neutralization is the correct one.

Let me now turn to a consideration of phrases involving a verbal word with a single high tone followed by a noun that contains a H that is subject to Neutralization. Examples are given in (63).

| | | | |
|---|---|---|---|
| (63) | a. | ku-afun-a nâzi | 'to chew a coconut' (cf. ku-afǔn-â, nazi) |
| | | ku-azim-a shôka | 'to borrow an axe' (cf. ku-azǐm-â, shoka) |
| | | ku-ar-á demu | 'to take a rag' (cf. ku-ǎr-â, demu) |
| | | ku-ar-a chí-demu | 'to take a small rag' (cf. chi-demu) |
| | | ku-ádz-á dzina | 'to call by name' (cf. ku-ádz-a, dzina) |
| | b. | a-na-jit-a ma-rênje | 'he's cooking pumpkins' (cf. a-na-jǐt-â, ma-renje) |
| | | a-na-andik-a chi-tânda | 'he's making a bed' (cf. a-na-andǐk-â, chi-tanda) |
| | | a-na-andik-a barûwa | 'he's writing a letter' (cf. baruwa) |
| | | a-na-tsong-a gungûhi | 'he's cutting a bed leg' (cf. a-na-tsǒng-â, gunguhi) |
| | | a-na-angamíz-a pêsa | 'he's losing money' (cf. a-na-angamíz-a, pesa) |
| | | a-na-vuw-a má-zobe | 'he's fishing for crabs' (cf. a-na-vǔw-â, ma-zobe) |

Each of the verb words in (63) has a H tone that will displace to the ultimate vowel of the verb on the first cycle. The nouns also have a high tone associated with them, but it is a high tone on the penultimate vowel; when the noun is considered by itself on the first cycle, High Tone Displacement will not be able to apply since this rule cannot affect penult highs. After the first cycle (I am assuming for the moment that only High Tone Displacement and High Doubling are cyclic rules; see below for discussion), we will have representations like the following:

```
L       HH L   L       H    H   L  L           H      H L
        | \                 |    |                    |       |
$ku-afun-a nazi$   $a-na-jit-a ma-renje$   $a-na-tsong-a gunguhi$

L       H    H  L
        |     |
$a-na-vuw-a ma-zobe$
```

In order to account for the falling tone in the case of *ku-afun-a nâzi* and *a-na-jit-a ma-rênje* we need to invoke the application of Neutralization and Low Attraction. The first rule will change the H on the penult vowel of the phrase to L, and the second rule will displace the H of the verbal word onto the low penult vowel of the noun. Of course, in order to maintain this analysis I must assume that Low Attraction, like High Tone Displacement, applies not just to the word but also to the phrase.

There is, however, one significant problem with appealing to Low Attraction to account for the data in (63) – namely, the fact that the H on the verbal word is attracted *across* a voiced obstruent in an example like *a-na-tsong-a gungûhi.* On the other hand, in *a-na-vuw-a má-zobe* the voiced obstruent at the beginning of the noun stem in *ma-zobe* does block reassociation of the verbal high with the penult low; instead, the verbal high must associate with the prefixal vowel. In the case of nouns, it is only a voiced obstruent immediately before the neutralized vowel that prevents a high from associating with that vowel (and causes the high to associate with the preceding vowel instead), whereas in verbs we saw that a voiced obstruent anywhere between the prefixal high and the neutralized vowel will block reassociation to the right of that voiced obstruent. Under the analysis that I have developed in this paper, which involves an appeal to a rule of Low Insertion in order to explain the role that voiced obstruents have in preventing Low Attraction and Displacement-to-Stem from reassociating highs across voiced obstruents, an ad hoc rule will be required. This rule will have to delete the L that Low Insertion assigns to the first obstruent of nouns like *gunguhi.* Or, alternatively, we will have to somehow formulate Low Insertion so that it will fail to assign a L to the initial consonant of *gunguhi.* Neither approach is particularly appealing, but I do not see any other solution that accounts for the facts in a better way. Consequently, I will simply assume that some such ad hoc modification of the rules will be required in order to explain the difference among *a-na-tsong-a gungûhi* (where the verbal H crosses a voiced obstruent) and *a-na-vuw-a má-zobe* (where the verbal H is blocked from crossing a voiced obstruent) and *á-vumikiz-e* (where a prefixal H cannot reassociate across a voiced obstruent). Only one additional point with respect to the appeal to Low Attraction in the derivation of the items in (63) needs to be made. The H that is affected by Low Attraction is located on the final vowel of the verb; in the cases discussed earlier, the H affected by this rule was located on a prefix. There seems to be no restriction as to the location of H that undergoes Low Attraction other than that it must be the first H preceding the neutralized vowel.

I turn now to the tonal pattern of phrases consisting of a verb with a single H followed by a noun that contains a H that does not neutralize. Examples are given in (64).

| | | | |
|---|---|---|---|
| (64) | a. | ku-anik-a ma-pémbâ | 'to put maize in the sun to dry' |
| | | | (cf. ku-anǐk-â, ma-pěmbâ) |
| | | ku-banang-a kándê | 'to spoil food' |
| | | | (cf. ku-banăng-â, kăndê) |
| | b. | a-na-vugur-a fúndô | 'he's untying a knot' |
| | | | (cf. a-na-vugŭr-â, fŭndô) |
| | | a-na-jit-á zódo | 'he's cooking mangos' |
| | | | (cf. a-na-jǐt-â, zódo) |
| | | a-na-tsor-a chí-dăfû | 'he's picking up a young coconut' |
| | | | (cf. a-na-tsŏr-â, chi-dăfû) |
| | | a-na-ragíz-a chi-tábu | 'he's ordering a book' |
| | | | (cf. a-na-ragíz-a, chi-tábu) |
| | | a-na-suw-a sáhánî | 'he's washing plates' |
| | | | (cf. a-na-sŭw-â, sahănî) |
| | c. | ni-na-azim-a chi-kárángô | 'I'm borrowing a frying pan' |
| | | | (cf. ni-na-azǐm-â, chi-karăngô) |

The most striking fact about the data in (64) is that the H associated with the verb in underlying structure has, for the most part, ended up on the following noun. In particular, it has ended up on the first vowel of the noun stem (hopping over the noun prefix in the process). The only cases where the H of the verb has not reached to the first vowel of the noun stem is when a voiced obstruent stands in the way. Thus (64) clearly involves the application of the rule that I have labelled Displacement-to-Stem, where that rule is able to apply at the phrasal level and not just the word level.

Consider the derivation of an example such as *ni-na-azim-a chi-kárángô* (64c). Underlyingly, there is a H on the verb stem and on the noun stem. On the first cycle, the H of the verb will displace to its ultimate vowel and the high of the noun will displace to its ultimate vowel. On the cycle that includes the entire phrase, the reapplication of High Tone Displacement will be vacuous (the rightmost H in the phrase is already associated with the ultimate vowel of the phrase). However, the H of the verb word will be eligible to undergo Displacement-to-Stem under the assumption that this rule affects the first H located before a stem (whether a verb or a noun stem). The reassociation of the verbal H with the first vowel of the noun stem produces the following representation:

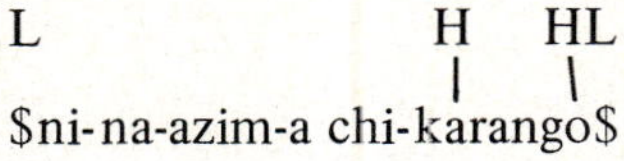


If the universal principles governing autosegmental representations come into play at this point, they will yield the appropriate phonetic form:

In an example such as *a-na-tsor-a chí-dǎfû* (64b), the verbal H cannot get associated with the first vowel of the noun stem since there is a voiced obstruent at the beginning of the stem. This voiced obstruent is linked to an inserted low tone, and Displacement-to-Stem cannot cross an association line. As a consequence, the verbal H must reassociate with the vowel that precedes the stem. In an example like *a-na-jit-á zódo,* the verbal H is also blocked from reassociating with the first vowel of the noun stem, but this time there is no prefixal vowel to which the verbal H can displace. As a consequence, the verbal H remains on the last vowel of the verb (where it came to be located as a result of the application of High Tone Displacement to the verb on the first cycle).[28]

*8.3. Phrases Involving Verbs with Two High Tones*

In this section I will consider the behavior of verb words with two high tones in their underlying structure when they are followed by a noun. In (65) I illustrate the situation where a low-toned noun follows.

| | | | |
|---|---|---|---|
| (65) | a. | a-na-chékéch-á ú-ngâ | 'he's sifting flour' (cf. a-na-chékéch-â, u-nga) |
| | | a-na-ézek-a bǎndâ | 'he's thatching a shed' (cf. a-na-ézěk-â, banda) |
| | | a-na-ádz-a mǔ-tû | 'he's mentioning s.o. by name' (cf. a-na-ádz-a, mu-tu) |
| | | a-na-tsíndz-á má-dzogǒrô | 'he's slaughtering roosters' (cf. a-na-tsíndz-â, ma-dzogoro) |
| | b. | a-ka-tsúkúts-á chí-róndâ | 'he has cleaned a wound' (cf. a-ka-tsúkúts-â, chi-ronda) |
| | | a-ka-tsúkúts-á chǐ-dǒndâ | *idem*. (cf. chi-donda) |

c. n-á-gwir-a dzogǒrô 'I caught a rooster'
(cf. n-á-gwǐr-â, dzogoro)

n-a-hénz-á mú-gǎngâ 'I looked for a doctor'
(cf. n-a-hénz-â, mu-ganga)

Clearly, the rightmost H of the verbal word ends up associated with the ultimate vowel of the noun. Interestingly, the first H of the verbal word displaces to the first vowel of the verb stem rather than to the first vowel of the noun stem. How is this fact to be explained? I suggest that the answer is simply that Displacement-to-Stem moves a H just to the closest stem. For example, given an underlying representation such as:

```
L      H   H                       L
       |   |
$[[#a-ka-tsukuts-a#] [#chi-ronda#]]$
```

High Tone Displacement will apply on the first cycle to move the rightmost H of the verb to the ultimate vowel of the verb. The first H of the verb will, however, remain located before the verb stem. Consequently, when Displacement-to-Stem tries to apply (regardless of whether it is a cyclic rule or if it is a non-cyclic, phrase-level rule) it will displace the prefixal H just to the verb stem (since that is the closest stem).

An example like *a-ka-tsúkúts-á chí-rôndâ* (65b) is interesting in that it provides another argument for the cyclic application of High Tone Displacement. Compare this example with *a-na-suw-a sáhánî* (64b). The relevant underlying forms are:

```
L   H   H                L        LH           H    L
    |   |                          |           |
$a-ka-tsukuts-a chi-ronda$        $a-na-suw-a sahani$
```

Notice that both representations have two high tones in their underlying structure, and in both cases the second H will associate with the ultimate vowel of the phrase via High Tone Displacement. But what about the first H? In the former case it displaces to the verb stem, while in the latter case it displaces to the noun stem. Without appeal to the cylic application of High Tone Displacement, there would be no explanation for this difference in behavior. Given the cycle, however, there is no problem. In the former case, the first H is not affected by High Tone Displacement on the verb cycle and remains located before the verb stem. In the latter case, High Tone Displacement does apply to the first H on the verb cycle, moving it to the ultimate vowel of the verb; as a consequence, on the second cycle the first H in the phrase will be located not before the verb stem but instead before the noun stem. As a consequence, the application of Displacement-to-Stem in the former case will associate the first H in the phrase with the verb stem whereas in the latter example the first H will associate with the noun stem. I conclude that this contrasting behavior provides independent evidence for the cyclicity of High Tone Displacement.

At this point I should observe that throughout this section I have been assuming that just High Tone Displacement and High Doubling are cyclic. This is by no means necessarily the case. Rules such as Low Insertion and Displacement-to-Stem could, for example, also be cyclic. I have not found any direct evidence to support the claim that they are cyclic, and thus I will leave this issue open at the present time. I should point out, however, that if Low Insertion is cyclic, it will necessitate a revision of my account of why High Tone Displacement is able to cross over voiced obstruents. Recall that I explained this fact by ordering High Tone Displacement before Low Insertion. Given that ordering, at the point where High Tone Displacement operates there are no association lines between voiced obstruents and tones to block displacement across them. However, if Low Insertion is cyclic, this ordering solution fails.

To see this, consider an example such as *ni-na-ezek-a bǎndâ,* which in its underlying structure has just one high tone, located on the verb stem. If Low Insertion were cyclic, then on the noun cycle a low tone would be associated with the initial consonant of *banda.* On the phrase cycle, the H of the verbal word would be separated from the ultimate vowel of the noun by a linked low tone. Thus in order to generate the correct results, High Tone Displacement would have to be allowed to cross an association line. Thus if the rule of Low Insertion is cyclic, then the rule ordering explanation of High Tone Displacement's ability to cross a voiced obstruent must be abandoned. However, since voiced obstruents still behave as though they have a low tone associated with them even when a high tone displaces across them to the ultimate vowel (i.e. they prevent a preceding high from associating with unlinked vowels to their right - cf. *a-na-tsíndz-á má-dzogǒrô*), we do not want to simply allow High Tone Displacement to cross these association lines - for crossing them would necessarily entail that the original lines be deleted. And if the line between the voiced obstruent and a low tone were deleted, we could not explain why these consonants block the spread of a preceding high tone onto unlinked vowels to the right of the voiced obstruent. The only means that I can see of salvaging the situation would be to formulate High Tone Displacement as a metathesis rule that takes the rightmost H of a word (phrase) and moves it past any associated low tones, linking it to the ultimate vowel. Thus if one wishes to maintain the ordering solution to the problem of the ability of High Tone Displacement to cross a voiced obstruent, Low Insertion must be non-cyclic; from this it will also follow that rules like Displacement-to-Stem and Low Attraction must also be non-cyclic, since they must follow Low Insertion.

I turn now to phrases where a verb with two high tones is followed by a noun which has a high tone subject to Neutralization. Examples appear in (66).

| | | | |
|---|---|---|---|
| (66) | a. | a-na-ézek-a ny-ûmba | 'he's thatching the house' (cf. a-na-ézěk-â, ny-umba) |
| | | a-ná-vwar-a chi-tâmbi | 'he's wearing a piece of cloth' (cf. a-ná-vwǎr-â, chi-tambi) |
| | | a-na-áfún-á chí-yogwe | 'he's chewing a sweet potato' (cf. a-na-áfún-â, chi-yogwe) |
| | | a-na-Bírík-á sálamu | 'he's sending greetings' (cf. a-na-Bírík-â, salamu) |
| | b. | ni-ká-vundz-a ru-kûni | 'I have broken a piece of firewood' (cf. ni-ká-vǔndz-â, ru-kuni) |
| | | ni-ka-ón-á simba | 'I have seen a lion' (cf. ni-ka-ôn-a, simba) |
| | c. | n-á-jit-a ma-rênje | 'I cooked pumpkins' (cf. n-á-jǐt-â, ma-renje) |
| | | n-á-jit-á dzungu | 'I cooked a sp. pumpkin' (cf. dzungu) |
| | | n-a-tsóng-á gungûhi | 'I carved a bed leg' (cf. n-a-tsóng-a, gunguhi) |

Clearly, the second H of the verb in these phrases displaces to(wards) the neutralized vowel in the noun; for instance, in the first two examples of (66a) the second H of the verb is able to associate with the neutralized vowel (because there are no voiced obstruents to block this association), while in *n-á-jit-á dzungu* (66c) the voiced obstruent *dz* prevents the second H of the verb from associating with the neutralized vowel. The first H in the verb word displaces to(wards) the first vowel of the verbal complex; for example, in *a-na-Bírík-á sálamu* (66a) the prefixal H associated with the /a/ subject prefix associates with the first vowel of /Birik/ since *B* is not a voiced obstruent and thus does not block Displacement-to-Stem, whereas in *a-ná-vwar-a chi-tâmbi* the H on /a/ can reassociate only as far as the prefix /na/ since the verb stem /vwar/ begins with a voiced obstruent.

The example *n-a-tsóng-á gungûhi* (66c) is of some interest. Recall that I noted earlier that when Low Attraction applies at the phrasal level it is allowed to reassociate a H past a voiced obstruent, provided that this voiced obstruent is located in the noun word and is not located immediately before the penult vowel. The present example shows, however, that the initial voiced obstruent of *gunguhi* must have a low associated with it in order to explain why in *n-a-tsóng-á gungûhi* the first H associated with the verb stem /tsong/ does not become associated (by the universal conventions) with the first vowel of *gunguhi* and why instead that vowel has low tone. It seems, then, that prior to the application of the general principles governing the association of unlinked tones and vowels, a low tone must be assigned to the initial consonant of *gunguhi*. But if it is the rule of Low Insertion that assigns this low, how can we explain why Low Attraction can skip over the initial consonant of *gunguhi* when it cannot skip over a voiced obstruent in the verb or the voiced obstruent located before the neutralized vowel of a noun? I have no explanation for this behavior of *gunguhi* and therefore must admit that it is potentially damaging to my attempt to explain the failure of Low Attraction and Displacement-to-Stem to displace past voiced obstruents in terms of the presence of an association line between these consonants and a low tone.

Given that the second H of the verb words in (66) displaces to the neutralized vowel and the first H displaces to the first vowel of the verbal complex, the remaining aspects of the tonal shape of the phrases in (66) are straightforward. If no voiced obstruents occur between the two H's in these phrases, then all of the unlinked vowels in between will associate with the H to the left. However, this will trigger the application of Fall Simplification to the neutralized vowel. Consequently, the H on the neutralized vowel will be lost. It is this application of Fall Simplification that accounts for examples such as *a-na-Bírík-á sálamu, a-na-áfún-á chí-yogwe,* and *ni-ka-ón-á simba.* If a voiced obstruent occurs between the two H's in the phrases in (66), then the unlinked vowels between the first H and that voiced obstruent will associate with the H while the unlinked vowels after the voiced obstruent will associate to the L of that consonant.

I will conclude this section by examining phrases where there is a verb with two H's followed by a noun that has a H that does not neutralize. Examples are given in (67).

| | | | |
|---|---|---|---|
| (67) | a. | a-na-áník-á má-pémbâ | 'he's putting maize in the sun to dry' (cf. a-na-áník-â, ma-pěmbâ) |
| | | a-na-tsún-á ŋónzî | 'he's skinning a sheep' (cf. a-na-tsûn-a, ŋǒnzî) |
| | | a-ná-vug-á dǒnâ | 'he's cooking hard maize porridge' (cf. a-ná-vug-a, dǒnâ) |
| | b. | n-a-ángámíz-a tánâ | 'I lost the bow' (cf. n-a-ángámíz-a, tǎnâ) |
| | | n-á-vugur-a fúndô | 'I untied the knot' (cf. n-á-vugǔr-â, fǔndô) |

n-a-tsúkúr-á má-pémbâ 'I carried the maize'
(cf. n-a-tsúkúr-â, ma-pěmbâ)

For the most part the data in (67) do not pose any special problems. Clearly, the H of the noun displaces to the ultimate vowel of the noun on the first cycle while the rightmost H of the verb displaces to the ultimate vowel of the verb on the first cycle. On the phrasal level, the high on the ultimate vowel of the verb displaces to the noun stem - cf. *n-á-vugur-a fúndô* - while the first H of the verb word displaces to(wards) the verb stem – cf. *a-na-tsún-á ŋónzî*. In an example such as *a-na-ánik-á má-pémbâ,* the unlinked vowels between the H on the first vowel of the verbal complex and the H on the first vowel of the noun stem all associate with the first of these H's in accordance with the general principles governing autosegmental representations. In *n-á-vugur-a fúndô,* on the other hand, the unlinked vowels between the H of the verb and the noun stem associate with the low tone of the initial consonant of the verb stem /vugur/.

The only problematic example in (67) is *a-ná-vug-á dŏnâ.* On the first cycle, the H of the noun can move to the ultimate vowel of that word but we would not expect the rightmost H of the verb to displace to the ultimate vowel of the verb due to the fact that this H is located on the penult vowel. Thus at the end of the first cycle we expect the following representation to emerge:

```
LH     H       HL
|      |       |
$a-na-vug-a dona$
```

When we apply Low Insertion to this representation, we will derive the following structure:

```
LH    LHL L   HL
|     ||/ |   |
$a-na-vug-a dona$
```

If we then apply Displacement-to-Stem, that rule will associate the first H with the vowel of /na/ since it will not be able to cross the association line connecting the *v* of /vug/ with a low tone. However, we would expect that Displacement-to-Stem would also be unable to move the H on /vug/ towards the noun stem since an association line stands in the way (namely, the association line between the final consonant of /vug/ and a low tone). However, to generate the correct phonetic representation, Displacement-to-Stem must be allowed to skip over the *g* of /vug/ but not the initial consonant of the noun *dŏnâ.* (All of this is, of course, reminiscent of the fact that Low Attraction was able to cross over a voiced obstruent in the example *n-a-tsóng-á gungûhi.*) At the present time, then, the most significant unresolved problem pertinent to the analysis I have developed here of Digo tonology is why in certain situations the rules of Low Attraction and Displacement-to-Stem are able to skip over a voiced obstruent and how this possibility is to be integrated into an analysis that employs the rule of Low Insertion to explain the general inability of these rules to cross voiced obstruents.

The present section represents just the beginnings of an analysis of the phrasal tonology of Digo. There are doubtless many complexities yet to be encountered. But the data analyzed here have been quite complex in themselves; however, I believe that the analysis that I have presented makes sense out of these very complicated facts and represents a real insight into the structure of Digo tones.

## 9. CONCLUSION

The Digo data analyzed in this chapter provide, I believe, interesting confirmation for the view of phonology that is generally referred to as "generative phonology", as well as for one specific model within that broader framework, namely, autosegmental phonology. According to the theory of generative phonology, surface phonetic shapes are sometimes the consequence of the application of a set of phonological rules applying (in a partially ordered fashion) to representations which may differ in significant respects from the phonetic shapes. Notice that the rules and representations which I have postulated in this study are entirely in accord with this view. For example, I have argued that there are many items which have a high tone associated with their penultimate vowel underlyingly - e.g. *ku-som-a* 'to read' (cf. *ku-somĕr-â* 'to read to') and *ny-umba* 'house' (cf. *ny-umbǎ-nî* 'in the house') - even though this high tone does not ever appear phonetically on that vowel. Indeed, I have shown that where a high tone appears on the surface has little direct connection with where this high originates in underlying structure - e.g. a high that appears on a noun in surface representation may originate on the preceding verb. I have also argued that a fairly complex set of rules (operating not just on words, but on phrases as well) mediates between the underlying forms and the surface structure, these language-specific rules being supplemented by various universal principles governing the association of unlinked tones and vowels. It is significant that there can be no question about whether these language-specific rules are (in some form) "psychologically real", for since they operate on phrases consisting of any verb followed by any noun, they can readily be shown to be fully productive and necessarily a part of the native speaker's knowledge of Digo.

Telex 81298 VAT Reg. No. 213 4152 13

| Date & tax point | Invoice No. |
| --- | --- |
| 04/12/84 | 510767 |
| Department | Account No. |
| E | H19415 |

Copies 1 Page 1 OF 1

| ur reference | Your reference | VAT rate % | Unit price £ | Total £ |
| --- | --- | --- | --- | --- |
| L374-01 | 24/10/83 | | 16.20 | 16.95 |

PACKING & INSURANCE £16.95

## w to pay for your books from Heffers

### Customers in the United Kingdom

ques: Cheques should be made payable to W. Heffer & Sons Ltd and sent to P.O. Box 33, Cambridge, England CB2 1TX.

k Giro: Payment may be made through any bank to Barclays Bank plc, Bene't Street, Cambridge, to our account number 30466581.

t Office Payment may be made at your local post office crediting our giro account number 252 8053.

### Customers Overseas

e countries listed below you may pay to our bank accounts **in your own currency;** please quote Heffer account number and the numbers of the invoices you are paying.

tralia: A.N.Z. Banking Group Ltd, Pitt & Hunter Streets, Sydney, N.S.W. 2001.
Account No. 43-31130.

ada: Royal Bank of Canada, 20 King Street West. Toronto, Ont. M5H 1C4.
Account No. 309.805.0.

mark: Copenhagen Handelsbank A/S, 2 Holmens Kanal, DK-1091 Copenhagen K.
Account No. 286730.

nce: Barclays Bank S.A., 33 Rue du 4 Septembre, 75002 Paris.
Account No. 175 020205 02 000171.

many: Deutsche Bank A.G., Rossmarkt 18, D-6000 Frankfurt (Main) 1.
Account No. 73/3436.

land: Amsterdam-Rotterdam Bank N.V., Leidseplein 25, Amsterdam, 1005 EJ.
Convertible Account No. 46.75.31.641;
*or* Postgiro (Nederland) Account No. 3903241.

y: Banca Commerciale Italiana, Piazza della Scala 6, 20121 Milan.
Estero Lire Account No. 970615/01/19.

an: Payments in Japanese Free Yen (not Domestic Yen) at the counter of an authorised foreign exchange bank for the credit of Fuji Bank Ltd., Otemachi I-Chome, Chiyodo-Ku, Tokyo. Savings Account No. 501886.

ain: Banco Central S.A., Division Internacional, Calle Serrano, 38, Madrid 1.
Pts. Convertibles Account No. 41003987.

itzerland: Schweizerische Bankgesellschaft, 45 Bahnhofstrasse, Zurich.
Account No. 383.780.01.

A: American Express International Banking Corp., Commercial Banking Division, New York Agency, P.O. Box 740, New York, N.Y. 10008.
Account No. 411843.

By International giro transfer, where available, quoting: British Postal Giro account (CCP) . 252 8053.

From any country send a bank draft, money order, UNESCO coupons or cheque in sterling or US lars to us in Cambridge, quoting your Heffer account number.

Ask any bank in any country to make payment to our account number 30466581 at Barclays nk plc, Bene't Street, Cambridge, through Barclays Bank International Ltd, Luton Branch, O. Box 22, 28 George Street, Luton, England LU1 2HW, and to quote your Heffer account number.
**yments must be made 'free of all charges to beneficiary'.**

heffers:

# INVOICE

Heffers Booksellers 20 Trinity Street Cambridge England CB2 3NG Telephone Cambridge (022

FRANCIS KATAMBA ESQ
DEPARTMENT OF LINGUISTICS & MODERN
ENGLISH LANGUAGE
UNIVERSITY OF LANCASTER
LANCASTER
LA1 4YW

| Location | Copies | Author/Title |
|---|---|---|
| H0524 | 1 | CLEMENTS & GOLDSMITH/AUTOSEQUENTIAL STUDIES IN BANTU TONE |

Please keep this invoice to check against your monthly statement. For payment arrangements see overleaf
Payment is due before the end of the month following receipt of the books.

TOTAL COST INCLUDING PO

The tonal pattern of Digo also fully supports the autosegmental approach to phonology. There can be no question but that the tones of Digo are quite separate from the segments that bear them; tones move from one vowel in a word to another vowel later in the word or even in the following word, quite unlike the segments that manifest the tones. Furthermore, I have shown the efficacy of assuming that the beginning and the end of a phrase have low tones associated with them even though a "boundary" is not a unit that bears tone, and I have also shown the usefulness of assuming that voiced obstruents in Digo have low tones associated with them.

Digo provides significant confirmatory evidence not only for the theory of generative phonology and, more specifically, the autosegmental approach to generative phonology, but also for the cyclic application of phonological rules. The question of cyclicity has been discussed for many years in generative phonology, but most of the crucial evidence for the cyclic application of phonological rules has come from stress phenomena. Digo tone provides a major new area of evidence in favor of the cyclic application of (some) rules. I do not believe, however, that the cyclic nature of the rules in Digo can be fully understood until more analysis has been done on the interaction of tone and syntax in Digo.

NOTES

1. See Goldsmith 1976b and Clements 1976 as well as Chapter 1 of this volume for an introduction to some of the basic concepts and principles of autosegmental phonology.
2. See Goldsmith 1976b.
3. See Goldsmith 1976b.
4. See Becker and Massamba (1980).
5. I am assuming that Leftwards High Spread, which adds an association line between an ultimate H and the penult vowel, is ordered after Neutralization. Given such an ordering, Neutralization cannot affect the output of Leftwards High Spread.
6. Notice that High Tone Displacement must be formulated so that it not only adds an association line between a high tone and the ultimate vowel, but alse *removes* the association line between the high tone and the vowel with which it was originally associated. Of course, if one adopted the view that the high tones are not yet linked to vowels at the point where High Tone Displacement operates, then this complication in the formulation of the rule would not be required. However, my analysis of Digo depends crucially on assuming that the high tones are associated with vowels prior to the application of this rule; consequently, I must stipulate in the formulation of the rule that the original association line is deleted. I will argue that there are two other displacement rules in Digo beside High Tone Displacement, and these other rules also involve deletion of the original association line between the displaced high tone and the vowel with which it is underlyingly associated.
7. I am assuming, of course, that High Tone Deletion precedes High Tone Displacement. Analogs of High Tone Deletion occur in such languages as Makua (see Cheng and Kisseberth 1979, 1980) and Tonga (see Goldsmith, this volume).

8. If High Tone Deletion were to be formulated as a purely phonological process, it would (presumably) say that if two high tones are associated with two vowels which are not separated from one another by a third vowel, then the second high tone is deleted. Later in the paper I will present cases where these phonological conditions are satisfied, but High Tone Deletion does not apply.

9. When an object prefix consists just of a vowel, then a high tone on this prefix is not phonetically very prominent when the following vowel is also high toned. When the next vowel is not high-toned, the high tone on the prefix is very clear. A high tone on a -CV- object prefix is always very clear.

10. See footnote 9.

11. When I say that a form such as **ǎ-ná-á-gurĭr-â* is expected, I am assuming that if subsequent to the application of High Tone Displacement we have a representation such as

```
LH         HL
 |          |
$a-na-a-gurir-a$
```

and if there are no other rules of a language-specific nature operative in Digo, then the general principles governing the association of unlinked tones and vowels would provide association lines that would result in the pronunciation indicated above, with rising tone on the first vowel. The various details of the general principles involved will be discussed briefly in the course of this paper.

12. It might appear that some rule such as High Tone Retraction could also explain examples like *ku-bundúg-a.* Although High Tone Displacement says that the H in the underlying structure of this word should displace to the ultimate vowel, in fact a high tone shows up on the penultimate vowel. If High Tone Retraction were allowed to apply to the output of High Tone Displacement, it would move the high away from the ultimate vowel onto the penultimate vowel just in the event a voiced obstruent intervenes. Although this would be a very appealing explanation of *ku-bundúg-a,* I will demonstrate in the section on phrasal tonology that something else appears to be going on in the derivation of *ku-bundúg-a* and other words like it.

13. I am assuming here a general principle that says that when unlinked vowels appear between two linked tones, the vowels associate with the tone to the left (see chapter 1). In the present examples, the correctness of this principle is not obvious, since the same phonetic results would obtain if the unlinked vowels between the two linked high tones were to associate to the right tone. Later cases arise just below where it is crucial that association under the above circumstances be to the left tone.

14. It should be pointed out that the stop portion of the prenasalized consonants *mb, nd, nj,* and *ng* does not behave as a voiced obstruent and thus must not be assigned a low tone by Low Insertion.

15. I will mention here just a few examples from the literature on Bantu: Beach (1924), Doke (1926), Carter (1962), and Fivaz (1970).

16. Since I have not yet given the justification for assuming a separate rule of Low Attraction, distinct from Displacement-to-Stem, I will not at this point enter into a discussion of how these two rules are sequenced with respect to one another. The matter is taken up in section 6.

17. Although one might attempt to explain the fact that the high associated with *ni-* ends up being associated with the *-a-* as a consequence of Displacement-to-Stem, to do so would require explaining why that rule did not succeed in reassociating the high tone in question with the verbal complex – i.e. why the high ends up on *-a-* rather than on the verb /san/. On the other hand, if we assume that the high on *ni-*

is unaffected by the displacement rules, then there is no difficulty in explaining why it ends up associated with *-a-*. Once the prefix *ni-* elides its vowel, the general principles governing unlinked tones will require the high that was formerly associated with the elided vowel to link with some vowel – and *-a-* is the only available vowel.

18. Fall Simplification must be restricted to penult falling tones due to the fact that a falling tone on an ultimate vowel is not simplified when it is preceded by a vowel that is associated with another high tone – cf. *a-na-púpút-â*.

19. Rising Tone Simplification must (obviously) apply after the general principles associating unlinked tones and vowels, since it is the application of these principles that creates the rising tone on the first vowel of a word that undergoes simplification.

20. I have not attempted to formalize Low Attraction here, but rather have tried to state as precisely as possible what this rule must do. The crucial aspects to the formalization of this rule are: the H affected by the rule must be followed by a penult low tone, and between the H and the penult low there may be other low tones (associated with voiced obstruents) but no highs; the H in question must associate as near to the penult low as possible without crossing an association line.

21. If we had an underlying structure where there were two high tones before the verbal complex and a high tone on the penult vowel, but the penult vowel were *not* also the first vowel of the verbal complex, then the two solutions sketched in the text would make different predictions. In this situation, the ordering of Displacement-to-Stem before Low Attraction would have the effect that the second prefixal high would first move to the beginning of the verbal complex (by virtue of the former rule) and then to the neutralized vowel (by virtue of the latter rule). The first prefixal high would remain in its original location. The ordering of Low Attraction before Displacement-to-Stem, on the other hand, would allow the rightmost of the prefixal highs to associate with the penult low tone (by virtue of Low Attraction) and the first prefixal high to associate with the first vowel of the verbal complex (by virtue of Displacement-to-Stem). At the present time, I do not have any data of the relevant structure and thus cannot determine which solution makes the correct prediction.

22. If one adopts the ordering where Low Attraction precedes Displacement-to-Stem and therefore places a condition on the latter rule that would render it inapplicable if the first vowel of the verbal complex already has a high tone associated with it, then another issue arises. Suppose that the rightmost of two prefixal highs cannot move all the way to the verbal complex due to the presence of a voiced obstruent at the beginning of that complex. This would mean that the first vowel of the verbal complex is not associated with a high tone. Would the leftmost prefixal high now be able to displace as far towards the stem as possible (without crossing an association line)? If not, the condition on Displacement-to-Stem suggested in the text would be inadequate and there would therefore be even more reason for adopting the ordering of Displacement-to-Stem before Low Attraction (since that ordering predicts that these two rules will always affect the *same* high tone, they cannot affect different high tones). Again, I have no data available to me which could clearly test these differing predictions.

23. One could obtain the pronunciation *a-réjezer-e* in another manner. Suppose that for some reason the high associated with the object prefix /a/ did not undergo Low Attraction. The H on this object prefix would also associate with the following vowel (the first vowel of the stem) due to the general principles associating unlinked vowels. The initial boundary (low) tone would combine with the high of the /a/ prefix. The following intermediate form would result: *ǎ-réjezer-e*. Rising Tone Simplification would convert this to the correct surface form. I reject this analysis

since (47) shows that a high on the object prefix *does* undergo Low Attraction in the imperative.

24. Although this explanation of *a-chékécher-e* is extremely appealing, there is a problem. For if there are two high tones associated with this verb stem in the imperative, the forms *chekecher-a* and *ni-chekecher-a* are inexplicable. They are pronounced as though they have no high tones. This pronunciation is easily explained if in underlying structure they simply have a high tone associated with the last vowel of the verb stem, since this high tone is subject to Neutralization. But if they also have a high tone associated with the first vowel of the verb stem, then there is no independent rule that would account for why it is missing in *chekecher-a* and *ni-chekecher-a* but present in *a-chékécher-e.* Thus while the latter form does clearly reflect the presence of an extra high tone (in contrast to *a-tsukûr-e* and *a-Birîk-e*), it is not entirely clear that this extra high should be attributed to a lexical high tone associated with the first vowel of /chekech/.

25. [For further discussion of this issue see Chapter 1 – *eds.*]

26. I should point out that it is not always easy, when words are pronounced in isolation under elicitation conditions, to distinguish between the regular mid-falling quality of a phrase penultimate low-toned vowel and the high-falling quality of words such as *a-na-sôm-a.* The difference is clear when the two types of words are placed in contrasting positions in complete sentences. Even in isolation the two word types can be distinguished in that a low-toned vowel before a high-fall is lower in pitch than a low-toned vowel before a mid-fall.

27. The attentive reader may have noted that these locative forms with the suffix *-ni* pattern tonally in a fashion that has some similarity to the plural imperatives (which also utilize a suffix *-ni*) cited but not discussed in the previous section.

28. Although when one considers just isolated words, the motivation for assuming that High Tone Displacement moves the rightmost H to the *ultimate* vowel is by no means overwhelmingly obvious, the phrasal evidence is more suggestive. Notice that in fact the H that displaces to the ultimate vowel of the verb on the verb cycle will very often actually appear phonetically on that vowel if it is prevented from displacing any further due to the presence of a voiced obstruent. Also, there are syntactic phrasal boundaries where Leftwards High Spread is inapplicable, and in this situation the displaced high manifests itself on the ultimate vowel. Consider, for example, the phrase *kuhegera nguruwé muhambo* 'to set a trap for a pig'. The high tone associated with the verb root /heg/ 'trap' displaces to the ultimate vowel of the low-toned noun *n-guruwe* 'pig'. However, High Tone Displacement cannot move the high tone onto the following noun – these two nouns are part of separate phrases as far as High Tone Displacement is concerned. When the phrase *kuhegera ngurǔwê* is pronounced in isolation, Leftwards High Spread applies; but that rule does not apply when *muhambo* 'trap' follows. The crucial point is that when Leftwards High Spread fails to apply, the displaced high tone actually manifests itself on the ultimate vowel of *n-guruwe.*

*Chapter 5*

# Tone in Zulu Nouns

Mary Laughren

Zulu is one of the S.E. Bantu languages of the Nguni group. It is spoken in Zululand and Natal in the Republic of South Africa.[1] This chapter presents an analysis of tone in Zulu nouns from the theoretical perspective of autosegmental phonology.[2]

I will show that the complex tonal alternations found in Zulu nouns are predictable on the basis of a small inventory of tonal melodies made up of high (H) and low (L) tones, together with a set of ordered tone rules. Rules of *Initial Tone Association* determine the manner in which designated tones of the characteristic tone melody (TM) are associated with tone-bearing units within the word. The output of these rules is subject to universal *Well-formedness Conditions* which have the function of assigning tones to tone-bearing units which have not yet received tones. Subsequently, rules of *Tone Association Adjustment* respecify tonal associations on the basis of information present in the tonal tier. Further rules apply to modify tonal association on the basis of information present in both tonal and segmental tiers. The output of the tone rules is assigned a surface phonetic realization by intonational rules. The universal Well-formedness Conditions continue to apply, where appropriate, at all stages in the derivation.[3]

A characteristic feature of Zulu is the important role played by *depressor consonants* – consonants marked by a distinctive feature corresponding phonetically to breathiness resulting from a slack configuration of the vocal cords. This phenomenon is discussed in some detail. A further feature of Zulu is the fact that certain lexical entries (morphemes, lexemes) are characterized by a tonal melody while others are not.[4] Furthermore, the lexical entry for some morphemes consists only of a tonal melody.

* This chapter is a revised version of "An Autosegmental Account of Tone in Zulu" (Laughren, 1981). I am very appreciative of the corrections, comments and additional information brought to my attention by the Zulu scholars D.K. Rycroft and J.S.M. Khumalo after reading the above-mentioned paper. I also wish to acknowledge with thanks the help and encouragement given me by G.N. Clements, whose ideas have been adopted and developed in several instances in this paper. Errors in the analysis, however, remain my sole responsibility.

The discussion proceeds as follows. Section 1 summarizes the theoretical framework. Section 2 presents a detailed examination of the underlying tonal melodies and of the major tone rules. In section 3 we examine the analysis of depressor consonants. Section 4 deals with a late rule of H Tone Spreading, and section 5 presents the rules assigning intonational contours to utterances on the basis of tonal configurations. Section 6 offers a brief conclusion and rule summary.

## 1. THEORETICAL FRAMEWORK[5]

The claim of autosegmental phonology is that certain defined phonological units or segments can be thought of as existing in an ordered sequence on a separate tier from other defined phonological units or segments. Hence tones belong to a tier called the *tonal melody tier* whereas consonants and vowels belong to a tier of segments defined by their inclusion in the set of consonants, the set of vowels, the set of nasals, the set of fricatives and so on. The phonemes of a given language are elements belonging to the intersection of several specified sets which are defined by distinctive feature notation: for example

$$\begin{bmatrix} +\text{ consonant} \\ +\text{ coronal} \\ +\text{ voiced} \\ +\text{ breathy} \end{bmatrix}$$

defines an element which is a member of the intersection of the sets of consonantal, coronal, voiced and breathy phonemes. In Zulu this element would be symbolized by the letter *d*.

If we say that these phonemes belong to either the consonantal set or to the set of vowels, then we see that there are severe restrictions on the manner in which these elements can be concatenated. This is regulated by the syllable structure imposed by each language. In Zulu syllables are underlyingly of the form V or CV.

Yet another level or tier which must be taken into account in a description of the interaction between the tonal melody tier and the segmental tier in Zulu is that of *stress*. Stress operates directly on the syllabic organization which dominates the segmental tier. Stress is assigned to certain syllables designated as [+ stressed] in the Zulu lexicon and also according to rules sensitive to the number of syllables in a word or phrase. In Zulu stress is one of the environmental determiners of tone reassociation (see section 3.1).[6]

In (1) we show the nature of the autosegmental tiers and the hierarchical organization of the tier of consonants (C) and vowels (V).

(1)

| | | | | | | |
|---|---|---|---|---|---|---|
| Syllabic organization: | \$ | \$ | \$ | \$ | \$ | ... |
| | \| | /\ | /\ | /\ | /\ | |
| Segmental tier: | V | CV | CV | CV | CV | ... |
| | [+ hi, + fr] | ... | | | | |
| Tonal melody tier:[7] | H | L | H | L | ... | |

The independence of the segmental tier and the tonal melody tier is reflected in the fact that identical sequences of segments may be distinguished in meaning by having contrastive tonal melodies, as in the examples in (2).[8]

(2) ì:ɓè:lé (LHLH) 'corn' *vs.* î:bé:lè (HLHL) 'breast'
ìsíkhò:và (LHL) 'owl' *vs.* ìsíkhò:vá (LHLH) 'banana plantation'

Similarly, words with the same tonal melody may be distinguished in meaning by the different segments (phonemes) of which they are composed. This is the case with *ì:ɓè:lé* 'corn' and *ìsíkhò:vá* 'banana plantation' which both have a LHLH tonal melody. Some morphemes have no intrinsic tonal melody in their lexical representation, but only have a segmental tier. This is the case with many nominal and verbal suffixes in Zulu. Other morphemes, such as the 'Pre-Prefixal' floating high tone posited by Khumalo (1981:129), have only a tonal representation in the lexicon.

Of course there is a relation between the elements on the segmental tier and those on the tonal melody tier. Strings of elements on the segmental tier will be said to be *characterized* by (or to *manifest*) the elements (that is, the tones) of the tonal melody tier. In formulating the relation between the two tiers we will see that both phonological and morphological conditioning is pertinent at different levels. The relation between the elements of the segmental tier and those of the tonal melody tier is given by the language-specific tone rules and the language-independent Well-formedness Conditions.

Analyses of vowel harmony and nasalization spreading (Goldsmith 1976a, b, Clements 1981b, Nash 1980) have required the positing of distinctive features such as [+round], [+nasal], and [+advanced tongue root] on a tier separate from that of the actual segments (= feature bundles) which manifest them. Elements of the segmental tier which are associated underlyingly with autosegments are called *opaque* elements. Those which are not associated with autosegments by the Well-formedness Conditions are called *neutral* elements. Here I will propose that underlying neutral elements can become opaque by the operation of rules which associate them with an autosegment already present in the autosegmental tier or inserted there by rule. This autosegment can then reassociate with further elements in the segmental tier. I will claim, then, that the depressor consonants of Zulu are opaque elements which become associated with a low tone in the tonal melody tier after the Initial Tone Association Rules and Well-formedness Conditions have applied to associate the tones of the lexically specified tonal melody with the tone-bearing units of the lexically specified segmental sequence.

Since phonological units exist on separate tiers, rules can apply to units on one tier independently of units which exist on another tier. Rules such as tonal metathesis can be envisaged as only applying to the tonal melody tier. Rules such as vowel deletion or assimilation apply only to the segmental tier. We will claim that in a given domain, all such uni-tier rules apply before rules which associate the elements of one tier with those of another.

If we posit a sequence of tone-bearing units (t) and a sequence of tones (T) existing on separate tiers, then the unmarked Initial Tone Association Rule will associate the first tone with the first tone-bearing unit. We will call this rule the Initial Tone Association Rule 1 (ITAR (1)), shown in (3).

(3) *Initial Tone Association Rule 1 (ITAR (1)):*

```
Segmental tier:        ⎡t   t   t   t . . .
                       ⎢|
Tonal melody tier      ⎣T  T  T . . .
```

While ITAR (1) would appear from studies done so far to be the unmarked or most widely applicable rule, other ITARs have been noted such as what Clements and Ford (1979) call ITAR (2). This rule, shown in (4), associates the first tone with the second tone-bearing unit.

(4) *Initial Tone Association Rule 2 (ITAR (2)):*

```
Segmental tier         ⎡t   t   t   t . . .
                       ⎢   /
Tonal melody tier:     ⎣T   T   T . . .
```

In Zulu (and Xhosa), as we shall see, there is an initial tone association rule which associates the first tone with the first two syllables or tone-bearing units: ITAR (2a), shown in (5).

(5) *Initial Tone Association Rule 2a (ITAR (2a)):*

Segmental tier: [t t t t ...

Tonal melody tier: [T T T ...

We will claim that all three rules apply in Zulu. Lexical entries for verbal and nominal roots as well as for some verbal suffixes characterized by a HL tonal melody must specify which ITAR determines the association of the melody to the tone-bearing units within their domain. L-initial tonal melodies always combine with ITAR (1). ITAR (2) appears to be derived from the very highly marked and unstable ITAR (2a) which would, it seems, no longer operate on roots in the Natal Coast dialect.[9] In the Kwa-Zulu dialect ITAR (2) and ITAR (2a) are in complementary distribution: ITAR (2a) applies within a domain containing 2 syllables, whereas ITAR (2) applies elsewhere.

The tones and tone-bearing units which are not associated after the application of the ITAR are associated according to well-formedness conditions which are taken to be universal rather than language specific.

*Well-formedness condition 1:* all tone-bearing units must be associated with at least one tone;

*Well-formedness condition 2:* no association lines cross.

Unassociated tones are not immediately deleted but remain in the tonal melody tier. The deletion of unassociated tones is carried out by rules motivated by the intonation component. Evidence for the retention of unassociated tones in the melody tier comes from the phenomenon of downstep, and will be discussed in section 5.

To account for the manner in which association takes place after the Initial Tone Association Rules(s) apply, a number of association conventions need to be given. The conventions laid out in Clements and Ford (1979) will be taken to hold for this work and will not be restated here.

The tone-bearing units referred to in the ITARs and Well-formedness Conditions must be specified for the language in question. In Zulu these are segment(s) composing the syllabic nucleus.[10]

## 2. ZULU TONAL MELODIES

The Zulu language has been analysed by Cope (1970), Rycroft (1963, 1979, 1980) and Khumalo (1981) as having two phonologically contrastive levels of pitch: high tone (H) and low tone (L). Both nominals and verbs have been divided by Cope and Rycroft into tonal classes according to the contrastive tonal melodies composed of H and L tones which have been recognized on stems. Four main tonal classes are recognized for the nominals and two or three for the verbs.[11]

Zulu nominal and verbal roots are assigned a distinctive tonal melody in their lexical entry. The tonal melody is an ordered sequence of H and L tones, that is of binary contrasting pitch levels. Hence a tonal melody characterizing a morpheme, be it a root or an affix, cannot consist of a sequence of like tones, LL . . . or HH . . , or be partially composed of such a sequence.

The number of melodies used in Zulu appears to be very limited. There are three main melodies which characterize the majority of nominal roots: L, HL and LHL. It is likely that the other melodies noted by Rycroft (1963: 50-51) are derived from these basic melodies. There are two melodies characterizing verbal roots: L and HL.

Nominals (nouns, adjectives and adverbs) and verbs have the same basic morphological structure. They consist of a root which can be followed by one or more suffixes, derivational and inflectional. This forms a stem to which one or more prefixes are attached.

Whereas all roots have both a segmental tier and tonal melody tier in their lexical representation, some affixes have only a segmental representation. This is the case with the diminutive suffixes attached to nominals which will be seen in later examples. Consequently these suffixes are incorporated into the domain of the root tonal melody for the purposes of tone association. Some morphemes suffixed to nominal stems have only a tonal melody in their lexical representation so that this melody is associated by the Well-formedness Conditions to available segments.

### *2.1 Tonal Classes*

As already noted, both Rycroft and Cope divide Zulu nominals and verbs into tonal classes. Xhosa has received a similar treatment (Westphal et. al. 1967). From the point of view of autosegmental theory, these tonal classes would be ordered paires or subsets of the Cartesian product of two finite sets: the set of tonal melodies and the set of ITARs. Since there are phonologically two ITARs operating in Zulu, ITAR (1) and ITAR (2/2a), and three principal tonal melodies for nominals, L, HL and LHL, a total of six ordered pairs would be theoretically possible. However because ITAR (2/2a) only combines with the HL melody, while ITAR (1) combines with all three tonal melodies, there are in fact only 4 ordered pairs which are exploited in Zulu.[12]

Rycroft's tonal classes A, B, C, and D, which correspond to Cope's classes I, IV, III and II respectively for nominal roots, could be characterized in terms of the present theory in the manner shown in Chart 1.[13]

CHART 1 Principal tonal classes of Zulu nouns.

| Rycroft: | Cope: | | present work (nouns): |
|---|---|---|---|
| *N and V* | *N* | *V* | *TM x ITAR* |
| A | I | II | (L, 1) |
| B | IV | I | (HL, 1) |
| C | III | I | (HL, 2/2a) |
| D (nominals only) | II | | (LHL, 1) |

Since a HL melody can combine with ITAR (1) or with ITAR (2/2a) this fact must be stated in the lexicon. It is in no way predictable synchronically. Since ITAR (1) is the most commonly used ITAR in Zulu we will not mark it specifically. We will only mark those HL melodies which combine with ITAR (2/2a). Thus the lexical entry for the root *bopho* 'cord' would contain (6) while that for *kole* 'school' would contain (7).

(6) $\begin{bmatrix} \text{bopho} \\ \text{HL (2)} \end{bmatrix}_{\text{nom. root}}$ 'cord'

(7) $\begin{bmatrix} \text{kole} \\ \text{HL} \end{bmatrix}_{\text{nom. root}}$ 'school'

*2.2 Domain of the Tonal Melody*

The domain of the pair (TM, ITAR) extends over the tone-bearing units of the segmental sequence it characterizes. If we have a lexical entry as shown in (8), then the domain of the pair (TM, ITAR) extends over the tone-bearing units (symbolized t) to the right of the bracket [ which defines the beginning of a domain. The domain extends as far as the following domain-initial bracket, [, or pause (marked //).

(8) $\begin{bmatrix} t_1^n \\ \text{(TM, ITAR)} \end{bmatrix}$

Where a segmental suffix follows the root and where this segmental suffix has no tonal melody, then the domain of the root tonal melody extends to include the root and suffix, both of which are dominated by the 'stem' node. Thus (9a) becomes (9b).

(9a) stem[ root[ $t^n$ (TM, ITAR) suffix[ $t^m$ (9b) stem[ $t^{n+m}$ (TM, ITAR)

A word such as *ábàfó* 'fellows' would include in its lexical representation the information shown in (10).

(10)

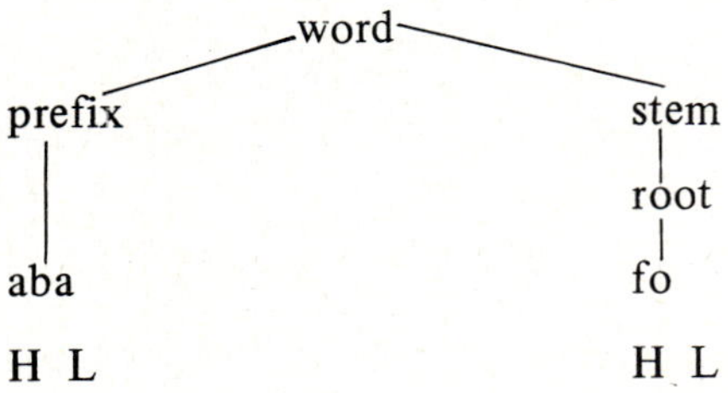


The word *ábàfánà* 'boys' would have the lexical representation shown in (11).

(11)

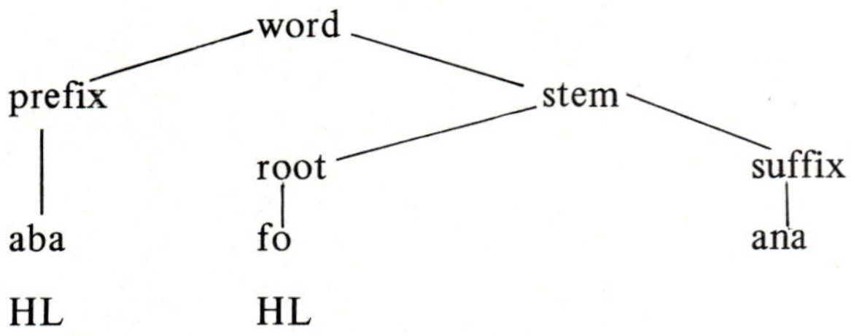


Because of a rule of vowel deletion: V + V → $\phi$ V, we get the surface form *abafana* and not **abafoana*. Since the diminutive suffix *-ana* has no tonal melody in its lexical entry, it enters the domain of the preceding root tonal melody in the way shown in (9a) and (9b). To simplify the representations we will only use domain-initial brackets [ and give the grammatical category of the morpheme(s) to the right by a label written to the left of the domain-initial bracket. Thus (10) will be represented as (12) and (11) as (13).

(12) word[ aba HL stem[ fo HL

(13) $_{\text{word}}$[ aba / HL ] $_{\text{stem}}$[ fo ana / HL ]

The initial Tone Association Rules apply within each tonal melody domain bounded by [. There are certain conditions on the application of the ITARs which we will examine later. Where ITAR (1) or (2/2a) fail to apply, the bracket preceding the tonal melody it combines with is erased and the latter is included in the domain of the preceding tonal melody. By convention the application of an ITAR within a domain causes the immediate left boundary to be erased.

*2.3 Tonal Metathesis*

Tonal metathesis, (14), is a rule that can be expressed with reference to the tonal tier without regard to the segmental tier.[14] Morphological conditioning is however pertinent since the rule only affects prefixal tonal melodies.

(14) *Tonal Metathesis*

HL → LH / $_{\text{prefix}}$[ ___ [ L

This rule (14) applies, for example, to (15). The class 2 prefix *aba-* has the tonal melody HL which is common to all 'full' prefixes.

(15) $_{\text{prefix}}$[ aba / HL ] $_{\text{stem}}$[ ntu / L ] 'people'

The application of (14) gives (16).

(16) $_{\text{prefix}}$[ aba / LH ] $_{\text{stem}}$[ ntu / L ]

The ITAR (1) then applies to give (17). Recall that by convention, brackets flanking a domain are erased after the application of the ITAR within the domain.

(17)
```
abantu
|    |
LH   L
```

The free H tone is then associated with the free tone-bearing unit of (17) by the Well-formedness Conditions, giving (18).

(18) abantu [àbántù]
| | |
L H L

Similarly with a noun such as *ìsí-khàthí* 'time' which has a root characterized by a LHL tonal melody, the HL melody of the class 7 prefix *isi-* is subject to the Tonal Metathesis rule (14). The derivation from the (abbreviated) lexical entry to the surface form is shown in (19).

(19) [isi HL]prefix [khathi LHL]stem 'time' (lexical entry)

[isi LH]prefix [khathi L HL]stem (by (14))

isikhathi
| |
LH L H L (by ITAR (1))

isikhathi [ìsíkhàthí] (by WFC)
| | | |
L H L H L

The unassociated L is deleted by a rule of Unassociated Tone Deletion (20) which deletes a tone (T) which remains unassociated immediately following or preceding a word boundary after all tone association rules have applied.

(20) *Unassociated Tone Deletion*

$T' \rightarrow \phi \;/\; \#\, \_\_\_$ (mirror image) (where T′ is an unassociated tone and # is a word boundary)

Tonal Metathesis[15] is not restricted to nominal prefixes. Where the tonal melody of a verbal prefix or verbal prefixes is HL followed by a verbal root characterized by L, rule (14) applies. In (21) the rule applies before the L toned stem *lima* 'plough', whereas it fails to apply before the HL toned stem *letha* 'bring' in (22).

(21) prefix [u + ya / HL] stem [lim + a / L] 'he/she is ploughing.'

prefix [uya / LH] stem [lima / L] (by (14))

uyalima<br>L H L [ùyálìmà] (by ITAR (1) and WFC)

(22) prefix [u + ya / HL] stem [leth + a / HL] 'he/she is bringing.'

uyaletha<br>H L H L [úyàléthà] (by ITAR (1) and WFC)

### *2.4 Nominal Prefixes*

Two series of noun class prefixes have been distinguished for Zulu.[16] These are traditionally called the 'long' or 'full' series and the 'short' series. Historically the 'full' series is derived from the 'short' series by the prefixation of a vowel to the CV prefix form, which gives a VCV form where the first V is identical with the second. This initial vowel seems to have been some sort of definite article, while the CV is the noun class morpheme. These two prefixal morphemes have so fused that the synchronic analysis into a VCV- 'full' series and a CV- 'short' series seems to reflect the synchronic reality, which gives a morphological contrast: 'definite' versus 'indefinite'. These series are in complementary distribution. The 'full' form is used for citation forms and in most constructions. The 'short' form is used in vocative constructions and after certain negative expressions such as *àkúkhò* and *àmúkhò* 'there's no . . .', 'it's not . . .'. All long form prefixes have a HL tonal melody whereas the short form prefixes have a L melody.

Certain morphemes can be prefixed to a noun, thus resulting in a complex prefix with concatenated tonal melodies. We will see an example of this with a copula in section 3.2.

### 2.5 *Downstep and Downdrift*

Some accounts of automatic downstep and downdrift only make reference to the tonal melody tier, so that the rule is formulated as in (23):

(23) H → ↓H / HL ______ [17]

In Zulu the presence of a downstepped or lowered H can always be attributed to an immediately preceding L tone in the tonal melody tier. In declarative utterances the pitch level of a H preceded by L is lower than the preceding H in the same tonal phrase, delimited by pauses, whether the preceding L is associated with a tone-bearing unit or not. A L preceded by a H which is in turn preceded by a L is lower in pitch than the former L, thus there is a general downdrift or falling intonational curve. The utterance final L tone is always very low or maximally low. This descending type of intonation, or downdrift, and final L lowering can be schematized as //⌉↓// 'declarative'. An intonation contour which eliminates downstepping and downdrift is used to characterize interrogative and some emotional types of utterances. This can be impressionistically characterized as // ————↓ // 'interrogative'. The raising of the overall pitch level is also used as an expressive device.[18]

At the level of lexical entries for morphemes and words, the downstepping feature is not phonologically distinctive. It is a surface phenomenon which is related to underlying tonal melodies. The phonological opposition between downstep and lack of downstep operates at the intonational level which is not the central concern of the present study. However, we will examine some aspects of downstep and intonation in Zulu in section 5.

### 2.6 *Conditions on the Application of ITARs*

Since the ITARs are language specific in that they define the relation between an element of the sequence of tones in a given tonal melody and a designated tone-bearing unit or units of the segmental sequence it characterizes, it is not surprising that this primary relation is subject to language specific constraints. Associated with these conditions are 'designated tone association rules' which refer to specific tones (in Zulu, H tones).

*Constraint 1:* ITARs cannot apply within a domain where $T = n$, $t = m$, and $m > n + 1$.

In other words, where the incorporation of segments into the domain of a stem tonal melody leads to a situation where the number of t (tone-bearing units) exceeds the number of T (tones) within the same domain by more than one, then the ITAR specified by the lexicon fails to apply. Where the ITAR fails to apply within the stem domain, then a rule applies which makes reference to a specific tone: the final H of the tonal melody characterizing the word, and to a specific tone-bearing unit: that of the antepenultimate syllable. This rule, Final High Tone Association (24), associates the last H of the sequence of tones created by the concatenation of the prefixal and root tonal melodies to the t of the antepenultimate syllable of the word.[19]

(24) *Final High Tone Association*

$$\begin{matrix} t & t & t \\ & & \\ H\,L & & \end{matrix} \quad \rightarrow \quad \begin{matrix} t & t & t \\ | & & \\ H & L & \end{matrix} \qquad / \_\_\_\_ \; \#$$

Thus a configuration such as (25a) becomes (25b), which is then subject to (24).

(25a) $\left[\begin{matrix} t & t \\ T & T \end{matrix}\right. \left[\begin{matrix} t^m \\ T^n \end{matrix}\right.$ (25b) $\left[\begin{matrix} t & t & t^m \\ T & T & T^n \end{matrix}\right.$

where $m > n + 1$

Since more than one toneless suffix can be incorporated into the domain of the root tonal melody, one can obtain forms like (26).

(26) [ root + suffixes
| 
ntu any (V) + any (V) + ana
L
stem

Since none of the suffixes in (26) has a characteristic lexical tonal melody, each one is incorporated into the domain of the root melody L, as in (27).

(27) [ ntwanyanyana
L
stem

Since the number of tone-bearing units (syllabic nuclei) t is four and the number of tones T is only one, the ITAR cannot apply due to Constraint 1. When this stem combines with a prefix to form a word the derivation shown in (28) occurs.

(28)
```
[aba   [ntwanyanyana      'the very tiny children'
[H L   [     L

 L H         L             (by (14))

 abantwanyanyana
           |
 L         H  L            (by (24))

 abantwanyanyana           (by WFC)   [àbàntwànyányànà]
 |/          |  |/
 L           H  L
```

Where there is no H in the tonal melody, then the L associates by virtue of the Well-formedness Condition (WFC). This is the case when for example a 'short' prefix is added to a stem characterized by L tone alone as in (29). By a rule not formalized here, the two adjacent L become a single L.

(29)
```
[ba    [ntwanyanyana      'O tiny children'
[L     [    L

 L                         (by Like Tone Simplification)

 bantwanyanyana
   \\ |//
     L                     (by WFC)     [bàntwànyànyànà]
```

Constraint 1 also affects the association of the tonal melody to verbal stems. In (30) ITAR (1) fails to apply within the domain of the stem *-cebisile*, and so following Tonal Metathesis (14) the Final High Tone Association rule (24) applies.

(30)
```
      [ba    [ceb + is + ile    'they enriched'
      [HL    [L
  word    stem

 LH     L                  (by (14))

 bacebisile                (by (24))
      |
 L    H L

 bacebisile                (by WFC)    [bàcèbísìlè]
 |/   | V
 L    H L
```

In (31) there is no H, so the WFC assures the association of the tonal melody with the tone-bearing units.

```
(31)        [si        [ceb + is + ile   'we enriched'
            [L         [L
        word      stem

           sicebisile                (by Like Tone Simplification and WFC)
            \ \|//
              L                                    [sìcèbìsìlè]
```

There is another constraint in Zulu which prevents the ITAR from applying. This constraint applies to the configuration shown in (32).

```
(32)      t          t
                     |
          L    H     L
```

Where Constraint 2 prevents the application of the ITAR, typically in the prefixal domain, then High Tone Association (33) applies.[20]

(33) *High Tone Association*

```
   t                  t            t
          →            \           |
   LH                 LH   / [ ___ L
```

(33) applies particularly in the domain of a 'full' prefix where Tonal Metathesis (14) causes the HL melody to become LH and where the segmental sequence only contains one tone-bearing unit, as in the monosyllabic noun class 9 prefix *iN-* or *i-*. The noun *ímfè* 'sweet reed' shown in (34) exemplifies this.

```
(34)      [im  [fe
          [HL  [L

     →     LH L              (by (14))

     →     imfe
           |  |
         L H  L              (by ITAR (1), (33))
```

In non-final position, the unassociated L is deleted by (20): however in prepausal context, the penultimate syllable is lengthened to include another tone-bearing unit which occasions changes in tonal association which in turn lead to the association of the initial L. This will be treated in detail in section 2.7.

The High tone association rules (24) and (33) can be seen as more specific rules of tone association than ITAR (1), (2) or (2a) since they associate a designated H tone with a designated t. We will call these rules the Designated Tone Association Rules (DTARs).

### *2.7 Tone and Vowel Length*

We have seen that each tonal melody in Zulu has a domain, and that the relation between the tones of the tonal melody and the tone-bearing units of the domain is defined by language specific tone association rules and universal Well-formedness Conditions.

The tone association rules of Zulu associate tones with the nucleus of a syllable. Phonetically long vowels exist in Zulu. [V:] can be the reflex of underlying (35a) or (35b), where $ is a syllable.

(35a) 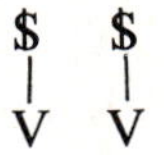

(35b) 

The Zulu nominal prefixes with long vowels, those realized as phonetically long in all positions and not just when in a penultimate syllable prepausally, are underlyingly of the (35a) type since they are reflexes of VCV where the intervocalic C is deleted by a late rule, shown in derivation (58) below.[21] Zulu nominal prefixes with a vowel plus a syllabic nasal are also underlyingly disyllabic.[22]

(35b) results from higher level prosodic and intonational processes. Prepausally the penultimate vowel is lengthened in declarative sentences where it is neither preceded nor followed immediately by a stressed vowel.[23] We will refer to this process as Penultimate Syllable Lengthening (36).

(36) *Penultimate Syllable Lengthening*

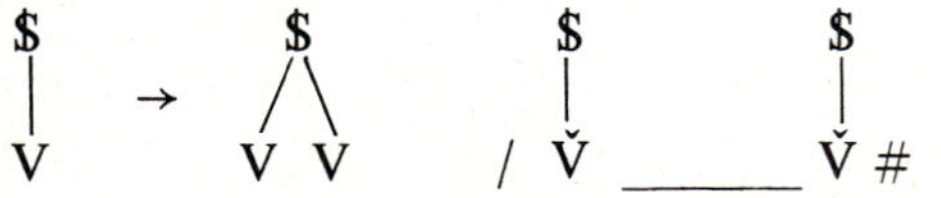

(declarative intonation) (V̌ = unstressed short vowel)

In Zulu, short syllables are only associated with one lexical tone in the surface representation. Syllables lengthened by (36) can carry two tones, thus (37a) and (37b) are permissable whereas (37c) is not.

(37a) 

(37b) 

(37c) 

Where certain processes (analysed as late rules) affecting tone association cause a configuration such as (37c) to exist, the Contour Tone Simplification Rule (38) applies causing the L to disassociate.

(38) *Contour Tone Simplification*

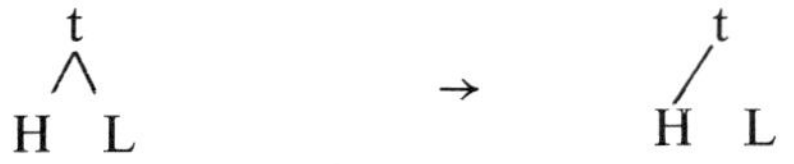


After the application of Penultimate Syllable Lengthening (36), any unassociated tone to the right of the tone associated with the lengthened syllable is associated with the lengthened syllable. If we accept that each V is a tone-bearing unit, then this association is predicted by the Well-formedness Condition. Thus (39a) becomes (39b).

(39a)

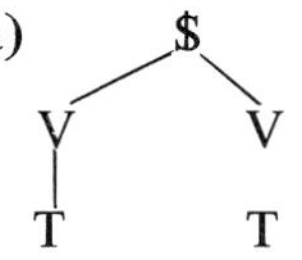


(39b)

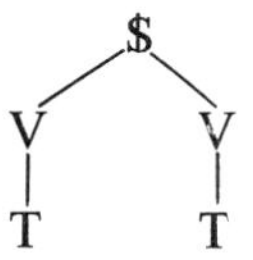


Where there is no unassociated tone, the tone associated with the lengthened syllable spreads to the second mora (or V) also by the Well-formedness Condition as in (40).

(40)

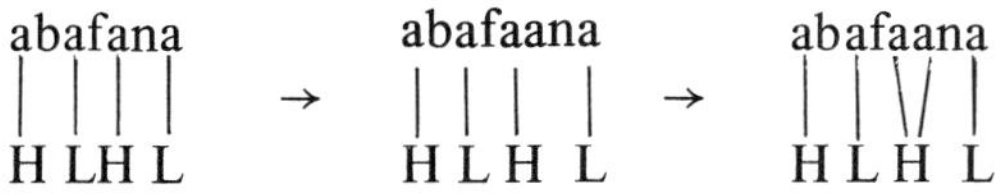


'the children'

(by ITAR and WFC) (by (36)) (by WFC)

Where an unassociated tone precedes a syllable which undergoes (36), then that unassociated tone associates with the first V of the lengthened syllable by a rule of Unassociated Tone Docking (41).

(41) *Unassociated Tone Docking*[24]

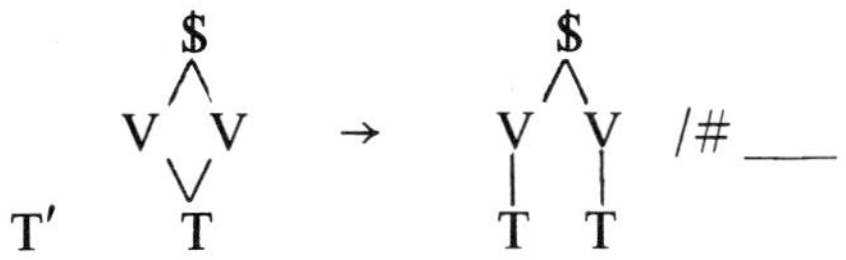


(where T′ is an unassociated tone)

The application of these rules is seen in (42), where the word *ímfè* 'sweet reed' seen in (34) undergoes rule (36).

```
(42) iimfe              iimfe        [ìːmfè]
      \/  |              |\  |
     LH   L      →       LH L
     (by (36), WFC)      (by (41))
```

*2.8 Derivations*

For a given lexical entry, the ITARs and the DTARs apply within bracketed domains. To show that rules are ordered and to see how they apply to words with roots of the four main tonal 'classes': L, ITAR (1), HL, ITAR (1), HL, ITAR (2/2a), LHL, ITAR (1), we will give the derivation for a sample of each type.

*2.8.1 Nouns with roots with L tonal melody*

```
(43a)   [àbántù]   'people'        (43b)   [àbántwànà]   'children'

 [aba  [ntu                         [aba  [ntu  + ana
 [H L  [  L                         [H L  [  L

 L H     L         (by (14))         L H     L         (by (14))

 abantu                             abantwana
 |     \                            |       /
 L H    L          (by ITAR (1))     L H    L          (by ITAR (1))

 abantu                             abantwana
 | |  |                             | |   /
 L H  L            (by WFC)          L H  L            (by WFC)
```

Prepausally (36) applies:

```
 abaantu                            abantwaana
 | |   /                            | |   | /
 L H  L            (by (36))         L H   L           (by 36))

 abaantu                            abantwaana
 | |/  |                            | |   |//
 L H   L           (by WFC)          L H   L           (by WFC)

 [àbáːntù]                          [àbántwàːnà]
```

In the following forms Constraint 1 blocks the operation of ITAR (1).

(43c) [àbàntwányànà] 'tiny children' (43d) [àbàntwànyányànà] 'very tiny children'

```
[aba [ntu + any + ana            [aba [ntu + any + any + ana
[H L [  L                        [H L [  L

L H    L        (by (14))        L H      L          (by (14))

abantwanyana                     abantwanyanyana
 L     H L      (by (24))        L           H L     (by (24))

abantwanyana                     abantwanyanyana
 L     H L      (by WFC)         L           H L     (by WFC)
```

Prepausally (36) would apply as for (43a) and (43b).

*2.8.2 Nouns with roots with HL, ITAR (1) tonal melody*

Nouns of this type behave like those with L roots with respect to the Initial and Designated Tone Association Rules and the Well-formedness Condition. The rule of Tonal Metathesis (14) does not however apply.

(44a) [ábàfó] 'youths' (44b) [ábàfánà] 'fellows'

```
[aba  [fo                        [aba  [f(o) + ana
[H L  [H L                       [H L  [  H L

 abafo                            abafana
 HL HL        (by ITAR (1))       HL HL        (by ITAR (1))

 abafo                            abafana
 H  LH L      (by WFC)            H L H L      (by WFC)
```

The unassociated L in (44a) is deleted by (20). In phrase final position, Penultimate Syllable Lengthening (36) applies:

```
abaafo                            abafaana
H L  H     (by (36) and WFC)      H L H L      (by (36), WFC)

[ábà:fó]                          [ábàfá:nà]
```

In (44c) Constraint 1 causes Final High Tone Association (24) to apply as it did in (43c) and (43d).

(44c) [ábàfànyányànà] 'tiny boys'

[aba [fo + any + any + ana
[H L [HL

abafanyanyana
H L H L (by (24))

abafanyanyana
H L H L (by WFC)

*2.8.3 Nouns with roots having LHL tonal melody*

Since the root tonal melody is L initial, Tonal Metathesis (14) applies.

(45a) [ìsíkhàthí] 'time'

[isi [khathi
[H L [ L H L

L H L H L (by (14))

isikhathi
L H L H L (by ITAR(1))

isikhathi
L H L H L (by WFC)

(45b) [ìsíkhàshánà] 'small time'

[isi [khath(i) + ana
[H L [ L H L

L H L H L (by (14))

isikhashana
L H L H L (by ITAR (1))

isikhashana
L H L H L (by WFC)

The unassociated L in (45a) is deleted by (20).

(45c) [ìsíkhàshányànà] 'tiny moment'

[isi [khath(i) + any + ana
[H L [ L H L

L H L H L (by (14))

isikhashanyana
L H L H L (by ITAR (1))

isikhashanyana
L H L H L (by WFC)

From the neighbouring Xhosa language we have an example of a 5-syllable stem with a LHL tonal melody.[25] Like the other tonal melodies this root melody can only associate within the domain of the stem where the number of syllables does not exceed the number of tones by more than one (Constraint 1). In (46) Final High Tone Association (24) applies as in (43c), (43d) and (44c).

(46) [àmáqhùqhùbányànà] 'very tiny swellings'

[ama [qhuqhub(a) + any + ana
[H L [ L H L

L H L H L (by (14))

amaqhuqhubanyana

L H L H L (by (24))

amaqhuqhubanyana

L H L H L (by WFC)

*2.8.4 Nouns with roots having HL, ITAR (2/2a) tonal melody*

Nouns with roots characterized by a HL melody which is associated by ITAR (2/2a) present much more variation both across dialects and according to phonological environments than do the other nouns. This variation is especially apparent with disyllabic stems. For nouns, these are stems made up of a root with no suffixes. Trisyllabic stems always undergo ITAR (2) which associates the initial tone, H, with the second tone-bearing unit.[26] Stems with more than 3 syllables fall under Constraint 1 which triggers the application of (24) as for other nouns. A possible exception is the dialect described by Rycroft (1963) which shows the H on the penultimate rather than the antepenultimate syllable of such words.[27]

In the Zulu dialect described by Cope (1970) and Rycroft (1963), the ITAR for disyllabic stems is ITAR (2a). This is evident from the non-final forms cited by Cope (1970: 120), repeated here in (47).

(47) úḿ!fáz̲í ... 'woman' umfazi
HL H L

í!nkósí ... 'chief' inkosi
HL H L

ísí!khwámá ... 'bag' isikhwama
H L H L

(!) represents downstep on the following H.

Non-final forms given by Rycroft (1963: 63) are reproduced in (48).

(48) í!nkósí ... 'chief' 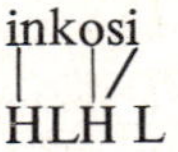

ísìbóphó ... 'cord' 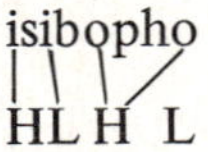

íz̲ìbóphó ... 'cords' 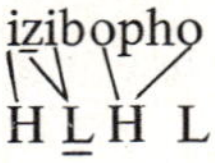

(The underlined consonants are "depressor consonants" whose effect on tone will be treated in section 3.)

Let us now consider examples from the dialect described by Rycroft (1979), which is somewhat different. This dialect, like that described by Cope (1970), maximalizes High Tone Spreading which causes the prefixal H to spread onto all the following tone-bearing units associated with L. This process will be discussed in detail in section 4.

(49) ámákhó!sí ... 'chiefs' 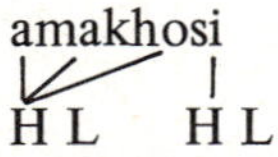

íz̲ìkhwàmá ... 'bags' 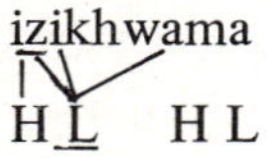

In the dialect exemplified by (49), it would at first appear that ITAR (2) and not ITAR (2a) applies, since the H of the root tonal melody is associated with the second syllable of the root and not the first and second as in the examples shown in (47) and (48). However when the penultimate syllable lengthening rule (36) applies phrase-finally, a certain number of adjustments in tone association occur which lead us to conclude that ITAR (2a) and not ITAR (2) applies. In this dialect, a rule called the Left Branch Deletion Rule (50) applies to any configuration where H preceded by L is associated to the tone-bearing units of two consecutive domain-final syllables. This rule does not apply in the dialect described by Cope (1970) and by Rycroft (1963).

(50) *Left-branch Deletion Rule*

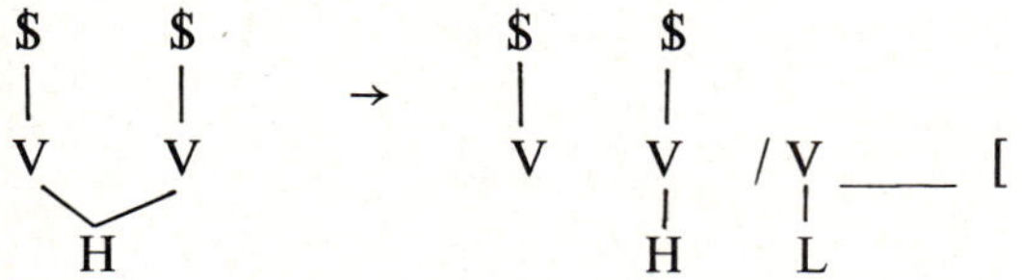

Notice that only forms which have undergone ITAR (2a) will be subject to this rule.

To illustrate the application of rules of tonal association to nouns of this class, we will give the derivation for *amakosi* 'chiefs' in all dialects.

(51) [ama / H L] [kosi / H L (2a)]

```
amakosi
|   |/
H L H L      (by ITAR (2a))

amakosi
| | |/
H L H L      (by WFC)    → [ámàkósí]  Cope (1970) and
                                     Rycroft (1963)
amakosi
| |  /
H L  H L     (by (50))

amakosi
|  |//
H L H L      (by WFC)    → [ámàkòsí]  Rycroft (1979) (before
                                     High Tone Spreading)
```

ITAR (2) and ITAR (2a) are in complementary distribution. The former applies to all trisyllabic stems whereas the latter applies only to disyllabic stems. It is possible that the evolution from ITAR (2a) to ITAR (2) came about as a result of Left Branch Deletion (50) becoming generalized. The existence of ITAR (2a) in trisyllabic stems in the Xhosa dialect points to the development of ITAR (2) from ITAR (2a).[28]

Left Branch Deletion (50) is a Tone Association Adjustment Rule which applies after the Initial Tone Association Rules and the Well-formedness Condition have applied. It is also sensitive to context since the prior application of the Penultimate Syllable Lengthening Rule (36) blocks the application of (50). Where (36) applies, then another adjustment rule, Right Branch Deletion (52), applies.

(52) *Right Branch Deletion*

This configuration, which is then subject to the WFC, arises in the case of disyllable HL (2a) stems after the application of Penultimate Syllable Lengthening (36), as is illustrated in (53).

(53) 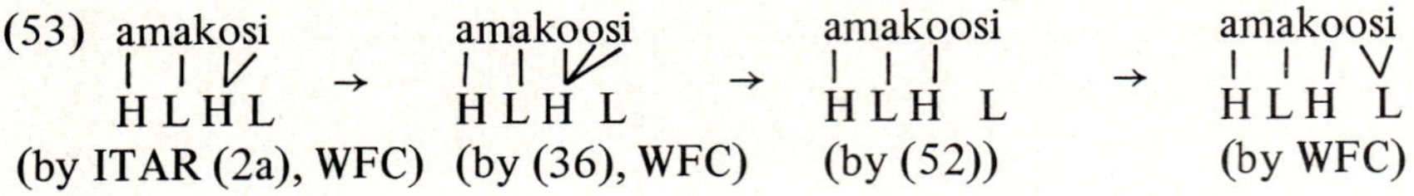

The last form in (53) is the surface form [ámàkô:sì] 'chiefs', which is attested in the dialects of Zulu described by both Cope (1970) and Rycroft (1963, 1979).

The association of the tonal melody HL (2/2a) to nouns with disyllabic stems is particularly complex. Linguists describing the data do not agree on surface representations or on the underlying phonological analysis, as is evident from comparing the work of Cope, Rycroft and Khumalo.

Khumalo (1981: vii) states that "There are two principal tonal dialects of Zulu, viz. the Natal Coast dialect, spoken in the urban areas along the Natal Coast, and the KwaZulu dialect, spoken in the rural and urban areas of KwaZulu." While both Cope and Rycroft distinguish two phonological contexts which condition variation in tonal realization on HL (2/2a) disyllabic-stem nouns (and verbs), Khumalo distinguishes three: 1) phrase final (//), 2) word final (#), and 3) word internal (in a compound) (+). In phrase final position the forms are different according to dialect. Examples provided by Khumalo are given in (54).[29]

(54)

| 1) ____ // KwaZulu / Natal | 2) ____ # | 3) ____ + | |
|---|---|---|---|
| úm̀!fâ:z̲ì ≃ úḿfà:!z̲í | úm̀fâz̲ì . . . | úm̀fà!z̲í | 'woman' |
| ínkô:sì ≃ ínkò:sí | ínkòsì . . . | ínkò!sí | 'chief' |
| ísì!khwâ:mà ≃ ísìkhwà:!má | ísìkhwàmà . . . | ísìkhwà!má | 'bag' |
| ísì!bô:phò ≃ ísìbò:phó | ísìbòphò . . . | ísìbò!phó | 'cord' |

From this data we conclude that in the Natal dialect of Zulu, ITAR (2a) no longer applies. Words with disyllabic stems behave in the same way as those with trisyllabic stems, that is the initial tone, H associates with the second tone-bearing unit by ITAR (2). Thus rules such as (50) and (52) do not apply. This development certainly goes in the direction of a considerable simplification of tonal association.

To account for phrase internal forms (context 2), it is necessary to posit a rule which causes the H to disassociate from the final syllable before a word boundary. This rule is formulated in (55).

(55) *Word-final High Tone Disassociation*

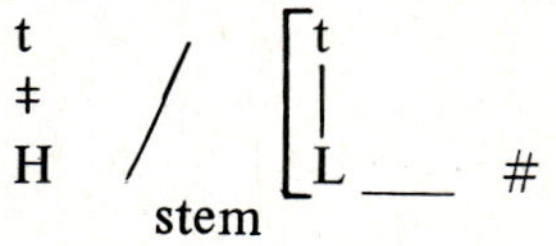

There is justification for (55) beyond nouns of the HL (2a/2) type since nouns of the type discussed in 2.8.3, those with LHL roots, also undergo this rule as is shown in data supplied by Khumalo (personal communication), reproduced in (56).

| (56) | 1) ____ // | 2) ____ # | 3) ____ + | |
|---|---|---|---|---|
| | ìzíndè:bé | ìzíndèbè . . . | ìzíndèbé | 'lips' |
| | ìsíkhò:vá | ìsíkhòvà . . . | ìsíkhòvá | 'banana plantation' |

Derivations of HL (2) nouns with trisyllabic and quadrisyllabic stems are shown in (57a) and (57b).

(57a) ama kos(i) + ana 'elder sons'
H L H L (2)

amakosana
|    /
H L  H L (by ITAR (2), (1))

amakosana
| V / /
H L  H L (by WFC)

amakosaana
| V V /
H L H L (by (36), WFC)

[ámàkòsá:nà]

(57b) ema kos(i) + an(a) + eni 'elder sons, LOCATIVE'
H L H L (2)

emakosaneni
|
H L  H L (by (24))

emakosaneni
| V / V
H L  H L (by WFC)

[émàkòsánènì]

## 2.9 *Compound Stems*

By compound stem we mean a stem made up of more than one morpheme characterized by a tonal melody. In Zulu there are many such stems, both in nouns and verbs, but we will only examine a few of these. (58), (59) and (60) provide examples of compound noun stems.[30]

(58) [ili HL]word [bhung(a)]stem [ane HL] 'beetle'

```
ili  bhung  ana
|      |     |
HL  H   L H  L            (by ITAR (1))

ilibhungana
|\ |  | |
H L HL H L                (by WFC)

iibhungana
|\  |  | |
HLHL H L                  (by Intervocalic Prefixal
                           Consonant Deletion)
```

[î:bhúng!ánà]

From (58) we see that Initial Tone Association takes place within each domain. The penultimate L remains unassociated and gives rise to the downstepped H on the penultimate syllable.

(59) [N L] [khom(o) L H L] [azi HL (2a)] 'O cow!'

```
N khom   azi
    |    |/
L  L HL H L          (by ITARs)

nkhomaazi            (by (36))

nkhomaazi            (by (52), (20), WFC)
   / /  \|
   L  H  L
```

[nkhòmâ:zì]

It is here assumed that a H unassociated at the end of a derivation is deleted and any sequence of like tones is simplified to a single tone. Thus in (59) the floating H is deleted and then the medial floating L is deleted because it follows another L. A final derivation follows.

(60) [isi HL] [vu HL] [vu HL] 'excessive heat'

```
isivuvu
| \ \ \
HL HLHL              (by ITARs, WFC)

isivuuvu             (by (36))
```

```
isivuuvu
I \ \\ \
H L HL H          (by WFC, (20))
```

[ísìvû:vú]

3. DEPRESSOR CONSONANTS

In Zulu as in the other Nguni languages there is a series of what are commonly called "depressor consonants". The phonetic character of these is, according to Cope, voiced and breathy, or "heavy" (Cope 1970: 113):

> I attribute to the distinctive feature of heaviness, which may be described as glottal friction with heavy voice, a combination of breath (+H) and voice (+v), neither of which is distinctive in itself. The light lenis jective stops and the light sonorants, nasals and nasal clicks have voice without breath, and the light fortis non-jective stops and clicks have breath without voice. It is only the heavy consonants that are depressors in tonological effect.

Rycroft and Ngcobo (1979: B7) state that depressor consonants are associated with breathy voice. Khumalo (1981: 19) attributes the phenomenon of pitch level depression "to the feature [+slack vocal cords]" which is a distinctive feature of the "depressor consonants" although the feature is also manifested on vowels adjacent to depressor consonants or in environments historically adjacent to them, as we shall se below.

Following Halle and Stevens (1971), Anderson (1974), and Stevens (1975), Khumalo (1981: 16-17) subcategorizes the Zulu phonemes in terms of four laryngeal feature categories: spread glottis, constricted glottis, stiff vocal cords, and slack vocal cords. The vowels, laterals, nasals and glides have a negative value for all four categories. The "depressor consonants" have a positive value for [spread glottis] and [slack vocal cords] and necessarily negative values for the other two features:

$$\begin{bmatrix} \text{+ spread glottis} \\ \text{−constricted glottis} \\ \text{−stiff vocal cords} \\ \text{+slack vocal cords} \end{bmatrix}$$

Since [+slack vocal cords] implies [+spread glottis] (the inverse does not hold), it is sufficient to isolate the feature [+slack vocal cords] ([+S]) as the distinctive feature which characterizes the subset of "depressor consonants" in the lexicon.

While the "depressor consonants" are the only phonemes characterized by the feature [+S] in the lexicon, this feature spreads by rule to other phonemes or segments in the speech chain. This feature also figures in the lexicon as a morpheme in its own right, associated by specific rules of word formation with other phonological units, as we shall see.

Before dealing with these rules, we will examine the relation between the depressor consonants and the tonal melody tier. To facilitate the presentation, following Rycroft (1963), all depressor consonants are underlined in the examples to floow.

### *3.1 Effect of Depressor Consonants on the Tonal Melody Tier*[31]

A depressor consonant (C), which is characterized in the lexicon by the feature [+S], associates by rule with the L associated with the tone-bearing unit or V adjacent to the C, thus causing that L to acquire extra low pitch which we will henceforth symbolize as L. This association of C with L and the subsequent lowering of the pitch level of L to L is given as (61), the Low Tone Lowering Rule. It applies after the rules of Tonal Metathesis (14), Initial Tone Association (3), (4), (5) and Tone Association Adjustment (41), (50), (52), (55) have applied.

(61) *Low Tone Lowering*[32]

VC → VC

L → L (mirror image)

The extra low pitch of the L tone associated with the depressor consonant compared with the L tone unassociated with a depressor consonant is shown in Doke's work (Doke, 1926 and Doke & Vilakazi, 1948), where actual pitch levels are numbered from 1 to 9. The highest level is 1, the lowest 9. Doke (1926: 245) gives the following pairs of illustrative examples, (62a) and (62b), (63a) and (63b), to which we have added the tones and association lines in accord with our analysis.

(62a) 3 2 2-8 9
isihla:lo 'seat'
L H L

(62b) 6 6 3-8 9
izihla:lo 'seats'
L HL

(63a) 22-43 9
isifu:ndo 'lesson'
H L H L

(63b) 2 6 3 9
izifu:ndo 'lessons'
H L H L

In terms of the autosegmental analysis that we are proposing, the lexical entry for (62a) and (62b) is shown in (64a) and (64b).

(64a) 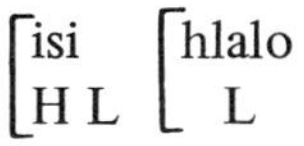 'seat' (64b) 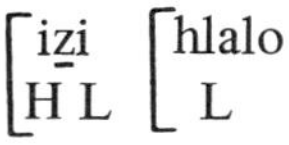 'seats'

Following the application of (14) and the ITARs and WFC we have the outputs shown in (65a) and (65b).

(65a) 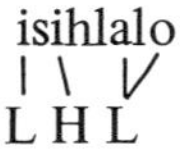 (65b) 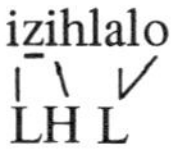

The application of (36) prepausally then gives the forms shown in (66a) and (66b).

(66a) 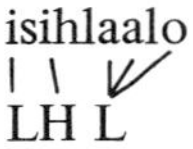 (66b) 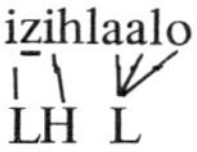

In comparing the pitch levels of the initial L of (62a) with that of (62b) we note that the initial level of the latter is 6, lower than that of the former which is 3. This is due to the operation of Low Tone Lowering (61) which associates the "depressor" consonant z̲ with the L associated with the adjacent V. This is shown in (67).

(67) 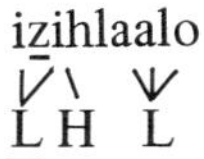

Where a depressor consonant precedes a V associated with a H, the L̲ associates with that V by virtue of Extra Low Tone Spreading (68).

(68) *Extra Low Tone Spreading*

This rule applies to the output of (67) to give (69).

(69) 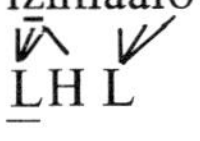

Where a V associated with the L̲ and H is in an unstressed (or non-prominent) syllable[33] symbolized V̌, the H disassociates from that V̌ and re-associates, if not blocked by a following 'depressor' consonant, with the V of the following syllable by virtue of High Tone Rightward Reassociation (70).

(70) *High Tone Rightward Reassociation*

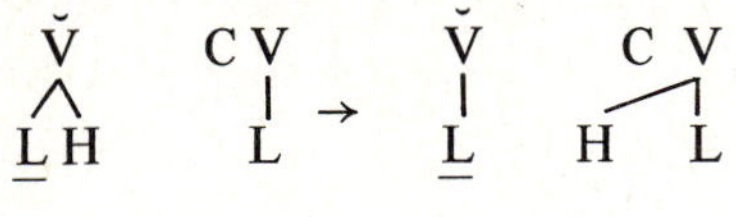


When (70) applies to (69) we get (71).

(71)

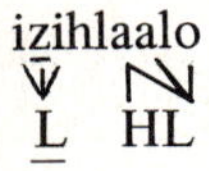


The HL contour on the first V of the penultimate syllable in (71) is then simplified by Contour Tone Simplification (38) to obtain (62b), repeated here as (72).

(72)

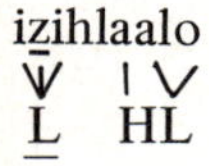


In phrase medial position where (36) does not apply then the derivations shown in (73) occur.

(73)

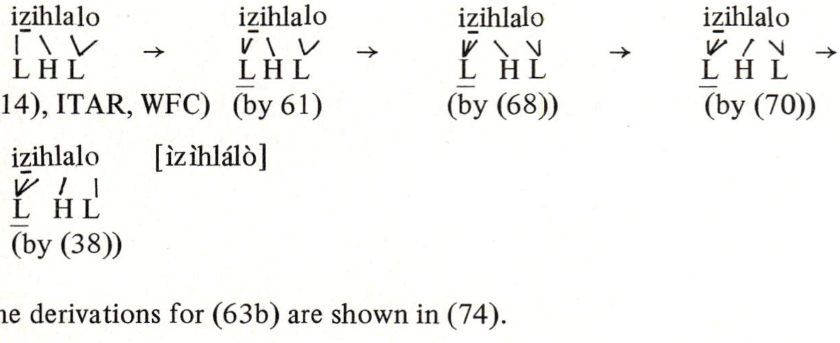


The derivations for (63b) are shown in (74).

(74)

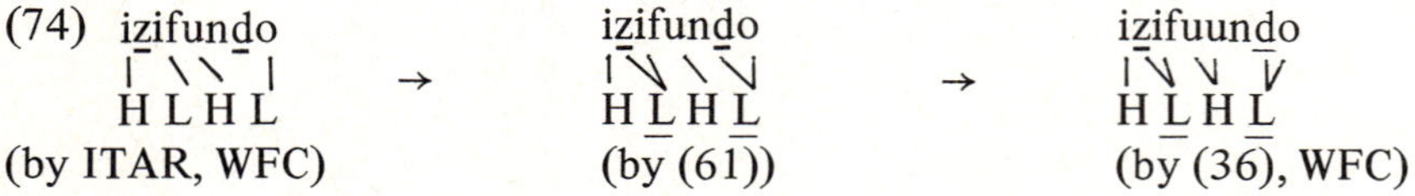


The 2-8 falling pitch on (62a) and the 2-4 falling pitch on (63a) reflect the influence of a late rule of H spreading, indicated in our representations by the dashed lines. In Zulu a L preceded by H is realized phonetically as a falling tone [\], dropping from below the pitch level of the preceding H when the L is associated with both morae of the lengthened penultimate syllable. Rycroft (1963: facing page 58) gives an impressionistic representation of (62a) which is in (75).

(75) isíhlalo

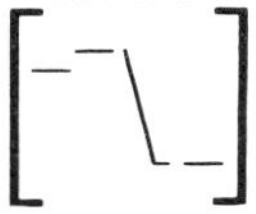

Rycroft does not indicate the effect of penultimate syllable lengthening but states that the context is phrase final.

The 2-4 falling pitch shown by Doke on (63a) is more problematical since Khumalo (1981: 49) notes a level tone when a L is associated with a short syllable. However it is perhaps possible that Doke obtained this form in very deliberate speech. Rycroft, like Doke, notes a short falling tone [`] dropping from the level of the preceding H to that of the following H, which is of course of a lower pitch because of downstep. An example given by Rycroft is shown in (76).

(76) ísikóle 'school'

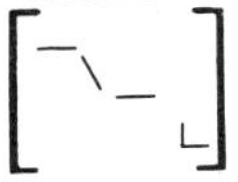

A H is realized as a level pitch [¯] as shown in (75) and (76). A L is always realized as a very low level pitch [_]. A V associated with both L and H has a rising pitch which levels out to a level high pitch in some instances depending on the rate of speech, thus [/] or [⌐]. A VV sequence (V V linked to H L) is realized as [⌉L]. A VV sequence (first V linked to L H, second V linked to L; i.e. LHL) is realized as [∩L].[34]

*3.2 Depressor Effect Without a Consonant*

The depressor effect, that is the lowering of the pitch of L tone (61), the spreading of a L tone onto a V associated by rule with a H tone (68), and the rightward displacement of a H tone (70), can be produced without the physical presence of a "depressor consonant" in the surface representation.

While the feature [+S] is a distinctive feature defining a subset of Zulu consonants, this feature, associated lexically with the "depressor consonants", spreads onto the following vowel in the speech chain by a rule of progressive assimilation or feature spreading. Since in the lexicon no vowels are defined by the feature [+S], any specification of vowels in the lexicon involving that feature would be redundant. The laryngeal features are only distinctive insofar as they are used to define subsets of obstruents. The progressive assimilation of the [+S] feature is shown in (77).

(77) CV → CV *or* V → V / C ___
[+S] [+S]

The intervocalic voiced consonants are deleted in some nominal prefixes of VCV structure in Zulu (see note 16). Where that consonant is a C, as in the class 10 prefix iziN-, then we see that the depressor-related rules apply before consonant deletion. This is shown in (79). While the other distinctive features are deleted along with the C, the laryngeal feature [+S] remains since it has been associated with a vowel which is not deleted. Following the deletion of C, there is regressive assimilation of the feature [+S] as shown in (78a) and illustrated in (79). Since any vowel immediately adjacent to a vowel which is [+S] assimilates that feature, the second rule of [+S] assimilation can be stated as in (78b).

(78) a. VCV V → V V (C deletion) → VV (regressive assimilation)

b. V → V / ___ V (mirror image)
+S +S

(79) [iziN HL] [gane HL] 'children'

→ izingane (HLHL) (by ITAR, WFC, (77)) → izingane (HL HL) (by (61), (68)) → i ingane (HLH L) (by C deletion, (78b))

→ iingaane (HL H L) (by (36), (38), WFC) [î:ngǎ:nè]

As mentioned above, while [+S] is associated in the lexicon with "depressor consonants", it is also given in the lexicon unassociated with any segment. To be realized or manifested in the surface representation,

[+S] must necessarily become associated with a specified segment, either a C or a V. Now it cannot associate with an obstruent defined in the lexicon as [−S] where this feature is distinctive, but it can be associated with any vowel, glide, lateral or nasal for which the laryngeal features are not distinctive.

In Zulu, the copulative prefix meaning 'it is . . .' is manifested on the surface for some nouns by a L tone, realized as L̲, associated with the initial vowel of the word which is pronounced with breathy voice or slack vocal cords. Since the copulative is elsewhere expressed by a L̲ tone prefix such as yh(i)-, ng(u)- and wh(u)- (see Khumalo, 1981: 133), we will assume that the laryngeal feature [+S] and the tonal melody L are given in the lexicon as a (partial) representation of the copulative morpheme, associated either with an unspecified C or with one of the prefixal Cs given above. Structurally, the position preceding the word-initial V would be occupied by a C. Where the C is not fully specified, that is where it has no distinctive feature specifications, it is phonetically uninterpreted.

Doke (1926: 212) compares a series of contrastive utterances including those reproduced here in (80a-d).

(80) a. $\overset{3}{\text{a}}\text{m}\overset{2}{\text{a}}\text{:ndl}\overset{9}{\text{a}}$ 'strength' b. $\overset{8}{\text{a}}\text{m}\overset{3}{\text{a}}\text{:ndl}\overset{9}{\text{a}}$ 'it is strength'

c. $\overset{2\text{-}4}{\text{u}}\text{:th}\overset{3}{\text{i}}$ 'stick' d. $\overset{8\text{-}3\text{-}5}{\text{u}}\text{:th}\overset{4}{\text{i}}$ 'it is a stick'

The lexical representations for (80a-d) are given in (81a-d).

(81) a. $\begin{bmatrix}\text{ama}\\ \text{H L}\end{bmatrix}$ $\begin{bmatrix}\text{an}\underline{\text{dla}}\\ \text{L}\end{bmatrix}$ b. $\begin{bmatrix}\underline{\text{C}}\\ \text{L}\end{bmatrix}$ $\begin{bmatrix}\text{ama}\\ \text{H L}\end{bmatrix}$ $\begin{bmatrix}\text{an}\underline{\text{dla}}\\ \text{L}\end{bmatrix}$

c. $\begin{bmatrix}\text{ulu}\\ \text{H L}\end{bmatrix}$ $\begin{bmatrix}\text{thi}\\ \text{H L}\end{bmatrix}$ d. $\begin{bmatrix}\underline{\text{C}}\\ \text{L}\end{bmatrix}$ $\begin{bmatrix}\text{ulu}\\ \text{H L}\end{bmatrix}$ $\begin{bmatrix}\text{thi}\\ \text{H L}\end{bmatrix}$

The derivations for (81a-d) are given in (82a-d).

(82) a. amandla (by (14), ITAR, WFC, (77))
LH L

b. Camandla (by (14), ITAR, WFC, (77))
LH L
(the prefixal L is deleted by Like Tone Simplification)

amaandla (by (36), WFC)
LH L

Camaandla (by (36), WFC)
L H L

amaandla (by (61))
L H L̲

Camaandla (by (61))
L̲ H L̲

```
c.  uluthi                              d. Culuthi
    | \ /                                  | \ \ |
    H L H L   (by ITAR, WFC)               L H LH  L   (by ITAR, WFC, (77))

    uluuthi                                Culuuthi
    | V /                                  | \V  |
    H L H L̸   (by (36), WFC,               L  HL  H L̸   (by (36), WFC,
              (20))                                      (20))

                                           Culuuthi
                                           V / |  |
                                           L HL   H     (by (61), (68), (70))
```

Where the *l* of the prefix *ulu-* is deleted, the resultant forms are (82c) [û:thí] and (82d) [ũ̂:thí] as indicated by Doke and shown in (80 c-d).

Khumalo (1981: 20) gives examples of dialectal variation involving the distribution of the feature [+S]. In the Natal Coast dialect, all deadjectival copulative prefixes of the form CV- are associated with [+S]. In the KwaZulu dialect on the other hand, only prefixes of the form CV- where C is [+nasal] are associated with [+S].

Since in the lexicon, laterals, nasals, glides and vowels are not associated with [+S], the association must take place by rule (as must be the case for the copulative prefix in (82b and d)). In the Natal Coast dialect, [+S] is part of the deadjectival copulative prefix morpheme, its association only being blocked by the presence of an obstruent which is inherently [–S] and which has two + values for the other laryngeal features. In the KwaZulu dialect, however, [+S] is only present in association with [+nasal] in the same morpheme.

The examples given by Khumalo (1981: 20) are reproduced here in (83 a-f).

```
(83)      NATAL COAST                                    KWAZULU

  a. [ +S  [                                   b. [     [
     [ ba  [ dala  →  badala                      [ ba  [ dala → badala
     [     [          / | |                       [     [          / | \
     [ HL  [ H L      HLH L                       [ HL  [ H L  HLH L

              [bá!dálà]      'they are old'             [bá!dálà]

  c. [ +S  [                                   d.  same as c.
     [ mi  [ ncana  →  mincane
     [     [           V  / |
     [ L   [ H  L      L  H L

              [mìncánè]      'they are small'
```

e. [ +S / lu / L ] [ khulu / H L ] → lukhulu (L H L)   f. [ lu / HL ] [ khulu / H L ] → lukhulu (HL H L)

[l̤ùkhúlù]   'it is big'   [lú!khúlù]

We note further that the prefixal tonal melody presents two allomorphs in function of the nature of the initial consonant. Where the prefixal consonant is *not* associated with [+S] then the tonal melody is H L, which is the underlying, unmarked tonal melody for those prefixes. However where the prefixal consonant is associated by rule with [+S] then the tonal melody is reduced to L. Such rules of allomorphy have to be stated in the grammar as they do not derive from general principles. Since in the lexicon *b* is [+constricted glottis, −slack vocal cords] it cannot be associated with the feature [+S]. However since the laryngeal features are not distinctive for laterals, nasals, vowels, and glides, they can be associated with these segments by rule, manifesting themselves in the surface representation. The feature [+S] characterizes the prefixal morpheme which is a syllable phonetically. In the surface representation this feature is only manifested by phonemes for which it is not lexically distinctive.

The dialectal variation in the distribution of the laryngeal features and the effect of the [+S] feature on the tonal melody tier clearly distinguishes these features from the non-laryngeal distinctive features.

Further examples of the use of the feature [+S] as a separate morpheme is in its use in imperative verb forms as cited by Khumalo (1981: 21-22). The feature [+S] is associated with the initial CV of the verb in the imperative, but it is absent in other forms of the verb such as the infinitive as is seen from comparing (84a) and (84b).

(84) a. [ +S / leth / H L ] [ a   'bring!'   b. [ uku / H L ] [ leth / H L ] [ a   'to bring'

→ [l̤éthà]   → [úkùléthà]

The imperative prefix yi- used with some verbs with C-initial roots is also characterized by [+S] (thus pronounced [y̤i]), and is associated with a L tonal melody.

The feature [+S] characterizes the first and second person singular and plural subject prefixes in the principal, positive constructions, whereas it is absent in other constructions and for third person prefixes. Where the prefix consists of a CV where the C has distinctive laryngeal features including [−S] such as s in the first person plural subject prefix si-, then [+S] can only associate with the V and not with the consonant, as was the case with ba- in 83(a). However, where the prefixal C has no distinctive laryngeal features, [+S] associates with both the C and the V of the prefix. Linked to [+S] in these cases is a tonal melody L (see Rycroft 1979: 33, 10.4).

The feature [+S] is apparently also used in a number of roots derived from English words which do not contain depressor consonants. Khumalo (1981: 22) gives the examples shown in (85).

(85)

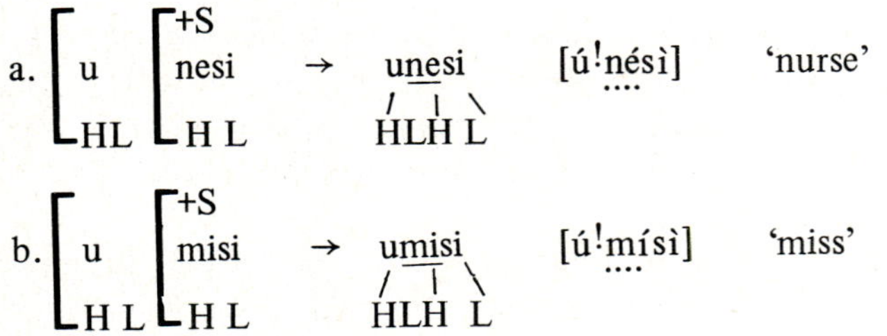


(85)

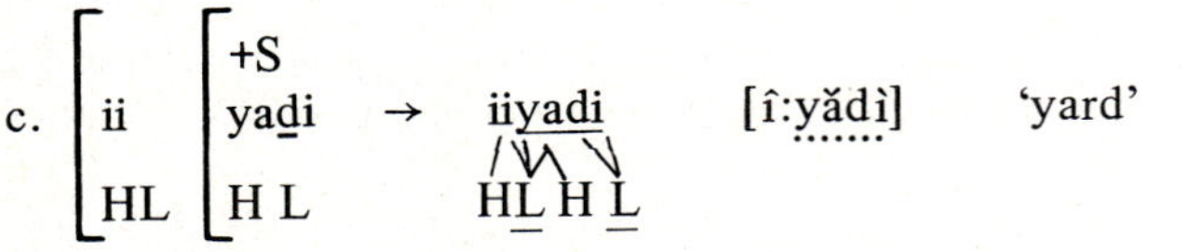


To summarize, while [+S] is a distinctive feature associated in the lexicon with the "depressor consonants", this feature is associated by rule with other C and V segments. Some of these rules are surface phonetic level rules, such as the regressive assimilation of the feature associated with the C onto the following V (77). Where [+S] is an element of a morpheme given in the lexicon, the feature then characterizes the initial syllable of the morpheme. Where the C is specified in the lexicon as [−S] and has a + value for some other laryngeal feature, then [+S] is only manifested by the initial V of the morpheme. Where the syllable is V initial, [+S] is manifested by that V.

The feature [+S] is an element of many morphemes, as illustrated briefly by Khumalo (1981) and summarized by Rycroft and Ngcobo (1979: B7, 3.8). It becomes clear that it is the feature [+S] through the intermediary of the C to which it is associated, whether lexically or by rule, to which the depressor effect on the L tone of the tonal melody is due. The influence of laryngeal features on the tonal melody tier has led some linguists to speculate on the possibility that these features are present on the tonal melody tier itself (see, for example, Yip 1982). This hypothesis is not explored in this paper, although I believe that it is worth further investigation.

### *3.3 Depressor Consonants between vowels associated with H*

Where the "depressor" consonant occurs between two Vs associated with H, then (61) fails to apply. This configuration (86) occurs with the words containing disyllabic stems with the HL (2a) tonal melody in the dialect described by Cope (1970).

```
(86) ...VC̲V #
        |/
        H L
```

This we take to be further proof that depressor consonant related rules apply after the ITARs (3), (4), (5), DTARs (24) and (33), and Tone Association Adjustment rules (50) and (52) have applied.

The examples in (87) taken from Cope (1970: 120-1) show that (61) fails to apply in this context.

```
(87) a. úḿ!fází ...        'woman'    b. í!nkúnzí ...     'bull'
        HL HL                            HL H  L

     c. úbú!hlúngú...      'pain'     d. í:!khándá ...    'head'
        H L  H  L                        H L  H L
```

Note that (. . .) represents phrase medial position.

The spreading of the prefixal H onto the second tone-bearing unit of the prefix in (87) is the result of High Tone Spreading which we will discuss in section 4.

In the dialect described by Rycroft (1979), Left Branch Deletion (50) applies to (87). Following the application of this rule, (61) applies as in (88).

```
(88) iz̲i-mb̲uz̲i      →  izimbuzi       →  izimbuzi    →   izimbuzi
     H L H L            H L    H L        H L̲  H L        H L̲    H L̸
  (by ITARs, WFC)     (by (77), (50))   (by (61))         (by (68), (20))

              [ízìmbùzǐ]   'goats'
```

According to Rycroft (1979: 17) the final H in (88) is seldom realized. This could be attributable to the two-way distinction made by Khumalo (1981) in phrase medial contexts: word internal and word final (see (56)). In the latter the final high tone disassociates and is deleted by (55).

If the Natal Coast dialect as described by Khumalo (1981) employs ITAR (2) and *not* ITAR (2a) as we have already proposed, then that dialect does not provide any evidence for the behaviour of a depressor consonant flanked by two vowels associated with H.

In the dialect described by Cope (1970) there is evidence that (36) which in turn triggers (52) applies before (61).

(89)

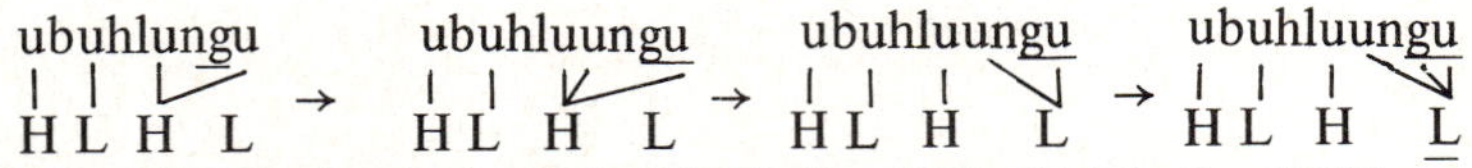


(by ITARs, WFC) (by (77), (36), WFC) (by (52), WFC) (by (61))

[úbúhlû:ngú] 'pain'

The H on the second syllable of the prefix in the surface representation is due to High Tone Spreading, to which we turn now.

## 4. HIGH TONE SPREADING

High Tone Spreading is a process which appears to be determined by both dialectal and performance factors. This rule is noted by Cope (1970) and by Rycroft (1979). It is tangentially noted by Westphal et. al. for Xhosa (1967). It is not noted by Rycroft (1963). Examples of high tone spreading are noted but not analyzed by Doke (1926).

Khumalo (1981: 60-61) vehemently denies the presence of any such process as High Tone Spreading in Zulu although he recognizes the presence of tonal assimilation rules which he calls Low Tone Raising Rules. These however effect a L followed by a H whereas High Tone Spreading affects a L preceded by a H.

According to Rycroft (1979: 19), High Tone "Spreading becomes less effective at a slow rate of utterance: later syllables on the 'spreading chain' tend to drop in pitch, to a lower level than the ensuing stem High tone (though this will still be downstepped in relation to the *first* prefixal High tone)."

High Tone Spreading is a simplification of the actual pitch contour or melody, so that a sequence of the type shown in (90) is converted into (91).

(90)

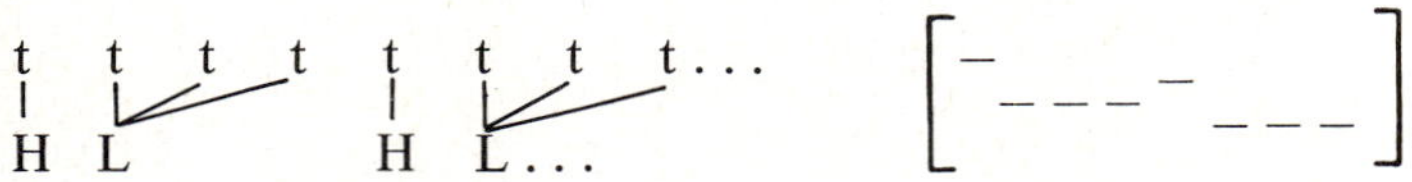


(91)

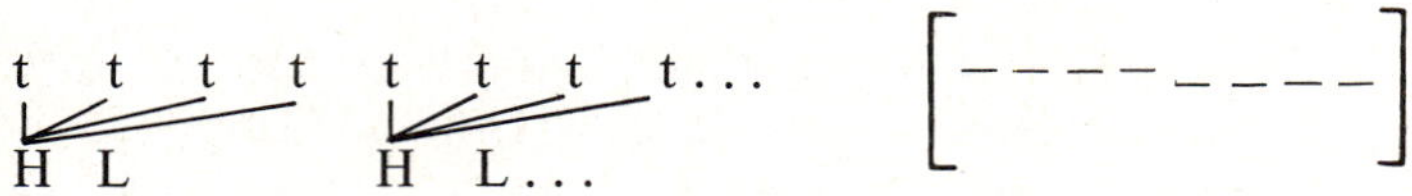

High Tone Spreading causes a H associated with a tone-bearing unit to spread rightwards and associate with a tone-bearing unit(s) previously associated with the following L. High Tone Spreading is of course blocked by the presence of an association line linking a segment associated with [+S] to a L̲.

A H cannot spread onto a tone-bearing unit associated with a H. Also the rule only applies to a H which is followed by a LH tonal sequence. Being a very late rule which applies to simplify the surface tonal melody after all tone association has been accomplished, it can apply within the domain of the H L tone sequence anywhere in the phrase (that is, the sequence of segments and tones between pauses) where the conditions are satisfied.

In those dialects where High Tone Spreading is maximalized, as in Rycroft (1979), the rightward spreading of the H causes the following L to be disassociated from all tone-bearing units and thus to become a floating L. Where High Tone Spreading is not maximalized, as in examples given in Cope (1970), the H may only spread onto one or two tone-bearing units associated with L while tone-bearing unit(s) to the right remain associated. In order to account for these variants, we formulate the rule as follows:

(92) *High Tone Spreading*

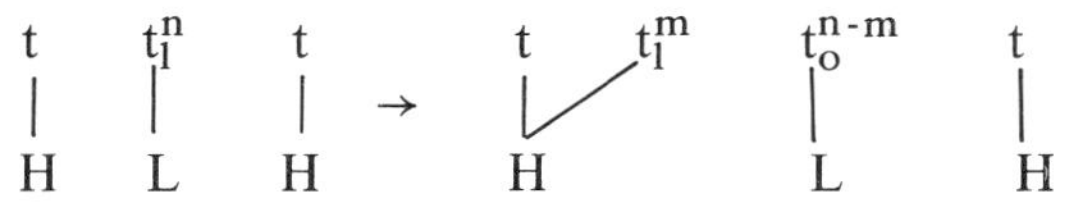


(where m ⩽ n)

By virtue of (92), (57a) *ámàkhòsánà* becomes (93) *ámákhó!sáná* (Rycroft, 1979: 15).

(93)

(= (57a)) (by (92))

Cope (1970: 119) gives two variants for (53) involving High Tone Spreading: *ámákhòsánà* or *ámákhó!sánà*. The derivations are shown in (94).

(94)

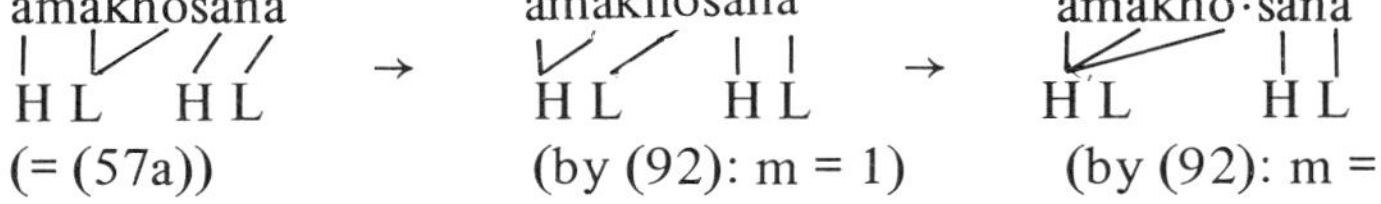


(= (57a)) (by (92): m = 1) (by (92): m = 2)

Since Cope (1970) does not give any indication as to the environment in which one or the other variant occurs, we cannot give the specific conditions (if any) which would allow us to predict the value of *m* in (92). However the passage already quoted by Rycroft (1979: 19) suggests that the rate of utterance may be the conditioning factor.

In the context of a word spoken in isolation, High Tone Spreading only affects prefixal H, since the conditions do not apply to the stem H. However within the context of a phrase made up of several words, the rule can apply wherever the necessary conditions are met. (95), an example from Cope (1970: 116), shows (92) applying to the H of the stem melody of *aba-fana* 'boys' in *ábá!fáná á''báyi!fúúnì* 'the boys don't want it'.

```
(95) abafana abayifuuni            ábá!fáná á''báyí!fúúnì
     | | \ | | | | V |      →      V   V---       V   V  |
     H L H L L H L H L             H L H L L     H L H   L
     (by ITAR, WFC, (36))          (by (92))
```

The L tones disassociated by (92) are not deleted but remain in the tonal melody tier and manifest their presence there by the lowered pitch of the H which follows them. The lowered or downstepped H is indicated by (!). Heightened or unstepped pitch, which is only noted by Cope (1970), is symbolized ('').

That High Tone Spreading (92) follows the depressor consonant related rules (61) and (68) can be seen by comparing (96) and (97).

```
(96) [aba  [fanyanyana     abafanyanyana       ábáfá!nyányànà
     [        [         →  | V    |  V      →  V---      \ V
     [H L  [ H L           H L    H  L         H L       H L
                           ((24), WFC)         (by (92))
                                                  'very tiny boys'

(97) [izi  [nqolanyana     izinqolanyana       ízìnqòlányànà
       _      [             _                   _
     [        [         →  | V    |  V      →  |\--   |  V
     [H L  [  H L          H L    H  L         H L    H  L
                                                 _
                           ((24), WFC)         (by (61))
                                                  'tiny wagons'
```

While (92) can apply to (96), it cannot apply to the output of (97). Due to the prior application of (61), which causes the 'depressor' consonant z̲ to associated with L (which is in turn realized as a L̲ tone), the structural description of this rule is not satisfied (z̲ is not a tone-bearing unit). Similarly in (98), the presence of a depressor consonant prevents High Tone Spreading from going beyond one syllable.

(98) [in [siz̲wanyana → insiz̲wanyana → insiz̲wanyana → ínsíz̲wànyánà
HL HL → H L H L → H L H L → H L H L
(by (24), WFC) (by (61), (68), (70), (38)) (by (92))
'a tiny youth'

5. DOWNSTEP AND UPSTEP

As we have already seen in section 2.5, the pitch level of a H preceded by L is lower than the pitch level of the preceding H within the same tonal phrase, whether the L is associated with a tone-bearing unit or not. Rycroft (1963: 58 facing) shows this difference in H levels impressionistically as in (99).

(99) ísìkó:lè 'school' ìsíkhà:thí 'time'

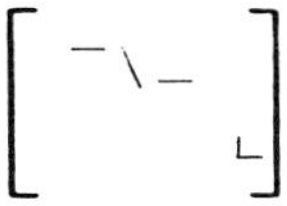

Doke (1926) shows the same phenomenon with his numbering system as in (100).

(100) a. ısiko:le (2 2-4 3 9) 'school' b. isikha:thi (3 2 3-5 4) 'time'

Khumalo (1981: 48) represents the lowering of the overall pitch level starting with the second H in a phrase in the way shown in (101).

(101) ábàfá:nà 'boys'

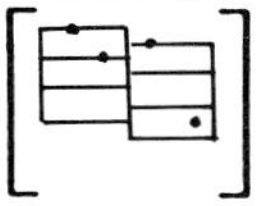

The downstep/downdrift phenomenon can be seen to extend to units larger than the word within the phrase. (102) is taken from Rycroft (1963: 61).

(102) // sìbónà í!nqólà é!ncá:nè // 'We see the small wagon.'
L H L HL H L HL H L

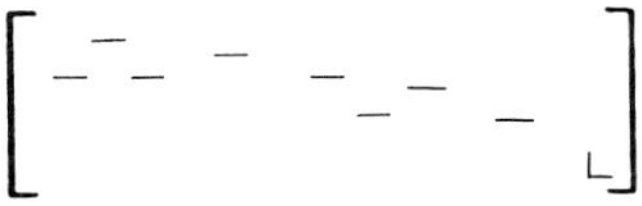

In normal to rapid speech, word-final vowels are deleted preceding a word beginning with a vowel. Consequently resyllabification occurs as in (103).

```
(103)   (C) V # V          (C) φ V
          \  |   |    →       \ /
            $    $              $
```

However the Initial Tone Association Rules (ITARs) still apply within the domains indicated in the lexical entry for each word. If we assume that these rules operate prior to the phrase-level rules such as (103), then we can account for the apparent deletion of unassociated tones at word boundaries as in (104) by Unassociated Tone Deletion (20). (104) is derived from (102).

```
(104)   // sì + bón # í + !nqól # é + !ncá:nè //
            |     |    |       |     |       | |
            L    HL̸   HL      HL̸    HL      H L
         [            –    –                           ]
         [  –                     –     –       –  ˪   ]
```

To explain the impressionistic pitch levels in (104) given by Rycroft (1963: 61) we must assume that all unassociated L are deleted preceding # (or $_{\text{word}}$[) since there is no downstep between the H associated with -bon and the H associated with i-, nor between the H associated with -nqol- and the H associated with e-. Word internally, however, we see that downstep occurs: the H on the stem of the nominals is lower than that on the prefix in both i+nqol- and e+ncane. We conclude, then, that the unassociated L is not deleted in these cases, which confirms our earlier assertions in section 2.3. Where like tones are adjacent within a phrase after tone association and other rules have applied, Like Tone Simplification occurs at the intonational level.

To transform (104) into the question: 'Are we seeing the small wagon?', the pitch level of all H is made identical, whether they are preceded by associated or unassociated L tones. This is shown is (105), taken from Rycroft (1963: 61).

```
(105)  // sì + bón # í + nqól # é-ncánè //? 'Are we seeing the small wagon?'
          |     |    |     /     |   | |
          L    HL̸   HL   HL̸    HL  H L
       [       –  –    –     –  –  ]
       [ –                        – ]
```

At first sight, it would seem that this intonational contour, which we have impressionistically schematized as //————↓// in section 2.5, could be explained in terms of the deletion of all unassociated tones from the tonal melody tier. The L̸ in (105) represent those unassociated L deleted by (20). The deletion of the remaining word-internal unassociated L tones would then be deleted by a special rule invoking the intonational structure characterizing an interrogative phrase.

More generally, we find that in interrogative phrases, both downstep and downdrift are suspended. This is seen in (106).[36]

(106) // sì-bíz # ìn + sízw # ě-ncánè //? 'Are we calling the small youth?'

L HL HL H L HL H L

The declarative counterpart to (106) is (107) where downstep and downdrift are evident.

(107) //sì-bíz # ìn + sízw # ě-ꜜncánè // 'We are calling the small youth.'

L HL HL HL HL H L

Since the presence of an associated L fails to cause downstep in (106) it is not sufficient to explain the lack of downstep in interrogative sentences by a simple rule of unassociated tone deletion. It has to be treated at a level which invokes the intonational contour structure.[37]

Cope (1970) describes a feature he calls *upstep*. The same phenomenon is recorded for Xhosa by Westphal who called it *up-lift* or *downdrift recovery* (Westphal, 1967).[38] Rycroft does not make reference to this feature. Khumalo claims that Cope and others have mistakenly been lead into positing this feature as a result of the wrong interpretation they have given to raised low tones.

> The interpretation of raised-low tones as phonological high tones has had a consequence: how does one interpret a high tone which is higher in pitch than the preceding high tone? (In our analysis this problem does not arise since the former would be classified a phonological low tone.) The resolution of this problem forced both Lanham and Cope into setting up 'tonal upsteps'. (Khumalo (1981: 61)).

All examples of upstep symbolized (") given by Cope occur preceded by an unassociated or floating L, which would normally produce downstep:

```
(108)   t   "t . . .
        |    |
        H  L H
```

In column 1 of (109) we reproduce some examples of upstep given by Cope (1970). In column II we give the form which would be predicted by our rules of tonal association excluding High Tone Spreading.

```
(109)     I                                   II
     a.   ábá!fáná á"báyí!fúnì                ábà!fánà à!báyì!fúnì
          |/  |/     |/   | |                 | | | | | / /  | |
          H L H L L  H L  H L                 H L H L L H L  H L
                                              'The children do not want it.'

     b.   sìbálá "íncwàd̲ǐ                     sìbálà !íncwàd̲ǐ
           | |/   |   |/|                      | | |  |   |/|
           L H L Ł H  L̲ H Ł                    L H L Ł H  L̲ H Ł
                                                   'We write a letter.'
```

A comparison of the examples in these two columns supports Khumalo's claim above that the misinterpretation of pitch on tone-bearing units associated with L between those associated with H lead Cope into positing upstep. This of course brings into question the status and nature of High Tone Spreading.

Cope (1970: 115) provides another example of upstep reproduced here as (110). This example is disputed by both Rycroft (personal communication) and Khumalo (personal communication). Rycroft claims that it is more likely to be interpreted as past tense, inferring an elided H tone suffix -é̲ and not -a̲. He adds that "the upstepping of the initial a̲- in the adjective *abancane* can optionally occur, which I analyse as an optional concomitant of the special inherent stress of the adjective prefix initial vowel, a-, which always has prominence there."

```
(110)  //sìbóna̸ # " ábá!fána̸ # " ábá!ncánè//  'We see the small boys.'
         | |        /   /          /      | |
         L H L     H L H L        H L     H L
```

Khumalo (pers. com.) gives what he considers the correct surface representation of (110) as (111), which is the form our rules predict.

```
(111)   sìbóna̸ !ábà!fá!na̸ ábà!ncáánè
         | \     | | |     | |   |/ |
         L H L  H L H L   H L   H L
```

From (111) we see that downstep occurs across word boundaries, unlike the indication given by Rycroft's data shown in (104). This would then lead us to claim that the floating L tones disassociated as a result of vowel deletion are not deleted, since it is their presence in the tonal melody tier which triggers downstep on the following H in function of the intonational structure. Consequently we are led to claim that in the dialect reported by Khumalo, Unassociated Tone Deletion (20) applies *before* vowel deletion at word boundaries (103) which causes the disassociation of tones, that is immediately after the ITARs, DTARs and Tone Association Adjustment rules (50) and (52). Whereas to account for Rycroft's data (see (104)), this rule applies following vowel deletion. To decide if these two variants really exist one would need to examine the phonetic data more closely, which we have been unable to do.

The declarative intonational structure which is characterized by downdrift is built up by grouping together the H L pairs in the tonal melody tier within any intonational phrase into constituents upon which a right-branching binary tree is built (see references in note 37). Each pair of sister nodes is labelled H L. This sort of configuration is shown in (112).

(112)

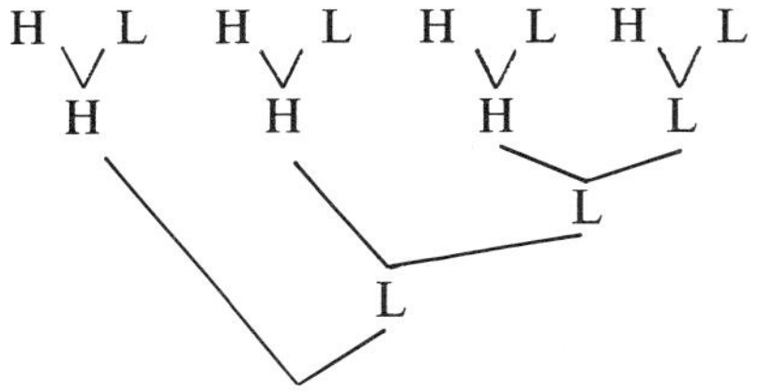


In contrast, the interrogative intonational structure, which is characterized by a maintenance of pitch level and the lowering of phrase final L as in declarative intonation, implies that a simple H L structure is built up on the actual melody tier as in (113).

(113)

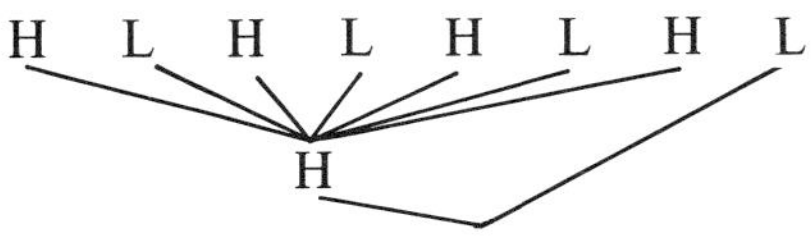


This tree expresses the fact that in interrogative phrases, only the final L tone is lowered. When the phrase ends in H, no structure is built. Since all tones except final L are dominated by H, all associated H have identical pitch and all associated L have identical pitch, namely lower than that of the H tones. Thus unassociated tones dominated by H are not interpreted at all, nor do they exercise any influence on neighbouring tones.

## 6. CONCLUSION AND TONAL RULE SUMMARY

We have shown that the tonal shape of Zulu nouns can be described in terms of lexical representations comprising two tiers, a tonal melody tier and a segmental tier, and a set of rules that assign tones to tone-bearing units and carry out reassociations on the basis of tonal and segmental information. These rules are sufficient to describe all the data recorded for Zulu nouns in the literature. While the tone of the Zulu verb is beyond the scope of the present study, it can be shown that many, if not most of the rules postulated here for the noun apply to verbal tone as well.

A summary of tone rules is given below.

(14) Tonal Metathesis

$$H\ L \rightarrow L\ H \ / \ {}_{word}[\_\_\_\_ \quad {}_{stem}[L$$

INITIAL TONE ASSOCIATION RULES:

(3) ITAR (1)

(4) ITAR (2)

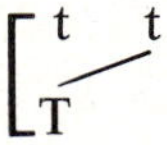


(5) ITAR (2a)

DESIGNATED TONE ASSOCIATION RULES:

(24) Final High Tone Association

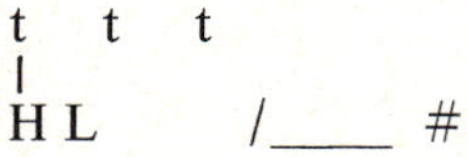


(33) High Tone Association

TONE ASSOCIATION ADJUSTMENT RULES:

(41) Unassociated Tone Docking

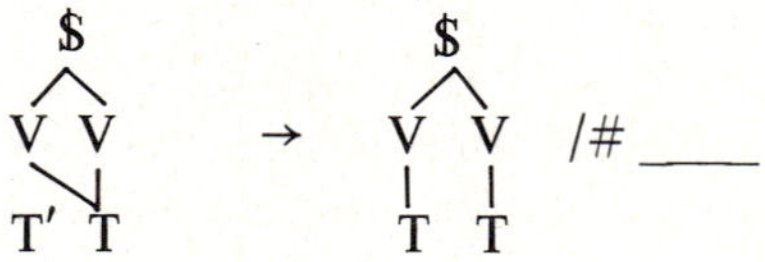

(50) Left Branch Deletion

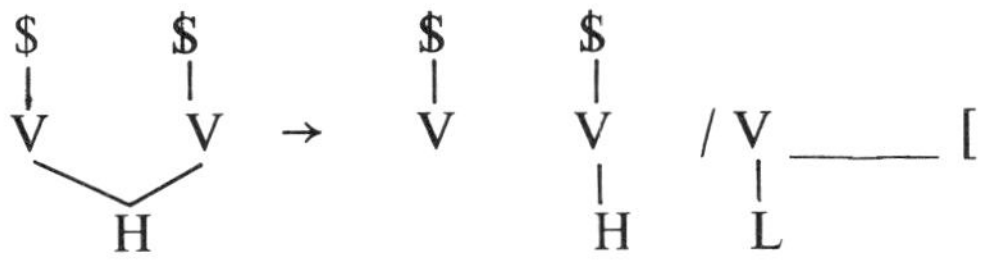


(52) Right Branch Deletion

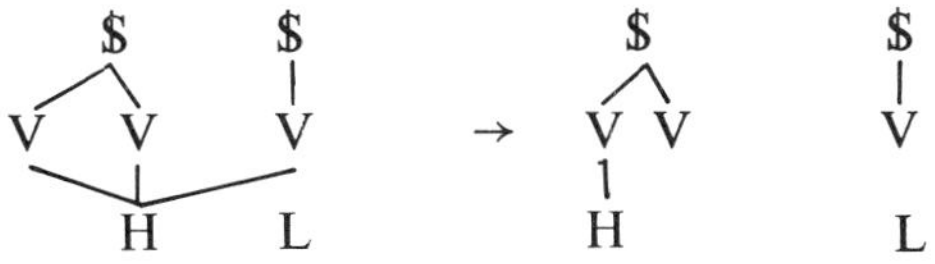


(55) Word-final High Tone Deletion

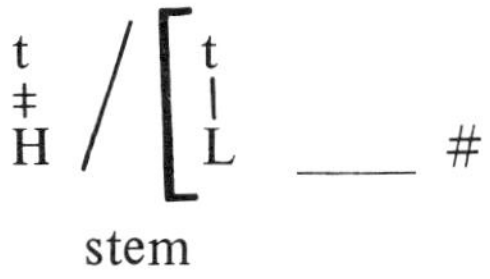


DEPRESSOR CONSONANT RELATED RULES:

(61) Low Tone Lowering

(mirror image)

(68) Extra Low Tone Spreading

(70) High Tone Rightward Reassociation

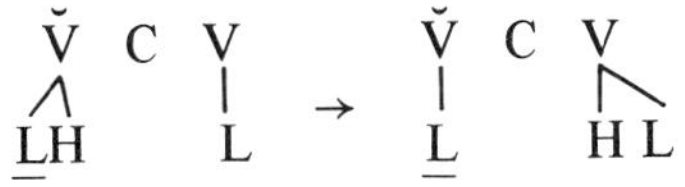


TONE DISASSOCIATION AND DELETION RULES:

(20) Unassociated Tone Deletion

$T' \rightarrow \phi$ / # ____

(mirror image)

(38) Contour Tone Simplification

SPREADING RULES:

(92) High Tone Spreading

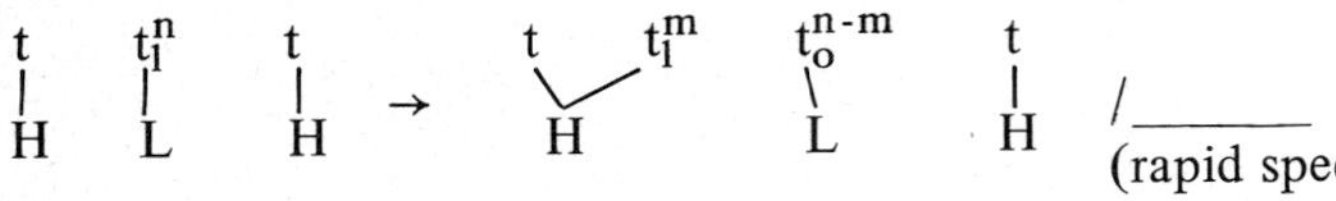


(rapid speech)

(where m ⩽ n)

INTONATION STRUCTURES:

(112) Declarative Intonational Structure

Tonal Melody Tier:

Intonation Structure:

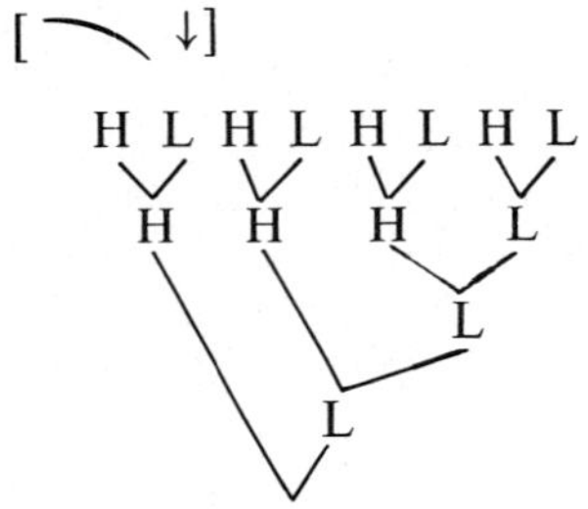


(113) Interrogative Intonational Structure [------ ↓]

Tonal Melody Tier:

Intonation Structure:

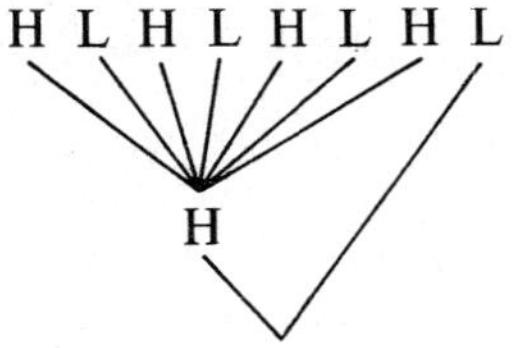


FOOTNOTES

1. The Zulu data for this paper has been taken from Doke (1926), Doke and Vilakazi (1948), Cope (1970), Rycroft (1963, 1979, 1980), Rycroft and Ngcobo (1979) and Khumalo (1981). Information on closely related and neighbouring languages, particularly Xhosa, has been taken from Louw (1971, 1979), Westphal (1951), and Westphal et. al. (1967).

2. The concept of autosegmental phonology was formalized and developed by Goldsmith (1975, 1976a, 1976b, 1981) and applied by him and other linguists such as Clements and Ford (1979, 1981) to the analysis of tone in African languages. Some

of the intuitions underlying autosegmental phonology had earlier been expressed in the work of linguists such as Stahlke (1971).

3. A summary of the language-specific rules governing tonal association in Zulu is given in section 6.

4. Cope (1970: 117-8) recognizes this fact for Zulu when he states:

> The language of the Nguni and Suthu groups also seem peculiar in that there is apparently a fundamental distinction in grammatical structure between morphemes with inherent tone and morphemes without it, between noun stems consisting of segmental and supra-segmental phonemes and verb stems consisting of segmental phonemes only.

This is reiterated by Khumalo (1981: 12).

5. Since the main tenets of autosegmental phonology are set out in the first chapter of this volume, we are dispensed from a detailed exposition in the present chapter. The universal Well-formedness Conditions assumed here are those set out in Clements and Ford (1979).

6. Stress appears to be interpreted differently by each Zuluist. Doke (1926) states that main stress generally falls on the penultimate syllable with secondary stress on other syllables usually beginning with the first syllable and then alternating syllables. Rycroft and Ngcobo (1979, B7) on the other hand state:

> Dynamic stress is potentially associated with the first syllable of each root or stem. In addition, certain words and formatives . . . have special *inherent* stress . . . which may take priority. In practice, actual realization of stress appears to be conditioned by speech rhythm requirements. In Zulu this seems to involve the principle of isochronous stress-timing . . . which may condition the neutralisation of a potential stress when an adjacent syllable has priority, or when (as in rapid speech) more syllables are crammed in, between the stress.

7. Compare the *segmental tier* given here with the P-base (containing the class of P-bearing units) and the *tonal melody tier* with the P-level (containing the class of P-segments in Clements (1981b: 135).

8. The examples in (2) come from Doke (1926: 208).

9. The data on which this statement is based was provided by Khumalo (personal communication) and is reproduced in section 2.8.4.

10. Clements (1980) has claimed that the tone-bearing unit is universally the V in the CV tier.

11. Cope (1970) only recognized two classes of verbs: tone class I and tone class II; however Rycroft (1979, 1980) recognizes three classes for Zulu verbs, and both Louw (1971) and Westphal (1951, 1967) recognize three corresponding classes in Xhosa. The differences noted by Cope and Rycroft for Zulu seem to arise from dialectal variation. Rycroft (1980: 34) states that "A three-way contrast applies in Xhosa, in the Zululand dialect of Zulu, and also possibly to some extent in Rhodesian Ndebele . . . Only a two-way tonal contrast appears to be observed in the Natal dialect of Zulu; other languages which certainly come within this category are Swati, and the Transvaal Ndebele dialects." However from Table 1 (Rycroft, 1980: 36) it is clear from a comparison of tri-syllabic verb stems that all dialects of Zulu distinguish three tonal classes for verbs. Khumalo's analysis (1981) of tonal melodies is quite different in some respects from that of either Cope or Rycroft. He gives a list of noun stems with a HLH melody and another with a LLH melody (Khumalo, 1980: 180). Rycroft (1963: 50) also notes these classes as being "less common"

than the four classes he goes on to describe in detail which are also the principal concern of this study.

12. Further investigation might reveal that yet another ITAR operates to account for the small class of nominals which Rycroft (1963: 50) classifies as class F(LLH), which is also noted by Khumalo (1981: 180) as LLH. Since tonal metathesis of the prefixal melody fails to take place with nouns of this class (Khumalo, personal communication), our analysis would lead us to posit that the Tonal Melody is HL and that the ITAR associates the H with the third tone-bearing unit of the stem. This must remain very tentative since we only have examples of trisyllabic roots. It would also seem likely that where a language develops several ITARs for a given tonal melody, the language in question is moving towards a pitch accent system.

13. We note that these four tone classes correspond to the maximum obtainable from Guthrie's formulae: IA, IB, IIA, IIB which is discussed in Carter (1973).

14. This rule was proposed by Marjan Groenhuis in an unpublished paper entitled "Tone in some Zulu Nouns" (1979). My thanks to G.N. Clements who brought this paper to my attention.

15. Khumalo (1981: 152) accounts for tonal metathesis in the prefix by his Low Prefix Tone Shift Rule. He further claims that the rule does not apply where the prefix contains a depressor consonant and the stem is trisyllabic. Thus he compares *ìsí-sèbénz̲ì* 'worker' with *íz̲ì-sèbénz̲ì* 'workers'. However in the data supplied by Rycroft (1979: 14) such a counterexample to the Tonal Metathesis Rule (14) is not noted. Rycroft gives the forms *ìz̲ì-khá!shánà* 'short times' and *ìz̲ǐ-nd̲l̲è!tshánà* 'small ears' which one would expect to behave in an analogous way to the example given by Khumalo. A tentative explanation of this seeming discrepancy is that trisyllabic words which fail to undergo (14) when in the plural are analysed not as having a LHL stem melody but as having a HL (2) tonal melody whereas their singular counterparts have a LHL melody. Since words which are based on disyllabic roots with a LHL melody are interpreted as having that melody in both singular and plural forms despite the addition of a toneless suffix, it is only a small set of trisyllabic roots which fail to undergo (14) when prefixed by iz̲i-. Since there is no LHL melody on verbal roots in our analysis, *sebenz-* as a verb root would have the melody HL (2). This question, however, is complex and requires further investigation.

16. The following list of Zulu noun class prefixes (with some alterations) is taken from Rycroft (1963: 48-49).

| Class | 'full' prefix series | 'short' prefix series |
|---|---|---|
| 1 | umu-/um̲-/umV- | mu-/m̲-/mV- |
| 1a | u- | φ |
| 2 | aba-/abV- | ba-/bV- |
| 2a | oo-/awoo- | bo-/φ |
| 3 | umu-/-um̲-/umV- | mu-/m̲-/mV- |
| 4 | imi-/im̲- | mi-/m̲- |
| 5 | ili-/ii- | li- |
| 6 | ama-/amV- | ma-/mV- |
| 7 | isi-/isV- | si-/sV- |
| 8 | izi-/izV- | zi-/zV- |
| 9 | iN-/i- | N-/φ |
| 10 | iziN-/iz̲i- | ziN-/zi- |
| 11 | uu-/ulu- | lu- |
| 14 | ubu-/ubV-/utsh(w)V- | bu-/bV-/tsh(w)V- |
| 15 & 17 | uku-/ukV- | ku-/kV- |
| 16 | pha- | pha- |

17. Such a formulation is given in Stewart (1971), who refers to the lowering of a H preceded by a L in turn preceded by a H as key lowering or register lowering. The symbol !, used to indicate downstep by Stewart, is analysed by him as a phonological element introduced into the tonal system. In our representation (↓) merely indicates that the pitch of the H to the right, symbolized (ˊ), is lower than that of the preceding H. In the interpretation developed in section 5, downstep is attributable to the intonational structure which is built up on the tonal melody tier; thus there is no such phonological element as !.
18. Some detailed accounts of pitch levels and contrasting intonational types are given by Doke (1926: 214-216).
19. Constraint 1 also holds in Xhosa. Westphal et. al. (1967:33) give many examples of what they call "tonal displacement" or "toneslip". This in fact corresponds to the association of the H to the tone-bearing unit of the antepenultimate syllable as specified by (24). (See also Westphal et. al., 1967; 21, 1.4). Khumalo (1981: 156) deals with this special H association by his Ante-penultimate Tone Shift rule.
20. Rule (33) also applies in Xhosa.
21. "Full" prefixes of classes 5 (<ili) and 11 (<ulu) are of this type; see note 16.
22. Syllabic nasals are derived from nasal consonant + vowel sequences from which the vowel has been deleted. This is treated in some detail in Doke (1926: 79).
23. Khumalo (1981) discusses in some detail the notion of "prominence" which is made up of three factors: stress, high tone and vowel length, and the concomitant notion of penultimate syllable prominence. The interaction of these prosodic features is certainly quite complex in Zulu. Tonal association is conditioned in certain cases by "prominence" features: stress, and vowel length. These features of course must be accounted for in any study of intonation in Zulu as well as in studies of the morpheme and word level. Stress and tone are connected in Zulu so that one cannot study the one without taking the other into account.
24. This rule does not apply in Xhosa. Compare (42) below with Xhosa *í:mfè* (Westphal et. al., 1967: 11).
25. Example taken from Westphal et. al. (1967: 22).
26. Louw (1971: 107) notes that in Ciskeian Xhosa the infinitive form of verbs with HL (2a) roots has the surface form showing the H associated with the first two syllables of the stem as in *úkù-bónísà* 'to show'. In other dialects of Xhosa, as in Zulu, the form is *úkù-bònísà*.
27. See Rycroft (1963: 64).
28. See footnote 26.
29. Verbs characterized by HL (2/2a) show the same dialect variation as nouns. See Khumalo (1981: 160-161) for examples with the root *-bon-* 'see'.
30. Examples taken from Khumalo (1981: 78-81).
31. The effect of consonants on the raising and lowering of the pitch level of adjacent vowels has been noted by a number of linguists examining very different languages. The development of the tonal split in some SE Asian languages has been connected with the presence of breathy or aspirated consonants which cause a lowering in the pitch, while glottalized consonants cause a raising of the pitch level. J.-M. Hombert, J.J. Ohala and W.E. Ewan (1979) provide a very good summary of the authors' experimental investigations into the nature of the effect of consonant features on pitch and also of some of the accounts in the literature that record the effect of certain features of consonants such as breathiness and glottalization on the pitch level of the neighbouring vowels (Punjabi, Tibeto-Burman, Hindi, Ndebele). Hombert (1978) also provides interesting data on the relation of the features +voice, +aspiration to pitch levels on adjacent vowels. It is interesting to note that in Zulu, the voiceless implosive, jective consonants have a glottalized release which Doke

(1926) indicates by the glottal stop after the consonant: pʔ, tʔ, tʃʔ, kʔ, ... Following a non-syllabic nasal consonant, all voiceless consonants have a glottalized release as shown by Doke (1926: 84-5). These consonants are never "depressors" in Zulu. Bearth and Link (1980) have recently described the correlation between low tone, or a high tone with an initial low on-glide and voiced, breathy consonants in the Ivory Coast language, Wobe.

32. This formulation of the rule was proposed by G.N. Clements (personal communication).

33. For a discussion of syllabic prominence in Zulu, see Khumalo (1981: 4-8).

34. Khumalo (1981) devotes chapter 2 to a detailed description and analysis of surface tonal realizations and phonetic realization rules.

35. Khumalo (1981) disputes the presence of upstep in Zulu claiming that a faulty analysis of the phonetic level leads Cope into positing upstep, where in fact according to Khumalo, downstep occurs.

36. In (106) and (107) the H tone associated by the ITAR with the prefixal vowel of *insizwa* disassociates as a result of (70) since this syllable is not stressed or 'prominent'. Since it cannot reassociate with the following syllable, already associated with the stem H, it is deleted along with the L by (20). However, when the L associated with *insizw-* spreads onto the prefix of the adjective *e-ncane*, H disassociation does not occur since this syllable is inherently stressed and prominent. That H does not disassociate by (70) from a stressed or prominent syllable is further borne out by examples such as (i) and (ii), supplied by Rycroft (personal communication). (>) indicates inherent stress or 'prominence'.

(i) sìbìzě i!nsízwà é!ncá:nè — 'We called the small boy'

L H HLH L HL H L

(ii) sìbìzî!nsízwě!ncá:nè

L HL H LHL H L

The inherent stress or prominence of the adjectival prefix as opposed to the unstressed, non-prominent noun prefix is syntactically demarcative. Doke (1926: 216) gives several examples which bear this out further. He contrasts NP (Noun indirect object) + NP (adjective) with NP (Noun indirect object) + NP (Noun direct object), where the distinction is only indicated on the surface by the pitch levels on the second NP prefix.

37. Clements (1983) and Huang (1980) present detailed analyses of downstep and upstep as a function of intonational structures. The formulation of the intonational rules of Zulu proposed below is largely based on the models proposed by Clements and Huang.

38. Westphal et al. (1967) refer to this phenomenon in Xhosa by several names: up-lift, down-drift recovery, up-step and escalation. Lanham (1960) refers to it as "crescendo".

*Chapter 6*

# Tone in Ci-Ruri

David P.B. Massamba

## 1. INTRODUCTION

The present discussion is based on the premise that Ci-Ruri, a Bantu language spoken in Tanzania, is an accent language, and that the tones which are exhibited in this language are surface manifestations of an underlying accent system.[1] In this respect Ci-Ruri distinguishes itself from Bantu languages that are non-accentual. The nature of tone in Ci-Ruri suggests that there are, in this language, two systems at work: an *accent* system and a *tone* system.

## 2. THE CI-RURI TONE SYSTEM

Four surface tones are exhibited in Ci-Ruri: Low (V̀), High (V́), Rising (V̌) and Falling (V̂). Strictly speaking, however, there are only two basic tones in this language, Low and High. Such tones are commonly referred to as *level* tones. The Rising and Falling tones are commonly referred to as *contour* tones. In Ci-Ruri, contour tones are a result of a combination of level tones; that is, Low + High → $\widehat{LH}$ (Rising) and High + Low → $\widehat{HL}$ (Falling). These will become evident as we go on with our discussion. The basic tones in Ci-Ruri (i.e., Low and High) are exemplified in (1).

(1) a) ò-kù-sùmíkà 'to tie'
pp-inf-tie
ò-kù-sàBúrà 'to dish out'
pp-inf-dish out
ò-kù-sùrúmùrà 'to untie'
pp-inf-untie
b) ò-kù-tàBùrà 'to tear apart'
pp-inf-tear apart
ò-kù-sòròtòrà 'to pull out'
pp-inf-pull out

pp = pre-prefix
inf = infinitive marker

As we can see from these examples, the only tones that are exhibited are Low and High. From the same examples we also note that there are two classes of verbs. On the one hand we find verbs with a High tone in their stems, and on the other we find others that exhibit only Low tones. This generalization would be maintained if we were to go through all Ci-Ruri infinitival forms of the sort given above. With respect to the tone melodies of the two classes, it is clear that in the first class (i.e., where a High tone is found) the melody is L H L, while in the latter it is Low through the entire word. However, as will soon be evident, the Basic Tone Melody in Ci-Ruri is Low-High-Low (henceforth, LHL).

## 3. THE CI-RURI ACCENT SYSTEM

Within the accent system, phonological segments (actually, syllables) are either accented or unaccented, and ultimately it is the accent that triggers the occurrence of the Basic Tone Melody. According to the analysis followed in this discussion, the accent (represented here by "*") is directly associated with the first Low Tone of the Basic Tone Melody (i.e., $\overset{*}{L}$ H L). In terms of an accent being associated with a 'Low Tone', Ci-Ruri is similar to Zambian Tonga where the Melody is H$\overset{*}{L}$.[2] The two languages differ, however, in that while in Ci-Ruri an accent triggers a High on the immediately following syllable, in Tonga a sequence of Highs is realized on the syllables that immediately precede the accent. In both cases the High is associated by the Well-formedness Condition. The following hypothetical example illustrates how the process of accentuation takes place in Ci-Ruri and Tonga:

(2)

Where there are no underlying accents, there is a Tonal Rule that inserts a Low tone in all words that have no tone. We will call such a Rule SURFACE-LOW-TONE ASSIGNMENT, or more formally:

(3) $V \dashrightarrow \underset{\substack{| \\ L}}{V} \;/\; \# X \;\_\_\_\; Y \#$   Cond: where $X \,\&\, Y \neq \ldots \overset{*}{V} \ldots$

At this point we can see why we said above that the Basic Tone Melody in this language is $\overset{*}{L}$ H L; verbs that exhibit a High tone in their stems are underlyingly accented while those that do not exhibit a High tone are underlyingly unaccented. Consequently, since the melody $\overset{*}{L}$ H L (in accented stems) is triggered by an accent, it is more basic than the melody L (in unaccented stems) which is derived by rule (3).

## 4. ACCENT REALIZATIONS

The tonal realization of accent depends on the environments in which it occurs. If an accent falls on an antepenultimate syllable or earlier in a word, it is realized as a High on the immediately following syllable (see the hypothetical example (2)). If it falls on the penultimate syllable, it will first hop back to the immediately preceding syllable, and it will then behave as an antepenultimate syllable accent. An antepenultimate syllable accent and a penultimate syllable accent are thus realized in the same manner: a High appears on the penult. Penultimate back-hopping is effected by the following rule:

(4) PENULTIMATE BACK-HOPPING

$$C\ V\ C\ \overset{*}{V}\ C\ V\ \#\ \dashrightarrow\ C\ \overset{*}{V}\ C\ V\ C\ V\ \#$$

On the other hand, if an accent falls on a phrase-final syllable, it will be realized as a Rise-Fall on the penultimate and ultimate syllables respectively. In such a case our analysis requires two tonal rules: Tone Simplification and Final High Spread. Tone Simplification says that when an accent falls on the ultimate syllable, the first 'Low Tone' which is directly associated with the accent will be disassociated. Thus:

(5) TONE SIMPLIFICATION

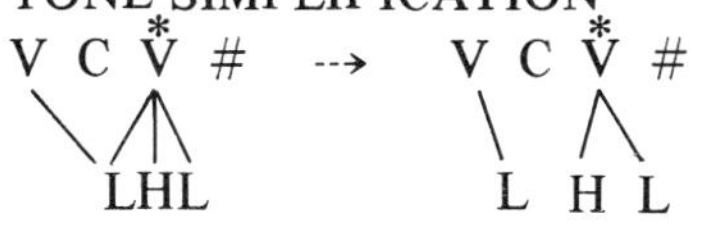


Final High Spread says that if a High tone falls on the final syllable of the stem, it will spread to the immediately preceding syllable. Thus:

(6) FINAL HIGH SPREAD

Given these two rules, the tonal realization of an accent on the final syllable of a stem proceeds as follows:

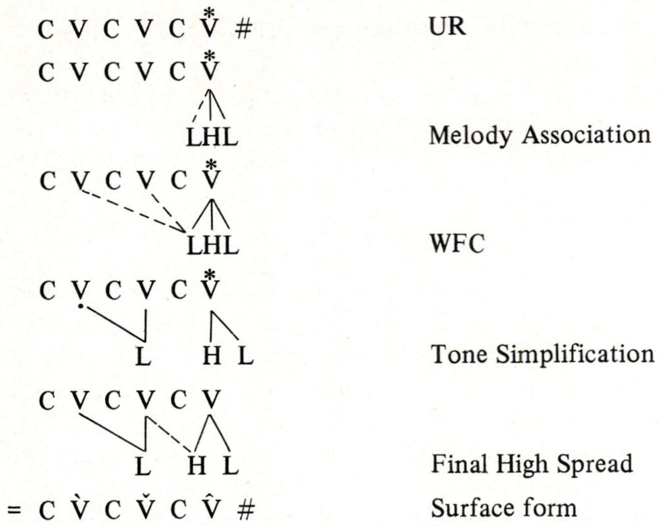


The functioning of all these rules will become clearer as we go on with our discussion. We may also point out here that in Ci-Ruri, as in many other Bantu languages, all accented verb stems have their underlying accent on the first syllable of the stem, although the accent can be realized tonally elsewhere.

## 5. TONAL REALIZATION OF ACCENTS IN CI-RURI INFINITIVES

### *5.1 The Ci-Ruri Verb System*

The Ci-Ruri Verb System has the agglutinating structure characteristic of Bantu languages. Ci-Ruri also has a pre-prefix which, although common in Bantu, is not found in every Bantu language. The structure of the verb cluster in this language is this:

(a) Infinitives:
pre-prefix + prefix + (object marker(s)) + root + (extension(s)) + final vowel

(b) Finite Verbs:
Either: tense marker + subject prefix + (object marker(s)) + root + (extension(s)) + final vowel
OR : subject prefix + tense marker + (object marker(s)) + root + (extension(s)) + final vowel

With finite verbs, we see that sometimes the tense marker precedes the subject prefix, and sometimes the subject prefix precedes the tense marker. This depends on the tenses involved.

In Ci-Ruri, verbs can also be further divided into two types: *simple* and *complex*. By "complex verbs", we mean all verbs which have one or two object markers in their clusters, and by "simple verbs", we mean those which do not have any object markers in their clusters. One might wonder why such a distinction is necessary at all. However, as one comes to grips with the accentual system of Ci-Ruri one realizes just how crucial such a distinction is. In this language the presence or absence of object markers has tremendous effects on the phonetic realization of tonal patterns in the verbs.

## *5.2 Accent Realization in Simple Infinitival Forms*

Having seen the different ways in which accents are realized tonally, we may now see how they work in real situations. Recall that in Ci-Ruri there are two classes of verb stems, accented and unaccented. In the case of the accented stems, the accent is on the first syllable, and in the case of the unaccented stems, surface tones are taken care of by the Surface-Low-Tone Assignment rule. Given all this preliminary information we can say that accentuation in Simple Infinitival forms follows the following procedure:

```
(7)     Accented Stems:
   (i)  ò-kù-sùrúmùrà              'to untie'

        Derived from:
                *
        o-ku-surumura              UR

                *
        o-ku-surumura
              | |  |
              L H  L               Melody Association

                *
        o-ku-surumura
         `\`\\| |  |/
              L H  L               WFC
```

This process extends to all accented Simple Infinitival forms. However, in cases where the accent falls on the penult, of Penultimate Back-Hopping (4) applies as shown in the example below:

```
   (ii) ò-kù-témà                  'to cut'

        Derived from:
                *
        o-ku-tema                  UR

             *
        o-ku-tema                  Penultimate Back Hopping
```

```
    *
o-ku-tema
  | / /
  L H L                 Melody Association

    *
o-ku-tema
 `\| / /
  L H L                 WFC
```

(8) Unaccented Stems:
ò-kù-sòròtòrà — 'to pull out'

Derived from:
o-ku-sorotora — UR

```
o-ku-sorotora
 \\|///
   L                    Surface-Low-Tone Assignment
```

## *5.3 Accent Realization in Complex Infinitival Forms*

Given what we have seen in (7) and (8), it is clear that in simple infinitival forms the process of accentuation is fairly simple. With complex infinitival forms, however, the situation is quite different. In 5.3.1 and in 5.3.2 below we examine how this is so.

### *5.3.1 Infinitival Forms with One Object Marker (OM)*

In Ci-Ruri verb clusters, object markers appear immediately preceding the stem. The shape of the OM is either -CV- or simply -V-, depending on the noun class of the object marker. Observe what happens in the forms below:

(9) Accent Stems:
(i) ò-kù-témà — 'to cut'
(ii) ò-kù-tèm-érà — 'to cut for'

but:
(iii) ò-kù-mù-témà — 'to cut him/her'
(iv) ò-kù-mù-tém-èrà — 'to cut for him/her'

We note here that in (9i) the High is on the first syllable of the stem, while in (9ii) the High is on the second syllable of the stem. Of course, this is what we expect given Penultimate Back-Hopping. However, when we look at (9iii) and (9iv) something rather strange seems to be happening. In these forms, the High is on the same syllable (i.e., the first syllable of the stem). One might argue that in (9iii) Penultimate Back-Hopping has also applied; but the problem is how to explain what has happened to (9iv). Why is the High in this form on the first syllable of the stem instead of being on the second syllable, as in (9ii)? Since the only difference that we see between the two forms is that in (9iv) there is an OM in the cluster while in (ii) there is none, the tonal difference between the two cases must be triggered by the OM. To make this fact even clearer, let us examine some examples containing verb stems that are underlyingly unaccented.

(10) Unaccented Stems:

| | |
|---|---|
| (i) ò-kù-gùrà | 'to buy' |
| (ii) ò-kù-gùr-ìrà | 'to buy for' |
| but | |
| (iii) ò-kù-mù-gúrà | 'to buy him/her' |
| (iv) ò-kù-mù-gúr-ìrà | 'to buy for him/her' |

Here we see that both (10i) and (10ii) have no High tone. This is expected, since the stems involved are underlyingly unaccented. However, when we look at (10iii) and (10iv) (where OMs appear), we find that a High shows up on the first syllable of the stem. We conclude, then, that the High that shows up on the first syllable of the stem in each of these forms is triggered by the OM; that is, the OMs that appear in these forms are accented. (In fact, in Ci-Ruri all OMs behave like the OM -mu-, i.e., they are all underlying accented.)

As far as (9iii) and (9iv) are concerned, one thing more needs to be said. Remember that the verb stem in all the forms in (9) is underlyingly accented, which means that in (9iii) and (9iv) there are two accents in each form: one on the stem and the other on the OM. Given this, we might expect the following surface manifestation of the accents:-

(11) 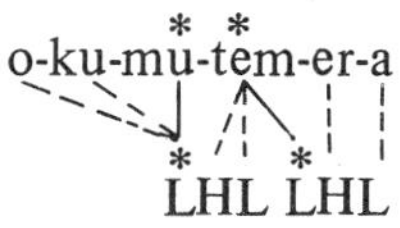

= *[ò-kù-mù-têm-ér-à]

However the correct form is: ò-kù-mù-tém-èr-à, as we have seen. Clearly our predictions give incorrect results. On the other hand, a closer look suggests that what has happened is that the accent on the stem has disappeared. In fact, in Ci-Ruri there is a rule by which a stem accent deletes if preceded by another accent. We state this rule more formally as follows:

(12) STEM ACCENT DELETION:

$$\overset{*}{V} + [_{\text{stem}}\overset{*}{V} \dashrightarrow \overset{*}{V} + [_{\text{stem}}V$$

Thus the non occurrence of the expected High on the second syllable of the stem in (9iv) is due to the fact that the accent that was supposed to trigger the High on the second syllable has been deleted by Stem Accent Deletion. We illustrate this process in (13):

```
            *  *
(13)   o-ku-mu-tem-er-a          UR

            *
       o-ku-mu-tem-er-a          Stem Accent Deletion

            *
       o-ku-mu-tem-er-a
        `- -\ ¦  /-/
            L H  L               Melody Association & WFC
```

### *5.3.2 Infinitival forms with two OMs*

In Ci-Ruri, two OMs may occur in a single verb cluster functioning as direct and indirect OMs. The two OMs are adjacent to each other and the indirect OM must precede the direct OM, except in cases where a 1st person pronoun is involved, in which case the order is reversed. Usually an occurrence of two OMs implies that an applicative suffix is involved.

When two OMs appear in a single verb cluster, the tonal results are surprising. Observe what happens in the following examples:-

(14) Accented Stems:

(i) ò-kù-Bà-lí-tèmĕrâ — 'to cut it for them'
pp-inf-them-it-cut-for

(ii) ò-kù-Bà-lí-sùmìk-ǐrâ — 'to tie it for them'
pp-inf-them-it-tie-for

(iii) ò-kù-Bà-lí-sùrùmùr-ǐrâ — 'to untie it for them'
pp-inf-them-it-untie-for

(15) Unaccented Stems:

(i) ò-kù-Bà-lí-gùr-ǐrâ — 'to buy it for them'
pp-inf-them-it-buy-for

(ii) ò-kù-Bà-lí-tàBùr-ǐrâ — 'to tear it apart for them'
pp-inf-them-it-tear apart

(iii) ò-kù-Bà-lí-sòròtòr-ĕrâ — 'to pull it out for them'
pp-inf-them-it-pull out for

In the examples given in (14), all the verb stems are underlyingly accented, while those in (15) are underlyingly unaccented. What is interesting to note here is the fact that in both cases the tone pattern is the same, i.e., a High on the second OM, a Rise-Fall on the penultimate and ultimate syllables respectively and a Low elsewhere. Thus the tonal difference between accented stems and unaccented stems has been neutralized. If we examine these examples more closely, we find that what has happened is that the expected High on the second syllable of accented verb stems has disappeared. This is no surprise because we know that the Stem Accent Deletion rule has applied. Note that once the Stem Accent Deletion rule has applied, all accented stems behave as though they were unaccented; hence the neutralization, e.g.

(16) Accented Stems:

| | |
|---|---|
|          *  *  *<br>o-ku-Ba-li-tem-era | UR |
|          *  *<br>o-ku-Ba-li-tem-era | Stem Accent Deletion |

Compare this with:

Unaccented Stems:

| | |
|---|---|
|          *  *<br>o-ku-Ba-li-gur-ira | UR |

Here we see clearly that after Stem Accent Deletion, accented stems become accentually similar to unaccented ones. A problem remains, however, for it is clear that even with the application of the Stem Accent Deletion rule, we will not get the pattern exhibited in (14) and (15). In fact, given what we have in these two cases we would expect something like:

(17)

| | |
|---|---|
|          *  *  *<br>o-ku-Ba-li-tem-era | UR |
|          *  *<br>o-ku-Ba-li-tem-era | Stem Accent Deletion |
|          *  *<br>o-ku-Ba-li-tem-era<br>LHLLHL | Melody Association & WFC |
| | = *[ò-kù-Bà-lî-tém-èrà] |

As can be seen, the account developed so far fails to account for the observed Rise-Fall pattern on the penultimate and ultimate syllables.

We pointed out in section 4 that the Rise-Fall pattern on the penultimate and ultimate syllables is a result of there being an accent on the ultimate syllable of the verb when in phrase-final position. We would like to suggest, therefore, that the accent on the second OM (i.e., the rightmost OM) has shifted to the final syllable in (14) and (15). According to this analysis, when two OMs appear in a single verb cluster, the accent on the rightmost OM shifts to the FV (final vowel). In fact, a more general statement would be to say that an OM accent will move to the FV whenever immediately preceded by another accent; or, more formally:

(18) OM ACCENT SHIFT:

```
*   ⊛
V  [V   X   V#
    OM
```

Given this rule, we can explain the appearance of the Rise-Fall pattern on the penultimate and ultimate syllables in the following way:

```
(19)  ò-kù-Bà-lí-sùmìk-ǐrâ        'to tie it for them'
      Derived from:
            *  *  *
      o-ku-Ba-li-sumik-ira        UR
            *  *
      o-ku-Ba-li-sumik-ira        Stem Accent Deletion
            *              *
      o-ku-Ba-li-sumik-ira        OM Accent Shift
            *              *
      o-ku-Ba-li-sumik-ira
           L H L     LHL          Melody Association, WFC, (5), (6)
```

Although we have said that an accent on a FV will be realized as a Rise-Fall on the penultimate and ultimate syllables, we must point out that this happens only when the word or form concerned is in phrase-final position; otherwise it is realized as a High on the next syllable, in the following word. In (19) above, for example, we know that there is an accent on the FV of the verb because if the form is followed by another word which is underlyingly unaccented, a High shows up on the first syllable of that word. Let us illustrate this with the following examples:

| | | |
|---|---|---|
| (20) | ò-kù-Bà-lí-sùmìk-ǐrâ | 'to tie it for them' |
| but: | | |
| | ò-kù-Bà-lí-sùmìk-ìrà lí-Bùì | 'to tie the stone for them' |
| | cf. lì-Bùì (in isolation) | |
| (21) | ò-kù-Bà-lí-sòròtòr-ěrâ | 'to pull it out for them' |
| but: | | |
| | ò-kù-Bà-lí-sòròtòr-èrà lí-Bùì | 'to pull the stone out for them' |

## 6. ACCENT & TONE IN FINITE VERBS

### *6.1 Tense & Tense Marking*

More interesting facts about the Ci-Ruri accent and tone system are found when one examines the nature of accentuation in tensed verb forms. Let us begin by pointing out that in Ci-Ruri, tense marking is accomplished by a combination of two factors, the segmental morphology and the tonology. Thus each tense is marked differently, and the difference can be either tonological or (segmentally) morphological. In Ci-Ruri certain tenses have an underlying accent while others do not. We will begin with those that do not have an underlying accent.

## *6.2 Tenses without an accent*

Of the major tenses in Ci-Ruri, there are only two tenses that have no underlying accent, the Present Perfect and Today Past tenses. We know that these tenses have no underlying accent of their own because if we compare them with their infinitive counterparts they turn out to have the same tone patterns, e.g.

| | | *Infinitive* | *Present Perfect* | *Today Past* |
|---|---|---|---|---|
| (22) | (a) | ò-kù-tèm-érà | nà-à-tèm-é-èyè | nà-à-tèm-érà |
| | | ò-kù-sùrúmùrà | nà-à-sùrúmù-ùyè | nà-à-sùrúmùrà |
| | | ò-kù-sùmíkà | nà-à-sùmík-ìrè | nà-à-sùmíkà |
| | (b) | ò-kù-gùr-ìrà | nà-à-gùr-ì-ìyè | nà-à-gùr-ìrà |
| | | ò-kù-tàBùr-ìrà | nà-à-tàBùr-ì-ìyè | nà-à-tàBùr-ìrà |
| | | ò-kù-sòròtòrà | nà-à-sòròtò-òyè | nà-à-sòròtòrà |

(a) = accented stems; (b) = unaccented stems.

Note that although these forms have the same tone patterns they are segmentally different. When OMs appear in these forms, the tonal representations are the same as in infinitives:

| (23) | *Infinitives* | *Present Perfect* | *Today Past* |
|---|---|---|---|
| | ò-kù-mù-tém-èrà | nà-à-mù-tém-è-èyè | nà-à-mù-tém-èrà |
| | ò-kù-mù-súmìkà | nà-à-mù-súmìk-ì-ìyè | nà-à-mù-súmìkà |
| | ò-kù-mù-gúr-ìrà | nà-à-mù-gúr-ì-ìyè | nà-à-mù-gúr-ìrà |

## *6.3 Tenses with an underlying accent*

Major tenses associated with underlying tense-specific accents in Ci-Ruri, are: Distant Past, Recent Past, Present Continuous and Distant Future. Of these we will discuss only two, the Distant Past Tense and the Present Continuous Tense.[3]

### *6.3.1 The Distant Past Tense*

In Ci-Ruri the Distant Past Tense is morphologically marked by the prefix -a-, which appears immediately following the subject prefix, and a suffix -ire. The surface tones in this tense are as follows:

(24) (a) Accented Stems:

| | |
|---|---|
| nà-à-tèm-érê | 'I cut' |
| nà-à-sùmík-ǐrê | 'I tried' |
| nà-à-sùrúmù-ǔyê | 'I untied' |

(b) Unaccented Stems:

| | |
|---|---|
| nà-à-gùr-írê | 'I bought' |
| nà-à-Bìrím-ǐrê | 'I ran' |
| nà-à-sòrótò-ǒyê | 'I pulled out' |

From these examples we note two important facts about this tense. First we note that the tonal difference between accented and unaccented stems has been neutralized; the two classes of stems now have the same tone patterns. Secondly, we note that there is a Falling tone on the FV in all the forms, regardless of whether their stems are accented or not, and a Rising tone in all forms whose stems have more than three syllables. What all this means is that at the underlying level the forms in this tense have an accent on the first and final syllables of the stem, i.e.

(25)

| *Accented Stems* | *Unaccented Stems* |
|---|---|
| ni-a-t$\overset{*}{e}$m-er$\overset{*}{e}$ | ni-a-g$\overset{*}{u}$r-ir$\overset{*}{e}$ |
| ni-a-s$\overset{*}{u}$mik-ir$\overset{*}{e}$ | ni-a-B$\overset{*}{i}$rim-ir$\overset{*}{e}$ |
| ni-a-s$\overset{*}{u}$rumu-uy$\overset{*}{e}$ | ni-a-s$\overset{*}{o}$roto-oy$\overset{*}{e}$ |

What happens in this tense is that both the prefix -a- and the suffix -ire have accentual properties. The suffix -ire is underlyingly associated with an accent (i.e., -ir$\overset{*}{e}$) while the prefix -a- is post-accenting (i.e., -à- = puts an accent on the immediately following syllable). This is effected by the following two rules:-

(26) SUFFIX ACCENT ASSOCIATION:

$$+\,[_{\text{suff.}}\,VCV\# \;\rightarrow\; +\,[_{\text{suff.}}\,VC\overset{*}{V}$$

cond: in the Distant Past

(27) PREFIX POST-ACCENTING:

$$\grave{a} + V \;\rightarrow\; a + \overset{*}{V}$$

Given the two rules (26) and (27), we can illustrate how the accents that trigger the surface forms are arrived at (we leave the further details of derivations for the reader):

```
(28)  Accented Stems.
            *
      ni-à-sumik-ire          UR
            *       *
      ni-à-sumik-ire          (26)
            *       *
      ni-a-sumik-ire          (27)

      Unaccented Stems.
      ni-à-gur-ire            UR
                    *
      ni-à-gur-ire            (26)
             *      *
      ni-a-gur-ire            (27)
```

When OMs appear in these forms, their effects are the same as we saw in the infinitives, e.g.

| (29) | *one OM* | *two OMs* |
|---|---|---|
| | nààmùtémĕrê | nààmùítèmèĕyê |
| | nààmùsúmìkǐrê | nààmùísùmìkììyê |
| | nààmùgúrǐrê | nààmùígùrììyê |
| | nààmùtáBùŭyê | nààmùítàBùrììyê |

We note from these examples that in the cases with one OM, the High appears on the first syllable of the stem instead of appearing on the second syllable. This is because of the Stem Accent Deletion rule. In the cases with two OMs, the High appears on the second OM and not on the second or first syllable of the stem. There are two reasons for this change. First, Stem Accent Deletion (12) applies, destroying the environments which trigger the appearance of a High on the second syllable of the stem. Secondly, the accent on the second OM (which would otherwise trigger a High on the first syllable of the stem) is moved to the FV by OM Accent Shift (18). Thus:

```
            *   *        *
(30)  ni-à-mu-sumik-ire           UR, (26)
            *            *
      ni-a-mu-sumik-ire           Stem Accent Deletion
      [naa-mu-súmik-ǐrê]          Output

            * * *             *
      ni-à-mu-i-sumik-ir-ire      UR, (26)
            * *               *
      ni-a-mu-isumik-ir-ire       Stem Accent Deletion
            * ⊛——————————————→*
      ni-a-mu-i-sumik-ir-ire      OM Accent Shift
      [naa-mu-í-sumik-i-ǐyê]      Output
```

*6.3.2 The Present Continuous Tense*

The present Continuous is the most irregular of all the tenses in Ci-Ruri.

Its irregularity can be seen both morphologically and tonologically. Morphologically, this tense is marked by an obligatory vowel prefix which occurs initially in all cases except the 3rd person singular (in which case this vowel occurs immediately following the subject prefix). Thus we have:

(31) è-nì-súmìkà 'I am tying'
TM-I-tie
ò-mù-súmìkà 'You(pl) are tying'
TM-you-tie
à-Bà-súmìkà 'They are tying'
TM-they-tie

but:

kà-à-sùmíkà '(S)he is tying'
(S)he-TM-tie

The complexity of tonal representation in this tense can be seen in the following examples:-

(32) Present Continuous
a) Accented stems

| | No OM | One OM | Two OMs |
|---|---|---|---|
| i) | è-nì-témà<br>TM-I-cut<br>kà-à-témà<br>(S)he-TM-cut | è-nì-í-těmâ<br>TM-I-it-cut<br>kà-à-ì-témà<br>(S)he-TM-it-cut | è-nì-Bá-ì-tèm-érâ<br>TM-I-them-it-cut-for<br>kà-à-Bà-í-tèm-ěrâ<br>(S)he-TM-them-it-cut-for |
| ii) | è-nì-súmìkà<br>TM-I-tie<br>kà-à-sùmíkà<br>(S)he-TM-tie | è-nì-í-sùmíkâ<br>TM-I-it-tie<br>kà-à-ì-súmìkà<br>(S)he-TM-it-tie | è-nì-Bá-ì-sùmík-ǐrâ<br>TM-I-them-it-tie-for<br>kà-à-Bà-í-sùmìk-ǐrâ<br>(S)he-TM-them-it-tie for |
| iii) | è-nì-súrùmùrà<br>TM-I-untie<br>kà-à-sùrúmùrà<br>(S)he-TM-untie | è-nì-í-sùrúmǔrâ<br>TM-I-it-untie<br>kà-à-ì-súrùmùrà<br>(S)he-TM-it-untie | è-nì-Bá-ì-sùrúmùr-ǐrâ<br>TM-I-them-it-untie-for<br>kà-à-Bà-í-sùrùmùr-ǐrâ<br>(S)he-TM-them-it-untie for |
| iv) | è-nì-súrùmùr-ìrà<br>TM-I-untie-for<br>kà-à-sùrúmùr-ìrà<br>(S)he-TM-untie-for | è-nì-í-sùrúmùr-ǐrâ<br>TM-I-it-untie-for<br>kà-à-ì-súrùmùr-ìrà<br>(S)he-TM-it-untie-for | ———<br><br>———<br> |

b) Unaccented stems

| | No OM | One OM | Two OMs |
|---|---|---|---|
| i) | è-nì-gúrâ<br>TM-I-buy<br>kà-à-gǔrâ<br>(S)he-TM-buy | è-nì-í-gǔrâ<br>TM-I-it-buy<br>kà-à-ì-gúrâ<br>(S)he-TM-it-buy | è-nì-Bá-ì-gùr-írà<br>TM-I-them-it-buy-for<br>kà-à-Bà-í-gùr-ǐrâ<br>(S)he-TM-them-it-buy for |
| ii) | è-nì-sákírà<br>TM-I-help<br>kà-à-sàkírà<br>(S)he-TM-help | è-nì-í-sàkírà<br>TM-I-it-help<br>kà-à-ì-sákírà<br>(S)he-TM-it-help | è-nì-Bá-ì-sàkír-ǐrâ<br>TM-I-them-it-help-for<br>kà-à-Bà-í-sàkìr-ǐrâ<br>(S)he-TM-them-it-help-for |
| iii) | è-nì-sórótǒrâ<br>TM-I-pull out<br>kà-à-sòrótǒrâ<br>(S)he-TM-pull out | è-nì-í-sòrótǒrâ<br>TM-I-it-pull out<br>kà-à-ì-sórótǒrâ<br>(S)he-TM-it-pull out | è-nì-Bá-ì-sòrótòr-ěrâ<br>TM-I-them-it-pull out for<br>kà-à-Bà-í-sòròtòr-ěrâ<br>(S)he-TM-them-it-pull out-for |
| iv) | è-nì-sórótòr-ěrâ<br>TM-I-pull out-for<br>kà-à-sòrótòr-ěrâ<br>(S)he-TM-pull out for | è-nì-í-sòrótòr-ěrâ<br>TM-I-it-pull out-for<br>kà-à-ì-sórótòr-ěrâ<br>(S)he-TM-it-pull out for | ———<br><br>——— |

In the forms in (32), the unaccented forms are interesting in that while their stems are underlyingly unaccented, we still find High, Rising and Falling tones. In fact, what is even more striking is the fact that in comparing the two sets of forms (i.e., accented and unaccented) we find that the unaccented ones show more complexity in their tonal patterns than the accented ones. One thing clearly common to all the verbs is that the subject prefixes are accented, at least when in non-initial position. In fact as a general rule in Ci-Ruri, all subject prefixes are underlyingly accented. However, when these prefixes appear in initial position they lose their accents; this rule applies to all initial accents, not just subject prefix accents.

Within the unaccented stems, if the stem has three syllables or less, an accent is put on the second syllable of the stem (which is also the final syllable if there are only two syllables). On the other hand, if the stem has *more* than three syllables, an accent will appear on the *final* syllable of the stem. As for the accented stems, since they are already underlyingly accented, no further accents will be assigned to them. Note, too, that all stem accents, except for cases involving 3rd person singular subject prefixes, are regularly deleted by the Stem Accent Deletion rule (though this may not *appear* to be true, due to the effects of the FV Accent Copy Rule, given in (35) below). There is one more thing that is common to both accented and unaccented verb stem forms. In both cases there is a rule of FV Accent Copying which requires that a FV accent be copied onto the first vowel of the stem in all stems of more than two syllables. However, this rule has one condition: if the stem is preceded by two or more syllables, and if one of them is accented, the rule will apply only if the accented syllable is *not* an OM.

In order to derive surface forms from underlying forms in the Present Continuous Tense the following rules are, therefore, necessary:

(33) PRESENT CONTINUOUS ACCENT ASSOCIATION:

(a) $V \dashrightarrow \overset{*}{V} / [_{\text{stem}} + V \text{——} (V)]\,\#$

(b) $V \dashrightarrow \overset{*}{V} / [_{\text{stem}} + V\ V\ V \ldots\ldots \text{——}]\,\#$

cond: where both (a) and (b) apply to non-3rd person singular unaccented stems.

(c) $V \dashrightarrow \overset{*}{V} / [V \ldots\ldots \text{——}]\,\#$

cond: where (c) applies only to forms with two OMs and 3rd person singular subject prefix.

(34) INITIAL ACCENT DELETION:

$\overset{*}{V} \dashrightarrow V / \#\text{——}$

(35) FINAL VOWEL ACCENT COPYING

(a) $\overset{*}{V} + [_{\text{stem}}\ \overleftarrow{\overset{*}{V}\ V\ V \ldots \overset{*}{V}}]\,\#$

(b) $\overset{*}{V}\ V(V) + [_{\text{stem}}\ \overleftarrow{\overset{*}{V}\ V\ V \ldots\ldots \overset{*}{V}}]\,\#$

cond: where the preceding $\overset{*}{V} \neq$ OM

Given what we have seen, it would seem that accent association in the Present Continuous Tense takes place as follows:

(36)

| *Objectless Accented Stems* | *Objectless Unaccented Stems* |
|---|---|
| e-n$\overset{*}{\text{i}}$-tema | e-n$\overset{*}{\text{i}}$-gur$\overset{*}{\text{a}}$ |
| ka-a-t$\overset{*}{\text{e}}$ma | ka-a-gur$\overset{*}{\text{a}}$ |
| e-n$\overset{*}{\text{i}}$-sumika | e-n$\overset{*}{\text{i}}$-s$\overset{*}{\text{a}}$kira |
| ka-a-s$\overset{*}{\text{u}}$mika | ka-a-s$\overset{*}{\text{a}}$kira |
| e-n$\overset{*}{\text{i}}$-surumura | e-n$\overset{*}{\text{i}}$-s$\overset{*}{\text{o}}$rotor$\overset{*}{\text{a}}$ |
| ka-a-s$\overset{*}{\text{u}}$rumura | ka-a-s$\overset{*}{\text{o}}$rotor$\overset{*}{\text{a}}$ |

| *One OM Accented Stems* | *One OM Unaccented Stems* |
|---|---|
| e-ni-mu-tema | e-ni-mu-gura |
| ka-a-mu-tema | ka-a-mu-gura |
| e-ni-mu-sumika | e-ni-mu-sakira |
| ka-a-mu-sumika | ka-a-mu-sakira |
| e-ni-mu-surumura | e-ni-mu-sorotora |
| ka-a-mu-surumura | ka-a-mu-sorotora |

| *Two OM Accented Stems* | *Two OM Unaccented Stems* |
|---|---|
| e-ni-Ba-i-tem-era | e-ni-Ba-i-gur-ira |
| ka-a-Ba-i-tem-era | ka-a-Ba-i-gur-ira |
| e-ni-Ba-i-sumik-ira | e-ni-Ba-i-sakir-ira |
| ka-a-Ba-i-sumik-ira | ka-a-Ba-i-sakir-ira |
| e-ni-Ba-i-surumur-ira | e-ni-Ba-i-sorotor-era |
| ka-a-Ba-i-surumur-ira | ka-a-Ba-i-sorotor-era |

A close examination of the accents given in the above forms reveals that certain accent rules such as Stem Accent Deletion, Penultimate Back-Hopping, Present Continuous Accent Association and OM Accent Shift have already been assumed. Before we illustrate how these rules work together to give the required surface manifestations, we must stress two points concerning the application of OM Accent Shift. First, if both OMs are preceded by an accent, they both shift to the FV. Second, the rule is restricted in such a way that if there is an accent in the way, the OM accent will not go beyond that accent; instead, it will stop there (i.e., it will not go to the FV). Given this we need to make a slight modification of our OM Accent Shift rule as follows:

(18′) OM ACCENT SHIFT:

(a) $[\overset{\circledast}{V}]_{OM} + [V \ldots\ldots V]_{stm}\ \# / \overset{*}{V} + \underline{\quad}$

(b) $[\overset{\circledast}{V}]_{OM} + [V \ldots \overset{*}{V} \ldots V]_{stm}\ \# / \overset{*}{V} + \underline{\quad}$

We will now illustrate how the process of accentuation in this tense takes place. We assume that the reader is now conversant with our system of derivations. We will, therefore, give derivations only up to a certain point and leave it to the reader to complete them.

(37) Accented Stems with no OM
[è-nì-súrùmùrà] 'I am untying'

Derived from:

```
   * *
e-ni-surumura                 UR
   *
e-ni-surumura                 Stem Accent Deletion
```

(b) Accented Stems with one OM

[è-nì-mú-sùrúmǔrâ] ‘I am untying him/her’

```
   *  *  *
e-ni-mu-surumura              UR
   *  *
e-ni-mu-surumura              Stem Accent Deletion
   *  o--------->
e-ni-mu-surumura              OM Accent Shift
   *     *<-----*
e-ni-mu-surumura              FV Accent Copying
```

(c) Accented Stems with two OMs

[è-nì-mú-ì-sùrúmùr-ǐrâ] ‘I am untying it for him/her’

Derived from:

```
   *  * *  *
e-ni-mu-i-surumur-ira         UR
   *  * *
e-ni-mu-i-surumur-ira         Stem Accent Deletion
   *  (o o)------------>
e-ni-mu-i-surumur-ira         OM Accent Shift
   *       *<---------*
e-ni-mu-i-surumur-ira         FV Accent Copying
   *       *         *
e-ni-mu-i-surumur-ira
```

(38) (a) Unaccented Stems with no OM

[è-nì-gúrâ] ‘I am buying’

Derived from:

```
   *
e-ni-gura                     UR
   *    *
e-ni-gura                     Present Contin. Accent Assoc.
```

(b) Unaccented Stems with one OM

[è-nì-mú-gǔrâ] ‘I am buying him/her’

Derived from:

```
   *  *
e-ni-mu-gura                  UR
   *  *    *
e-ni-mu-gura                  Present Contin. Accent Assoc.
   *  o--->*
e-ni-mu-gura                  OM Accent Shift
   *       *
e-ni-mu-gura
```

(c) Unaccented Stems with two OMs

[è-nì-mú-ì-gùr-írà] ‘I am buying it for him/her’

Derived from:

```
   *  * *
e-ni-mu-i-gur-ira             UR
   *  * *       *
e-ni-mu-i-gur-ira             Present Cont. Accent Assoc.
   *  (o o)---->*
e-ni-mu-i-gur-ira             OM Accent Shift
```

e-nì-mu-i-gùr-ira    Penultimate Back-Hopping
e-nì-mu-i-gùr-ira

7. ACCENT & TONE IN NOUNS

Synchronically, Ci-Ruri Nouns can be divided into three tonal classes as shown below:-

(39) Tonal Classes of Nouns in Ci-Ruri:

| Class I | Class II | Class III |
|---|---|---|
| òmwàánà 'child' | àBàyǎrâ 'girls' | omusasi 'mad person' |
| àBàgásì 'women' | èciBǔyâ 'gourd' | emisimu 'arrows' |
| òmùrúmè 'man/husband' | òBùgǒrô 'snuff' | aBasaani 'friends' |
| òmùtèékì 'cook' | àmǎtî 'trees' | omuwofu 'blind person' |

The examples given above are just a representative sample of the many words in the three tonal classes of Ci-Ruri nouns. We note from these examples that Class I nouns have a High on the penultimate syllable and a Low elsewhere; Class II nouns have a Rise-Fall pattern on the penultimate and ultimate syllables respectively and a Low elsewhere; Class III nouns have Low tones throughout.

Given the tone patterns in these classes, it is clear that Class I is a class of nominal stems in which an accent is associated with the first syllable of the stem; Class II is a class of nominal stems in which an accent is associated with the final syllable of the stem, and Class III is a class of nominal stems in which neither one of the syllables is associated with an accent. This is illustrated in the following table:-

(40) Accent Association in Nouns

| Class I | Class II | Class III |
|---|---|---|
| o-mu-a*na | a-Ba-yara* | o-mu-sasi |
| a-Ba-ga*si | e-ci-Buyu* | e-mi-simu |
| o-mu-ru*me | o-Bu-goro* | a-Ba-saani |
| o-mu-te*eki | a-mati* | o-mu-wofu |

It should be recalled that Penultimate Back-Hopping applies in cases like those in Class I where an accent appears on the penult. Also, wherever applicable the rules of Tone Simplification, Final High Spread and Surface-Low-Tone Assignment apply. Let us illustrate the nature of accentuation in Ci-Ruri Nouns with the following two examples from Class I and II:

(41) (a) Class I

| | |
|---|---|
| o-mu-ru*me (accent on ru) | UR |
| o-mu-rume (accent hops from ru to mu) | Penultimate Back-Hopping |
| o-mu*-rume (accent on mu) / L H L | Melody Association & WFC |

(b) Class II

| | |
|---|---|
| o-Bu-goro* (accent on final o) | UR |
| o-Bu-goro* (accent on final o) / LHL | Melody Association & WFC |
| o-Bu-goro / L HL | Tone Simplification & Final High Spread |

8. CONCLUSION

In this paper we have given a brief account of the accentual and tonal system of Ci-Ruri. We have looked at infinitives, finite verbs and nouns, and have seen that the Basic Tone Melody in Ci-Ruri is L* H L in which, according to our analysis, the accent is directly associated with the first Low tone. We have also seen that in Ci-Ruri there are two classes of verbs, those that are underlyingly accented and those that are underlyingly unaccented; and that there are three classes of nouns, those with an accent on the first syllable of the stem, those with an accent on the final syllable of the stem and those with no accent.

FOOTNOTES

1. For a more detailed discussion of whether or not Ci-Ruri is an accent language, see Massamba (1982).
2. The case for an accent being associated with the "Low Tone" of the Basic Tone Melody in Tonga has been convincingly argued by Goldsmith (1981 and this volume).
3. Again, for a better understanding of this see Massamba (1982), in which both affirmative and negative forms are discussed in detail.

*Chapter 7*

# Stem Tone Assignment in Shona

David Odden

Although Shona is typical among Bantu languages in that it has only the two simple lexical tonal contrasts in verb stems, H and L, Shona presents some rather interesting and complicated patterns in the surface manifestation of these basic tonal contrasts. In particular, the surface sequence of tones which appears in the verb stem depends on a considerable number of factors, including lexical tone, the number of syllables within a stem, presence or absence of reduplication, and the tone of the prefix which precedes the verb stem, as well as the presence of a morphosyntactically conditioned melody consisting solely of a sequence of tones, mapped onto the stem and modified by the application of various optional and obligatory rules. It is then the goal of this chapter to outline the tonal structure of the verb stem in the Karanga dialect of Shona, concentrating primarily on the problems of stem tone conjugation.

In the first section of this chapter, I shall briefly discuss the role of contour tones in the grammar of Karanga Shona. For additional information and discussion of contour tones in Shona, the reader is referred to Odden (1981), Chapter Four. In the second section of this chapter, I discuss the problem of stem tone conjugation. I argue that this phenomenon can be accounted for by mapping the tone melody HHLB onto the stem, and applying various rules to the derived representations. Finally, in the last section of the chapter, I touch on certain areas of theoretical interest where the analysis of stem tone in Shona brings out evidence bearing on these issues. I discuss there the problem of the relationship between the tonal melody HHLB and the rule mapping that melody on the verb stem; I argue that there are other tonal melodies associated with different morphological constructions which require different tone mapping rules. I also discuss the place of the Wellformedness Conditions in phonological derivations, and propose that these conditions apply after any rule referring to an unassociated vowel.

## 1. CONTOUR TONES

There are, at the underlying level, no distinctive contour tones in Shona, although there are contour tones in surface representations, due to non-contrastive variation in H tones. Despite the lack of contrastive rising and falling tones at the surface, it can be argued that at a deeper level of the grammar, more than one tonal autosegment may be associated with a vowel. One of the environments where contour tones arise in derivations consists of vowel sequences. I argue in Odden (1981) that the diminutive suffix *-aná* combines with the preceding vowel to form a single syllable, and that the tone of the final stem vowel combines with the underlying L tone of the diminutive suffix vowel *-a* to form a contour tone. If the noun stem ends in a H tone, the combination of H plus L tones yields a falling tone. If that derived falling tone happens to stand after a L tone, a general Decontouring rule will apply which deletes every tone on a contour tone except the first tone. Examples of the diminutive are provided in (1).

| | | |
|---|---|---|
| (1) | mwaná | 'child' |
| | mwanáná | 'little child' |
| | dhongí | 'donkey' |
| | dhongwáná | 'little donkey' |
| | dengú | 'basket' |
| | dengwáná | 'little basket' |

The underlying form of *mwanáná* is *mwaná+aná*. Application of the vowel combination rule yields the form *mwanâná*, to which the Decontouring rule (2) then applies, giving the surface form *mwanáná*.

(2) 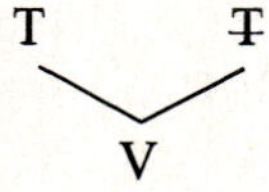


Not every derived falling tone will undergo Decontouring and thus appear as a H tone on the surface. When the derived falling tone stands after a H tone, a Fall Simplication rule applies to delete the initial H tone of the falling tone. This rule can be seen to apply to the diminutive nouns in (3), whose stems end in the tone pattern HH.

| | | |
|---|---|---|
| (3) | hárí | 'pot' |
| | hádyaná | 'little pot' |
| | mbúdzí | 'goat' |
| | mbúdzaná | 'little goat' |
| | murúmé | 'man' |
| | murúnyaná | 'brother-in-law' (lit. 'little man') |

Application of the vowel combination process to the underlying form *mbúdzí+aná* yields the form *mbúdzâná,* to which the Fall Simplification rule (4) applies and yields the surface form *mbúdzaná*.

(4)

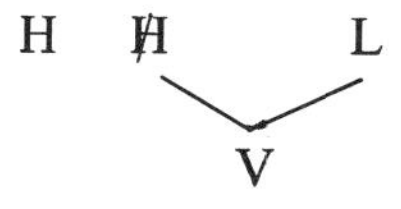


The Fall Simplification rule also applies to the habitual prefix *-nô-* which can be argued to bear an underlying falling tone. When the subject prefix standing before the prefix *nô* bears a L tone, Fall Simplification cannot apply, so the Decontouring rule applies to the falling tone of that prefix, yielding a H tone.

| | | |
|---|---|---|
| (5) | ndi-nó-bika | 'I cook' |
| | ti-nó-bika | 'we cook' |
| | ndi-nó-tórá | 'I take' |
| | ti-nó-tórá | 'we take' |

If, on the other hand, the preceding prefix bears a H tone, the Fall Simplification rule will apply, and deletes the H tone element of the falling tone.

| | | |
|---|---|---|
| (6) | á-no-bika | 'he cooks' |
| | vá-no-bika | 'they cook' |
| | á-no-tórá | 'he takes' |

Under the assumption that the prefix *nô* bears an underlying falling tone, the derivation of the surface form *ánobika* 'he cooks' is given in (7).

(7)

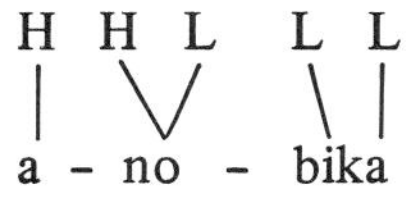


underlying

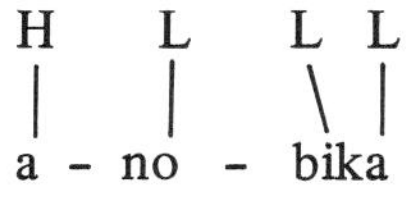


Fall Simplification

On the other hand, when the preceding subject prefix bears a L tone, Fall Simplification is inapplicable, so Decontouring applies, yielding a H tone on the prefix *-nô-*, as shown in the derivation of *ndinóbika* 'I cook' in (8).

(8)
```
 L  H  L    L  L
 |   \/     \  |
ndi - no  -  bika        underlying

 L  H       L  L
 |   \      \  |
ndi - no  -  bika        Decontouring
```

2. STEM TONE ASSIGNMENT

Having outlined the role of contour tones in the grammar of Shona in the preceding section, I shall now turn to a consideration of the process of stem tone conjugation. When a verb appears in one of a wide range of morphosyntactic environments, such as the Conditional, Relative Clause, Negative, or Reflexive, inter alia, a certain tonal pattern is found on the stem. The tone pattern to be discussed here corresponds approximately to Fivaz's Tone Conjugation V and Va (Fivaz (1970)) for the Zezuru dialect. There are, however, differences between the Karanga and Zezuru dialects in the area of stem tone conjugation. The general tonal structure of this type of verb is summarized below using the past tense negative of the L toned verb root *-bik-* 'cook' and the H toned verb roots *-p-* 'give' and *-tór-* 'take'.

| | | |
|---|---|---|
| (9) | handáká-biká | 'I didn't cook' |
| | handáká-bikísa | 'I didn't make cook' |
| | handáká-bikísíra | 'I didn't make cook for' |
| | handáká-bikísísira | 'I didn't make cook for a lot' |
| | handáká-bikísísirana | 'I didn't make cook a lot for each other' |
| | handáká-bikísírisisana | 'I didn't make cook a lot for each other' |
| | handáka-pá | 'I didn't give' |
| | handáka-tóra | 'I didn't take' |
| | handáka-tóresá | 'I didn't make take' |
| | handáka-tóréserá | 'I didn't make take for' |
| | handáka-tóréséraná | 'I didn't make take for each other' |
| | handáka-tóréséresaná | 'I didn't make take for each other a lot' |
| | handáka-tóréséresesaná | 'I didn't make take for each other a lot' |

Depending primarily on the number of syllables in the verb stem and the underlying tone of the verb root, the tones of the nonassertive verb stem will conform to the pattern in (10).[1]

(10)

| | *L Toned Stem* | *H Toned Stem* |
|---|---|---|
| | LH | HL |
| | LHL | HLH |
| | LHHL | HHLH |
| | LHHLL | HHHLH |
| | LHHLLL | HHHLLH |
| | LHHLLLL | HHHLLLH |

The tone pattern outlined above is encountered in numerous morphosyntactic environments. Examples below illustrate a portion of the range of forms having this tone pattern, using one H toned and one L toned stem.

(11)

| | | |
|---|---|---|
| | handízaká-biká | 'I didn't cook' |
| | handízaká-tóra | 'I didn't take' |
| | handá-tóra | 'I didn't take (today)' |
| | handá-biká | 'I didn't cook (today)' |
| | zvandáká-biká | 'when I cooked' |
| | zvandáka-tóra | 'when I took' |
| | wandáká-biká | 'what I cooked' |
| | wandáka-tóra | 'what I took' |
| | ndicházví-biká | 'I will cook myself' |
| | ndicházvi-tóra | 'I will take myself' |
| | ndáká-biká | 'I having cooked' |
| | ndáka-tóra | 'I having taken' |
| | kana ndíchá-biká | 'if I will cook' |
| | kana ndícha-tóra | 'if I will take' |

It can thus be seen that this tonal pattern occurs in a wide range of verbal forms, involving syntactic information as well as morphological information. In Odden (1981) I discuss the characterization of this class of verbs. I shall concentrate on the rules accounting for this pattern here.

From a purely surface-oriented viewpoint, a large number of highly specific rules would be necessary in order to account for the wide range of actual tones in the verbal stem. Each of these rules would be conditioned by the full range of morphosyntactic environments where the tone pattern appears, as well as by phonological information regarding the number of syllables in the stem and the lexical tone of the root. For example, one rule is necessary to place a final H tone on forms such as *handákábiká* 'I didn't cook'. This rule places a H tone on the final vowel of L toned verbs which have two syllables in the stem.

(12) $$L \rightarrow H \,/\, [L \_\_\_\_ \# \qquad \left\{ \begin{array}{l} \text{Relative Clause} \\ \text{Negative} \\ \text{Conditional} \\ \text{Reflexive} \\ \quad \vdots \end{array} \right\}$$

Another rule would assign H tones to the second and third stem vowels, providing that a L tone also stands to the right of both of the focal vowels. This rule would attempt to account for the H tones of the form *handákábikísa* and *handákábikísíra,* and is constrained so that a H tone is not assigned to the final vowels of the form *handákábikísa*.

(13) $$L^2 \rightarrow H \,/\, L \_\_\_\_ L \qquad \left\{ \begin{array}{l} \text{Relative Clause} \\ \text{Negative} \\ \text{Conditional} \\ \text{Reflexive} \\ \quad \vdots \end{array} \right\}$$

Similarly, an additional series of rules is necessary to account for the tone pattern of H toned verbs. One rule assigns a H tone to the final vowel of the stem when that vowel is preceded by at least two syllables, accounting for the H tone in the form *handákatóresá*.

(14) $$L \rightarrow H \,/\, H\, T_1 \_\_\_\_ \# \qquad \left\{ \begin{array}{l} \text{Relative Clause} \\ \text{Negative} \\ \text{Conditional} \\ \text{Reflexive} \\ \quad \vdots \end{array} \right\}$$

This rule assigns H tone to all H toned verb stems in the relevant morpho-syntactic environment, provided that the final vowel is not immediately preceded by the lexical H tone. Finally, another rule would be needed to assign H tones on the second and third syllables of the stem, providing that at least two tones, either H or L, remain immediately to the right. This rule will account for the medial single H tone in four syllable stems, such as *handákatóréserá*, and for the two medial H tones in the five syllable stem *handákatóréséraná*.

(15) $$L^2 \rightarrow H \,/\, H \_\_\_\_ T_2 \qquad \left\{ \begin{array}{l} \text{Relative Clause} \\ \text{Negative} \\ \text{Conditional} \\ \text{Reflexive} \\ \quad \vdots \end{array} \right\}$$

This surface-oriented approach outlined here is highly unsatisfactory, since it fails to explain the tonal patterns of the verb stem in a unified manner, and instead relies on a collection of ad hoc rules. Moreover, this approach cannot explain the presence of a H tone in the monosyllabic stem *-pa* of the form *handákapá* 'I gave' nor the L tone in the same stem in the form *handápa* 'I gave (today)'. It is therefore worthwhile investigating a more abstract analysis to see if it is possible to account for these data in a more elegant fashion. I shall presently pursue an analysis which is capable not only of accounting for the data in (9), but which also accounts for additional data which the purely surface analysis cannot account for.

Under the analysis I propose here, it is assumed that a single sequence of tones is mapped onto all verb stems, regardless of syllable structure or underlying lexical tones. The addition of this tonal sequence is triggered once in the grammar, conditioned by the presence of the relevant combination of morphosyntactic features, such as Relative Clause or Negative. Tonal rules subsequently act upon the stem bearing this tone pattern to derive the surface tones of the verb.

Certain aspects of the abstracted tone pattern are apparent even from the surface tones illustrated above in (10). For example, the tone of the final vowel is identical to the lexical tone of the root, at least for all verb stems having more than two syllables. Furthermore, the two syllables immediately following the root syllable bear H tones, providing that those two H tones are not in final position. I therefore assume that in both H toned verb stems and L toned verb stems, a morphological rule adds to the tone of the verb stem the unassociated sequence *HHLB*, where B is a variable interpreted as H when the lexical tone of the root is H, and L when this tone is L.

After the morphologically conditioned sequence of tones is inserted into the verbal stem, that tone sequence is mapped onto the vowels of the stem by a Mapping rule, which states:[2]

(16) Associate the first H tone with the first unassociated vowel and the second H tone with the next unassociated vowel: If for either H tone there is no unassociated vowel, then associate that H tone with the previously associated vowel to the left. Lastly, associate the tone pair LB with the final vowel of the stem. If the stem bears two final vowels, associate the pair with the leftmost available final vowel.

I shall illustrate below the way in which this tone schema allows a unified account of the tonal patterns under consideration.

I take into consideration first the L toned verb roots. Application of the mapping rule to the underlying form *handákábikisira* yields the phonetic form directly, since the tone pair LB is realised first as LL, and is then automatically simplified to L tone by application of a universal convention which states that two identical tones may not be adjacent on the same vowel.[3]

```
(17)            LHHLB
                |
    handáká-bik-is-ir-a        underlying

                L HHL
                | | | |
    handáká-bik-is-ir-a        Mapping
```

In the derivation in (18), only three stem syllables are available for the tone melody to be associated with. Application of Mapping places a H tone on the second and third syllables, and also places the pair LB on the final vowel. The pair LB is realised as LL, which automatically simplifies to L, with the result that the final syllable of the verb stem bears a falling tone preceded by a H tone. The independently motivated Fall Simplification rule discussed in the previous section then applies and deletes the H tone element of the falling tone, resulting in the surface tone pattern LHL for the stem vowels.

```
(18)            LHHLB
                |
    handáká-bik-is-a           underlying

                L HHL
                | | \/
    handáká-bik-is-a           Mapping

                L HL
                | | |
    handáká-bik-is-a           Fall Simplification
```

Finally, in (19), the entire tonal sequence HHLB is mapped onto the final vowel. The first H tone is associated with the final vowel and, since there are no unassociated vowels for the second H tone to associate with, that tone associates with the previously associated final vowel as well. Due to the application of the convention preventing adjacent identical tones on one vowel, that H tone is deleted. Finally, the pair LB is associated with the final vowel (which is now associated with a H tone) and is realised as LL, which simplifies to L. This yields, after application of Mapping, a falling tone on the final vowel, which is preceded by a L tone. Fall Simplification will not be applicable, so Decontouring will apply instead, giving the surface stem tone pattern LH.

(19)

```
            L H H L  B
            |
handáká-bik-a            underlying

            L H L
            | \/
handáká-bik-a            Mapping

            L  H
            |  |
handáká-bik-a            Decontouring
```

Despite the disparate tonal patterns of the stem depending on the number of syllables in the stem, the tonal melody HHLB acting in conjunction with independently motivated rules can account for all varieties of L toned stems in a wide range of morphosyntactic forms.

Not only does the tonal pattern abstracted in the present analysis account for L toned stems, it also generalises to all H toned verb stems. In the derivation of L toned stems, it may not be apparent what reason there is for mapping the tone pair LB onto the final vowel, since that tone sequence is invariably simplified to a single L tone on the surface, at least for L toned verb stems. However, in a H toned stem, B will be realised as a H tone, with the consequence that the final vowel bears a rising tone which does not undergo automatic simplification to a single tone. As shown by the data in (20), the L tone element of that rising tone is shifted off of the final vowel onto the penultimate vowel, provided that vowel is not also the root initial vowel.

| | | |
|---|---|---|
| (20) | handáka-tóra | 'I didn't take' |
| | handáka-tóresá | 'I didn't make take' |
| | handáka-tóréserá | 'I didn't make take for' |
| | handáka-tóréséraná | 'I didn't make take for each other' |

In order to account for the movement of the L tone onto the penultimate vowel, I propose the following Leftward Shift Rule.

(21) *Leftward Shift*

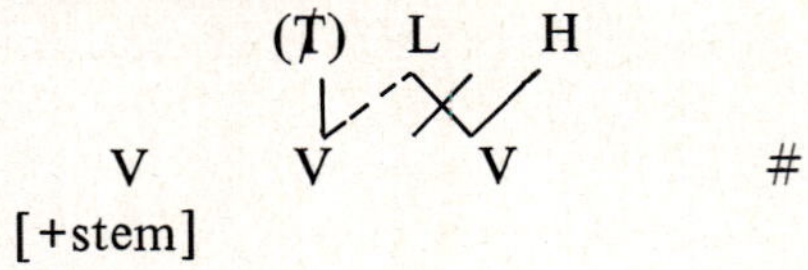


The application of Mapping and Leftward Shift to the H toned stem *-toreserana* yields the surface form *handákatóréséraná*, as shown in (22).

(22)

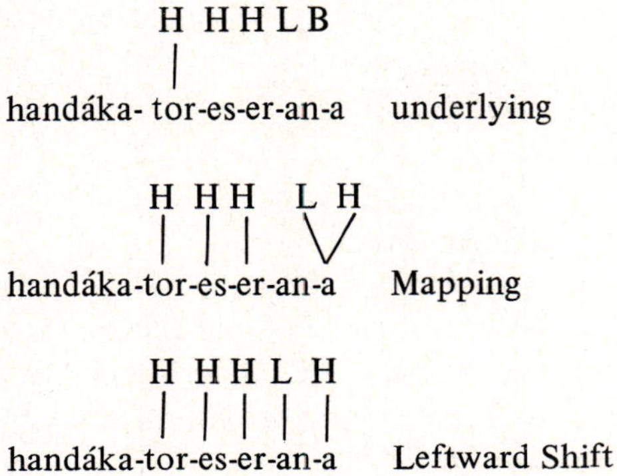


In this derivation, the penultimate vowel bears no tone, so the L tone of the final vowel merely moves onto that vowel.

In the derivation of (23), after simplication of Mapping to the underlying H toned stem *toresera*, the final rising tone is preceded by a H tone, namely the H tone of the melody HHLB. That H tone is replaced by the L tone of the final vowel, giving the surface form *handákatóréserá* 'I didn't make take for'.

(23)

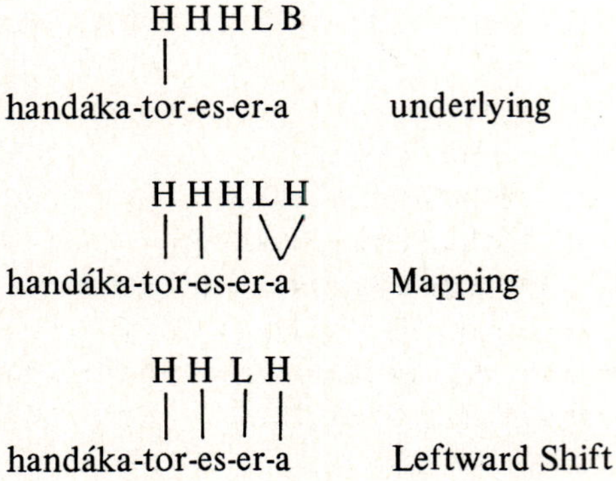


In (24), the derivation of the trisyllabic stem *-toresa* is given. Application of Mapping associates the initial H tone with the second stem vowel and the second H tone with the final stem vowel. The tone pair LB is also associated with the final vowel, yielding the stem tone pattern H H *HLH*. The Fall Simplification rule can apply to this structure, since a H tone on the penultimate vowel precedes a combination of H and L on the final vowel. The application of Fall Simplification removes that H tone, which then creates a structure to which Leftward Shift may apply. After application of Leftward Shift, the surface pattern HLH results.

(24)

| | | |
|---|---|---|
| H HHLB | | |
| handáka-tor-es-a | | underlying |
| H HHLH | | |
| handáka-tor-es-a | | Mapping |
| H HLH | | |
| handáka-tor-es-a | | Fall Simplification |
| H L H | | |
| handáka-tor-es-a | | Leftward Shift |

Fall Simplification must crucially precede Leftward Shift, since Fall Simplification removes the initial H tone on the final vowel in the preceding derivation, which would otherwise block the application of Leftward Shift.

Proceding to a shorter verb stem in (25), *-tora*, the entire sequence HHLB is placed on the final vowel, yielding the stem tone pattern H *HLH*. Analogous to the derivation in (24), a H tone stands on the penultimate vowel before the sequence *HL* associated with a single vowel, the final vowel. Fall Simplification applies and deletes the initial H tone of the falling contour tone. Leftward Shift cannot apply to the output of Fall Simplification in this case, since the Leftward Shift rule has been stated so as to require the presence of at least one stem vowel preceding the focal vowel which receives the shifted H tone. Decontouring (2) will therefore apply to the contoured *LH* tone on the final vowel, yielding the surface pattern HL for the verb stem.

(25)

| | | |
|---|---|---|
| H HHLB | | |
| handáka-tor-a | | underlying |

HHLH
handáka-tor-a Mapping

HLH
handáka-tor-a Fall Simplification

H L
handáka-tor-a Decontouring

Finally, if the verb stem has only one vowel, as in the verb stem *-pa* 'give' in (26), the entire tone melody HHLB is mapped onto the single stem vowel. Fall Simplification is inapplicable in the example in (26), since the complex tone on the root is preceded by a L tone (*-ka*) rather than a H tone. Decontouring will therefore delete each tone which stands to the right of the root initial H tone.

(26) HHHLB
handáka-pa underlying

HLH
handáka-pa Mapping

H
handáka-pa Decontouring

One prediction of the present analysis, which can be shown to be true, is that in case a monosyllabic verb stem stands after a phonetically H toned prefix, the complex tone of the verb stem will be in the correct environment to undergo Fall Simplification, and should consequently appear as a L tone on the surface. As demonstrated below in (27), a monosyllabic verb stem can appear on the surface with either a H tone or a L tone; it has a H tone when the preceding prefix bears a L tone, and a L tone when the preceding prefix bears a H tone.

(27) handá-pa 'I didn't give (today)'
handákamú-pa 'I didn't give him'
handízaká-pa 'I didn't give'

| | |
|---|---|
| handáka-pá | 'I didn't give' |
| handámu-pá | 'I didn't give him (today)' |
| handízakámu-pá | 'I didn't give him' |
| zvandáka-pá | 'when I gave' |

While the correlation between stem tone and prefix tone might have been an isolated phenomenon in the grammar, unrelated to any other facts of the language, this distribution of tones is automatically expected under the present analysis. The derivation of the form *handápa* 'I didn't give (today)' is given in (28), to contrast with the derivation of *handákapá* 'I didn't give' in (26).

(28)

| | |
|---|---|
| H H H L B<br>\|<br>handá-pa | underlying |
| H L H<br>\\\|/<br>handá-pa | Mapping |
| L H<br>\\/<br>handá-pa | Fall Simplification |
| L<br>\|<br>handá-pa | Decontouring |

The tonal pattern HHLB which is proposed here is therefore able to explain the wide range of phonetic tones appearing on stems bearing an underlying H tone, regardless of the length of the stem.

Up to this point, I have discussed how the tonal melody HHLB is associated with verb stems which have no more than five syllables in the case of H toned stems and four syllables in the case of L toned stems. However, since verbal stems can be considerably longer, it is interesting to see what happens in the case of rather long examples. For any verb stem which has more syllables than tones in the melody, there is a certain degree of flexibility in the phonetic tones of the vowels which are not associated with the melodic tones. By application of a rule of Leftward Spreading, the final L tone of the melody HHLB may spread leftward onto any number of consecutive unassociated vowels, and any vowels not associated with the final L by Leftward Spreading will then be associated with the H tone of the melody by the Wellformedness Conditions. In

(29), additional data is provided where the number of stem syllables excedes the number of tones to be associated with those syllables.

| | | |
|---|---|---|
| (29) | handáká-bikísísirana | 'I didn't make cook for each other a lot' |
| | handáká-bikísísírana | id. |
| | handáká-bikísísírána | id. |
| | *handáká-bikísísíráná | |
| | handáka-tóréséseraná | 'I didn't make take for each other a lot' |
| | handáka-tóréséséraná | id. |
| | *handáka-tórésésérá ná | |
| | *handáka-tóréseseraná | |
| | handáka-shámwárídzisisiraná | 'I didn't make befriend for each other a lot' |
| | handáka-shámwárídzísisiraná | id. |
| | handáka-shámwárídzísísiraná | id. |
| | handáka-shámwárídzísísíraná | id. |
| | *handáka-shámwárídzísísíráná | |

In order to account for this alternation between H tones and L tones, I propose the following optional rule of Leftward Spreading.

(30) 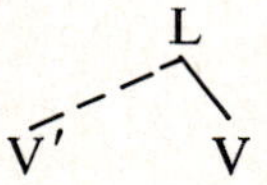

(optional, iterative)

This rule associates the final L tone of the melody with one or more members of a preceding sequence of unassociated stem vowels. Any vowels not associated with the final L by application of Leftward Spreading will then be associated with the preceding H tone by application of the Wellformedness Conditions. The derivation of the form *handákábikísísirana* is given in (31); in this derivation, the final L tone of the melody associates with every unassociated vowel.

(31)

```
            L HHLB
            |
handáká-bik-is-is-ir-an-a        underlying

            L HH    L
            | | |   |
handáká-bik-is-is-ir-an-a        Mapping
```

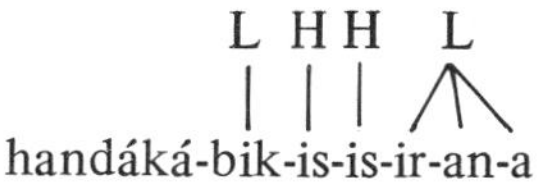

Leftward Spreading

In the derivation of the alternative form *handákábikísísírana*, the L tone of the melody associates with all but the leftmost unassociated vowel. That vowel is then associated with the preceding H tone by application of the Wellformedness Conditions.

(32)

Leftward Spreading

Wellformedness Conditions

Finally, in the derivation of the form *handákábikisisirána*, the Leftward Spreading rule does not apply at all, so the Wellformedness Conditions spread the final melodic H tone onto all of the unassociated vowels.

(33)

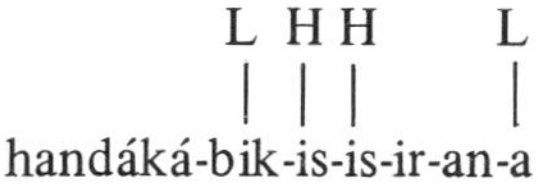

Mapping

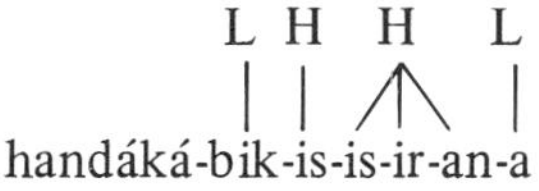

Wellformedness Conditions

It should be noted that, although all of the forms in (29) are possible, there is a definite preference for forms where Leftward Spreading does not apply. Thus, forms like *handákábikisisirána* and *handákashámwár-ídzísísíraná* are preferred to the forms *handákábikísísirana* or *handákashámwáridzisisiraná*. It is also interesting that the forms where Leftward Spreading does not apply are clearly the most common, and that application of Leftward Spreading to one versus three vowels is no better or worse. Furthermore, in one grammatical context (imperative with object prefixes), application of Leftward Spreading maximally leftward is preferred over nonapplication; thus, the form *vá-shamwáridzisirane* is preferred to the form *vá-shamwáridzísíráne* 'make them befriend for each other!'.

The interaction between verb stem reduplication, the number of stem syllables, and the tone mapping rule which associates the melody with the stem provides some interesting evidence which confirms certain facts of the language automatically, where these facts could not be predicted by other possible analyses. When a verb stem is reduplicated, it is important to consider how many syllables appear in the lefthand reduplicated element. It is not the case in Shona that the reduplicated stem is tonologically identical to a nonreduplicated stem. When the lefthand element contains two syllables, both copies of the verb stem are taken as a single domain for mapping the tonal melody. Thus, the reduplicated stem *bikabika* 'cook frequently' behaves tonologically like the nonreduplicated stem *bikisira*, and the reduplicated stem *bikabikisa* 'make cook frequently' behaves tonologically just like nonreduplicated stems such as *bikisirana*.

| | | |
|---|---|---|
| (34) | handáká-bikábíka | 'I didn't repeatedly cook' |
| | handáká-bikísíra | 'I didn't make cook for' |
| | handáká-bikábíkisa | 'I didn't make cook repeatedly' |
| | handáká-bikísírana | 'I didn't make cook for each other' |
| | handáka-tórátorá | 'I didn't take frequently' |
| | handáka-tóreserá | 'I didn't make take for' |
| | handáka-tórátóresá | 'I didn't make take frequently' |
| | handáka-tóréséraná | 'I didn't make take for each other' |

On the other hand, when the lefthand element of the reduplication contains three or more syllables, then the entire tonal melody is mapped onto the first member of the stem, thus making the reduplicated stem *bikisabikisa* 'make cook frequently' tonologically distinct from the nonreduplicated stem *bikisisirana*, which has the same number of syllables.[4]

| | | |
|---|---|---|
| (35) | handáká-bikísabikisa | 'I didn't make cook frequently' |
| | handáká-bikísírabikisira | 'I didn't make cook for frequently' |
| | handáka-tóresátoresa | 'I didn't make take frequently' |
| | handáka-tóreserátoresera | 'I didn't make take for frequently' |
| | *handáká-bikísábíkísa | |
| | *handáka-tórésátoresá | |

The particular behavioral distinction between stems with two syllables in (34) and stems with more syllables in (35) can be shown to be a consequence of the analysis proposed here, along with general conventions on tone association rules which prevent association lines from crossing. Considering first the derivation of the form *handákábikábíka*, it is observed that the Mapping rule associates the first H tone of the melody with the second stem vowel *-a* and the second H tone of the melody with the third vowel of the stem, *-i-* in the righthand reduplicated element. Finally, the pair of tones LB is associated with the final vowel *a*, which appears in word-final position (recall that the term "final vowel" is used here in the technical sense of note 2).

(36)

```
             L HHLB
             |
handáká-bik-a-bik-a        underlying

             L H HLB
             | |
handáká-bik-a-bik-a        Mapping

             L H H LB
             | | |
handáká-bik-a-bik-a        Mapping

             L H H L
             | | | |
handáká-bik-a-bik-a        Mapping
```

In the example under consideration, the Mapping rule must draw an association line between the sequence LB and the word-final "final" vowel *-a-*. If Mapping were to attempt to draw an association line between the medial vowel *-a-* in the stem *bikabika*, it would be necessary to cross the association line between the final melodic H tone and the vowel *i* in the righthand reduplicated element. It is therefore impossible to associate the tonal pair LB with the leftmost "final" vowel, so it must be associated with the rightmost final vowel.

On the other hand, in the derivation of the longer forms, represented in (37), a different situation obtains, as a result of the additional vowel in the leftmost stem copy. The first H tone associates with the vowel *i* in the first stem copy, and the second H tone associates with the vowel in the leftmost copy. The tone pair LB may also associate with the medial vowel *-a-*, since to do so does not cross any association lines, and the Mapping rule stated above requires that the tone pair LB be associated with the leftmost stem-final vowel. The derivation of the form *handáká-bikísabikisa* is given below to clarify this point.

(37)

```
             L HHLB
             |
handáká-bik-is-a-bik-is-a        underlying
```

L H H L B

handáká-bik-*i*s-a-bik-is-a Mapping

L H H L B

handáká-bik-is-*a*-bik-is-a Mapping

L H H L

handáká-bik-is-*a*-bik-is-a Mapping

The derivation then proceeds as expected, with Fall Simplification applying to the complex HL tone on the final vowel.

The analysis given here can explain why the tone melody is restricted to the first stem copy, just in case there are three or more vowels in the first stem. The facts of reduplication also support the decision to assign two H tones to the tone melody, since a crucial fact which prevents the tone pair LB from being associated with the first stem in the form *handáká-bikábíka* is the fact that the vowel *i* of the rightmost stem is associated with the second melodic H tone. Let us imagine that an analysis were proposed whereby the tone melody is HLB, and the melodic H tone copies onto the following unassociated vowel. In that case, Mapping would assign the melodic H tone to the final vowel *a*, and would furthermore assign the tones LB to that same vowel.

(38) L H L B

handáká-bik-a-bik-a underlying

L H L B

handáká-bik-*a*-bik-a Mapping

L H L

handáká-bik-*a*-bik-a Mapping

After application of Decontouring, the ungrammatical form **handáká-bikábika* would result.[5]

In summary, the tonal melody HHLB which I have proposed here is able to account for a considerable range of tonal alternations in the verb stem, where surface-oriented rules cannot describe these data with similar elegance. Despite the complex array of conditioning factors, the occurring forms can be predicted and the ungrammatical forms blocked without directly referring to these properties, through the application of the few phonological rules proposed here.

## 3. THEORETICAL IMPLICATIONS

In this last section, I would like to touch on two theoretical implications which the analysis of Shona stem tone raises for phonological theory. I would first like to argue that the tone mapping rule (16) must be stated to apply specifically to the tone melody HHLB, since other tonal melodies are mapped onto words by different tone mapping rules. I will then discuss a question concerning the status of the Well-formedness Conditions.

There are two other tonal melodies employed in verbs in Shona, which occur in two relatively restricted verbal forms. In the subjunctive, the tone melody L is mapped onto the final vowel of the verb stem. The insertion of the melody L on the final vowel of the verb has two effects on the surface. It prevents the lexical H tone from appearing on the final vowel (where a lexical H tone would otherwise be spread onto the two syllables after the root-initial syllable, as in the infinitive form *kutórésèra* 'to make take for'). Secondly, the insertion of the melody L on the final vowel in the subjunctive creates a falling tone on the final vowel of a monosyllabic verb stem which undergoes Fall Simplification and appears as a L tone on the surface. Examples of the subjunctive are given in (39).

| | | |
|---|---|---|
| (39) | hándíríme[6] | 'let me plow' |
| | hándírímire | 'let me plow for' |
| | hándírímisire | 'let me plow for intensively' |
| | hándípe | 'let me give' |
| | hándítóre | 'let me take' |
| | hándítórése | 'let me make take' |
| | hándítóRésére[7] | 'let me make take for' |

The form *hándípe* is derived as shown in (40).

```
(40)  H  H H   L
      |  \ \
      ha-ndi-pe              underlying

      H  H H L
      |  \ \/
      ha-ndi-pe              Mapping of Subjunctive Melody
```

H H L
| \ |
ha-ndi-pe Fall Simplification

I propose that the tonal melody L is mapped onto the stem by the rule in (41).

(41) Associate the L tone with the rightmost final vowel.

This mapping rule is stated so that if the stem contains two final vowels (in the sense of note 2) in a reduplicated form, the melodic L tone is associated with the final vowel which appears at the end of the word. Inspection of the data in (42) confirms that a reduplicated H toned verb stem allows the lexical H tone to spread onto the leftmost final vowel of the stem *-toretore*.

| | | |
|---|---|---|
| (42) | hándítórétóre | 'let me take frequently' |
| | hándítórétórese | 'let me make take frequently' |
| | hándítórésétorese[8] | 'let me take frequently' |

The mapping rule (41) associates the subjunctive L tone with the word-final vowel, and the Tone Tripling rule (see note 7) spreads the lexical H tone to the following two syllables.

(43) H HH L
| | |
ha-ndi-tor-e-tor-e underlying

H HH L
| | | |
ha-ndi-tor-e-tor-e Mapping

H H H L
| | /|\ |
ha-ndi-tor-e-tor-e Tone Tripling

If the melodic L tone were associated with the first final vowel, as in the derivation (44), the incorrect form **hánd́ítóretorese* would be generated.

(44) H HH L
| | |
ha-ndi-tor-e-tor-es-e underlying

```
H   H H L
|   | | |
ha-ndi-tor-e-tor-es-e      Mapping

*hándítóretorese           other rules
```

It can therefore be seen that the L tone melody of the subjunctive differs crucially from the LB melody of the subordinate clause verbs in that the former melody is mapped onto the rightmost final vowel in the case of reduplication, whereas the latter melody is mapped onto the leftmost final vowel.

There are six verb stems in Shona which have a perfective form; this tense is constructed by adding the final vowel *-e*, modifying the stem tone, and changing a preceding stem vowel *a* to *e*. Although the basic stem of the verb may have either a H or a L tone, in the perfective the distinction between H and L toned stems is neutralized. Thus the L toned stem *-gar-* seen in the form *kugara* 'to sit' and the H toned stem *-zár-* seen in the form *kuzárá* 'to be full' both have the same surface tone pattern in the perfective. In the forms given below, when the subject prefix bears a L tone, the vowels of the stem all bear a H tone.

| | | |
|---|---|---|
| (45) | ndi-géré | 'I am seated' (-gar-) |
| | ndi-vété | 'I am asleep (-vát-) |
| | ndi-zéré | 'I am full' (-zár-) |
| | ndi-míré | 'I am quiet' (-mír-) |
| | ndi-nyéréré | 'I am silent' (-nyánár-) |
| | ndi-réré | 'I am asleep' (-rar-) |

If the subject prefix bears a H tone, the initial stem tone is lowered in the case of bisyllabic stems, and the two nonfinal H tones are lowered in the case of the trisyllabic stem *-nyerere*.

| | | |
|---|---|---|
| (46) | á-geré | 'he is seated' |
| | á-veté | 'he is asleep' |
| | á-zeré | 'he is full' |
| | á-miré | 'he is quiet' |
| | á-nyereré | 'he is silent' |
| | á-reré | 'he is asleep' |

Under the analysis proposed here, the perfective is characterized by the melody HH, where the first H replaces the lexical tone of the root and is spread to any nonfinal stem vowel, and the second H is associated with the final vowel of the stem. Accordingly, the form *ndinyéréré* has the following tonal representation.

(47)

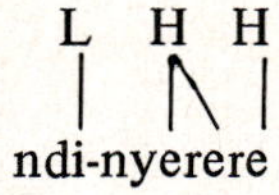


Following up on this analysis, the lowering of two surface H tones in the form *ányereré* derives from a similar underlying tonal form, where a rule such as (48) lowers the stem-initial H tone autosegment.

(48) H → L / H + ——— (perfective)

The application of this rule is illustrated in (49).

(49)

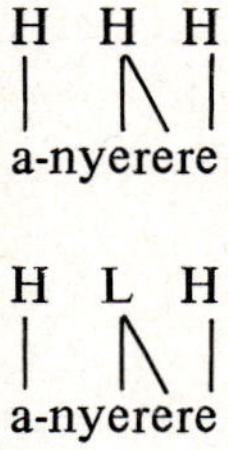


underlying

Perfective Lowering

Note, however, that the melody HH employed in the perfective is mapped by a significantly different principle than was employed in mapping the tones HH of the melody HHLB. The perfective tone mapping rule must replace the lexical tone of the root with the first melodic tone; moreover, the second H of the perfective melody HH is assigned to the final vowel, whereas in the subordinate clause melody HHLB, the second H tone is mapped onto the next leftmost stem vowel. It must therefore be concluded that the mapping rule employed for the perfective melody cannot be the same mapping rule as is employed for assigning the melody HHLB to the verb stem.

I have argued here for the existence of three separate tone melodies in Shona, each of which is associated with a distinct mapping rule. A similar situation is encountered by Laughren (this volume), where she argues for Zulu that noun stems selecting the tone melody HL must be lexically specified as undergoing one of two different initial association rules. Similarly, Kisseberth (this volume) argues that the imperative in Digo is formed with a H tone which is associated with the penultimate syllable of the stem by a special association rule. One might take a similar approach in a language like Kimatuumbi, where verbal stem tone is assigned according to various morphological conditions. For example, in the subjunctive, a H tone is associated with the fourth mora after the subject prefix.[9]

| | | |
|---|---|---|
| (50) | nį-teleké | 'I should cook' |
| | nį-kį-teléke | 'I should coǫk it' |
| | nį-bųųndáye | 'I should blunt' |
| | nį-ka-bųų́ndaye | 'I should go and blunt' |
| | nį-ka-kį-bų́ųndaye | 'I should go and blunt it' |

In the present progressive subordinate form of the Kimatuumbi verb (one of the tenses for which the tonal melody HHLB is selected in Shona), a H tone is mapped onto the second stem vowel after the subject prefix *-á-*.

| | | |
|---|---|---|
| (51) | pa-á-temá | 'while he is chopping' |
| | pa-á-kaáta | 'while he is cutting' |
| | pa-á-teléka | 'while he is cooking' |
| | pa-á-kį-téleka | 'while he is cooking it' |

In both cases, the tone melody is the same, namely H. In the case of the subjunctive, this melodic tone is mapped onto the fourth vowel after the subject prefix, while in the case of the present progressive, it is mapped onto the second vowel. There is also a melody HH in Kimatuumbi, which may be mapped onto the first and third stem morae in agent nominalizations, or onto the second and last morae in subordinate perfective verbs. Thus, the suggestion that the three stem-tone melodies in Shona each have their own mapping rules is supported by parallel situations in other Bantu languages.

A second theoretical implication of the present analysis relates to the question of where the Wellformedness Conditions come into effect in the grammar. Returning to the derivation of verbs such as *-bikisisirana*, it will be recalled that the application of Mapping yields the structure in (52).

```
(52)            L  H H       L
                |  |  |      |
      handáká-bik-is-is-ir-an-a      output of Mapping
```

According to the position taken in Clements and Ford (1979:182),

> the initial tone association rule(s) enter associations between single tones and single tone-bearing units, leaving other tones and tone-bearing units unassociated. Associations among the latter are governed by a set of principles of well-formedness which are hypoth-

> esized to be language-independent . . . Applying persistently through a derivation, they guarantee that the phonetic output is physically interpretable.

If one interprets this position as indicating that the Wellformedness Conditions apply at all stages in the derivation, one might expect these conditions to apply to the representation (52), to yield the form (53).

(53)

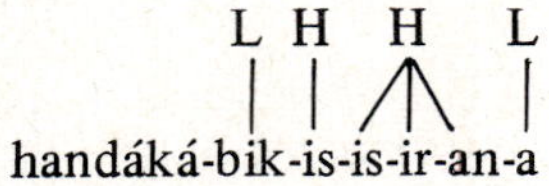

Wellformedness Conditions

Although the form *handákábikísísírána* is grammatical, the form *handáká-bikísísirana*, which is also grammatical, could not be generated if the Wellformedness Conditions apply immediately after Mapping. In fact, it is necessary that the Wellformedness Conditions not apply until after the application of Leftward Spreading, in order to guarantee that Leftward Spreading has a chance to apply to the structure in (52).

One would not, however, want to conclude that the initial application of the Wellformedness Conditions is governed by a language-specific ordering statement in Shona. Rather, the applicability of the Wellformedness Conditions may be predicted by the following principle:

(54) The Wellformedness Conditions come into effect after the last rule in the grammar which refers to an unassociated vowel in its structural description.

The crucial characterization of the place in the grammar where the Wellformedness Conditions come into effect is not only that they apply after the Initial Tone Association Rule(s), which associate single free tones with single free vowels (Haraguchi (1977)), but that they apply after any rule referring to free vowels. It is in fact hard to imagine how a grammar could be constructed which has a rule referring to a free vowel, but where that rule applies after the Wellformedness Conditions, which assure that all free vowels bear a tone.

In conclusion, I have offered an analysis of the subordinate clause stem-tone alternations, arguing that the tone melody HHLB is associated with the verb stem in the relevant morphosyntactic environments. I have also argued that the Mapping rule associating that melody with the verb stem must be stated to refer to that particular melody; different melodies require different Mapping rules. Finally, I have proposed that the application of the Wellformedness Conditions is delayed until the last rule of the grammar which refers to a free vowel.

NOTES

This chapter is an abbreviated version of Chapter Five of Odden (1981), and was presented at the Tenth Annual Conference on African Linguistics at Urbana, April 1979. The data for this paper were collected during 1977-1981 from Kokerai Rugara, a native speaker of the Karanga dialect of Shona, to whom I owe a great debt of thanks. Although this paper addresses only the Karanga dialect of Shona, a similar analysis can be given of the other dialects, at least to the extent that the facts are similar. I would like to thank Chuck Kisseberth, Mike Kenstowicz, John Goldsmith, Nick Clements, Susan Stucky, Mary Odden and Winifred Wood for helpful comments and suggestions on this paper. Research for this paper was supported by a University of Illinois Fellowship provided by the Department of Linguistics, a FLAS Fellowship in African Languages provided by the African Studies Center, and NSF Grant BNS-7924523, to whom I give thanks.

1. The tone pattern of monosyllabic verb stems such as *-pa* 'give' is more complex and cannot be easily extracted for this chart. These verbs will be discussed later.
2. This Mapping rule gives preference to mapping a tone onto an unassociated vowel over an associated vowel, and a vowel on the left over a vowel on the right. This preference is presumably universal, and is expressed in one of the Wellformedness Conditions of Clements and Ford (1979). Therefore, the Mapping rule could be simplified to eliminate the hierarchy of vowels which the tones are associated with. In this rule, the term "final vowel" is used in the technical sense employed in Bantu linguistics to refer to the suffix *-a*, *-e*, or *-i* which appears after all other stem formatives. The selection of the final vowel is based on morphological criteria. The final vowel has numerous unique properties to which phonological and morphological rules refer. When a verb stem is reduplicated, viz. *-bikabika* 'cook frequently', the stem contains two final vowels. This has an effect on the Mapping of the melodic tones onto reduplicated stems, as I shall discuss later.
3. It is assumed in all following derivations that lexical tones are already associated. The element "B" in all representations stands for a copy of the root tone. In order not to clutter the figures, tones of syllables preceding the stem are not represented autosegmentally.
4. As argued in Odden (1981), there is a rule in the grammar which inserts a L tone over toneless vowels. This rule applies to the final toneless vowels of the forms in (35).
5. Although reduplicated stems are often tonologically indistinguishable from nonreduplicated stems in Bantu languages, this is not always the case. As seen in Shona, reduplicated stems are not identical to simple stems, and as argued in Odden (in press), reduplicated stems in Kimatuumbi are not tonologically identical to nonreduplicated stems.
6. This has the underlying form *hándírime*, to which the Root Raising rule (discussed in Odden 1981) applies, changing root-initial L tone to H when preceded by H and followed by L.
7. The last two H tones in this form come from a rule discussed in Odden (1981) which spreads the lexical H tone two syllables rightward; this rule accounts for the three stem-internal H tones in *kutóréséra* which derives from underlying *kutóresera*. The Tone Tripling rule appears to apply to only one syllable in *hándítórése*, and not at all in *hándítóre*, but in fact the final H tone which derives from Tone Tripling becomes L because of the subjunctive L tone melody, which is assigned to the final vowel.

8. It might be thought that Leftward Spread (30) should apply here to give **hándí-tóresetorese*. This can be prevented by applying Tone Tripling (footnote 7) before Leftward Spreading. The correct form *hándítórésétorese* will then derive by applying Leftward Spreading maximally to the left. Since Leftward Spreading is optional, *hándítórésétórése* would result from not applying the rule at all. My data are not sufficient to allow me to confidently declare that this form is grammatical. On the one hand, my data include the forms *ngándípútsísírísise* 'let me break intensively for' as acceptable, **ngándípútsísísírise* (id.) as ungrammatical, and *ngándípútsísírise* (id.) as questionable.

9. The principles of tone assignment in verbs are discussed in Odden (in press).

*Chapter 8*

# Principles of Tone Assignment in Kikuyu

George N. Clements

## 1. INTRODUCTION

This chapter examines the principles that account for the tonal realization of Kikuyu words.[1] Kikuyu is one of the few Bantu languages whose tone has received detailed examination in the earlier descriptive literature. Armstrong's 1940 study (reprinted as Armstrong 1967) presents over 250 pages of tonal transcriptions representing the speech of an educated speaker in his late forties at the time the study appeared. This work is an extremely valuable source of information due to the comprehensiveness of its coverage and the accuracy of the author's phonetic observations. This important record is supplemented by the extensive data on noun tones included as an introduction to Benson's 1964 dictionary. However, neither Armstrong nor Benson offer a phonological analysis of their data, presenting instead lists of forms arranged into "tone classes". Greenberg (1948) is the first to notice that Armstrong's various tonal classes for verbs can be reduced to two, corresponding to verb roots bearing Proto-Bantu H tone and L tone. A further advance is made by Ford (1975), who shows that the multiple tone levels recorded by Armstrong and Benson are derivable from two underlying tones, H and L, together with phonemic downstep.

With a tone system of considerable richness and complexity, Kikuyu is of unusual interest in the context of current research on Bantu tone and accent. Many of its tonal characteristics reflect structural features of Proto-Bantu, both lexically and grammatically. If we are correct in assuming that Bantu accent systems have developed out of tonal systems rather than vice-versa (see Chapter 1 for discussion), then Kikuyu seems to offer a plausible approximation to the type of system which (abstracting from its considerable overlay of recently-acquired tone rules) might have stood at the point of departure for the current split into tone systems and accent systems. Kikuyu offers, then, a perspective of interest both to the Bantuist and to the historical phonologist.

The most striking feature in the development of the tone system of modern Kikuyu is the process of tone shift, which caused each etymological tone to be realized one syllable to the right. This process is not only a historical one, but survives as a central rule of the synchronic phonology, where it gives rise to a pervasive and highly regular system of tonal displacements in the verb. One result of this process is that word-final L tones do not become lost, but survive in the form of "downsteps" which, while never overtly pronounced themselves, play a crucial role in the tonal and intonational realization of longer phrases and sentences. Previous works have examined the comparative evidence for tone shift (Clements and Ford 1979) and the synchronic system of phrase-level tone sandhi (Clements and Ford 1981). The present study takes these works as a point of departure, and examines the synchronic evidence showing that tone shift survives as a central process in the tonal phonology of the word.

It will emerge from the following discussion that floating tones play an important role in the synchronic phonology of the Kikuyu word. These tones arise both from the "overcrowding" effect created by the tone shift process, according to which word-final tones are left without a tone-bearing unit of their own, and from the morphological structure of the word, in which underlying tones are frequently in excess of available tone-bearing units, even if the process of tone shift is disregarded. It will be shown that there are three types of floating tones: floating H tones, which have no consequences for tonal realization except where they are subsequently associated with tone-bearing units by rule, and two types of floating L tones: those that act as downstep operators, symbolized !, and those that do not. Both types of floating L tones play a grammatical role in the morphology of the finite verb, and undergo rules which are fully as regular as those that affect "audible" tones. While this result generally confirms earlier work on Kikuyu tone, it provides even more substantial evidence that floating tones, far from being the "abstract" elements they have sometimes been held to be, are fully concrete, learnable components of phonological representation.

A further area of theoretical interest concerns the tonal morphology of the verb. The Kikuyu verb, like that of other Bantu languages, is a highly complex, agglutinative entity involving two tiers of structure: the tonal tier and the segmental tier (that is, the tier upon which consonants and vowels are arrayed).[2] Formatives making up the verb are of three types: those that are specified for both tonal and segmental properties, those that are specified for tonal properties alone, and those that are specified for segmental properties alone. Much of the complexity of the verbal morphology arises from the interaction of formatives of these three types. In particular, it will be shown that the rules of tone assignment largely disregard the morphological relation between tones and tone-bearing units, with the result that tones are quite typically associated with segmental material characterizing other formatives than their own. This result owes primarily to two factors: first, the process of tone shift itself, and second, the fact that the domain of tone association in Kikuyu is the word, rather than the morpheme. In the latter respect Kikuyu appears to be quite different from tone languages like Tiv (see Pulleyblank 1983), but not unlike tone languages such as Shanghai, in which a process of tone shift similar to that of Kikuyu shows the domain of tone association to be the (compound) word (see Wright 1983).

The process of tone shift may be characterized in a preliminary way as a rule that applies to representations in which tones have not yet become associated with tone-bearing units, linking the first tone in the word to the second tone-bearing unit, as follows (t = tone-bearing unit, T = tone):

(1)

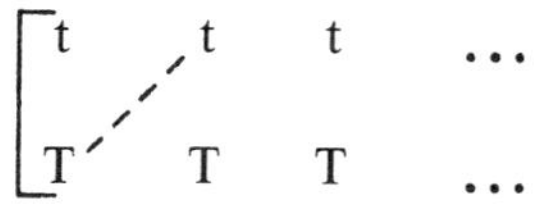

This rule should be understood as affecting only those tones and tone-bearing units that are not yet associated. Remaining unassociated tones and tone-bearing units are then linked by the usual conventions of autosegmental phonology (see Chapter 1). We will return to the precise formal characterization of tone shift in a later section; for the present, the account given in (1), which follows the analysis in Clements and Ford (1979), will be adopted for the purposes of exposition.

In order not to introduce unnecessary clutter in the transcriptions, the following conventions will be adopted. Syllables bearing H tone are marked with an acute accent (´), syllables bearing rising tone are marked with an inverted circumflex accent (ˇ), and syllables bearing L tone are unmarked. No consonants are syllabic, hence no consonants bear surface tone. Vowel sequences constitute single syllables unless they are separated by a dot. Thus, [riá] represents a single syllable bearing H tone, [riǎ] represents a single syllable bearing rising tone, [ria] represents a single syllable bearing L tone, and [ri.á] represents two syllables bearing L and H tone, successively. These representations can be converted into narrow transcriptions by applying the following two rules in order: (i) copy an acute accent onto a preceding tautosyllabic vowel, and (ii) introduce a grave accent (`) over any vowel not bearing an accent. Thus: [riá] → [ríá] (by (i)); [ria] → [rìà] (by (ii)); [riǎ] → [rìǎ] (by (ii)); [ri.á] → [rì.á] (by (ii)). These rules are merely transcriptional, and do not designate any difference in realization from the broader system of transcription which will be used from now on.

We begin by examining tone assignment in nouns (section 2), and then proceed to the verb. Sections 3-5 develop an analysis of the most general of the rules applying to verb forms. While only a few tenses are specifically dealt with in these sections, the analysis presented here extends to all the verb forms falling within the scope of this study, as summarized in Appendix A.

The next sections examine the rules that determine the form of the underlying melody itself. These rules, which I term "melody composition rules", have the function both of inserting grammatical tones and of modifying the tone melodies constructed by earlier rules. Sections 6 and 7 review the main features of verbal morphology that are relevant to this study, and section 8 provides a closer examination of the intricate problem of floating tone suffixes.

In section 9 we formulate the rules that express the major redundancies in the tone melody. We find that underlying tone melodies need not be specified tense by tense, but are a function of the lexically-given form of each element and a small set of rules that modify them under certain grammatical conditions. Section 10 provides a summary.

## 2. TONE ASSIGNMENT IN NOUNS

We begin with an examination of tone assignment in the Kikuyu noun. Most Kikuyu nouns, like those of other Bantu languages, consist of a noun class prefix of the shape CV, V, or N, and a following stem of one or more syllables. Noun tones vary according to the context in which the noun occurs. The forms in (2) illustrate nouns formed from bisyllabic stems. In these nouns the initial CV sequence is the noun class prefix. The forms given in column A are those that appear sentence-finally after affirmative verb forms that do not induce H Tone Spread upon following words (see section 8.2), such as *ɲɔníré* 'I saw' (Current Past Completive). Those given in column B represent the tonal shape of these nouns as they appear in isolation, or after certain negative verb forms such as *ndinɔɔ́na* 'I didn't see'.

| (2) | tone class | | A | B | |
|---|---|---|---|---|---|
| | 1. | LL | kemore | kemore | 'torch' |
| | 2. | LH | moγatɛ̌ | moγatɛ | 'bread' |
| | 3. | HL | moγɛká | moγɛká | 'rug' |
| | 4. | HH | maγɔkɔ́ | maγɔkɔ | 'bark' |
| | 5. | LHL | kaɲamǒ | kaɲamǒ | 'small animal' |
| | 6. | HLHL | karání | karání | 'clerk' |

The large majority of Kikuyu nouns formed from bisyllabic stems fall into one of these six tone classes.[3]

It will be noticed first of all that the tone of the noun class prefix is L in all cases. This is easily explained on the assumption that noun class prefixes are underlyingly L-toned. If we set aside the last tone class for the time being, we notice that in all cases, the second syllable also bears L tone. This is explained on the assumption that the L tone of the prefix spreads one syllable to the right by the principle of tone shift (1). Thus tonal contrasts are restricted to the final syllable of these nouns, which bear one of three surface tones: H, L, and LH (rising). And yet, although there are only three contrasting tonal patterns in these five words, nevertheless five distinct classes must be recognized, since we find five distinct patterns of alternation.

Suppose we consider the hypothesis that the underlying tone melodies characterizing each of these tone classes consists of the L tone of the prefix plus the tone melody indicated at the left in (2). Thus the full tone melody for a noun of tone class 1 is LLL, that for tone class 2 is LLH, and so forth. Under this assumption, the surface tones given in column A are readily accounted for. We may assume that tone shift applies regularly in nouns, assigning the first tone to the second syllable, and that subsequently the association conventions map tones onto the remaining syllables in the following way:[4]

(3) Association Conventions

a. Associate free tones with free tone-bearing units from left to right until no free tones or tone-bearing units remain.

b. Associate any remaining free tone-bearing unit with the nearest accessible tone.

By convention (3a) the second tone of the melody (that is, the first tone of the noun stem) is associated with the third syllable. By convention (3b) the first tone is associated with the first syllable. These principles give us the following derivations for tone classes 1, 3, and 4:

(4)

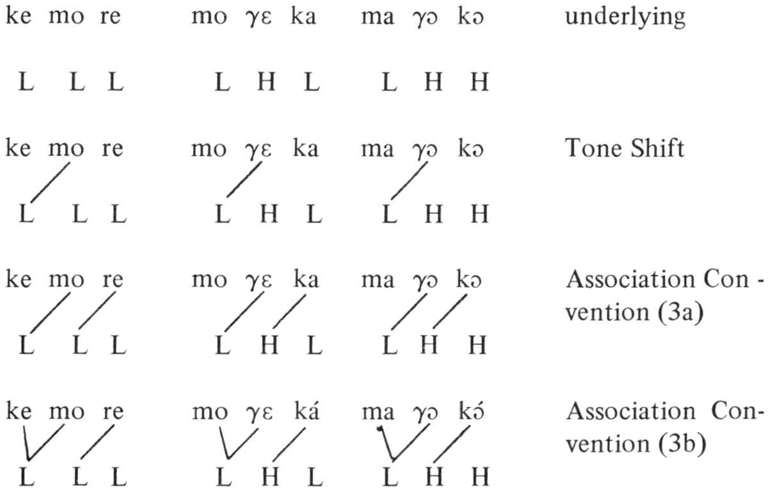

In order to account for tone classes 2 and 5, in which we find a rising tone on the final syllable, it will be necessary to assume an additional rule which associates a floating H tone with the preceding syllable, if it bears L tone. This rule is stated below (σ = syllable):

(5) H Tone Association

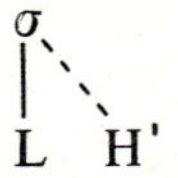


Here and elsewhere the prime (') is used in the statement of tone rules to indicate floating tones. Thus, rule (5) applies uniquely to floating H tones. We now have the following derivations of tone classes 2 and 5.

(6)

| | | |
|---|---|---|
| mo γa tε<br>L L H | ka ɲa mo<br>L L H L | underlying |
| mo γa tε<br>L L H | ka ɲa mo<br>L L H L | Tone Shift, Association Conventions |
| mo γa tε̌<br>L L H | ka ɲa mǒ<br>L L H L | H Tone Association |

We shall return to the analysis of tone class 6 shortly.

While these rules and principles account correctly for the tonal shapes of nouns in column A, it will be remarked that they have done so only at the cost of generating floating tones at the end of words. This can be regarded as a harmless consequence of the analysis, assuming that floating tones are, by general convention, unpronounced; but what is the evidence for including these apparently superfluous tones in underlying tone melodies in the first place?

First, it will be recalled that although only three distinct surface patterns occur in contexts A and B, five tone classes must be recognized since there are five distinct patterns of alternation. The present analysis accounts for this five-way distinction by making maximal use of the combinatory possibilities available in a system with just two tones, H and L. Thus the first four tone classes represent all possible ordered pairs formed from the set {H, L}; to obtain the fifth it is of course necessary to introduce a three member melody. This analysis accounts for the five-way contrast using strictly phonological means.

There is, nevertheless, a simpler alternative available that would give us the same result. Suppose we replaced the geminate tone melodies HH and LL with the single-member melodies H and L. We would still be able to generate the correct surface patterns in these two classes, while not generating the apparently superfluous floating tones (they would still be needed, of course, to distinguish classes 2, 3, and 5). This alternative would, in fact, be imposed by theories of tone incorporating what has been called the Obligatory Contour Principle, which disallows geminate tone sequences characterizing single morphemes (Leben 1978). For the present, we have little reason to decide between these alternatives, so let us suspend judgment until we have evidence that can discriminate between them.

A source of evidence for an analysis which generates floating L tones at the ends of nouns belonging to tone classes 1, 3, and 5 comes from a consideration of the column B forms. We have so far not raised the question of how these are to be accounted for. But we now see that, given the tone melodies proposed for each tone class in (2) (or the somewhat simpler set of melodies assumed in the alternative just discussed), we can predict the column B forms by a very simple principle: lower a H tone (or a H tone sequence) occurring in absolute final position.[5] This rule will apply to tone classes 2 and 4, in which a H tone occurs finally in the melody, but it will not apply in any of the other classes. This rule may be stated as the rule of Flattening, given below:

(7) Flattening

$$H_Q \rightarrow L \;/\; \underline{\quad}\,]_S$$

The subscript Q is used to indicate that the rule applies to each member of a H tone sequence occurring in the stated context. Thus it will lower both the single H tone occurring at the end of *moɣatɛ̌*, 'bread' (tone class 2) and the pair of H tones occurring at the end of *maɣɔ́kɔ́* 'bark' (tone class 4). (It might be supposed that the subscript Q notation could be eliminated if the second alternative is accepted, according to which the underlying stem melody for class 4 is H. It is independently necessary, however, to account for the application of Flattening to words with sequences of word-final H-toned syllables, such as *moanákɛ́* 'young man' or *keriríkániá* 'reminder', which acquire L tones throughout in the B contexts, as well as for its application to word-final H tone sequences in verbs where each H tone in the sequence can be shown to characterize a separate formative; see section 8 for further discussion of the operation of Flattening in verbs).

A third source of justification for the floating tones generated by the analysis given above comes from the tonal realization of words in sequences. Whenever a noun of tone classes 1, 3, or 5 occurs non-finally with no following modifiers, it introduces downstep on any following words in the sentence. Nouns of tone classes 2 and 4 do not have this effect. This phenomenon may be illustrated by proper nouns drawn from each of the tone classes 1-5. In (8), the first two columns exhibit the tonal shape exhibited by these nouns in contexts A and B, as before; these columns establish their tone class membership. In the third column these nouns are placed in a sentential context where their downstep-inducing behavior is exhibited. Each sentence may be glossed 'buy X a good rug', where *γorera* is the singular imperative of - *γorer* - 'buy for', and *moεγa* 'good' is the postnominal modifier of *moγεka* 'rug'. (For the further tonal alternations illustrated in these examples, including the rightward displacement of the downstep following the nouns of tone classes 3 and 5, see Clements and Ford (1981)).

(8)

| tone class | | A | B | | | |
|---|---|---|---|---|---|---|
| 1. | LL | moremi | moremi | γorerá moremi | ! moγεká | moεγa |
| 2. | LH | ngoγě | ngoγe | γorerá ngoγe | móγεká | moεγa |
| 3. | HL | kama.ú | kama.ú | γorerá kama.u | móγέ!ká | moεγa |
| 4. | HH | wamboγó | wamboγo | γorerá wamboγó | móγε ká | moεγa |
| 5. | LHL | kariokǐ | kariokǐ | γorerá karioki | móγέ!ká | moεγa |

It will be seen that a downstep appears to the right of the target noun in classes 1, 3, and 5, but not in tone classes 2 and 4. The appearance of this downstep correlates with nouns whose tone melodies end in a floating L tone after the operation of tone shift and the Association Conventions; that is, with the exact complement of the class of nouns which undergo Flattening in context B. If we assume that floating L tones are interpreted as downstep operators by the intonational rules, this correlation of facts is fully accounted for.[6]

To summarize the discussion so far, we have seen good evidence in favor of an analysis which generates floating L tones at the end of nouns of tone classes 1, 3, and 5. In particular, the downstep data given in (8) show that the alternative analysis briefly considered above, which replaced geminate tone melodies with single-tone melodies, is unable to account for the appearance of downstep at the end of nouns of tone class 1, since under this hypothesis no floating tones would be generated there. We will therefore adopt the analysis which permits sequences of geminate tones in the lexical entries of noun stems. Under this analysis, the four reconstructed tone classes of Proto-Bantu nouns (LL, LH, HL, HH) are retained at the level of underlying representations in Kikuyu, where they occur along with two others (LHL, HLHL) which are apparently Kikuyu innovations.

We see, then, that in spite of the striking surface effects of tone shift, Kikuyu nouns retain most of the basic structural features of the ancestral system at the level of underlying representation. The evidence from nouns shows that Kikuyu is a true "lexical tone language" in the sense of Pike (1948), and that underlying representations contain L tones as well as H tones, in contrast to some Bantu tonal systems that have apparently lost this underlying distinction (see the contributions to this volume by Kisseberth and by Hyman and Byarushengo).

We have not yet considered the analysis of nouns of tone class 6. Before doing so, let us consider the tonal behavior of nouns whose first stem syllable contains a long vowel. Representative nouns are given in (9).

| (9) | tone class | | A | B | |
|---|---|---|---|---|---|
| | 1. | LL | keβaata | keβaata | 'type of dance' |
| | 2. | LH | keroomǐ | keroomi | 'cheetah' |
| | 3. | HL | moraatá | moraatá | 'friend' |
| | 4. | HH | moðeeγí | moðeeγi | 'elder's staff' |
| | 5. | LHL | kariokǐ | kariokǐ | (man's name) |
| | 6. | HLHL | matoórǎ | matoórǎ | 'villages' |

As these forms show, nouns formed from bisyllabic stems of the shape CVVCV fall into the same six tone classes as do nouns with short initial stem syllables. The tone patterns displayed in (9) are identical to those given in (2) except that in class 6 we find a rising tone on the final syllable instead of a H tone. Setting the latter forms aside for a moment, we can account for the remaining forms by assuming that syllable weight plays no role in tone assignment in Kikuyu nouns. This follows with no further qualification from the analysis given earlier, in which the tone-bearing unit with respect to Tone Shift (1) and the Association Conventions (3) was taken to be the syllable; the rules and principles of initial tone association assign tones to syllables without regard to their weight.[7]

Now let us consider the analysis of tone class 6. Examining the last row of forms in (9) above, we see that the underlying stem tone melody for this class must be HLHL. The first three tones of this melody are justified by the fact that they appear overtly in both contexts A and B. The final L tone is justified by the fact that these nouns do not undergo Flattening. (It can also be shown that these nouns induce downsteps on following words.) What is curious about these nouns is that their tone melody cannot be assigned by the rules of association given so far. These rules would assign the first H tone of the melody to the final syllable, leaving all remaining tones afloat; their surface realization would then be identical to nouns of tone class 3:

(10)

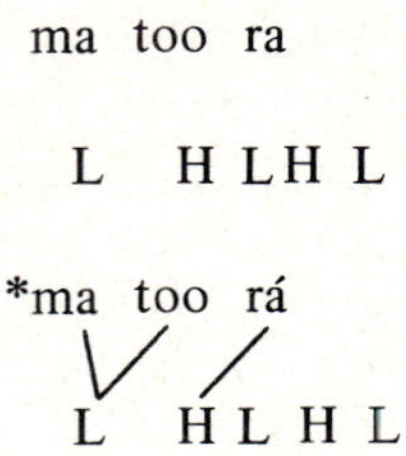


underlying

Tone Shift, Association Conventions

Note also that H Tone Association (5) cannot apply since its structural description is not satisfied.

In order to account for tone assignment in nouns of this class, it will be assumed that the final H tone of the melody is lexically associated with the final syllable. Thus, the underlying representation of *karani* (see (2) ) and *matoora* will be as follows:

(11)

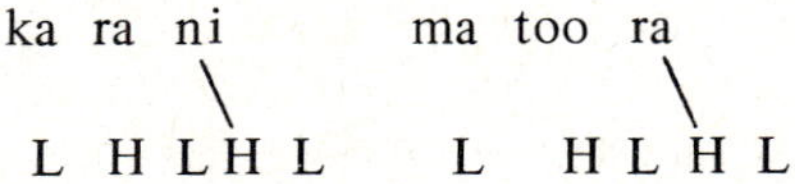


Tone Shift and the Association Conventions then apply in the usual way. Note that the first H tone of the melody cannot be associated with the last syllable, since it is already associated with a tone, and is thus not subject to Association Convention (3a):

(12)

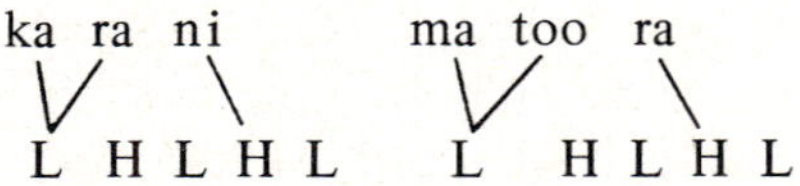


H Tone Association (5), however, is defined upon the representations in (12), and thus applies as follows:

(13)

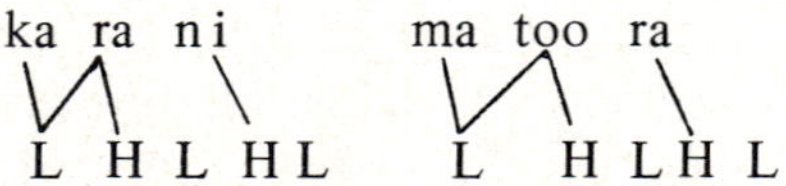


This creates a representation with a rising tone on the penultimate syllable. This rising tone is subject to a rule of simplification which is described and motivated in Clements and Ford (1981, 345-6). By this rule, a rising tone simplifies to H before the sequences ꜜH or L, and to L nonfinally elsewhere:

(14) Rising Tone Simplification

a.

b.

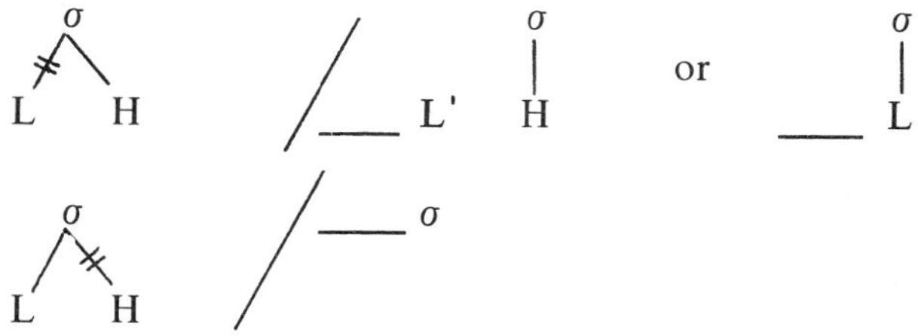


(the double stroke through an association line is an instruction to delete it). Note that rule (14a) is defined on the forms in (13), and applies to yield the following:

(15)

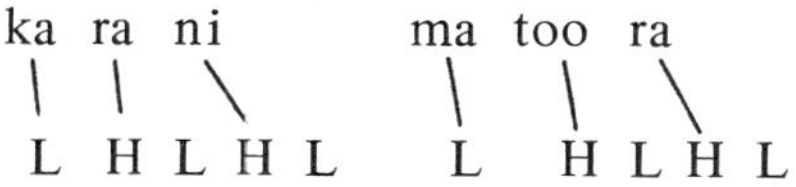


We have now derived one of the surface alternants of *karani*, namely the alternant that appears before a L-tone-initial modifier, where we find a downstep between the two H tones of the final syllables (see Armstrong 1967, 255 for examples). In other contexts the (medial) L tone either associates to the final syllable, replacing the H tone (Armstrong, 255-6), or is deleted, as in contexts A and B illustrated in (2); as these rules are of little generality we will not state them here. The surface form of *matoora* is derived by associating the (medial) floating L tone with the final syllable; this rule, applying only in the context following long vowels, explains the complementary distribution between class 6 forms with final rising tones (which always have a long vowel in the penultimate syllable) and those with final H tones (which always have penultimate short vowels).[8]

## 3. TONE ASSIGNMENT IN VERBS

The process of tone shift is even more strikingly illustrated in verbs, to which we now turn. As in other Bantu languages, the Kikuyu verb has a highly agglutinative structure involving both prefixes and suffixes. The following schema illustrates the maximal expansion of the finite verb; only the subject prefix, root, and final vowel are obligatory members of this schema:[9]

(16) finite verb → (*ne*) SP (*ti*) (T) (D) (OP) (*e*) root (X*) FV

Thus, the finite verb consists of a selection of the following constituents: the focus particle *ne*, the subject prefix (SP), the negative formative *ti*, one or two tense prefixes (T), a directive prefix (D), an object prefix (OP), the reflexive prefix *e*, the simple verbal radical or root, one or more stem extensions (X), and a final vowel (FV). Only one object prefix is possible. It precedes the reflexive prefix *e*, except for the first person singular object prefix which follows it. Stem extensions are of three types: semantically empty suffixes or root expansions which may be considered part of the extended radical itself, grammatical suffixes associated with such general meanings as 'causative', 'reciprocal', and 'passive', and suffixes of the tense/aspect system, which together with the tense prefix determine the tense/aspect category of any verb. Tense/aspect suffixes follow all others except for the imperfect suffix *-aγ-*, which precedes certain suffixes of the second category. The final vowel, which plays a significant role in the tonal system, consists of the single vowel *-a* or *-ɛ*. The root together with all suffixes will be referred to here as the *verbal stem.*

Tone shift as it affects verbs can be illustrated by forms drawn from the Current Habitual (CH) and Current Past Completive (CPC) tenses, given in (17) and (18) below.

(17) Current Habitual (CH)

L tone root: -rɔr- 'look at'

| | | | |
|---|---|---|---|
| to rɔr aγ a | 'we look at' | má rɔ́r aγ a | 'they look at' |
| to mo rɔr aγ a | 'we look at him/her' | má mó rɔr aγ a | 'they look at him/her' |
| to ma rɔ́r aγ a | 'we look at them' | má má rɔ̂r aγ a | 'they look at them' |

H tone root: -tom- 'send'

| | | | |
|---|---|---|---|
| to tom áγ a | 'we send' | má tóm áγ a | 'they send' |
| to mo tom áγ a | 'we send him/her' | má mó tom áγ a | 'they send him/her' |
| to ma tóm áγ a | 'we send them' | má má tóm áγ a | 'they send them' |

In these examples, as in those in (18), *to-* is the subject prefix 'we' and *ma-* is the subject prefix 'they'. The first row of forms in each set contains no object prefix. The suffix *-aγ-* is the habitual suffix, and *-a* is the final vowel. The forms in the second row contain the object prefix *mo-* 'him/her', and the forms in the third row contain the object prefix *ma-* 'them'. (Here and below spaces will be used to separate formatives. However, these divisions will not always correspond to syllable divisions; in particular, an intervocalic consonant is always syllabified with the vowel to its right at the surface level. Thus, the syllabification of the first form is *to-rɔ-ra-γa*.)

(18) Current Past Completive (CPC)

L tone root: -rɔr- 'look at'

| | | | |
|---|---|---|---|
| to rɔr ir ɛ́ | 'we looked at' | má rɔ́r ir ɛ́ | 'they looked at' |
| to mo rɔr ir ɛ́ | 'we looked at him/her' | má mó rɔr ir ɛ́ | 'they looked at him/her' |
| to ma rɔ́r ir ɛ́ | 'we looked at them' | má má rɔ́r ir ɛ́ | 'they looked at them' |

H tone root: -tom- 'send'

| | | | |
|---|---|---|---|
| to tom ír ɛ́ | 'we sent' | má tóm ír ɛ́ | 'they sent' |
| to mo tom ír ɛ́ | 'we sent him/her' | má mó tom ír ɛ́ | 'they sent him/her' |
| to ma tóm ír ɛ́ | 'we sent them' | má má tóm ír ɛ́ | 'they sent them' |

These forms are arranged in the same way as those in (17). Note that the tense/aspect suffix here is *-ir-*, and the final vowel is *-ɛ-*

If we examine the tones in the forms in (17) and (18) we see that only the first and last formatives maintain a fixed tone throughout each paradigm. The other formatives show a pattern of tone alternation which correlates with the identity of the formative to their immediate left. Thus, all formatives are H after the formatives *-tom-*, *ma-*, and *-ir-*, and all formatives are L after the formatives *to-*, *mo-*, *-rɔr-*, and *-aγ-*. This suggests that we attribute underlying H tone to the first of these sets, and underlying L tone to the second; the principle of tone shift will then account for all forms. To confirm this, all we need to do is to "undo" the effect of Tone Shift by copying each tone one formative leftward, as shown in (19) and (20). Each formative is now seen to have a single invariant tonal shape, which (in the case of the prefixes and roots) corresponds to the tones reconstructed for these formatives in Proto-Bantu.[10]

(19) Current Habitual (prior to tone shift)

| | | | |
|---|---|---|---|
| to rɔr aγ a | má rɔr aγ a | to tóm aγ a | má tóm aγ a |
| to mo rɔr aγ a | má mo rɔr aγ a | to mo tóm aγ a | má mo tóm aγ a |
| to má rɔr aγ a | má má rɔr aγ a | to má tóm aγ a | má má tóm aγ a |

(20) Current Past Completive (prior to tone shift)

| | | | |
|---|---|---|---|
| to rɔr ír ɛ́ | má rɔr ír ɛ́ | to tóm ír ɛ́ | má tóm ír ɛ́ |
| to mo rɔr ír ɛ́ | má mo rɔr ír ɛ́ | to mo tóm ír ɛ́ | má mo tóm ír ɛ́ |
| to má rɔr ír ɛ́ | má má rɔr ír ɛ́ | to má tóm ír ɛ́ | má má tóm ír ɛ́ |

One feature of the underlying forms given in (19) and (20) deserves comment. It will be noticed that the aspect suffixes, *-aγ-* and *-ir-*, bear the same tone as the final vowel. In fact, it is a regular property of Kikuyu verbs that aspect suffixes never contribute a distinctive tone of their own to the underlying tone melody. This fact may be accounted for by assuming that these formatives are underlyingly toneless. If we then postulate that the final vowel *-a-* of the Current Habitual is characterized by lexical L tone, and the final vowel *-ɛ* of the Current Past Completive by lexical H tone, we may account for all surface tones by the principle of tone shift (1). The following derivations of *mámótomáγa* 'they send him/her' and *tomarɔ́rirɛ́* 'we looked at them' illustrate:

(21)
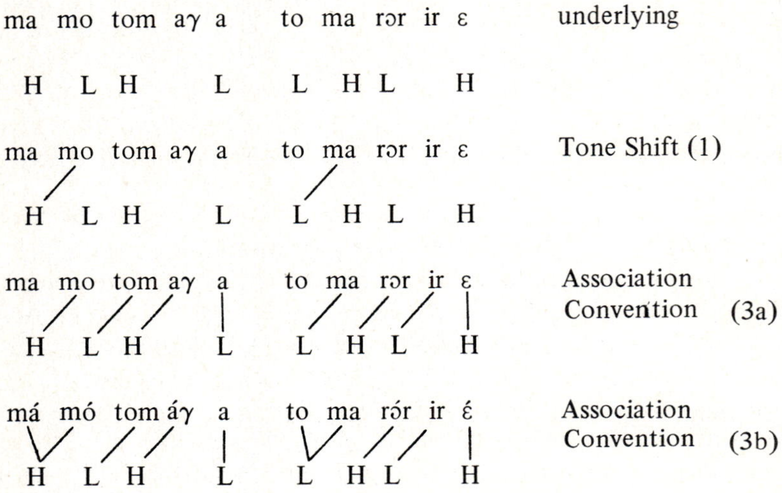


This derivation is perfectly analogous to that given in (4). Notice in particular that Association Convention (3a) pairs off unassociated tones with unassociated syllables from left to right, in a one-to-one fashion, thus assigning the tone of the root to the suffix syllable and the tone of the final vowel to the final vowel itself.

This analysis provides strong independent support for the principle of tone shift, initially postulated to account for nouns alone. In the subsequent discussion we will see that this principle holds throughout the system of verbal inflection, although in many cases it interacts with other rules that make its operation less transparent on the surface.

We have so far only examined tenses in which the tense prefix is absent. Tense prefixes are of the shape CV or V. Prefixes of the latter type present an apparent problem for the view that the tone-bearing unit is the syllable. Consider the forms below, which represent the Immediate Perfect (IP).

(22) Immediate Perfect (IP)

| | | | |
|---|---|---|---|
| to a rɔ́r a | ma á rɔ́r a | to a tóm á | ma á tom á |
| to a mó rɔr a | ma á mó rɔr a | to a mó tom á | ma á mó tom á |
| to a má rɔ́r a | ma á ma rɔ́r a | to a má tóm á | ma á ma tóm á |

The format here is the same as in our earlier examples, except that glosses have been omitted. It will be recalled that vowel sequences in all cases form single surface syllables, which bear the tone written over the second vowel. Thus, for example, *maátomá* consists of three syllables bearing H, L, and H tone respectively.

The H tone found on *-rɔr-, mo-*, and *ma-* in the first column of forms suggests that the underlying tone of the tense prefix *-a-* is H. The underlying tone of the subject prefix *to-*, on the other hand, must be L, since that is the tone it bears on the surface. However, given the principles assumed so far, we would expect the L tone of the subject prefix to be associated with the second syllable: that is with the three formatives *-rɔr-, mo-*, and *ma-* that in fact bear H tone. Apparently, then, this L tone does not spread as expected. How can we account for this seeming idiosyncracy?

The solution to the puzzle lies in the assumption that the initial domain of syllabification is not the word, but the formative, and that moreover, it is at this level of the derivation that Tone Shift and the Association Conventions apply. Surface syllables are formed by a subsequent rule that fuses vowel sequences into single syllables. We will formulate the rule of Syllable Fusion as follows:

(23) Syllable Fusion

This rule deletes the second of two successive syllable nodes if the second syllable is vowel-initial. This vowel then reassociates (together with any floating tones that result from the deletion of the syllable) to the first syllable node. (The reassociations may in fact be the consequence of a general convention on autosegmental representation, according to which segments "set afloat" by the operation of a rule affecting another tier reassociate to the syllable that conditioned the deletion, that is, to the syllable that appears as the left or right context of the rule in question; see Clements and Ford (1979, 207)).

Given this rule, we have the following derivations of the forms in the first column of (22):[11]

(24)

| to a rɔr a | to a mo rɔr a | to a ma rɔr a | underlying |
|---|---|---|---|
| L H L L | L H L L L | L H H L L | |
| to a rɔr a | to a mo rɔr a | to a ma rɔr a | Tone Shift, AC's |
| \|/ / / | \|/ / / / | \|/ / / / | |
| L H L L | L H L L L | L H H L L | |

```
toa  rɔ́r   a      toa  mó   rɔr   a      toa  má  rɔ́r    a     Syllable
 |    |   /        |    /    |   /         |    |    |    /      Fusion
 L H L L           L H    L  L  L          L H   H   L   L
```

The rule of Syllable Fusion illustrated here is not restricted to certain verb forms alone, but applies obligatorily across morpheme boundaries within the word, and optionally across word boundaries, where it also has important consequences for tonal realization; see Armstrong, chapter 1 and Clements and Ford (1979, 193-5) for further examples and discussion.

Notice that our analysis in (24) has generated Floating L tones at the end of each verb form. We will see independent justification for these floating tones in the later discussion.

To complete our account of (22), we must account for the fact that the first formative following the tense prefix *-a-* bears L tone instead of the expected H just in case the tones to its immediate left and right are both H; see *maámarɔ́ra, maátomá*, and *maámatómá*. Under our present analysis, this indicates that *-a-* bears underlying L tone in this environment. We may account for this fact by postulating a lexical rule which lowers the prefix tone when flanked by H tones. Although this rule applies in no other tense, it need not be specifically restricted to the Immediate Perfect since no other tense prefixes happen to satisfy its structural description.

(25) Tense Prefix Lowering

$$H \rightarrow L \;/\; H + \begin{bmatrix} \underline{\qquad} \\ \text{+tense} \\ \text{prefix} \end{bmatrix} + \; H$$

We will see a full derivation involving this rule in (37), below. It does not appear to be crucially ordered with respect to the other rules discussed so far.

We have so far assumed that verbal extensions, including tense/aspect suffixes, are underlyingly toneless, while the final vowel bears a contrastive underlying tone of its own. We have not, however, seen any evidence directly confirming these assumptions; as far as the examples considered so far are concerned, we might just as well have assumed that the final vowel is toneless, and verbal extensions bear contrastive underlying tone. Both analyses would account equally well for the forms in (17), (18), and (22). We turn to relevant evidence now.

As noted earlier, longer verbal stems may be created from shorter ones by adding stem extensions of various sorts. Under the hypothesis that such extensions are toneless, they should acquire their tones through the principles of tone assignment given so far. Thus, the first extension in a series should be assigned the tone of the root, and the second and all subsequent extensions should be assigned the tone of the final vowel:

(26)

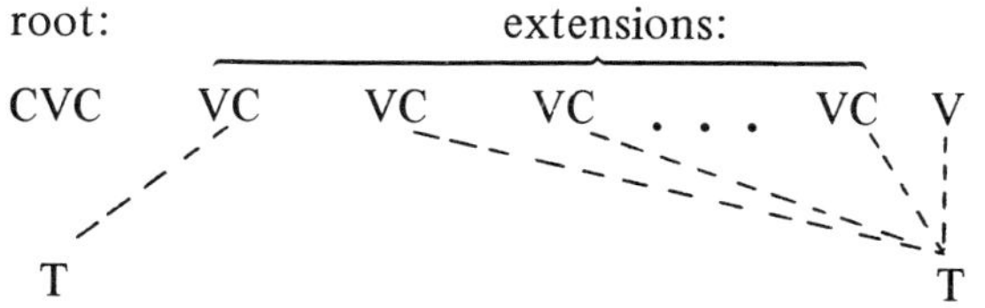


This is exactly the pattern that we find. Examples of longer stems are given in (27) – (29) for each of the three tenses examined so far, with shorter stems repeated at the beginning of each set for comparison.[12]

(27) Current Habitual (CH)

| | | |
|---|---|---|
| L stems: | torɔraγa | 'we look at' |
| | totɛŋɛraγa | 'we run' |
| | toγaraγaraγia | 'we roll' |
| H stems: | totomáγa | 'we send' |
| | tohetókaγa | 'we go past' |
| | toriríkanaγa | 'we remember' |

(28) Current Past Completive (CPC)

| | | |
|---|---|---|
| L stems: | torɔrirɛ́ | 'we looked at' |
| | totɛŋɛrírɛ́ | 'we ran' |
| | toγaraγáririɛ́ | 'we rolled' |
| H stems: | totomírɛ́ | 'we sent' |
| | tohetókírɛ́ | 'we went past' |
| | toriríkánírɛ́ | 'we remembered' |

(29) Immediate Perfect (IP)

| | | |
|---|---|---|
| L stems: | toarɔ́ra | 'we have just looked at' |
| | toatɛ́ŋɛra | 'we have just run' |
| | toaγáraγariɛ | 'we have just rolled' |
| H stems: | toatómá | 'we have just sent' |
| | toahétóka | 'we have just gone past' |
| | toaríríkana | 'we have just remembered' |

We see that in all cases, the second syllable of the stem (the first extension suffix) bears the tone of the verb root, while subsequent syllables bear the tone of the final vowel: L in (27) and (29), H in (28). This is in accordance with (26). It can be seen that the longer stems of (29) provide the crucial evidence for the identity of the final vowel tone in the Immediate Perfect; here the L tone characterizing this vowel in underlying representation only appears overtly when the stem has three or more syllables, as in the final two examples. The derivation of *toarírikana* is given below:

```
(30)  to  a   rir   i k  an  a          underlying

       L  H    H           L

      to   a   rir   i k  an  a         Tone Shift, Association Convention
      \/  /    /          \/
      H   H    H           L

      toa   rír     ík  an  a           Syllable Fusion
       /     /      /    \/
      L     H      H     L
```

4. THE STABLE SUFFIX

We have so far examined verb forms in which the final vowel is characterized by a single tone, L or H. This tone is assigned to tone-bearing units by the regular principles of tone assignment applying to both verbs and nouns.

In contrast to the tense forms examined up to now, some tense forms are characterized by a tonal "appendix" of the shape LH, which is added to the right of the full tone melody. In such forms, the L tone of the "appendix" is always associated with the final vowel, no matter how long the verbal stem may be. The H tone associates with the final vowel by H Tone Association (5), yielding a rising tone. The *ne*-form of the Current Past Completive will illustrate.

(31) Current Past Completive (*ne*-form)

| | | |
|---|---|---|
| L stems: | némárɔ́r'írɛ̌ | 'they looked at' |
| | nématɛ́ŋɛrírɛ̌ | 'they ran' |
| | némáɣáraɣárírìɛ̌ | 'they rolled' |
| | némákúmuðákúmú'ðírɛ̌ | 'they scrubbed a little more' |
| H stems: | némátómírɛ̌ | 'they sent' |
| | némáhétókírɛ̌ | 'they went past' |
| | némárírikánírɛ̌ | 'they remembered' |
| | némáhétókáhétókeírɛ̌ | 'they passed by several times' |

We return in just a moment to a discussion of the downstep in the form *némárɔ́r'írɛ̌*. We see that in these forms, all syllables after the second stem syllable bear H tone except for the last, which bears LH (rising) tone. This can be explained on the assumption that this tense form is characterized by the tonal "appendix" just mentioned. If we suppose that the L tone of this appendix is associated prior to the operation of the general rules of tone assignment, then we have derivations like the following:

(32)

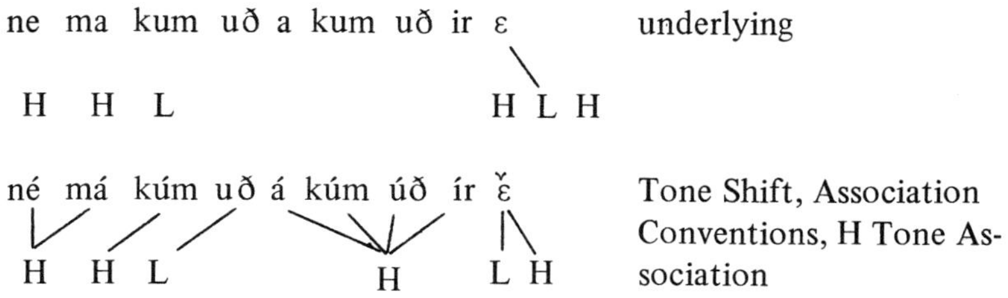


Since the LH "appendix" always falls on the final vowel, regardless of the inherent tone of this vowel, I will refer to this tone sequence as the *stable suffix*. The stable suffix is always added to the right of the stem melody, and thus occurs to the right of the tone of the final vowel; this latter tone can be called the *mobile suffix*, due to its property of associating leftward to toneless suffixes.

Similar derivations account for all forms but the first, which contains an internal downstep. The derivation of this form proceeds much as in (32), except that after the operation of the Association Conventions, there are two applications of H Tone Association:

(33)

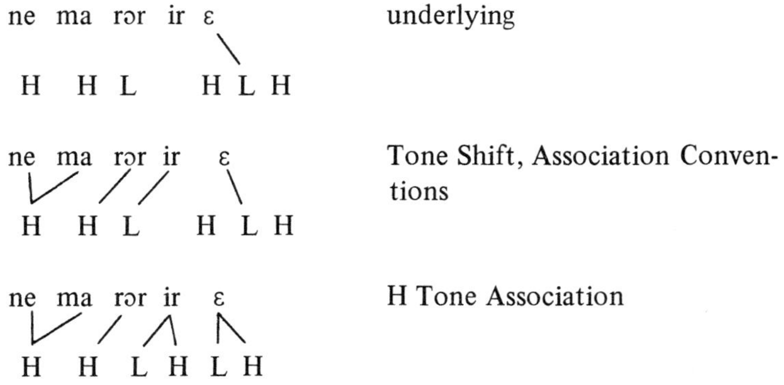


At this point we have produced a form with an incorrect rising tone on the penultimate syllable. This is subject to the rule of Rising Tone Simplification (14), which will delete the association between the L of the first LH sequence and the syllable to which it is linked. This rule gives the following result:

(34) né má rɔ́r! ír ɛ̌ — Rising Tone Simplification

H H L H L H

We see, then, that the occurrence of downstep in this form is predicted by the regular operation of the rules and principles given so far.

We may select examples from the *ne*-form of the Current Habitual to illustrate the tone sequence formed by the concatenation of the L mobile suffix and the LH stable suffix.

(35) Current Habitual: *ne*-form

| | | |
|---|---|---|
| L stems: | némárɔ́raγǎ | 'they look at' |
| | némátɛ́ŋɛraγǎ | 'they run' |
| | némáγáraγaraγiǎ | 'they roll' |
| H stems: | némátómáγǎ | 'they send' |
| | némáhétókaγǎ | 'they go past' |
| | némáríríkanaγǎ | 'they remember' |

We see that these forms pattern exactly like those in (31), except that here we find L tones in place of the H tones that represented the "mobile" tonal suffix in (31). Here, then, the "mobile" suffix is L. We may confirm this analysis by observing that the mobile tonal suffix which occurs before a stable tonal suffix is generally identical to the mobile tonal suffix in the related tense forms that lack the stable tonal suffix. Thus, we have already seen that the mobile tonal suffix of the Current Past Completive is H both in the simple (*ne*-less) form (18) and in the *ne*-form, which has the stable suffix (31). Similarly, the mobile suffix in the Current Habitual is L, regardless of whether the stable suffix is present or not (compare (17) and (35)). Although there are exceptions to which we will turn below, it is generally the case that the mobile tone remains constant throughout all the forms of a given tense, whether the stable suffix is present or not. Further confirmation comes from the *ne*-form of the Immediate Perfect. We have already seen that the mobile suffix in the simple (*ne*-less) form of this tense is L; the same is true of the *ne*-form, as is confirmed by the final member of each of the following sets:

(36) Immediate Perfect: *ne*-form

| | | |
|---|---|---|
| L stems: | némaárɔ́rǎ | 'they have just looked at' |
| | némaátɛ́ŋɛrǎ | 'they have just run' |
| | némaáγáraγariɛ̌ | 'they have just rolled' |
| H stems: | némaá!tómǎ | 'they have just sent' |
| | némaáhetókǎ | 'they have just gone past' |
| | némaárirííkanǎ | 'they have just remembered' |

Once again, the downstep appearing in *némaá!tómǎ* is predicted by our analysis. Parallel derivations of this form and *némaáhetókǎ* are given below.

(37)

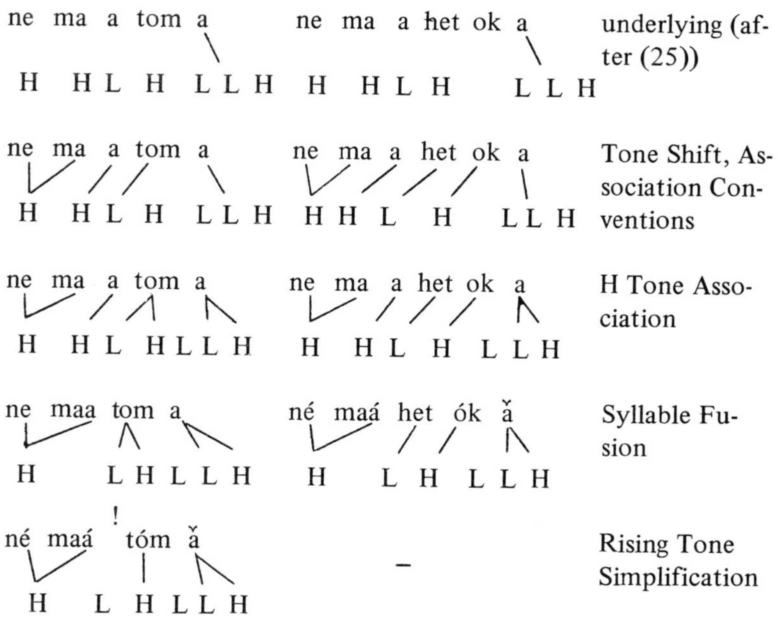


Notice that the application of Syllable Fusion to the third line of this derivation will cause the second H tone to reassociate to the preceding syllable; the next line assumes that whenever two identical tones come to be associated to the same tone-bearing unit, they degeminate to a single tone. Nothing of importance hangs on this convention, however. Of more importance is the set of floating L tones generated by this derivation. While this and other derivations generate floating L tones quite freely, only floating L tones flanked on both sides by H tones are ever interpreted word-internally as downsteps. We shall formalize this constraint in terms of a downstep interpretation rule in the later discussion (section 8.2); for the moment, it is sufficient to note that the output of (37) correctly predicts the surface realization of these forms. It should be noted in particular that the downstep in *némaá!tómǎ* is derived in the same way as the downstep in the earlier example *némárɔ́r!írɛ̌*, even though its source is different: in the previous case it arose from the lexical L tone of the root *-rɔr-*, while in the present case it arises from the derived L tone of the tense prefix *-a-*. The derivations in (33-4) and (37) thus offer a particularly convincing source of confirmation for the principles of tone association proposed up to this point.

## 5. TONE ASSIGNMENT AND SYLLABLE WEIGHT

We have now examined tone assignment in verbs with simple radicals of the shape CVC (*-rɔr-*, *-tom-*) or with extended radicals of the shape CVCVC (*-tɛŋɛr-*, *-hetok-*) or CVCVCVC (*-γaraγar-*, *-ririkan-*). As we have seen, the verbal stem as a whole contains just two underlying tones (or, in tense forms with the stable suffix, four) no matter what the length of the stem. These tones are regularly mapped onto stem syllables by the principles given in the last two sections.

Let us now consider tone assignment in verbs whose initial radical syllable is heavy, that is of the form CVVC. Unlike in nouns, where syllable weight played only a marginal role in tone assignment, we find that verbs show an apparent irregularity in certain tense forms if they contain a L-toned root of the form CVVC. The following paradigm of forms from two of the tenses seen earlier will illustrate.

(38) Current Habitual (CH)

a. L tone root: -ɲiit- 'take hold'

| | |
|---|---|
| to ɲiit aγa | má ɲiít aγa |
| to mo ɲiit aγa | má mó ɲiit aγa |
| to ma ɲiít aγa | má má ɲiít aγa |

b. H tone root: -haat- 'sweep'

| | |
|---|---|
| to haat áγa | má haát áγa |
| to mo haat áγa | má mó haat áγa |
| to ma haát áγa | má má haát áγa |

(39) Current Past Completive (CPC)

a. L tone root: -ɲiit- 'take hold'

| | |
|---|---|
| to ɲiit ˊírɛ́ | má ɲiit írɛ́ |
| to mo ɲiit írɛ́ | má mó ɲiit ˊírɛ́ |
| to má ɲiit írɛ́ | má má ɲiit írɛ́ |

b. H tone root: -haat- 'sweep'

| | |
|---|---|
| to haat írɛ́ | má haát írɛ́ |
| to mo haat írɛ́ | má mó haat írɛ́ |
| to ma haát írɛ́ | má má haát írɛ́ |

Of interest are the forms in (39a). Under the principles given earlier, we would have expected the lexical L tone of the root to shift to the first syllable of the suffix, but this syllable bears the H tone of the "mobile" suffix. Moreover, we would have expected the H tone of the prefix *ma-* to shift to the root, but this retains its lexical L tone in all cases. A final anomaly in this paradigm is that the L tone of the prefix *to-* fails to spread to the prefix *ma-* in the third example. In fact, the only evidence that

Tone Shift is operative here at all consists in the form *mámóɲiitírɛ́*, where the H tone of the prefix *ma-* has shifted onto the prefix *mo-*. Notice that these irregularities are local to the paradigm in (39a); all other paradigms are regular.

On the evidence of these forms, it might at first be supposed that verb roots like *-ɲiit-* consist not of one, but of two tone-bearing units. This assumption would allow derivations like the following, for *mámóɲiitírɛ́*:

(40)

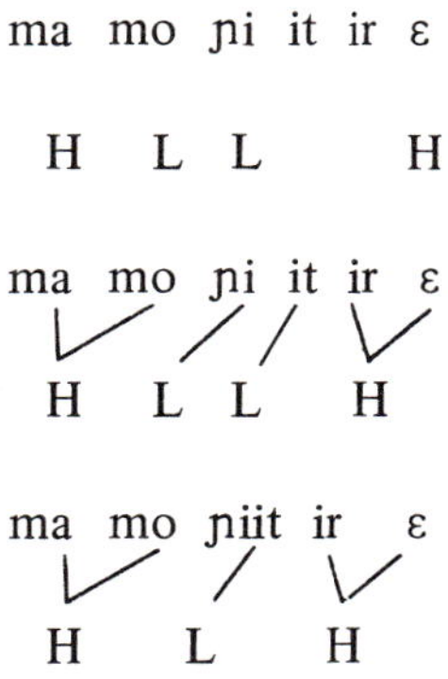


underlying

Tone Shift, Association Conventions

Syllable Fusion

An analogous derivation could be given for *máɲiitírɛ́* and *mámáɲiitírɛ́*, if we assume, in addition, that the falling tone created on the root syllable by Syllable Fusion is simplified to L by a further rule. One problem with this approach is that it does not account in any obvious way for the form *tomáɲiitírɛ́*, where we expect the H tone of *ma-* to shift to the root. An otherwise unmotivated rule would be needed to account for the failure of Tone Shift here.

However, a more serious objection to this approach involves the fact that long syllables within single roots cannot generally be treated as two tone-bearing units in Kikuyu. We have already seen that initial tone association in nouns disregards syllable weight; in other words, long syllables count as one tone-bearing unit, just as short syllables do (cf. (9)). One might entertain the hypothesis that verb roots differ from nouns just in taking the mora, rather than the syllable, as the tone-bearing unit. Although on the face of it, the paradigms given in (38) and (39b) might seem to contradict this idea, it turns out that these forms do not present insuperable difficulties for this analysis, since one can find independent motivation for the extra rules that would be needed to account for these forms.

Rather conclusive evidence against this analysis, however, can be cited from deverbal nouns whose base consists of L-toned verb roots of the shape CVVC. As the following examples show, such deverbal nouns can fall into any one of the six noun tone classes discussed in section 2.

(41) Deverbal nouns formed from L-toned CVVC verb roots:

| tone class | A | B | gloss | verbal base | |
|---|---|---|---|---|---|
| 1. LL | iγeera | iγeera | 'fetching' | -γeer- | 'fetch' |
| 2. LH | mohεεhǒ | mohεεho | 'whisper' | -hεεh- | 'whisper' |
| 3. HL | moγuuciá | moγuuciá | 'wire-puller' | -γuuci- | 'pull wire' |
| 4. HH | okeeγú | okeeγu | 'stupidity' | -keeγ- | 'be stupid' |
| 5. LHL | ikuu.ǎ | ikuu.ǎ | 'carrier' | -kuu- | 'carry' |
| 6. HLHL | mocoókǎ | mocoókǎ | 'something reappearing' | -cook- | 'return' |

This table shows that deverbal nouns are assigned tones by the same principles according to which nondeverbal nouns are assigned tones, and hence that the initial CVVC of the noun stem counts as a single tone-bearing unit. (There are no additional tone classes of bisyllabic noun stems whose membership consists uniquely of deverbal nouns formed from CVVC verb roots.) Thus if we were to maintain the analysis summarized in (40) we would be forced to assume that the number of tone-bearing units contained in a CVVC root is a function of the category (noun or verb) of the word in which it is contained, a highly implausible result. And we would still not have accounted for the anomalous form *tomáɲiitírέ*.

Let us consider, then, an alternative solution that preserves our original assumption that the tone-bearing unit is the syllable, regardless of syllable weight. If we examine the forms in (39a) once again, we see that they have three properties that distinguish them from all regular forms: (i) the root vowel is long, (ii) the root vowel bears lexical L tone, and (iii) the mobile suffix bears lexical H tone. It is just when these three characteristics are simultaneously present that we find the apparent failure of Tone Shift to apply. In order to account for these forms we will postulate the existence of a rule that operates prior to Tone Shift and the Association Conventions, associating the lexical L tone of a verb root with a heavy root syllable just in case a H tone follows. Tone Shift and the Association Conventions then apply to the output of this rule. It is formulated in (42):

(42) Heavy Syllable Lowering

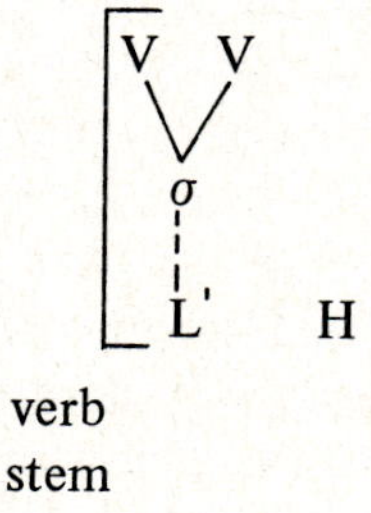

The derivation of *mámóɲiitíré* is given below.

```
(43)  ma  mo  ɲiit ir  ɛ          underlying

        H   L   L   H

      ma  mo  ɲiit ir  ɛ          Heavy Syllable Lowering
               |
        H   L   L   H

      má  mó ɲiit  ír  ɛ́          Tone Shift, Association Conventions
       |/      |    \/
        H   L   L   H
```

Crucial to this derivation is the fact that the first L tone of the melody cannot be associated under the Association Conventions, since there is no free tone-bearing unit for it to be paired with. It therefore remains afloat. As we have noted earlier, word-internal floating L tones operate as downsteps only when flanked on both sides by H tones; as this is not the case in (43), there is no downstep in the surface form. The derivations of *máɲiitíré* and the problem form *tomáɲiitíré* follow.

```
(44)  ma  ɲiit ir  ɛ      to  ma  ɲiit ir  ɛ     underlying

       H   L    H         L   H   L    H

      ma  ɲiit ir  ɛ      to  ma  ɲiit ir  ɛ     Heavy Syllable Lowering
           |                       |
       H   L    H         L   H   L    H

      má  ɲiit ír  ɛ́      to  ma  ɲiit ir  ɛ     Tone Shift, Association
      |    |    \/         |/       |    \/      Conventions
       H   L    H         L   H   L    H

           —              to  má  ɲiit ír  ɛ́     H Tone Association, Rising
                          |   |    |    \|       Tone Simplification
                          L   H   L    H
```

These derivations are perfectly straightforward, involving only the rules introduced up to this point.

What we have learned from our discussion of the forms in (39a) is that syllable weight may play a role in tone systems, just as it is known to do in stress systems. The operation of Heavy Syllable Lowering, taking precedence over the more general principles of tone assignment observed elsewhere in Kikuyu, is analogous to the rules assigning stress to heavy syllables found very widely in stress systems, and which also take precedence over the more general rules of stress assignment, such as rules of alternating stress (see, for example, Prince 1983). It seems that a unitary notion of "heavy syllable" is involved in both cases.

The rule of Heavy Syllable Lowering must be a Kikuyu innovation, since its very existence presupposes Tone Shift, itself a Kikuyu innovation;[13] if Kikuyu did not have Tone Shift, the rule of Heavy Syllable Lowering would apply with no observable effect. The existence of Heavy Syllable Lowering, rather than weakening our original hypothesis that the tone-bearing unit is the syllable, actually strengthens it, since it accounts for the range of forms in (38), (39), and (41) in a much more straightforward way than the alternative hypothesis sketched in (40) was able to do. There is rather good evidence that in regard to this feature, too, Kikuyu retains fundamental properties of the Proto-Bantu system. It is known that the syllable, rather than the mora was the domain within which the reconstructed H vs. L tones contrasted in Proto-Bantu (Guthrie 1967-71, Meeussen 1967); thus in the vast majority of cases, CVVC roots are reconstructed with a uniform H or L tone.[14]

There is a further rule of Kikuyu that is conditioned by syllable weight. The following forms illustrate the tonal behavior of verbs in the Current Progressive (CP) tense. This tense is formed by prefixing the formatives /ra + a/ to the stem; no tense/aspect suffix occurs with it. It can be shown that the tone sequence characterizing the tense prefixes is HL, and that the mobile suffix in this tense is H.

(45) Current Progressive (CP)

a. L tone root: -rɔr-

| | |
|---|---|
| to raa rɔ́r ǎ* | má raá rɔ́r ǎ* |
| to raa mó rɔr ǎ* | má raá mó rɔr ǎ* |
| to raá ma rɔ́r ǎ | má raá ma rɔ́r ǎ |

b. H tone root: -tom-

| | |
|---|---|
| to raá tom á | má raá tom á |
| to raa mó tom á* | má raá mó tom á* |
| to raá ma tóm á | má raá ma tóm á |

Six forms, marked with an asterisk, show an unexpected H tone on the syllable following *raa*. According to the rules established so far, the derivations of *toraarɔ́rǎ* and *toraátomá* should proceed as follows:

(46)

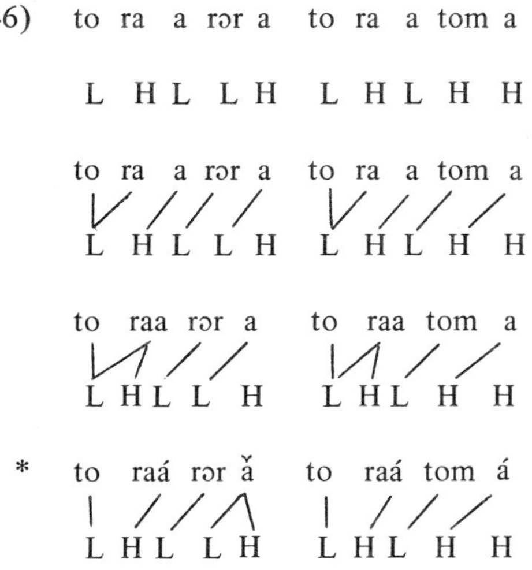


underlying

Tone Shift, Association Conventions

Syllable Fusion

H Tone Association, Rising Tone Simplification

The first of these derivations gives the incorrect output, with a H tone on the second surface syllable rather than the third. All of the other forms marked with an asterisk in (45) are deviant in exactly the same respect.

Examining the deviant cases more closely, we see that if H tone is predicted to fall on a heavy syllable and the two syllables following it both bear L tone, the H tone shifts to the first of these, displacing the original L. At the same time, the syllable that originally bore the H loses it. The rule involved here may be provisionally formulated as follows; we will see a way of simplifying this rule below.

(47) Heavy Syllable Shift (provisional formulation)

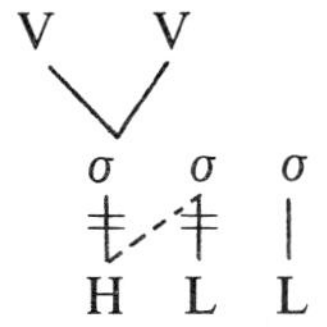


The syllable which becomes toneless as a result of the operation of this rule receives the tone of the preceding syllable through the reapplication of the Association Conventions.[15] Thus, this rule applies to the final line of (46) to create the following surface form:

(48)

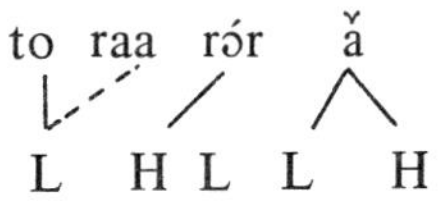


Heavy Syllable Shift, Association Conventions

Note that the disassociated L tone does not become interpreted as downstep since it is not flanked by two H tones.

Heavy Syllable Shift is not restricted to sequences of prefix vowels, but affects any heavy syllable containing vowels belonging to two formatives. A further source of such syllables is the prefix-stem juncture, when the stem is vowel-initial. The following paradigm illustrates the tonal behavior of the stem *-ikarera* 'sit on' in the Current Habitual. (Recall that here as elsewhere, vowel sequences are to be interpreted as single surface syllables, bearing the tone written over the second of the vowels.)

(49) Current Habitual (L tone root)

| | |
|---|---|
| to ik ar aγ er a | ma ík ár aγ er a* |
| to mo ik ar aγ er a | má mo ík ar aγ er a |
| to ma ik ár aγ er a* | má ma ík ár aγ er a* |

Here as before I have marked with an asterisk the forms that exhibit the effects of Heavy Syllable Shift. As is normal (see Barlow 1960:78), the imperfect aspect suffix *-aγ-* precedes the applied suffix *-er-*. The mobile tonal suffix in this tense, it will be recalled, is L.

Heavy Syllable Shift applies here exactly as in the earlier forms. The following example illustrates.

(50)

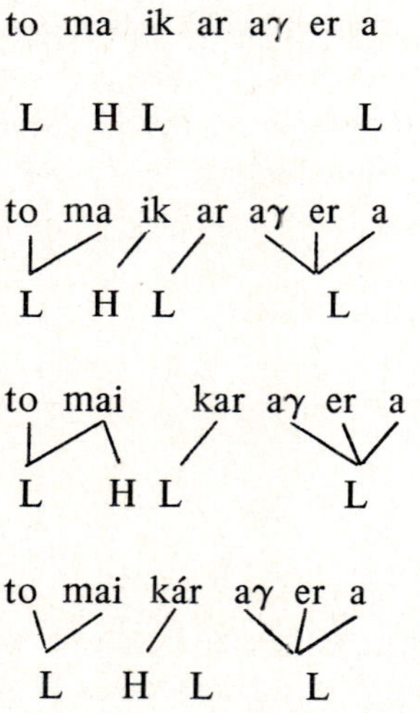


underlying

Tone Shift, Association Conventions

Syllable Fusion

Heavy Syllable Shift

The one form that our rules do not yet derive correctly is *mámoikaraγera*; we would expect a falling tone on the second syllable. The derivation goes as follows:

(51)

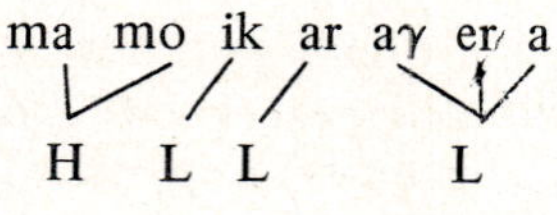


(after Tone Shift, Association Conventions)

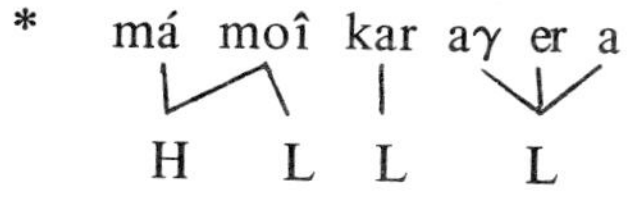


Syllable Fusion

Falling tones created by Syllable Fusion normally simplify to H if the next syllable bears L tone, and to L if the next syllable bears H tone. A provisional statement of the Falling Tone Simplification rule is given below:

(52) Falling Tone Simplification

This rule applies to the final line of (51) to derive the correct surface form:

(53)

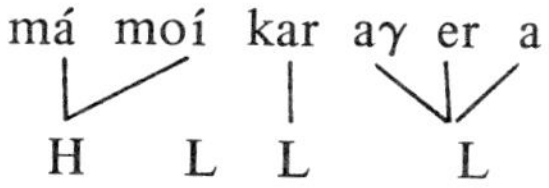


Falling Tone Simplification

Having motivated the rule of Falling Tone Simplification, we may return to the provisional formulation of Heavy Syllable Shift given in (47). We may now see that the statement of this rule is unnecessarily complicated, since the delinking of the L tone is independently accounted for by Falling Tone Simplification. In fact, given (52) the rule may be restated as follows:

(54) Heavy Syllable Shift (final formulation)

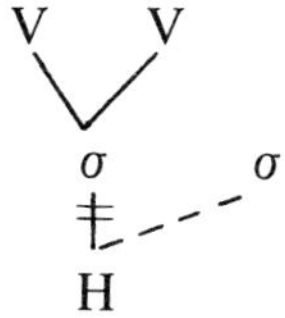


In this formulation, the rule states that a H tone is shifted off a heavy syllable onto the following syllable, with no further tonal conditions. Notice that if the next following syllable bears L tone, as in the examples seen so far, the first case of Falling Tone Simplification (52a) will be applicable, and the falling tone created by Heavy Syllable Shift will be simplified to H. If, on the other hand, the next following syllable bears H tone, the second case of Falling Tone Simplification applies, and the falling tone simplifies to L. Thus no further conditions need be placed on the rule. The derivation of *toraátomá* (46) correctly continues as follows, immediately following Syllable Fusion:

(55)

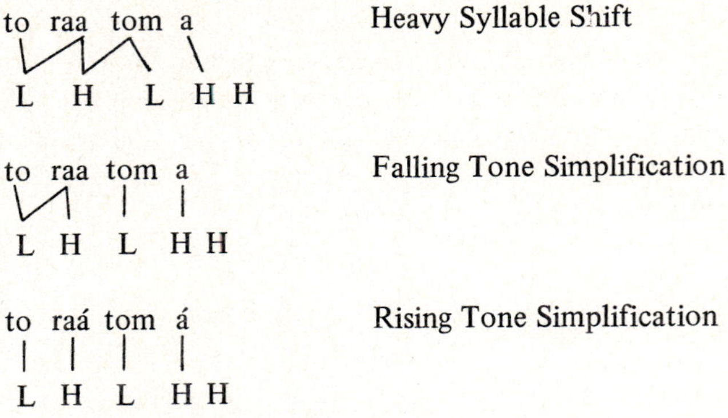


As noted earlier, Heavy Syllable Shift applies only to heavy syllables formed from two distinct formatives. It does not affect heavy syllables contained entirely within roots. Thus this rule does not apply to *tomaɲiitaɣa* in (38a) or similar forms. In order to account for this restriction we might insert a morpheme boundary "+" between the two Vs of (54), or condition this rule in other ways; as I know of no further evidence bearing on the exact formulation of this restriction[16] I will leave (54) as it stands, merely taking informal note of the fact that monomorphemic vowel sequences do not undergo it.

The following list of rules summarizes the analysis up to this point.

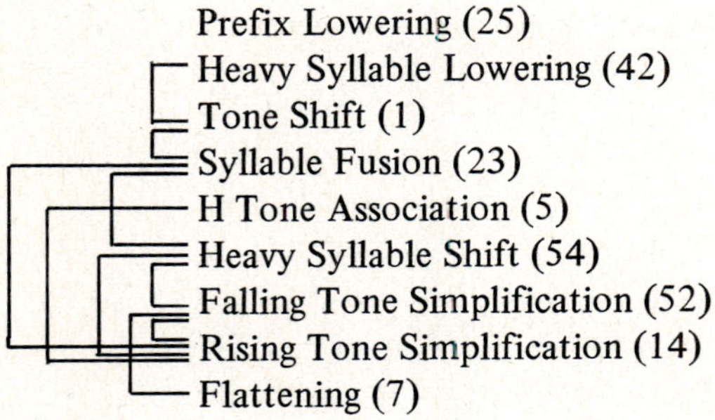


6. AFFIRMATIVE TENSES: NONTONAL MORPHOLOGY

The analysis presented up to this point extends with few additional complications to the full set of main clause affirmative tenses examined in this study (see Table I, below). A *main clause tense* is understood here as one which may occur in a simple declarative sentence, or in the main clause of a complex declarative sentence. This definition includes the consecutive tenses, but excludes the conditional tenses (see Barlow (1960) for an inventory of Kikuyu tenses, including those not examined in this study).

The main clause affirmative tenses, excluding the consecutive tenses, can be characterized in terms of the Cartesian product of the following two sets of tense and aspect formatives:

| (56) | tense prefixes: | aspect suffixes: |
|---|---|---|
| | ∅ | aγ |
| | e+ko | eet |
| | ra+a | ir |
| | a | ∅ |
| | re+e | |
| | ka+a | |

I use the terms "tense prefix" and "aspect suffix" for convenience. The suffixes correlate well with aspectual categories in the analysis of Johnson (1980, 1981) and the prefixes correlate only slightly less consistently with tense categories; thus these terms are of mnemonic value, if not rigorously accurate. The tense prefixes, except for *-a-*, are analyzed as consisting of two formatives on the basis of tonal, rather than semantic evidence. (56) characterizes 24 theoretically possible combinations; of these, 21 actually occur. The missing combinations are /re+e...ir/, /ka+a...eet/, and /ka+a...ir/. Two of the occurring tenses, /e+ko...ir/ and /re+e...eet/, were not examined in detail and are not included in this study.

Consecutive tenses are those that may occur in noninitial clauses of consecutive constructions. Four of the six considered here are formed by combining one of the prefixes *-ka-*, *-a-*, *-ra-+-a-*, and *-ke-* with the final vowel *-a-*. The final two are prefixless tenses formed with the final vowel *-ɛ-*, and are homophonous both segmentally and tonally with the subjunctive tenses.

The twenty-five tenses considered in this study are listed in Table I. In this table, each tense is identified by its "tense sign", that is, by the combination of tense prefix, aspect suffix and final vowel that uniquely identifies it. Two tenses, the Immediate Perfect (tense 12) and the Current Past Consecutive (tense 21) are segmentally homophonous but (as we shall see) tonally distinct. The final vowel is given after each aspect suffix without separation; it appears as *-ɛ-* after *-eet-* and *-ir-* and in tenses 24 and 25 (homophonous with the subjunctive), and as *-a-* elsewhere.

Table I: Kikuyu Main Clause Affirmative Tenses

| | *Tense Sign* | *Name* | *Armstrong* | *Barlow* |
|---|---|---|---|---|
| 1. | ∅ . . . a | Stative Present | – | 128-29 |
| 2. | ∅ . . . aγa | Current Habitual | 6 | 37-8, 140 |
| 3. | ∅ . . . eetε | Current Perfect | 4 | 50-1, 134-5 |
| 4. | ∅ . . . irε | Current Past Completive | 1 | 33, 132 |
| 5. | e+ko . . . a | Current Future | 8 | 41-3, 129-30 |
| 6. | e+ko . . . aγa | Current Past Imperfect | – | 141, 143 |
| 7. | e+ko . . . eetε | Current Past Perfect | – | 135 |
| 8. | ra+a . . . a | Current Progressive | – | 130, 137 |
| 9. | ra+a . . . aγa | Near Past Imperfect | – | 141-2 |
| 10. | ra+a . . . eetε | Near Past Perfect | – | 135-6 |
| 11. | ra+a . . . irε | Near Past Completive | 2 | 61-2, 132 |
| 12. | a . . . a | Immediate Perfect | 5 | 53-5, 133-4 |
| 13. | a . . . aγa | Remote Past Imperfect | 7 | 142 |
| 14. | a . . . eetε | Remote Past Perfect | – | 136 |
| 15. | a . . . irε | Remote Past Completive | 3 | 58, 132-3 |
| 16. | re+e . . . a | Near Future | 9 | 84-5, 131 |
| 17. | re+e . . . aγa | Near Future Imperfect | – | 143-4 |
| 18. | ka+a . . . a | Remote Future | 10 | 46, 131 |
| 19. | ka+a . . . aγa | Remote Future Imperfect | – | 144 |
| 20. | ka . . . a | Current Consecutive | 11 | 73, 149-50 |
| 21. | a . . . a | Current Past Consecutive | 12 | 150-1 |
| 22. | ra+a . . . a | Near Past Consecutive | 13 | 69-70, 150 |
| 23. | ke . . . a | Remote Past Consecutive | 14 | 65-6, 150 |
| 24. | ∅ . . . ε | Future Consecutive/ Subjunctive | – | 151 |
| 25. | ∅ . . . aγε | Future Imperfect Consecutive/ Imperfect Subjunctive | – | – |

References to relevant description in Armstrong (1967) and Barlow (1960) are given at the right; numbers under Armstrong give her tense numbering, and numbers under Barlow give page references.

## 7. AFFIRMATIVE TENSES: TONAL MORPHOLOGY

We now consider the tonal morphology of the verb tenses listed in Table I. Each tense occurs in up to four formally distinguished tonal forms. These are given below:

(57) a. *ne*-form
b. simple form
c. subject relative form
d. general relative form

The choice among these forms is determined by a complex set of syntactic and discourse factors, which cannot be examined in any detail here; however, as the last two forms have not been distinguished from the simple form (57b) in the previous literature, some brief discussion is called for. The *ne*-form is marked by the presence of the focus marker, *ne*, which is prefixed to the entire verbal word. This form is generally used when the verb falls within the scope of focus; see Barlow (1960, 34; 117-8; 263-4) and Armstrong (1967, chapter 14) for discussion and examples. The simple form is characteristically used when the focus of the sentence falls exclusively on a postverbal constituent which remains *in situ*, that is, which is not preposed with the focus marker *ne*. It is tonally distinguished from the *ne*-form by the fact that the final vowel never bears the stable tonal suffix.[17] The relative forms are used to register the fact that an element of the clause has been extracted from that clause to a position preceding it. Characteristic uses are in (i) relative clauses, (ii) clauses with preposed focused constituents, and (iii) clauses with preposed question words (WH-words); the latter environment may be a special case of (ii).

Relative tonal forms are differentiated into two subtypes, which I will call the *subject relative form* and the *general relative form*. The subject relative form is used in subject relative clauses (i.e. those in which the head of the relative clause functions as the subject of the relative clause) when the head noun is a member of noun class 1, 4 or 9, or when it is the 3rd person singular independent pronoun *wɛɛ*; the general relative is used in all other cases. The subject relative differs from the general relative in three respects: (i) the subject prefix bears L tone, (ii) the subject prefix *o-* replaces *a-* in class 1, and (iii) the final vowel never bears the stable suffix, but only the mobile suffix in all cases.[18]

Let us consider now the underlying tone melody for each tense. In general, this is simply a concatenation of the underlying tones of each of the formatives that constitute it, with a few qualifications. First, the subject prefix bears underlying H tone in the *ne*-forms and general relative forms; as we shall see later, this is a consequence of a general rule of Subject Prefix Raising which replaces the base tone of the subject prefix with H whenever it is not sentence-initial. Second, the base tone of the subject prefix is replaced with L in the subject relative, as noted above, and is deleted before the three tense prefixes *-ree-*, *-kaa-*, and *-eko-*. Third, the reflexive prefix *-e-* loses its basic H tone and ceases to constitute a tone-bearing unit after the tense prefixes *-raa-*, *-a-*, and *-ree-*. Fourth, the final vowel cannot be assigned a constant underlying tone; rather, its tone (the "mobile suffix") must be specified on a tense-by-tense basis. This fact suggests that the mobile suffix is not a part of the same formative as the final vowel but is an independent tonal formative on its own. Finally, the tonal melody as constructed so far is completed with the adjunction of up to three tonal suffixes: the stable suffix LH as described earlier, the floating suffix T*, and the downstep suffix *!*. The latter two suffixes will be examined in some detail in the next section.

Underlying tones of each position class in the schema (16) are given below; I omit the negative prefix *-ti-* which does not occur in the tenses discussed in this work.

(58) underlying tones of verbal formatives:

*ne-*: H

SP: in the subject relative form, the SP bears L tone if the noun head is the independent pronoun *wɛɛ* or is a noun of class 1, 4, or 9, otherwise it bears H tone; in all other tense forms, the SP bears H tone except for the four personal classes (1st and 2nd persons sg. and pl.) which bear L tone.

T: *e+ko*, HL
*ra+a*, HL
*a*, H (if the aspect suffix is absent)
L (if the aspect suffix is present)
*re+e*, LH
*ka+a*, LL

D: the directive prefix *-ke-* bears H tone.

OP: the object prefixes have underlying L tone in the singular personal classes and in classes 1, 4, and 9, and H in all others.

*-e-*: the reflexive prefix *-e-* has underlying H tone.

*roots*: have underlying H or L tone.

X: extension suffixes are toneless.

FV: the final vowel is characterized by a H or L mobile suffix, specified according to the tense and, in a few cases, to the tense form.[19]

It will be noted that if we analyze the longer tense prefixes as consisting of two formatives, as proposed earlier, then all prefixes in the Kikuyu verb have one, and only one tone each. On the other hand, the suffixes do not, in general, show this property; indeed, if we adopt the suggestion made just above according to which the final vowel and the mobile suffix are distinct formatives, then verbal suffixes in Kikuyu consist *exclusively* of segmental suffixes without tones, and tonal suffixes without segmental support.

## 8. FLOATING TONE SUFFIXES

The tonal melody of a Kikuyu verb may end in one or more floating tone suffixes: the stable suffix LH discussed in section 4, the floating suffix T*, and the downstep suffix ꜜ. The latter two will be discussed in this section.

### *8.1. The Downstep Suffix*

Let us return to a problem that was left unexplained in our treatment of nouns in section 2. In considering the tone classes represented in (2), we noted that noun tones varied according to context; in particular, it was shown that the tone forms in column B were derivable from those represented in column A by a rule of Flattening (7), which lowers H tones to L in absolute sentence-final position. The problem is the following: why does Flattening not apply to the forms of column A? These forms are also sentence-final, occurring after certain tense forms such as the Current Past Completive (simple form). It appears to be some property of the verb that blocks the operation of Flattening, as it is only the (first) object of the verb that ever displays this immunity.

There is a second anomaly involving the set of verbs that convey immunity to Flattening to their objects: these verbs are exceptions to Flattening themselves. Representative examples are given in (59). These examples illustrate the *ne*-form of the three tenses examined in the earlier discussion, the Current Habitual (CH), the Current Past Completive (CPC), and the Immediate Perfect (IP); in all cases, the tonal melody ends in the stable suffix (see section 4 for further examples).

| | | | |
|---|---|---|---|
| (59) | CH: | némárɔ́raγa mókandá | 'they look at a rope' |
| | | némámórɔraγǎ | 'they look at him' |
| | CPC: | némárɔ́ꜜrírɛ mókandá | 'they looked at a rope' |
| | | némámórɔrírɛ̌ | 'they looked at him' |
| | IP: | némaárɔ́ra mókandá | 'they have just looked at a rope' |
| | | némaámórɔrǎ | 'they have just looked at him' |

The noun object, *mókandá*, belongs to the stem tone class HH, and thus appears as *mokanda* in isolation, *mokandá* after verbs like *ɲɔniré* which do not trigger H Tone Spread (see below, section 8.2), and as *mókandá* after verbs which do trigger this rule, as in the examples given above. (We return shortly to a discussion of why some verbs trigger this rule and others do not.) What is of interest in these examples is the behavior of the word-final H tones, which resist Flattening in all cases.[20] Without exception, verbs that convey immunity to Flattening to their objects are exceptions to Flattening themselves. How are we to explain this fact?

The answer, as shown in detail in Clements and Ford (1981), is that the verb forms in question have a morphological final downstep in their tone melody, which regularly permutes to the right of any following object, should there be one.[21] The occurrence of this downstep can be represented as follows, where NP = the noun object, and $]_S$ = sentence-final position:

(60) a. V ! $]_S$ (verb is sentence-final)

b. V NP ! $]_S$ (object is sentence-final)

c. V NP ! X$]_S$ (object is sentence-internal)

The situations schematized in (60a,b) are illustrated in (59). A better transcription of the first pair of examples, then, would be the following:

| | | |
|---|---|---|
| (61) | némárɔ́raγa mókandá ! | 'they look at a rope' |
| | némámórɔraγǎ ! | 'they look at it' |

We see that the failure of Flattening to apply in these forms is attributable to the fact that the word-final H tones are not, in fact, sentence-final, but precede the downstep (which, it will be recalled, is formally characterized as a floating L tone).

Certain verb forms, on the other hand, fail to "immunize" their objects from Flattening. On the analysis given above, these verb forms should be lacking the downstep suffix. Accordingly, they should undergo Flattening themselves. This is in fact the case, as is shown in (62), illustrating the general relative form of the same three tenses given in (59).

| | | | |
|---|---|---|---|
| (62) | CH: | ando ! marɔ́raγa mókanda | 'people who look at a rope' |
| | | mondo ! marɔ́raγa | 'someone who they look at' |
| | CPC: | ando ! marɔ́ ! rírɛ | 'people who looked at a rope' |
| | | mondo ! marɔ́ ! rírɛ | 'someone who they looked at' |
| | IP: | ando ! maarɔ́ra mókanda | 'people who have just looked at a rope' |
| | | mondo ! maarɔ́ra | 'someone who they have just looked at' |

That the general relative form of these tenses ends in the stable suffix LH is shown, among other things, by the fact that the final H is displaced onto the initial syllable of the noun object (this is the regular effect of H Tone Spread, see next section). This H tone, as well as the final H of *mokandá*, undergoes Flattening in sentence-final position. All "non-immunizing" verb forms show this behavior. This is explained by the fact that they do not end in the downstep suffix.

The analysis given above receives striking confirmation from an examination of forms illustrating case (60c). Under the present analysis, we expect to find a downstep appearing to the right of a sentence-internal noun object if the verb has the downstep suffix and no downstep otherwise. This prediction is correct. The following example, drawn from Clements, McCloskey, Maling, and Zaenen (1983) illustrates; the verb *ahɛírɛ́* is in the Current Past Imperfect, simple form:

(63) mondo ! .ahɛírɛ́ moanákɛ́ káγó!kó roociíně !
'someone gave the boy a small chicken this morning'

The first object is *moanákɛ́* 'boy' and the second object is *káγó!kó* (underlyingly /kaγokó/, stem tone class HH) 'small chicken'. In conformity with the schema (60c), we find a downstep to the right of the first object, appearing internally in *káγó!kó* where it is placed by a regular rule of Downstep Displacement.[22] Now compare this with the following sentence, illustrating the general relative form of the same tense which, under our hypothesis, does not have the final downstep. We expect no downstep to appear following the first object, and this expectation is confirmed:

(64) né roociíně móndo !.ahɛí!rɛ́ moanákɛ́ káγoko *t*
'this morning someone gave the boy a small chicken'

"*t*" marks the spot from which the adverbial complement is extracted.[23] The internal downstep in the verb is not at issue here, this being the first (L tone) element of the stable suffix which is disassociated by case (a) of Rising Tone Simplification (14). The point here is that no downstep appears to the right of the first object *moanákɛ́*, showing that the verb-final downstep is not present, exactly as claimed above.[24] Countless further examples can be offered to confirm this point.

We thus see that some tense forms have a final downstep suffix in their melody, while others do not. The distribution of this element is very simple: it appears after all main-clause affirmative nonrelative tense forms and nowhere else. Thus, all such tense forms pattern exactly like the ones illustrated in (59) and (63), providing they have a final H tone in their tone melody preceding the downstep suffix, and all other tense forms pattern like those illustrated in (62) and (64). Clements, McCloskey, Maling, and Zaenen (1983) propose that all affirmative verb forms end in the downstep suffix, which is deleted by a syntax-sensitive rule; a different interpretation will be offered in section 9.

### *8.2. The Floating T* Suffix*

In the preceding discussion we have seen several examples of forms exhibiting the effect of a rule of H Tone Spread, which causes a word-final H tone to displace onto the first syllable of a following word: see (8), (59), (62), (64). Further examples of this rule are given below:

| | | |
|---|---|---|
| (65) | né kémore | 'it's a torch' |
| | né móγatɛ̌ | 'it's bread' |
| | né móγɛká | 'it's a rug' |
| | né máγɔkɔ́ | 'it's bark' |

| | | |
|---|---|---|
| (66) | kemore kenɛnɛ́ | 'a big torch' |
| | moγatɛ mónɛnɛ́ | 'big bread' |
| | moγɛká mónɛnɛ́ | 'a big rug' |
| | maγɔkɔ́ mánɛnɛ́ | 'big bark' |

The nouns in these examples are familiar from the discussion in section 2. Comparing the forms of the nouns in (65) and (66), we see that the H-toned focus marker *ne* causes a following L-toned syllable to bear H tone. Moreover, comparing the forms of the adjective in (66), we see that the first syllable bears H tone just in case the stem melody of the preceding noun is H-final. These forms, too, illustrate the effect of H Tone Spread.[25]

(67) H Tone Spread

Notice that the falling tone created by this rule is subject to Falling Tone Simplification (52). If the falling tone precedes a L-toned syllable, it will simplify to H by case (a) of this rule; this is the case illustrated in the examples of (62), (65) and (66). If, on the other hand, the falling tone precedes a H-toned syllable, it will simplify to L by case (b) of this rule, restoring the status quo antes. This case is illustrated by the following forms, in which H Tone Spread has applied only to have its effects erased by Falling Tone Simplification:

| | | | |
|---|---|---|---|
| (68) | né moaná | (stem tone class HL) | 'it's a child' |
| | né maitó | (stem tone class HH) | 'it's my mother' |

| | | |
|---|---|---|
| (69) | moγatɛ́ moɛγá (→ moɛγa) | 'good bread' |
| | moγɛká moɛγá (→ moɛγa) | 'a good rug' |
| | maγɔkɔ́ mɛɛγá (→ mɛɛγa) | 'good bark' |

In the latter set of examples, the underlying final H tone of the adjective undergoes Flattening after having triggered Falling Tone Simplification. The H tone of *moγatɛ́* is due to Rising Tone Simplification (14), case (a). Note that this set of forms establishes the partial ordering:

Falling Tone Simplification (52)
Rising Tone Simplification (14)
Flattening (7)

as given at the end of section 5.[26]

Curiously, certain verb forms do not condition H Tone Spread, even though their final syllable bears H tone. The simple form of the Current Past Completive, used to provide the context for the column A forms of nouns in (2), is one example. More generally, we find that the set of exceptions coincides with the simple form and the subject relative form of verb tenses formed without tense prefixes; thus, tenses 1-4 and 24-25 of Table I.

Verbs that do not condition H Tone Spread have a second interesting property; they fail to undergo Flattening. This property is illustrated in (70):

(70) Current Past Completive (subject relative form)

| | |
|---|---|
| mondo ! ororirɛ́ mokanda | 'someone who looked at a rope' |
| mondo ! omorɔrirɛ́ | 'someone who looked at him' |

Similar examples can be given for the other prefixless tenses in the simple and subject relative forms. These tense forms fail both to condition H Tone Spread on the following word, and to undergo Flattening themselves, even in the subject relative form (the failure to flatten in the simple form follows, of course, from the presence of the downstep suffix as explained in the previous section).

We have earlier seen that a similar conjunction of properties lent itself to a plausible explanation in terms of a floating tone suffix: in that case, a floating downstep suffix. Suppose we postulate a floating tone suffix in the tone melody of the tense forms under discussion here, which is distinct both from H tone and from the downstep suffix. Let us provisionally call this suffix T*. This tone must be distinct from H tone, since otherwise it would not explain the set of properties illustrated in (70). It must also be distinct from the downstep suffix, of course, since otherwise it would be interpreted as a downstep by the phonetic realization rules; moreover, it would undergo the other rules to which the downstep suffix is subject, namely Downstep Permutation (as discussed earlier) and Downstep Displacement (as discussed in Clements and Ford 1981)). If we consider it a third tone of some sort, we can explain the exact pattern of exceptionality of the tense forms in question to both H Tone Spread and Flattening.

A clue to the identity of this tone comes from certain forms of verb tenses formed without aspect suffixes. We may illustrate with the simple form of the Immediate Perfect. As we know from the previous discussion (section 3), this tense is characterized by a L mobile suffix. This tone appears overtly on the final vowel of verbs with trisyllabic stems, as illustrated in the second and fourth examples below:

| | | | |
|---|---|---|---|
| (71) | L stems: | toarɔ́ra mokandá | 'we have just looked at a rope' |
| | | toakíɲera mokandá | 'we have just caught up with a rope' |
| | H stems: | toatómá mokandá | 'we have just sent a rope' |
| | | toahétóka mokandá | 'we have just overtaken a rope' |

The form of interest is *toatómá*. In this form the H tone of the root is assigned to the final vowel, and hence the L tone mobile suffix has no chance to surface. What is of interest here is the fact that *toatómá* does not condition H Tone Spread. We may easily account for this fact if we assume that the mobile L tone remains in the representation even if it is unassociated with any syllable. Its presence will block the application of H Tone Spread, which does not provide for the existence of a floating L tone between the spreading H tone and the L tone associated with the syllable that follows (see (67)).

If the failure of *toatómá* to condition H Tone Spread is due to the presence of a floating L tone at the end of its tone melody, then we would expect this same floating L tone to block the application of Flattening to all forms of the verb in this tense that occur in sentence-final position. This expectation is confirmed: this verb fails to undergo Flattening in the subject relative.[27]

(72) mondo ! waamótomá /o+a+mo+tom+a/ 'the person who sent him'

cf. mondo ! waamóhetóka 'the person who overtook him'

The exceptionality of this form to Flattening is thus an automatic consequence of the analysis, following from our assumption that unmapped tones are not deleted but survive in representations as floating tones.

Now it will be noticed that the characteristics of the floating L tone occurring after *toatómá* and *waamótomá* in these examples are exactly those of the tonal suffix T* that we observed earlier: it blocks H Tone Spread, blocks Flattening, and fails to be interpreted as downstep. The identity of this tone is now revealed: it must be a L tone, since it shows up as such in the longer stems of (71) and (72). If T* is a floating L tone, however, what is the identity of the floating downstep suffix?

It seems that this question cannot be answered on purely synchronic grounds, since the floating tone that acts as a downstep operator never associates with a tone-bearing unit in Kikuyu, and hence never reveals its identity. It must, in any case, be distinct from H, for the same reasons that T* had to be: if it were a H tone, we would not have any straightforward way of explaining the fact that it blocks H Tone Spread and Flattening, both of which apply to H tones. In its phonological behavior, it seems closer to a L tone than to a H. This is because in other languages, downstep operators are normally interpretable as floating L tones; floating H tones are rarely if ever known to serve this function. It seems most appropriate to consider this tone a variety of L tone, distinguished from other floating L tones by a special mark of some sort. We will indicate this tone as follows: $\bar{L}$, where the superscript is a feature indicating that this tone is to be interpreted as the downstep operator. We may now assume that $\bar{L}$ tones are derived from L tones, by the following two rules. The first of these turns a L tone into a $\bar{L}$ tone if it occurs finally in the tone melody of a noun, and the second performs the same operation on floating L tones that are flanked on both sides by H tones, word-internally.

(73) $L \rightarrow \bar{L} \; / \; \_\_\_ \; ]_N$

(74) $L' \rightarrow \bar{L} \; / \; H\_\_H$ (word-internally)

The floating downstep suffix of section 8.1 will be introduced by rule, as we will see shortly. Hence, there are no occurrences of $\bar{L}$ in underlying representations.

Under this analysis, the rules of Kikuyu freely generate floating L tones (and for that matter, floating H tones). Only those underlying L tones that occur under the conditions cited in (73)-(74) become interpreted as downsteps. Thus the rules of downstep interpretation are crucially sensitive to the distinction between two types of floating L tones, and operate only on those which have received the special mark introduced by rules (73) and (74). This analysis accounts, among other things, for the many cases in our earlier derivations where floating L tones were generated that never became interpreted as downsteps; notice that in all such cases, the conditions of rules (73) and (74) were not satisfied.

The analysis of the floating tone suffixes T* (=L) and ! (=$\overline{L}$) is summarized in Table II.

Table II: Characteristics of the Floating Tone Suffixes

| | | T* | ! |
|---|---|---|---|
| A. | Phonological behavior: | | |
| | 1. interpreted as downstep | – | + |
| | 2. undergoes DS Permutation | – | + |
| | 3. undergoes DS Displacement | – | + |
| | 4. blocks Flattening (in object) | – | + |
| | 5. blocks Flattening (in verb) | + | + |
| | 6. blocks H Tone Spread (onto object) | + | – |
| B. | Distribution (verb-finally): | | |
| | 1. *ne*-form | – | + |
| | 2. simple form | +[1] | + |
| | 3. subject relative | +[1] | – |
| | 4. general relative | – | – |

[1] only if verb form has no tense prefix

### 8.3. *Floating Tone Suffixes: a Diachronic Interpretation*

While the identity of the downstep suffix is not synchronically recoverable, its historical source is clear, at least in general outline. It is known that pre-tone-shift Kikuyu, like several of its present-day neighbors, had a three-way surface tonal distinction between H, L, and $\overline{L}$, where the latter symbol is here to be interpreted as extra-L tone (Clements and Ford 1979). This latter tone only occurred on the final syllables of words, where it may already have been realized as a downstep operator. When tone shift was introduced, the $\overline{L}$ tone was displaced to the right of the word, becoming the present-day downstep operator. As this tone was not pronounced, the three-way surface distinction between H, L. and $\overline{L}$ was replaced by a two-way surface distinction between H and L.

An illustration suggestive of the way this process might have taken place can be drawn from a comparison between certain verb forms in Kikuyu and the closely-related Kikamba language. Unpublished materials collected by Kevin Ford show that the main clause affirmative tenses in Kikamba are formed with the following tonal suffixes, among others: H, L, L$\overline{L}$, HL, HH$\overline{L}$, LH$\overline{L}$. The final two tones of three-member suffix melodies are realized as contour tones on the final vowel, and the final tone of a two-member melody associates exclusively with the final vowel; the first (or only) tone in each case is the mobile suffix, which associates to all remaining noninitial vowels in the stem. Notice that L̄ is in complementary distribution with L, occurring only word-finally after L or as the second member of a contour tone.

Now let us suppose that a system of this type undergoes tone shift of the Kikuyu type. As a result, the final L and L̄ tones of all multimember tonal suffixes will be shifted off the verb, losing their segmental support, and L̄ (but not L) will continue to serve its function as a downstep operator. Notice in particular that the surface contrast between the HL and the HHL̄ suffix sequences will be merged, yielding a single "mobile" H tone, except that the first will be followed by a floating L tone and the second by a floating L̄ tone which will now be in contrast with it, just as in modern Kikuyu.

In support of this reconstruction one can cite rather close parallels between certain cognate forms in Kamba and Kikuyu. Compare the following (*-kam-* is a H-toned root; CH = Current Habitual; CPC = Current Past Completive; the circumflex accent ˆ transcribes HL̄):

| | | | | | |
|---|---|---|---|---|---|
| (75) | | | *Kikamba* | *Kikuyu* | |
| a. | CH | *ne*-form: | netokáma.â | nétókámáγǎ! | 'we milk' |
| | | simple form: | tokáma.a | tokamáγa | |
| | | subj. rel.: | okáma.a | okamáγa | |
| b. | CPC | *ne*-form: | nétókámi.ɛ̂ | nétókámírɛ̌! | 'we milked' |
| | | simple form: | tokámí.ɛ | tokamírɛ́ | |
| | | subj. rel.: | okámí.ɛ | okamírɛ́ | |

These forms are tonally parallel in all cases except the very first, where the two initial syllables of Kikamba have L tone. Setting these aside, the Kikuyu forms can be derived from the Kikamba forms by shifting each tone one syllable rightward and applying H Tone Association. Notice that while a floating L̄ will be generated to the right of the *ne*-forms in Kikuyu, a floating L tone will be generated to the right of the others. These floating tones can be given a straightforward respective interpretation as the ! and T* we have postulated in the present-day language on synchronic grounds.

The parallel between Kikamba and Kikuyu cannot be pursued much farther than this. Notice that the distribution of L and L̄ is determined purely on phonological grounds in Kikamba verbs, while the distribution of ! and T* in Kikuyu is determined on morphological grounds, as we have seen (Table II). In particular, Kikuyu has generalized ! to all and only nonrelative tenses, and T* to all and only prefixless tenses. If a system like that of Kikamba were to be postulated as the source of the Kikuyu system, we would have to allow for a considerable degree of restructuring. The exact nature of the way in which ! and T* developed in Kikuyu must await a detailed comparative study.

## 9. THE MELODY COMPOSITION RULES

We have now reviewed the tonal structure of the verb at the level of underlying representation – that is, at the level providing the input to the tone rules of sections 2-5. And yet we have already noticed that the tonal formulae summarized in Appendix A contain a considerable amount of redundancy. It is not necessary for the Kikuyu speaker to learn each tonal melody as a separate entity, tense by tense and tonal form by tonal form. Rather, it is sufficient to learn the basic tones for each formative as given in (58) together with a few simple rules to determine the underlying tonal melody for any given tense form. The rules in question will be called the *melody composition* rules, and comprise a set of morphologically conditioned rules that precede the set of tone rules proper.

In order to express the regularities exhibited in Appendix A, let us assume that the tone melodies given there represent the output of a set of inflectional rules that assign affixes to derivational bases. The affixes introduced may consist of tones alone, segments alone, or both tones and segments. The inflectional rules are organized into ordered sets, and the rules within each set apply disjunctively, introducing the mutually exclusive affixes that correspond to the various "position classes" represented in Appendix A. These rules have access to the set of phonological, syntactic and morphological properties that inflectional rules normally have access to, and thus may make reference to features of tense, aspect, noun class, polarity, and the like. Finally, melody composition rules not only introduce affixes but may make adjustments in affixes already assigned.

I will begin with the rules affecting prefixes and then pass to the rules for suffixes. Prefixes are for the most part straightforward, occurring generally with their underlying values; only the subject prefixes offer complexities.

We have claimed that subject prefixes in the nonrelative and general relative tonal forms have underlying H tone except for the first and second persons (singular and plural), which bear L tone. This analysis is justified by contrasts such as the following, where the verb is the L-toned root *-kiɲ-* 'arrive' (Current Past Completive, simple form):

| | | |
|---|---|---|
| (76) | tokiɲirɛ́ | 'we arrived' |
| | mákíɲirɛ́ | 'they arrived' |

We can explain the contrast on the first two syllables if we assume that the prefix *to-* has basic L tone, and the prefix *ma-* has basic H tone. The contrast found in (76) is only found, however, in sentence-initial position; sentence-internally, the same subject prefixes bear underlying H tone, as the following examples illustrate (the grave accent ` is used for the extra-L tone found under question intonation):

| | | | |
|---|---|---|---|
| (77) | a. | nétókí!ɲirɛ̌ | 'we arrived' |
| | | néré tókí!ɲírɛ̀ | 'when did we arrive?' |
| | b. | némákí!ɲirɛ̌ | 'they arrived' |
| | | néré mákí!ɲírɛ̀ | 'when did they arrive?' |

These examples are in the *ne*-form of the Current Past Completive. The downstep corresponds to the L tone of the root, parallel to the examples seen earlier in (31). What is of interest here is the fact that the subject prefix in (77a) must be regarded as bearing underlying H tone, as indicated by the tone of the following syllable.

We have seen that the subject prefix is replaced by H in another environment as well: the general relative form. In this form, of course, the verb is normally sentence-internal, and so the appearance of H here can be regarded as simply another instance of the raising of the basic tone to H in sentence-internal position. But this solution runs into trouble when we consider the subject relative form. In this form, as we recall from the earlier discussion, the subject prefix is always L-toned; and moreover, the usual class 1 prefix *a*- is replaced by *o*-. Our rule of Subject Prefix Raising must be conditioned in such a way as not to affect the subject relative form.

This problem has a relatively straightforward solution if we consider the suggestion made in note 18, according to which the subject relative form does not involve merely the replacement of one prefix by another, but the replacement of an entire prefix series – the so-called verbal prefix series – with another – the pronominal prefix series (which appears independently in pronouns and certain noun qualifiers). We may then restrict the Subject Prefix Raising Rule in the appropriate way:

(78) Subject Prefix Raising

$$\mathrm{T} \rightarrow \mathrm{H} \;/\; \mathrm{T} \left[ \frac{\qquad}{\text{+verbal pfx}} \right]$$

Two other rules account for variants in the shape of the subject prefix. First, the subject prefix tone is replaced by L in the Remote Past Consecutive, and by H in all other consecutive tenses. (These tenses do not have a subject relative form and hence the rules in question need not make reference to the feature [+verbal pfx]). These rules apply disjunctively.

(79) Subject Prefix Tone Replacement (Consecutive Tenses)

a. $$\mathrm{T} \rightarrow \mathrm{L} \;/\; {}_{\mathrm{V}}\!\left[ \left[ \frac{\qquad}{\text{Rem Past Consec}} \right. \right]$$

b. $$\mathrm{T} \rightarrow \mathrm{H} \;/\; {}_{\mathrm{V}}\!\left[ \left[ \frac{\qquad}{\text{Consec}} \right. \right]$$

Second, the subject prefix tone is deleted in all nonconsecutive future tenses. In all these tenses, we find a bisyllabic tense prefix. However, the deletion rule cannot be conditioned solely by the form of the tense prefix, since there are bisyllabic tense prefixes in nonfuture tenses that do *not* condition the deletion. Hence, the feature [+ future] must be mentioned in any case, and the rule might just as well be conditioned by this feature (and the feature [ – consecutive]) alone. We thus have the following:

(80) Subject Prefix Tone Deletion (future tenses)

$$T \rightarrow \emptyset \ / \ \_\_ \begin{bmatrix} -\text{consec} \\ +\text{future ts} \end{bmatrix}$$

Let us turn now to the suffixes. As noted earlier, it is not possible to assign an invariant underlying tone to the final vowel. It seems preferable to consider this suffix as toneless, and to consider the mobile suffix as a distinct formative in its own right. Let us assume that this formative is inserted according to appropriate morphological conditions, by the following rules of word formation, applying in the order given:

(81) Mobile Suffix Insertion

a. $$\emptyset \rightarrow L \ / \ \left[ \begin{bmatrix} \_\_\_\_ \\ \text{Stative Present} \\ \text{(gen. relative)} \end{bmatrix} \right]_V$$

b. $$\emptyset \rightarrow H \ / \ \left[ \begin{bmatrix} \_\_\_\_ \\ \text{Current/Near Future} \\ \text{(simple form)} \end{bmatrix} \right]_V$$

c. $$\emptyset \rightarrow H \ / \ \left[ \begin{bmatrix} \_\_\_\_ \\ \text{Stative Present} \\ \text{Current Perfect} \\ \text{Current Past Completive} \\ \text{Current Progressive} \\ \text{Near Past Imperfect} \\ \text{Remote Past (Imperfect,} \\ \text{Perfect, Completive)} \\ \text{Near Past Consecutive} \\ \text{Future Consecutive} \\ \text{Future Imperfect Conse-} \\ \text{cutive} \end{bmatrix} \right]_V$$

d. $$\emptyset \rightarrow L \ / \ \_\_]_V$$

Since these rules form a disjunctive set and are ordered from the most specific to the least specific, the final rule (81d) will apply as the "default" case. The rules in (81) should be regarded as straightforward rules of inflection; the fact that the same formative is assigned to a variety of mutually exclusive grammatical categories is not by any means an unusual feature of such rules.

Proceeding now to the remaining tonal suffixes, we next encounter the stable suffix, LH. This is inserted in the following set of tenses:

(82) Stable Suffix Insertion

$\emptyset \rightarrow$ LH / [ [ ____ (in *ne*-form and general relative)

Stative Present
Current Habitual
Current Perfect
Current Past Completive
Immediate Perfect
Near Future
Near Future Imperfect
Remote Future
Remote Future Imperfect
Current Past Consecutive ] $]_V$

This rule is overtly general, and inserts the stable suffix incorrectly in the Current Perfect, *ne*-form; I assume a separate rule to delete this. I also assume a rule stating that the L tone of the stable suffix is immediately associated with the final vowel. Neither of these rules will be given a specific statement here.

Next in turn is the floating L tone T*, which, as we have seen, has the curious property of occurring only in tenses lacking an overt tense prefix. We can further say that it occurs in *all* such tenses; although we have no evidence for its presence in the Current Habitual, we have no evidence for its absence either. There is in fact a very straightforward way of explaining its curious distribution. Suppose we say that the floating tone T* is introduced as the "default" case by a rule occurring as the final rule in the set of (disjunctively ordered) rules assigning tense affixes. Just in case no tense prefix is assigned, the following rule applies:

(83) T* Insertion

$\emptyset \rightarrow$ L / ___ $]_V$ (simple form and subject relative)

No further information need be stipulated. As this rule is ordered after rules (81) and (82), T* will occur to the right of the tonal suffixes inserted by these rules. By disjunctivity, this suffix cannot be introduced if any tense prefix has been introduced. As this rule has no exception as stated, it will apply to *all* remaining tenses, hence, to all prefixless tenses, giving us exactly the right results.

In fact, this rule has one rather curious exception. T* is not inserted in the Future Consecutive and Future Imperfect Consecutive (homophonous with the corresponding subjunctive tenses) just in case an object prefix is present. This exception would be quite difficult to explain or motivate if (83) were regarded as a rule applying independently of the set of tense prefix rules. If, however, we regard it as a member of this set of rules, and if we regard words as being "built up" from the inner layers of derivation to the outer layers, then this exception seems much less arbitrary than it otherwise would: the object prefixes occur in the next layer of prefixes down, and thus can be referred to by the rules assigning tense affixes without violating conditions of adjacency (Siegel 1978). This exception, then, provides some rather interesting confirmation for the correctness of our solution.[28]

The final member of the string of floating tone suffixes is the downstep suffix, which occurs only in nonrelative tenses, and in all such tenses provided they are (i) affirmative, (ii) main-clause, and (iii) nonconsecutive.[29] Following suggestions made to me independently by Frank Heny and David Odden, I will formulate this rule as a rule inserting the downstep to the right of the first major phrase $\bar{\bar{X}}$ occurring as a right complement to the verb, if there is one, and otherwise to the immediate right of the verb. This solution allows us to eliminate the rule of Downstep Permutation assumed in Clements and Ford (1979, 1981). (V = verb).

(84) Downstep Insertion

$$\emptyset \rightarrow \bar{L} \; / \; \begin{bmatrix} \text{V} \\ \text{+affirmative} \\ \text{–relative} \\ \text{–consecutive} \\ \text{–conditional} \end{bmatrix} \; (\bar{\bar{X}}) \; \_\_$$

In this formulation, the downstep is inserted outside the domain of the verb proper. Exceptionally, the downstep is absent in the Future Consecutive and the Future Imperfect Consecutive; I assume that (84) is to be further conditioned so as not to insert it in these tenses.

I add one brief comment on the final column in Appendix A. This column indicates whether a given tense does (+) or does not (–) undergo Downstep Permutation. Under the analysis assumed here, this translates into an indication whether the tense in question does (+) or does not (–) allow the expression in parentheses to be included as part of the rule. Thus, downstep occurs to the left, rather than to the right of a following phrasal category in tense 23 (under the alternative analysis referred to in note 29), and in all nonfinite forms of the verb, listed in Appendix A as forms A-C. These forms can be idiosyncratically marked as exceptions to the longer expansion of (84).

Rules (78) – (84) constitute the largest part of the melody composition component of Kikuyu. One important rule remains to be discussed, however, and we turn to this now.

Whenever a verb follows a noun subject with a L-final stem melody, its first syllable does not bear its (lexically given) basic tone, but always bears L tone at the level of entry to the tone rules proper. This L tone appears on the surface if the preceding noun ends in an overt L tone itself:

(85) ando ꜝ nemákíꜝɲírɛ̌ 'people arrived'
ando ꜝ makíɲirɛ̂ rè? 'when did people arrive?'

(the tense is the Current Past Completive). This L tone cannot be attributed to spreading from the final tone of the noun, since spreading would shift the downstep (created, it will be recalled, from the final L tone of nouns whose stem tone class is L-final by (73)) to the *right* of the first syllable of the verb:

(86) * 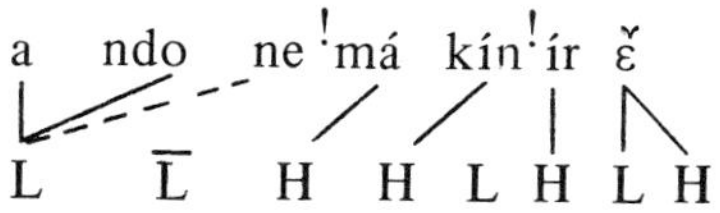


Moreover, it can be shown that the first syllable of such verbs bears underlying L tone not only after nouns ending in overt L tone, but after nouns ending in H tone followed by downstep (that is, nouns of stem tone class HL). Consider the following examples (in all cases, the vowel sequences occurring across word boundaries are unfused):

(87) a. moremi ꜝ atɛ́mírɛ́ motě 'Mũrĩmi cut a tree' (LL)
b. wamboɣó átɛ́mírɛ́ motě 'Wambũgũ cut a tree (HH)
c. ngoɣe átɛ́mírɛ́ motě 'Ngũgí cut a tree' (LH)
d. kama.ú áꜝtɛ́mírɛ́ motě 'Kamau cut a tree' (HL)

(stem tone classes given at the right). The first example is parallel to those of (85). The next two give no evidence of a L tone. The final example, however, shows the effect of the rule of Downstep Displacement, which shifts a downstep rightward across L tones if a H precedes, causing the intervening L tones to raise to H (see Clements and Ford 1981). For this rule to have operated, the initial tone of the verb must have been L in its input.

We see, then, that the initial tone of a verb melody is L if the immediately preceding tone in the sentence is L, and H otherwise. Somehow, a L tone must be introduced into the verb melody; but crucially, this L tone cannot be subsequently subject to Tone Shift, since it does not associate with the second syllable of the verb, nor does it cause a general shift of all tones one syllable rightward beyond the positions we would expect them to have under Tone Shift. It seems, moreover, unlikely that this L tone should be treated as some sort of boundary tone, since the subject-verb unit is a very tightly-knit one, both in terms of syntax and phrasing.

There is a rather simple solution to this problem, that turns out to have interesting consequences for our account of Tone Shift. Suppose we say that a "spurious" L tone is inserted at the beginning of every word in Kikuyu, thus (W = noun, verb, adjective):

(88) Spurious L Tone Insertion

$$\emptyset \rightarrow L \;/\; {}_{W}[\_\_$$

An immediate result is that we may eliminate the rule of Tone Shift (1), since normal left-to-right mapping as defined by Association Convention (3a) will assign all tones to all syllables correctly.

The spurious L tone produces incorrect results in just two cases. First, as we know, the L tone does not appear sentence-initially in verbs, and hence must be deleted in this position; thus we have the following:[30]

(89) Spurious L Tone Deletion

$$L \rightarrow \emptyset \;/\; {}_{S}[\;{}_{V}[\;\_\_$$

The second example of (76) thus undergoes the following derivation:

(90)

```
ma  kiɲ  ir  ɛ        underlying

  H   L      H

ma  kiɲ  ir  ɛ        (88)

L   H    L   H

ma  kiɲ  ir  ɛ        Association Convention (3a)
|    |   |   |
L    H   L   H
```

```
ma  kiɲ  ir  ɛ           (89)
     |    |  |
     H    L  H

má  kíɲ  ir  έ           Association Convention (3b)
  \  |    |  |
     H    L  H
```

Assuming that (89) is ordered after the initial application of Association Convention (3a), Tone Shift can be eliminated; the shift of each tone rightward can now be regarded as an effect of the insertion of the spurious L tone.

The other case where (88) applies overgenerally is after words ending in H tones with no following downstep (87b,c). We must therefore add the rule:

(91) Spurious L Tone Raising

$$L \rightarrow \emptyset \; / \; H \;\; {}_{W}[ \; \_\_$$

I have formulated this rule as a deletion rule. The preceding H tone will associate with the now-toneless syllable under Association Convention (3b), accounting correctly for (87b, c).

This analysis accounts for all facts that the original Tone Shift rule (1) was introduced to account for, and additionally extends to the set of forms represented by (85) and (87). The new analysis of tone shift can be illustrated by the following derivation of the sentence *totomirέ mokandá* 'we sent a rope' (Current Past Completive, simple form):

```
(92)  to   tom   ir  ɛ       mo   ka nda        (after (81), (83))

      L    H       H L        L    H   H

      to   tom   ir  ɛ       mo   ka nda        (84)

      L    H     H   L        L    H   H L̄

      to   tom   ir  ɛ       mo   ka nda        (88)

      L    L    HH   L        L    L H  H L̄
```

```
to  tom  ir ɛ     mo   ka nda          Association Convention (3a)
|   |    |  |     |    |  |
L   L    H  H  L  L    L  H  H  L̄

to  tom  ír ɛ́     mo   ka ndá          (89), Association Conven-
  `-|    |  |     |    |  /            tion (3b)
    L    H  H  L  L    L  H  H  L̄
```

H Tone Spread and Flattening fail to apply to the output of these rules since the floating L and L̄ tones block them. No further rules apply.

## 10. SUMMARY: THE ORGANIZATION OF A TONAL GRAMMAR

The analysis of Kikuyu tone assignment developed in the preceding pages is summarized in the following list of rules. This list assumes that tone rules do not form a single, undifferentiated component but rather fall into sets of sub-components: (i) the melody composition rules, (ii) the initial tone association rules, and (iii) the tone rules proper. The Association Conventions are ordered by a universal statement at the end of the initial tone association rule component, and apply thereafter whenever they have an opportunity to do so. (See Laughren's contribution to this volume for a similar conception of the internal organization of the tone component.)

I. Melody composition rules (members of disjunctive sets are grouped together under the same subheading)
   a. Mobile Suffix Insertion (81)
   b. Stable Suffix Insertion (82)
   c. Tense Prefix Lowering (25)
      T* Insertion (83)
   d. Subject Prefix Tone Replacement (79)
      Subject Prefix Tone Deletion (80)
      Subject Prefix Raising (78)
   e. Downstep Insertion (84)
   f. Spurious L Tone Insertion (88)

II. Initial tone association rules
   Heavy Syllable Lowering (42)
   Association Conventions (3)

III. Tone Rules proper

Spurious L Tone Deletion (89)
Spurious L Tone Raising (91)
H Tone Association (5)
Heavy Syllable Shift (54)
H Tone Spread (67)
Falling Tone Simplification (52)
Rising Tone Simplification (14)
Flattening (7)

## NOTES

1. Kikuyu is a central Kenyan Bantu language spoken in the area of Nairobi and the districts to the north by a population approaching 2.5 million speakers. Guthrie classifies it in his zone E, group 50, while Heine, on lexicostatistic evidence, places it in one of 25 parallel subgroups of the Eastern Highland subgroup of the Congo branch (see Guthrie 1967-71, Heine 1973).
2. This is a convenient simplification. For more extended discussion of syllable organization, postulating an intervening CV-tier, see McCarthy 1981, Clements and Keyser 1983.
3. A seventh tone class of bisyllabic noun stems is listed in Benson as "disyllabic class 5"; this class, which has a very small membership, is not discussed here.
4. I assume here the set of conventions given in Clements (1981b). These conventions are similar in empirical effect to the conventions stated in Clements and Ford (1979), but are somewhat simpler. Notice that we might, as an alternative, have taken (3a) and (3b) together as defining a single, indissociable association convention as proposed by Halle and Vergnaud (1982). In factoring out (3a) and (3b) as separate conventions, the claim is made that step (3b) may apply or reapply to relevant strings regardless of whether (3a) has applied. The discussion of Kikuyu which follows offers no strong grounds for choosing between these two interpretations, since decisive configurations seldom arise (see, however, note 15). In fact, recent work suggests that (3) may be overly strong whether interpreted in my sense or in Halle and Vergnaud's. It may be that one or the other of these proposed conventions should be assigned the status of unmarked, widely recurrent tone rules rather than universal conventions in any strong sense of this term. For further discussion and alternative proposals see Pulleyblank (1983), Clark (forthcoming), as well as Chapter 1 above.

In the statement given in (3b), an "accessible" tone is to be understood as one to which a tone-bearing unit can be associated without crossing an association line.
5. We shall see in section 8.2 below why this rule does not apply to the forms in column A.
6. The expected downstep after *moɣɛka* in (8) is deleted by an independently motivated rule (Clements and Ford 1981, 328); see also (66).
7. This observation is already implicit in the tonal classification given in Benson (1964), where CVCV stems and CVVCV stems are treated alike. More generally, no loss of tonal distinctiveness, in Guthrie's sense, has been found to correlate with any particular syllable type; the tonal classes of Proto-Bantu are well preserved in Kikuyu noun stems of all canonic forms. In verbs, on the other hand, we shall see that syllable weight plays a significant role. The claim made here is that syllable weight is irrelevant to underlying noun tone classes and also to the principles of initial tone association that map underlying tone melodies onto tone-bearing units in

nouns. One type of exception to this statement will be examined just below (see (15) and the following discussion).

8. The correspondences between the tone classes proposed in this section and those given by Armstrong and Benson are as follows:

| *this classification* | *Armstrong* | *Benson* |
|---|---|---|
| 1. LL | *mondo* class | disyllabic 1 |
| 2. LH | *mote* class | disyllabic 2 |
| 3. HL | *mbori* class | disyllabic 3 |
| 4. HH | *ŋgoko* class | disyllabic 4 |
| 5. LHL | *ɲamo* class | disyllabic 6 |
| 6. HLHL | { *ɲjata* class<br>{ *ðiimbo* class | disyllabic 7,8 |

I have claimed that Armstrong's *ɲjata* and *ðiimbo* classes, as well as Benson's disyllabic classes 7 and 8, form a single class in nouns with bisyllabic stems, the tonal realization of the final syllable depending on the weight of the penultimate syllable. An apparent exception is *morɔra* 'share of free beer', given with a final rising tone by Armstrong (1967: 261); Benson, however, lists it with a final H tone (1964:405), consistently with the present analysis.

9. Some details are omitted. See Barlow (1960) for a full treatment of Kikuyu morphology, as well as Johnson (1980, 1981) for detailed discussion of the Kikuyu tense/aspect system. My system of nomenclature for Kikuyu tense/aspect categories is based upon Johnson's, with a few minor departures.

10. No tonal reconstructions have as yet been published for tense/aspect formatives.

11. I indicate the application of Syllable Fusion in the third line by removing the space separating the fused vowels. This is, of course, merely a space-saving notational convention; fuller phonological representations would include the syllable tier, and we would thus have derivations like the following, for *toarɔ́ra*:

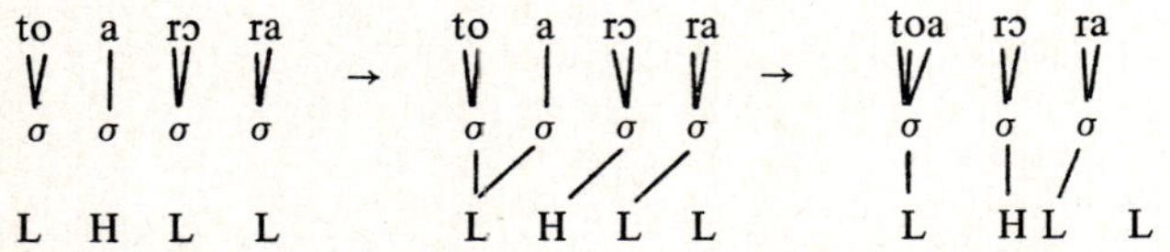


As the principles of syllabification are relatively straightforward as far as the forms discussed in this chapter are concerned, I have omitted the syllable tier in my derivations; the reader may easily reconstitute it.

12. The third example in (27-9) illustrates the behavior of reduplicated stems; further examples are given in (31). As these forms show, the reduplication of the stem must take place before the suffixation of *-aɣ-* and *-ir-*, as well as of *-i-* 'causative'. Thus we have: *ɣara* → *ɣaraɣara* → *ɣaraɣarira* → *ɣaraɣariria* (and eventually *ɣaraɣariris*, by a rule changing final *-a* to -ɛ after front vowels). The reduplication rule motivates the traditional treatment of suffixes such as these as infixes.

13. Tone Shift is a Kikuyu innovation because it does not occur in Kikuyu's closest linguistic relatives. Cases of tone shift described elsewhere in Africa must be due to independent innovations.

14. Exceptions include **-nį̀nį̀* 'small', **-tá̀ànò* 'five', in some reconstructions. See Guthrie (1967-71), Meeussen (1979, 1980).

15. This rule provides some evidence for the account of the Association Conventions given in (3). Under alternative interpretations, such as those suggested by Halle and Vergnaud (1982) and Pulleyblank (1983), see note 4, the rule would have to

be further complicated by an explicit statement to the effect that the first syllable mentioned in (47) is associated with whatever tone immediately precedes the H tone.

16. This restriction cannot be derived from the principle of strict cyclicity, as might be at first supposed, since crucial reference to syllable structure exempts a form from this principle; see Clements and Keyser (1983, §5.3.2).

17. The sole exception to this statement is the Current Past Consecutive.

18. The subject prefix forms used in subject relative clauses are homophonous with the members of the pronominal prefix series, suggesting that this series replaces the normal verbal prefix series in subject relative clauses (Meeussen 1967). This argues that subject relative clauses have the formal status of noun determiners in Kikuyu. It should be emphasized that the discontinuous dependency holding between the subject prefix tone and the tonal suffixes is exact, and permits no exceptions: whenever the L tone of the subject prefix is present, the stable suffix must be absent (the reverse implication holds only in certain tense forms, as shown in Appendix A). While Mrs. Gacũi showed occasional hesitation whether to use the stable tone or not for certain class 4 and 9 relative forms (no such hesitation being noted in class 1), the choice of the L-toned prefix always implied the absence of the stable suffix. Thus, we find

(i) ngoko éhetókeétɛ́ 'the chicken which has passed by' (class 9)

(ii) ngoko íhétókeêtɛ 'the chickens which have passed by' (class 10)

but never *ngoko éhetókeêtɛ* or *ngoko éhétókeétɛ́* as variants of (i). (The final tone sequence of (ii) is the normal sentence-final realization of the stable suffix in this tense form, determined by Flattening (7)).

19. The mobile tonal suffix, as noted earlier, is described as characterizing the final vowel, rather than the aspect suffix, since the mobile suffix is present whether or not an aspect suffix is present; thus, the presence or absence of the aspect suffix does not affect the structure of the melody.

20. Some speakers optionally reduce a final rising tone to L under all circumstances.

21. More generally, this rule permutes the downstep to the right of the first following phrasal constituent, of whatever category; see section 9 below for a fuller account.

22. See Clements and Ford (1981) for discussion of this rule, which is also exemplified in (8) and (87).

23. This symbol conventionally represents a phonetically unpronounced "trace".

24. The initial H tone occurring on *káγoko* is due to H Tone Spread; see discussion in next section.

25. Noun-final downsteps are deleted before a noun modifier, explaining their absence after *kemore* and *moγɛká*. Also, the failure of Flattening to apply to *moγatɛ* and *maγɔkɔ́* in (65) owes to the fact that *ne*, used as an independent copula, ends in downstep, which permutes to the right of its following complement, "immunizing" it from Flattening. These points are discussed in Clements and Ford (1981). The final L tone of *moγatɛ̀* in (66) is due to Rising Tone Simplification (14), case (b).

26. The treatment of H Tone Spread presented in this section allows us to eliminate the use of the ad hoc feature [+fused] required in Clements and Ford (1981, 341).

27. Flattening takes place in the general relative however, since this form terminates with the LH stable suffix, which follows the mobile suffix.

28. It has been suggested to me by Victoria Bergvall that the object prefixes display some of the characteristics of pronouns, and should perhaps be regarded as word-internal clitics. If this analysis is correct, and if my analysis of the T* suffix is correct as well, we are led to the surprising conclusion that cliticization rules may precede – or be ordered among – rules of the inflectional morphology.

29. However, Appendix A indicates two alternative analyses of the Remote Past Consecutive, under one of which Downstep Insertion must apply in this tense. The feature [ – conditional] in (84) excludes the non-main-clause tenses.
30. This rule can perhaps be generalized to words of all categories, since it would apply to nouns with no audible effects. Notice, however, that we cannot collapse (88) and (89) into a single rule of sentence-internal L tone insertion, since we would then be unable to account for the fact that we find tone shift in *all* words, whether they exhibit the spurious L tone on the surface or not.

ACKNOWLEDGEMENTS

Earlier versions of portions of this study were presented at the U.S.C./ U.C.L.A. Workshop on the Formal Treatment of Non-segmental Properties in Phonology, Lake Arrowhead, California, May 1981, and at the 13th Annual Conference on African Linguistics, Montréal, April-May 1982. I thank John Goldsmith, Larry Hyman, and Douglas Pulleyblank for helpful discussion of various of the issues raised in this study; I would also like to acknowledge the research support provided by the Harvard Graduate Society and the Marion and Jasper Whiting Foundation. Particular recognition is due to Rebecca Gacũi of Nairobi, Kenya, upon whose speech the present study is based. During the year 1980-1981, which she spent in Cambridge, Mass., Mrs. Gacũi took valuable time from her studies and her family responsibilities to assist me in the task of verifying the tonal paradigms for all tenses reported in this study, part of which had been gathered in earlier work with Mrs. Lillian Mwan ĩki, also of Nairobi. Mrs. Gacũi was born in Nakuru District in 1948, and divided her time between there and her family home in Limuru Division, Kiambu District during the years of her schooling. In spite of her Kikuyu-English-Swahili trilingualism, Mrs. Gacũi at no time showed any hesitation in providing the Kikuyu forms I requested from her. The internal consistency of her tonal forms, which held up against frequent rechecking after substantial lapses of time, and their nearly exceptionless coincidence with the tonal forms recorded by Armstrong and Benson provide the strongest possible assurance that they are fully representative of contemporary Southern Kikuyu speech.

Appendix A: Summary of Tense Forms

| | *SP* | *TP* | *OP* | *ROOT* | *FV* | *T** | *!* | *DP* |
|---|---|---|---|---|---|---|---|---|
| 1. Stative Present (∅ . . . a) | | | | | | | | |
| *ne*-form | H | – | B | B | HLH | – | ! | + |
| simple form | B | – | B | B | H | T* | ! | + |
| subject relative | B | – | B | B | H | T* | – | 0 |
| general relative | H | – | B | B | LLH | – | – | 0 |
| 2. Current Habitual (∅ . . . aγa) | | | | | | | | |
| *ne*-form | H | – | B | B | LLH | – | ! | + |
| simple form | B | – | B | B | L | 0 | ! | + |
| subject relative | B | – | B | B | L | 0 | – | 0 |
| general relative | H | – | B | B | LLH | – | – | 0 |
| 3. Current Perfect (∅ . . .eetε) | | | | | | | | |
| *ne*-form | H | – | B | B | H | – | ! | + |
| simple form | B | – | B | B | H | T* | ! | + |
| subject relative | B | – | B | B | H | T* | – | 0 |
| general relative | H | – | B | B | HLH | – | – | 0 |
| 4. Current Past Completive (∅ . . . irε) | | | | | | | | |
| *ne*-form | H | – | B | B | HLH | – | ! | + |
| simple form | B | – | B | B | H | T* | ! | + |
| subject relative | B | – | B | B | H | T* | – | 0 |
| general relative | H | – | B | B | HLH | – | – | 0 |
| 5. Current Future (e+ko . . . a) | | | | | | | | |
| *ne*-form | ∅ | HL | B | B | L | – | ! | + |
| simple form | ∅ | HL | B | B | H | – | ! | + |
| subj/gen relative | ∅ | HL | B | B | L | – | – | 0 |
| 6. Current Past Imperfect (e+ko . . . aγa): same as above | | | | | | | | |
| 7. Current Past Perfect (e+ko . . . eetε): same as above | | | | | | | | |
| 8. Current Progressive (ra+a . . . a) | | | | | | | | |
| *ne*-form | H | HL | B | B | H | – | ! | + |
| simple form | B | HL | B | B | H | – | ! | + |
| subj/gen relative | B/H | HL | B | B | H | – | – | 0 |
| 9. Near Past Imperfect (ra+a . . . aγa): same as above | | | | | | | | |
| 10. Near Past Perfect (ra+a . . . eetε) | | | | | | | | |
| *ne*-form | H | HL | B | B | L | – | ! | + |
| simple form | B | HL | B | B | L | – | ! | + |
| subj/gen relative | H | HL | B | B | L | – | – | 0 |
| 11. Near Past Completive (ra+a . . . irε): same as above | | | | | | | | |
| 12. Immediate Perfect (a . . . a) | | | | | | | | |
| *ne*-form | H | H | B | B | LLH | – | ! | + |
| simple form | B | H | B | B | L | – | ! | + |
| subject relative | B | H | B | B | L | – | – | 0 |
| general relative | H | H | B | B | LLH | – | – | 0 |

| | *SP* | *TP* | *OP* | *ROOT* | *FV* | *T** | *!* | *DP* |
|---|---|---|---|---|---|---|---|---|
| 13. Remote Past Imperfect (a . . . aγa) | | | | | | | | |
| *ne*-form | H | L | B | B | H | – | ! | + |
| simple form | B | L | B | B | H | – | ! | + |
| subj/gen relative | B/H | L | B | B | H | – | – | 0 |
| 14. Remote Past Perfect (a . . . eetε): same as above | | | | | | | | |
| 15. Remote Past Completive (a . . . irε): same as above | | | | | | | | |
| 16. Near Future (re+e . . . a) | | | | | | | | |
| *ne*-form | ∅ | LH | B | B | LLH | – | ! | + |
| simple form | ∅ | LH | B | B | H | – | ! | + |
| subject relative | ∅ | LH | B | B | L | – | – | 0 |
| general relative | ∅ | LH | B | B | LLH | – | – | 0 |
| 17. Near Future Imperfect (re+e . . . aγa): same as above | | | | | | | | |
| 18. Remote Future (ka+a . . . a) | | | | | | | | |
| *ne*-form | ∅ | LL | B | B | LLH | – | ! | + |
| simple form | ∅ | LL | B | B | L | – | ! | + |
| subject relative | ∅ | LL | B | B | L | – | – | 0 |
| general relative | ∅ | LL | B | B | LLH | – | – | 0 |
| 19. Remote Future Imperfect (ka+a . . . aγa): same as above | | | | | | | | |
| 20. Current Consecutive (ka . . . a) | | | | | | | | |
| simple/gen relative | H | L | B | B | L | – | – | 0 |
| 21. Current Past Consecutive (a . . . a) | | | | | | | | |
| simple gen/relative | H | L | B | B | LLH | – | – | 0 |
| 22. Near Past Consecutive (ra+a . . . a) | | | | | | | | |
| simple/gen relative | H | HL | B | B | H | – | – | 0 |
| 23. Remote Past Consecutive (ke . . . a) | | | | | | | | |
| simple/gen relative | L | H | H | H | H | – | ! | – |
| (alternative: | L | H! | L | L | L | – | – | –) |
| 24. Future Consecutive/Subjunctive (∅ . . . ε) | | | | | | | | |
| simple form: no OP | H | – | – | H | H | T* | – | 0 |
| simple form: OP | H | – | B | B | H | – | – | 0 |
| 25. Future Imperfect Consecutive/Imperfect Subjunctive (∅ . . .aγε): same as above | | | | | | | | |
| A. Infinitive (ko . . . a) | – | L | B | B | L | 0 | ! | – |
| B. Singular Imperative: | | | | | | | | |
| no OP (∅ . . . a) | – | – | – | B | H(L) | T* | – | 0 |
| OP (∅ . . . ε) | – | – | B | B | H | 0 | ! | – |
| C. Plural Imperative: | | | | | | | | |
| no OP (∅ . . . aa.i) | – | – | – | B | HLH | 0 | ! | – |
| OP (∅ . . . εε. i) | – | – | B | B | HLH | 0 | ! | – |

Key to Appendix A

abbrevations:

| | |
|---|---|
| SP: | Subject Prefix |
| TP: | Tense Prefix |
| OP: | Object Prefix |
| FV: | Final Vowel |
| T*: | Floating $\underline{L}$ Tone |
| !: | Floating $\bar{L}$ Tone |
| DP: | Downstep Permutation |

| | |
|---|---|
| B: | Base Tone (as given in lexicon) |
| B/H: | B in subject relative, H in general relative |
| H(L): | L tone is present and preassociated with FV if in sentence-final position, otherwise H occurs alone |
| –: | (in first seven columns) absent; (in last column) rule does not apply |
| 0: | (in sixth column) presence is indeterminate; (in last column) rule is not defined. |

NOTES

1. In the FV column, the mobile suffix and the stable suffix are given without separation.
2. In the Stative Present, the final tone of the stable suffix is preassociated with the FV; in all other tenses the first tone of the stable suffix is preassociated with the FV.
3. The *ne*-form and the subject relative form are not used in tenses 20-25; the general relative is not used in tenses 24 and 25.
4. Two alternative analyses, each consistent with the data, are given for tense 23.
5. The H tone of the HL sequence characterizing the TP *e+ko* is preassociated with the second syllable *-ko*.
6. Suppletive forms of the imperative, not given here, are used for L roots of the canonic form CVCV or shorter, and H roots of the canonic form CV (see forms in Armstrong 1967).

# Bibliography

Abbreviations:

| | |
|---|---|
| ACAL: | Annual Conference on African Linguistics |
| ALS: | African Language Studies |
| AS: | African Studies |
| AuÜ : | Afrika und Übersee |
| CLS: | Chicago Linguistic Society |
| HSP: | Harvard Studies in Phonology |
| IJAL: | International Journal of American Linguistics |
| IULC: | Indiana University Linguistics Club |
| JAL: | Journal of African Languages |
| JALL: | Journal of African Languages and Linguistics |
| JLR: | Journal of Linguistic Research |
| LA: | Linguistic Analysis |
| Lg: | Language |
| LI: | Linguistic Inquiry |
| NELS: | North Eastern Linguistics Society |
| SAL: | Studies in African Languages |
| SCOPIL: | Southern California Occasional Papers in Linguistics |
| SELAF: | Société d'Etudes Linguistiques et Anthropologiques de France |
| SLS: | Studies in the Linguistic Sciences |


Anderson, Stephen R. 1974. *The Organization of Phonology*. Academic Press, New York.

Armstrong, Lilias E. 1967. *The Phonetic and Tonal Structure of Kikuyu*. Dawson of Pall Mall, for the International African Institute, London.

Barlow, A. Ruffell. 1960. *Studies in Kikuyu Grammar and Idiom*. William Blackwood & Sons, for the Foreign Mission Committee of the Church of Scotland, Edinburgh.

Batibo, Herman, 1976. A New Approach to Sukuma Tone. In Hyman (ed.), 241-257.

Beach, D. 1924. The Science of Tonetics and its Application to Bantu Languages. *Bantu Studies* 2, 75-106.

Bearth, T. and C. Link. 1980. The Tone Puzzle of Wobe. SAL 11.2, 147-207.

Becker, Lee A. and D.P.B. Massamba. 1980. Ci-Ruri Tonology (a Preliminary View). SLS 10.1, 1-13.

Bennett, Tina L. 1977. Interrogatives. In Byarushengo et. al., 171-88.

Benson, T.G. (ed). 1964. *Kikuyu-English Dictionary*. Oxford University Press, London.

Bouquiaux, L., L.M. Hyman, and J. Voorhoeve, eds. 1980. *L'expansion bantoue: Actes du colloque international du CNRS, Viviers, 4-16 avril 1977*. II: *L'expansion bantoue*, vol. 2. SELAF numéro spécial 9, Paris.

Byarushengo, Ernest R. 1975. An Examination of the Segmental Phonology of Haya. Unpublished M.A. thesis, University of Dar es Salaam.

Byarushengo, Ernest R. 1977. Preliminaries. In Byarushengo et. al., 1-15.

Byarushengo, E.R., A. Duranti, and L.M. Hyman, eds. 1977. *Haya Grammatical Structure*. SCOPIL 6, University of Southern California, Los Angeles.

Byarushengo, E.R., L.M. Hyman, and S. Tanenbaum. 1976. Tone, Accent, and Assertion in Haya. In Hyman (ed.), 183-205.

Carter, Hazel. 1962. *Notes on the Tonal System of Northern Rhodesian Plateau Tonga*. Her Majesty's Stationery Office, London.

Carter, Hazel. 1971. Morphotonology of Zambian Tonga: Some Developments of Meeussen's System – I. ALS 12, 1-30.

Carter, Hazel. 1972. Morphotonology of Zambian Tonga: Some Developments of Meeussen's System – II. ALS 13, 52-97.

Carter, Hazel. 1973. Tonal Data in *Comparative Bantu*. ALS 14, 36-52.

Cheng, C. - C. and C.W. Kisseberth. 1979. Ikorovere Makua Tonology (part 1). SLS 9.1, 31-63.

Cheng, C. - C. and C.W. Kisseberth. 1980. Ikorovere Makua Tonology (part 2). SLS 10.1, 15-44.

Cheng, C. - C. and C.W. Kisseberth. 1981. Ikorovere Makua Tonology (part 3). SLS 11.1, 181-202.

Chomsky, Noam and M. Halle. 1968. *The Sound Pattern of English*. Harper & Row, N.Y.

Clark, Mary. Forthcoming. *The Tonal System of Igbo*. Foris Publications, Dordrecht.

Clements, G.N. 1976. Vowel Harmony in Nonlinear Generative Phonology: An Autosegmental Model. IULC, Bloomington.

Clements, G.N. 1979. The Description of Terraced-level Tone Languages. Lg 55.3, 536-558.

Clements, G.N. 1980. The Tone-bearing Unit. Presented to the Conference on Tone and Tonal Representation, University of Massachusetts, Amherst, Mass.

Clements, G.N. (ed.). 1981a. *Harvard Studies in Phonology*, vol. 2. IULC, Bloomington.

Clements, G.N., 1981b. Akan Vowel Harmony: a Nonlinear Analysis. HSP 2, 108-177. Reprinted in Goyvaerts (ed.), forthcoming.

Clements, G.N. 1981c. An Outline of LuGanda Syllable Structure. SAL Supplement 8, 12-16.

Clements, G.N. 1983. The Hierarchical Representation of Tone Features. In Ivan R. Dihoff, ed., *Current Approaches to African Linguistics*, vol. 1. Foris Publications, Dordrecht.

Clements, G.N. and K.C. Ford. 1979. Kikuyu Tone Shift and its Synchronic Consequences. LI 10.2, 179-210.

Clements, G.N. and K.C. Ford. 1981. On the Phonological Status of Downstep in Kikuyu. In Goyvaerts (ed.), 309-357.

Clements, G.N. and S.J. Keyser. 1983. *CV Phonology: a Generative Theory of the Syllable*. MIT Press, Cambridge.

Clements, G.N., J. McCloskey, J. Maling, and A. Zaenen. 1983. String-vacuous Rule Application. LI 14.1, 1-17.

Cole, Desmond T. 1967. *Some Features of Ganda Linguistic Structure*. Witwatersrand University Press, Johannesburg.

Cook, Thomas L. 1979. Internal Reconstruction Applied to a Case of Disymmetry in the Efik Verbal System. Presented to the Colloquium on Grammatical Change, University of Leiden, September 17-18.

Cope, A.T. 1970. Zulu Tonal Morphology. JAL 9.3, 111-152.

Doke, C.M. 1926. *The Phonetics of the Zulu Language*. Witwatersrand University Press, Johannesburg.

Doke, C.M. and B.W. Vilakazi. 1948. *Zulu-English Dictionary*. 2nd edition revised with addendum, 1958. Witwatersrand University Press, Johannesburg.

Fivaz, D. 1970. Shona Morphophonemics and Morphosyntax. Unpublished Ph.D. dissertation, University of the Witwatersrand.

Ford, Kevin C. 1975. The Tones of Nouns in Kikuyu. SAL 6.1, 23-48.

Fromkin, Victoria A. (ed.) 1978. *Tone: a Linguistic Survey*. Academic Press, N.Y.

Givón, Talmy. 1978. Negation in Language: Pragmatics, Function, Ontology. In Peter Cole, ed., *Syntax and Semantics vol. 9: Pragmatics*. Academic Press, N.Y.

Goldsmith, John. 1974a. A Fragment of a Grammar of Igbo. Unpublished ms., MIT.

Goldsmith, John. 1974b. English as a Tone Language. Unpublished ms., MIT. Appears with revisions in Goyvaerts (ed.) 1981, 287-308.

Goldsmith, John. 1974c. An Autosegmental Typology of Tone: and How Japanese Fits In. In E. Kaisse and J. Hankamer, eds., NELS 5. Department of Linguistics, Harvard University, Cambridge.

Goldsmith, John. 1974d. Autosegmental Phonology. Unpublished manuscript, MIT.

Goldsmith, John. 1975. Tone Melodies and the Autosegment. In R.K. Herbert, ed., ACAL 6, *Ohio State Working Papers in Linguistics* no. 20, 135-147.

Goldsmith, John. 1976a. An Overview of Autosegmental Phonology. LA 2, 23-68.

Goldsmith, John. 1976b. *Autosegmental Phonology*. MIT Ph.D. dissertation. Published by Garland Publishing Inc., N.Y., 1979.

Goldsmith, John, 1979. The Aims of Autosegmental Phonology. In Daniel Dinnsen, ed., *Current Approaches to Phonological Theory*. Indiana University Press, Bloomington.

Goldsmith, John. 1982. Accent Systems. In Harry van der Hulst and Norval Smith, eds., *The Structure of Phonological Representations*, vol. 1. Foris Publications, Dordrecht.

Goldsmith, John. 1983. Accent in Tonga: an Autosegmental Account. In Ivan R. Dihoff, ed. *Current Approaches to African Linguistics*, vol. 1. Foris Publications, Dordrecht.

Goldsmith, John. Forthcoming. A Note on Tone in Sukuma. In Goyvaerts (ed.).

Goyvaerts, Didier L. (ed.). 1981. *Phonology in the 1980's*. Story-Scientia, Ghent.

Goyvaerts, Didier L. (ed.) Forthcoming. *African Linguistics: Essays in Memory of M.W.K. Semikenke*. John Benjamins, Amsterdam.

Greenberg, Joseph H. 1948. The Tonal System of Proto-Bantu. *Word* 4, 196-201.

Groenhuis, Marjan. 1979. Tone in Some Zulu Nouns. Unpublished ms., Rijksuniversiteit te Groningen.

Guthrie, Malcolm. 1967-71. *Comparative Bantu*. 4 vols. Gregg International Publishers, Farnborough, Hants.

Hachipola, Jerome. 1982. Another Look at the Tonga Accentual System. Unpublished ms., Indiana University.

Halle, Morris and P. Kiparsky, 1981. Review of *Histoire de l'accentuation slave*, by Paul Garde. Lg 57, 150-181.

Halle, Morris and K.N. Stevens. 1971. A Note on Laryngeal Features. *Quarterly Progress Report* no. 101, Research Laboratory of Electronics, MIT, 198-213.

Halle, Morris and J.-R. Vergnaud. 1980. Three-dimensional Phonology. JLR 1.1, 83-105.

Halle, Morris, and J.-R. Vergnaud. 1982. On the Framework of Autosegmental Phonology. In Harry van der Hulst and Norval Smith, eds., *The Structure of Phonological Representations*, vol. 1. Foris Publications, Dordrecht.

Haraguchi, Shosuke. 1977. *The Tone Pattern of Japanese: an Autosegmental Theory of Tone*. Kaitakusha, Tokyo.

Heine, Bernd. 1973. Zur genetischen Gliederung der Bantu-Sprachen. AuÜ 56, 164-185.

Hombert, J.-M. 1978. Consonant Types, Vowel Quality, and Tone. In Fromkin (ed.), 77-111.

Hombert, J.-M., J.J. Ohala, and W.G. Ewan. 1979. Phonetic Explanations for the Development of Tones. Lg. 55.1, 37-59.

Huang, C.T.J. 1980. The Metrical Structure of Terraced-level Tones. In John T. Jensen, ed., NELS 11. Cahiers Linguistiques d'Ottawa vol. 9. Department of Linguistics, University of Ottawa, 257-70.

Huang, C.T.J. Forthcoming. The Autosegmental and Metrical Nature of Tone Terracing. In Goyvaerts (ed.). [Revised version of Huang 1980].

Hyman, Larry M. 1973. The Role of Consonant Types in Natural Tonal Assimilations. In Hyman (ed.) *Consonant Types and Tones*, SCOPIL no. 1, 151-179.

Hyman, Larry M. (ed.) *Studies in Bantu Tonology*. SCOPIL no. 3.

Hyman, Larry M. 1978. Tone and/or Accent. In Donna Jo Napoli, ed., *Elements of Tone, Stress, and Intonation,* 1-20. Georgetown University Press, Washington, D.C.

Hyman, Larry M. (ed.) *Aghem Grammatical Structure*. SCOPIL no. 7.

Hyman, Larry M. 1981. Tonal Accent in Somali. SAL 12, 169-203.

Hyman, Larry M. 1982a. Globality and the Accentual Analysis of Luganda Tone. JLR 2.3, 1-40.

Hyman, Larry M. 1982b. Against Asterisks in Luganda and Bantu Tonology: a Reply to Hyman (1982a). Unpublished ms., University of Southern California.

Hyman, Larry M. and R.G. Schuh. 1974. Universals of Tone Rules: Evidence from West Africa. LI 5, 81-115.

Hyman, Larry M. and J.R. Watters. 1980. Auxiliary Focus. Presented to the Conference on Auxiliaries, Fourth Annual Round Table in Linguistics, Rijksuniversiteit te Groningen, July 4-8, 1980.

Jakobson, Roman. 1971. *Selected Writings*, vol. 1. Mouton, The Hague.

Johnson, Marion R. 1980. A Semantic Description of Tense and Reference in the Kikuyu Verb. SAL 11.3, 269-320.

Johnson, Marion R. 1981. A Unified Temporal Theory of Tense and Aspect. In P.J. Tedeschi and A. Zaenen, eds., *Syntax and Semantics* vol. 14: *Tense and Aspect*, 145-175. Academic Press, N.Y.

Kähler-Meyer, Emmi. 1963. Bantu-Tonsprachen und -Nichttonsprachen in Tanganyika. *Zeitschrift für Phonetik, Sprachwissenschaft, und Kommunikationsforschung* 16, 101-112.

Kähler-Meyer, E. 1967-68. The Tones in Urbantu. AuÜ 51, 81-90.

Kahn, Daniel. 1976. *Syllable-based Generalizations in English Phonology*. MIT Ph.D. dissertation. Published by Garland Publishing Inc., N.Y., 1980.

Khumalo, J.S.M. 1981. Zulu Tonology. Unpublished Master of Arts Dissertation, University of the Witwatersrand, Johannesburg.

Kiparsky, Paul. 1973a. Phonological Representations. In Osamu Fujimura, ed., *Three Dimensions of Linguistic Theory*. TEC Co., Tokyo.

Kiparsky, Paul. 1973b. Elsewhere in Phonology. In Stephen R. Anderson and Paul Kiparsky, eds., *A Festschrift for Morris Halle*. Holt, Rinehart, and Winston, N.Y.

Kiparsky, Paul. 1982. *Explanation in Phonology*. Foris Publications, Dordrecht.

Lanham, L.W. 1958. The Tonemes of Xhosa. ALS 17, 65-81.

Lanham, L.W. 1960. The Comparative Phonology of Nguni. Unpublished Ph.D. dissertation, University of the Witwatersrand, Johannesburg.

Laughren, Mary. 1981. An Autosegmental Account of Tones in Zulu. HSP 2, 218-310.

Leben, William R. 1971. Suprasegmental and Segmental Representations of Tone. SAL Supplement 2, 183-200.

Leben, William R. 1973. Suprasegmental Phonology. MIT Ph.D. dissertation, published by Garland Publishing Inc., N.Y.

Leben, William R. 1976. The Tones in English Intonation. LA 2, 69-107.

Leben, William R. 1978. The Representation of Tone. In Fromkin (ed.), 177-219.

Louw, J.A. 1971. The Tonal Paradigm of the Verb in Xhosa. In *Afrikanische Sprachen und Kulturen: ein Querschnitt*. Deutsches Institut für Afrika-forschung, Hamburg, 102-113.

Louw, J.A. 1979. Some Remarks on Nguni Tone. LIMI 7.1/2, 45- 49.

Luce, Jan. 1981. A Phonetic Investigation of Accent in Tonga and English. Unpublished ms., Indiana University.

Massamba, David P.B. 1977. A Comparative Study of the Ruri, Jita, and Kwaya 'Languages' of the Eastern Shores of Lake Nyanza (Victoria). Unpublished M.A. dissertation, University of Dar es Salaam.

Massamba, David P.B. 1982. Aspects of Accent and Tone in Ci-Ruri. Unpublished Ph.D. dissertation, Indiana University.

McCarthy, John. 1979. Formal Problems in Semitic Phonology and Morphology. Unpublished MIT Ph.D. dissertation. Distributed by the IULC.

McCarthy, John. 1981. A Prosodic Theory of Nonconcatenative Morphology. LI 12.3, 373-418.

McCarthy, John. 1983. A Prosodic Account of Arabic Broken Plurals. In Ivan R. Dihoff, ed. *Current Approaches to African Linguistics*, vol. 1. Foris Publications, Dordrecht.

McCawley, James. 1964. What is a Tone Language? Presented to the Summer Meeting of the Linguistic Society of America.

McCawley, James. 1970. Some Tonal Systems That Come Close to Being Pitch Accent Systems but Don't Quite Make It. CLS 6, 526-532.

McCawley, James. 1973. Some Tonga Tone Rules. In Stephen R. Anderson and Paul Kiparsky, eds. *A Festschrift for Morris Halle*. Holt, Rinehart, and Winston, N.Y.

McCawley, James. 1978. What is a Tone Language? In V. Fromkin (ed.), 113-131.

Meeussen, A.E. 1954. *Linguistische schets van het Bangubangu*. Annalen van het Koninklijk Museum van Belgisch Kongo. Terveuren: Linguistiek, deel 5.

Meeussen, A.E. 1963. Morphotonology of the Tonga Verb. JAL 2, 72-92.

Meeussen, A.E. 1965. A Preliminary Tonal Analysis of Ganda Verb Forms. JAL 4, 108-113.

Meeussen, A.E. 1967. Bantu Grammatical Reconstructions. *Annales du Musée Royal de l'Afrique Centrale* no. 61, 80 - 121, Tervuren.

Meeussen, A.E. 1979. Vowel Length in Proto-Bantu. JALL 1.1, 1-7.

Meeussen, A.E. 1980. *Bantu Lexical Reconstructions*. Archives d'Anthropologie/ Schrief voor Antropologie, vol. 27, Tervuren.

Mould, Martin. 1979. Reconstructing Bantu Tense Systems. Paper presented to the 10th ACAL, University of Illinois, April 5-7, 1979.

Mukarovsky, Hans. 1976/77. *A Study of Western Nigritic*. 2 vols. Afro-Pub, Vienna.

Nash, David G. 1980. Topics in Warlpiri Grammar. Unpublished Ph.D. dissertation, MIT.

Odden, David. 1981. Problems in Tone Assignment in Shona. Unpublished Ph.D. dissertation, University of Illinois.

Odden, David. Forthcoming. An Accentual Approach to Tone in Kimatuumbi. In Goyvaerts (ed.).

Paulian, Christiane. 1975. Le kikuya, langue teke du Congo. SELAF 49-50, Paris.

Phillipson, David. 1977a. The Spread of the Bantu Languages. *Scientific American* 236, 106-114.

Phillipson, David. 1977b. *The Later Prehistory of Eastern and Southern Africa*. Heinemann, London.

Pierrehumbert, Janet B. 1980. The Phonology and Phonetics of English Intonation. Unpublished Ph.D. dissertation, MIT.

Pratt, Mary. 1972. Tone in Some Kikuyu Verb Forms. SAL 3, 325-377.

Pike, Kenneth L. 1948. *Tone Languages*. The University of Michigan Press, Ann Arbor.

Prince, Alan S. 1983. Relating to the Grid. LI 14.1, 19-100.

Pulleyblank, Douglas. 1982. Accent in Kimatuumbi. Presented to the 13th ACAL, Montreal. To appear in J. Kaye, H. Koopman, D. Sportiche, and A. Dugas, eds., *Current Approaches to African Linguistics* vol. 2, Foris Publications, Dordrecht.

Pulleyblank, Douglas. 1983. Tone in Lexical Phonology. Unpublished Ph.D. dissertation, MIT.

Rycroft, D.K. 1963. Tone in Zulu Nouns. ALS 4, 43-68.

Rycroft, D.K. 1979. Tonal Formulae for Nguni. LIMI 7.1/2, 5-44.

Rycroft, D.K. 1980. Nguni Tonal Typology and Common Bantu. ALS 17, 33-76.

Rycroft, D.K. and A.B. Ncobo. 1979. *Say it in Zulu*. Manual and Tapes. School of Oriental and African Studies, London.

Schachter, Paul and Victoria Fromkin. 1968. *A Phonology of Akan: Akuapem, Asante, and Fante. Working Papers in Phonetics* 9, Department of Linguistics, UCLA.

Schadeberg, Thilo. 1979. Über die Töne der Verbalen Formen im Rimi. AuÜ 57.

Siegel, Dorothy. 1978. The Adjacency Constraint and the Theory of Morphology. In Mark J. Stein, ed., NELS 8. Department of Linguistics, University of Massachusetts, Amherst, Mass.

Smith, Neilson V. 1968. Tone in Ewe. *Quarterly Progress Report* no. 88, Research Laboratory of Electronics, MIT, 290-304. Reprinted in Eric Fudge, ed., *Phonology*, Penguin, London, 1973.

Stahlke, Herbert. 1971. The Noun Prefix in Ewe. SAL Supplement 2, 141-159.

Steriade, Donca. 1982. Incomplete Syllabification and Segmental Extrametricality. Presented to the West Coast Conference on Formal Linguistics, Stanford University, January 1982.

Stevens, Kenneth N. 1975. Modes of Conversion of Airflow to Sound, and Their Utilization in Speech. Presented to the 8th International Congress of Phonetic Sciences, Leeds, England.

Stevick, Earl. 1969a. Pitch and Duration in Ganda. JAL 8, 1-28.

Stevick, Earl. 1969b. Tone in Bantu. IJAL 35, 330-341.

Stewart, John M. 1971. Niger-Congo, Kwa. In Thomas A. Sebeok, ed., *Current Trends in Linguistics*, vol. 7, 179-212. Mouton, The Hague.

Stewart, John M. 1980. The Asante Twi Tone Shift. To appear in Ivan R. Dihoff, ed., *Current Approaches to African Linguistics* vol. 1, Foris Publications, Dordrecht.

Tanenbaum, Sarah. 1977. Left- and Right-dislocation. In Byarushengo, Duranti, and Hyman (eds.), 161-170.

Van Spaandonck, Marcel. 1967. *Morfotonologische Analyse in Bantutalen*. Academische Proefschrift, Rijksuniversiteit te Ghent. French translation: *L'analyse morphotonologique dans les langues bantoues*. SELAF 23-24, 1971.

Voorhoeve, Jan. 1973. Safwa as a Restricted Tone System. SAL 4, 1-22.

Wang, William S.-Y. 1967. Phonological Features of Tone. IJAL 33, 93-105.

Weidert, Alfons. 1981. *Tonologie: Ergebnisse, Analysen, Vermutungen*. Niemeyer Verlag, Tübingen.

Westphal, E.O.J. 1951. The Tone of Verb Stems in Xhosa. AS 10.3, 107-111.

Westphal, E.O.J., M. Notshweleka, and S.M. Tindleni. 1967. *Tonal Profiles of Xhosa Nominals and Verbo-nominals*. University of Cape Town. Communication from the School of African Studies. Department of African Languages no. 32.

Williams, Edwin. 1976. Underlying Tone in Margi and Igbo. LI 7, 463 - 484.

Woo, Nancy. 1969. Prosody and Phonology. Unpublished Ph.D. dissertation, MIT. Distributed by the IULC, Bloomington.

Wright, Martha S. 1983. A Metrical Approach to Tone Sandhi in Chinese Dialects. Unpublished Ph.D. dissertation, University of Massachusetts, Amherst, Mass.

Yip, Moira. J.W. 1980. The Tonal Phonology of Chinese. Unpublished Ph.D. dissertation, MIT. Distributed by the IULC, Bloomington.

Yip. Moira. J.W. 1982. Against a Segmental Analysis of Zahao and Thai. LA 9.1, 79-94.

# List of Contributors


ERNEST R. BYARUSHENGO, Department of African Linguistics, University of Dar es Salaam, and Department of Linguistics, University of Southern California, Los Angeles, California

GEORGE N. CLEMENTS, Department of Modern Languages and Linguistics, Cornell University, Ithaca, New York

JOHN A. GOLDSMITH, Department of Linguistics, Indiana University, and Department of Linguistics, University of Chicago, Chicago, Illinois

LARRY M. HYMAN, Department of Linguistics, University of Southern California, Los Angeles, California

CHARLES W. KISSEBERTH, Department of Linguistics, University of Illinois, Urbana, Illinois

MARY LAUGHREN, Department of Education, Northern Territory, Australia and Department of Linguistics and Philosophy, M.I.T., Cambridge, Massachusetts

DAVID P.B. MASSAMBA, Kiswahili Institute, University of Dar es Salaam

DAVID ODDEN, Department of Linguistics, Yale University, New Haven, Connecticut